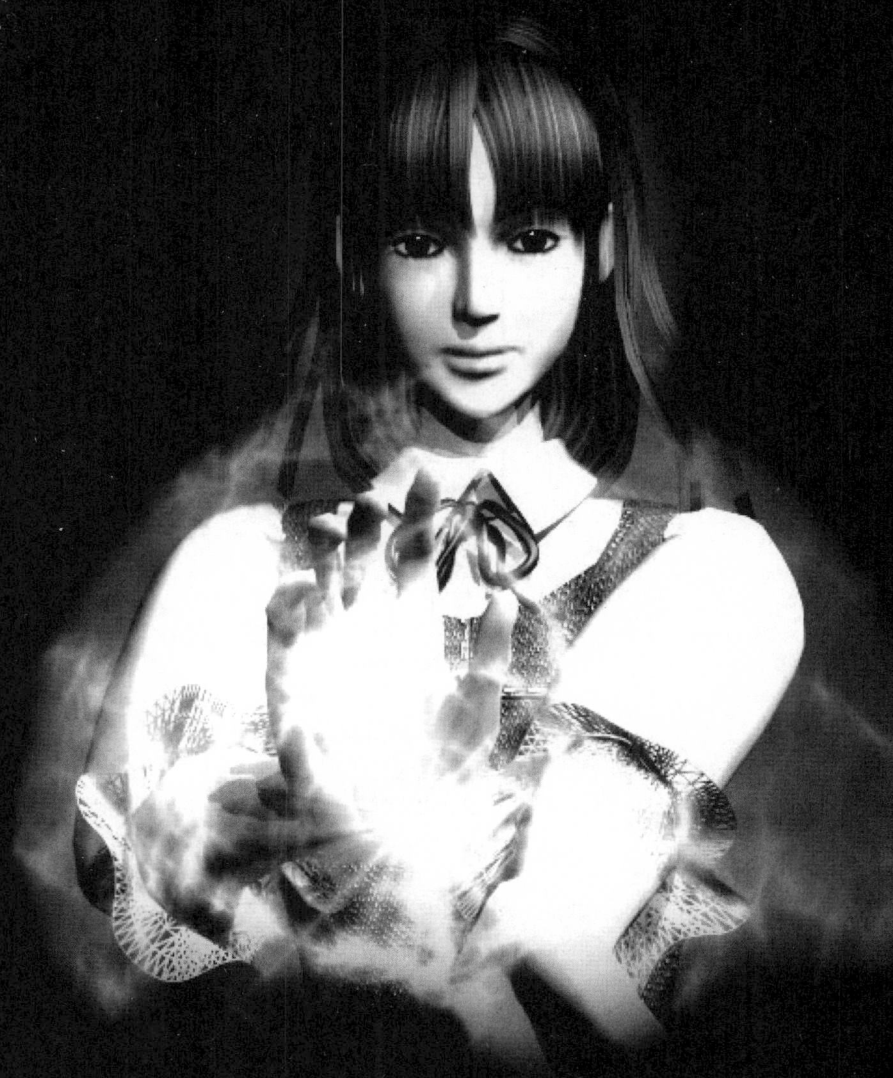

Translators

Kevin Liu

Jean Yen

Editors

Darren W. Jenkins

Nicole Curry

Production Artists

Will Chen

Kai-Chieh Yu

Gary Lin

Kelly Lin

US Cover Design

Hiep Ho

Lettering Fonts

Comicraft

www.comicbookfonts.com

President

Robin Kuo

Redmoon V1 © Mina Hwang

Originally published in Korea in 1988 by Seung-chul Pack

English translation rights arranged through

World Netgames, Inc.

Publisher

ComicsOne Corporation

47257 Fremont Blvd.

Fremont, CA 94538

www.ComicsOne.com

First Edition: September 2001

ISBN 1-58899-093-1

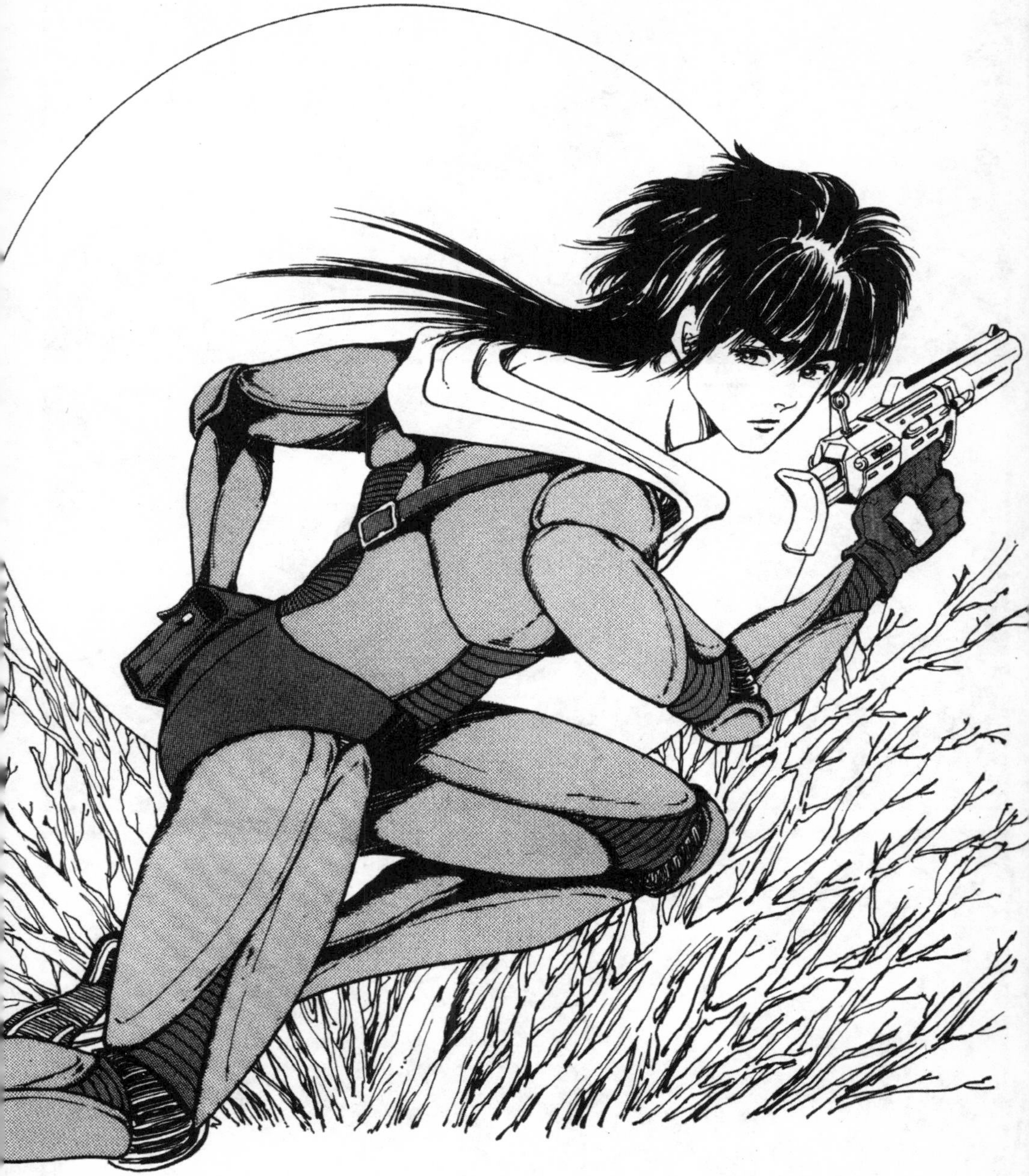

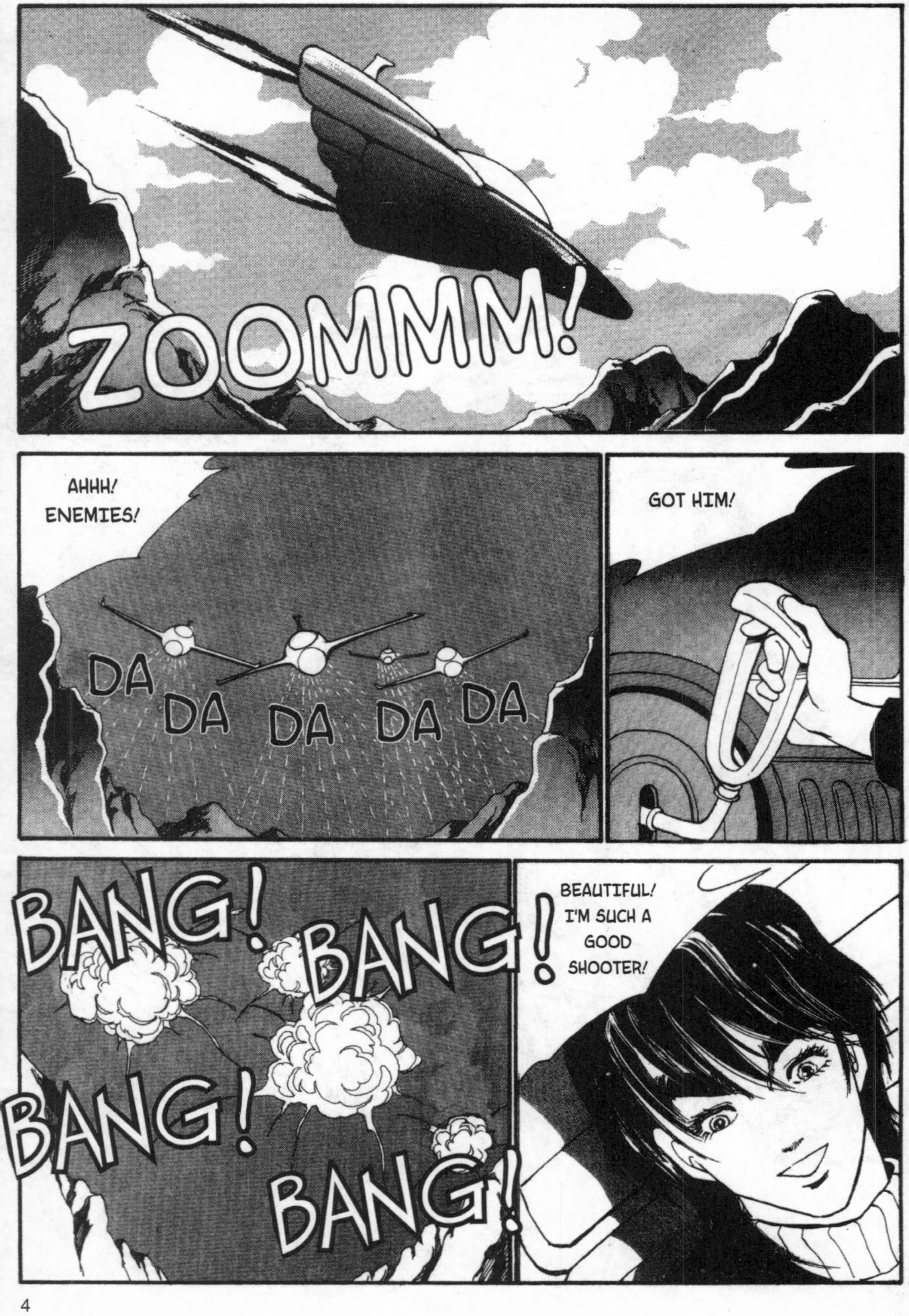
ZOOMMM!
AHHH! ENEMIES!
DA DA DA DA DA
GOT HIM!
BANG! BANG! BANG! BANG!
BEAUTIFUL! I'M SUCH A GOOD SHOOTER!

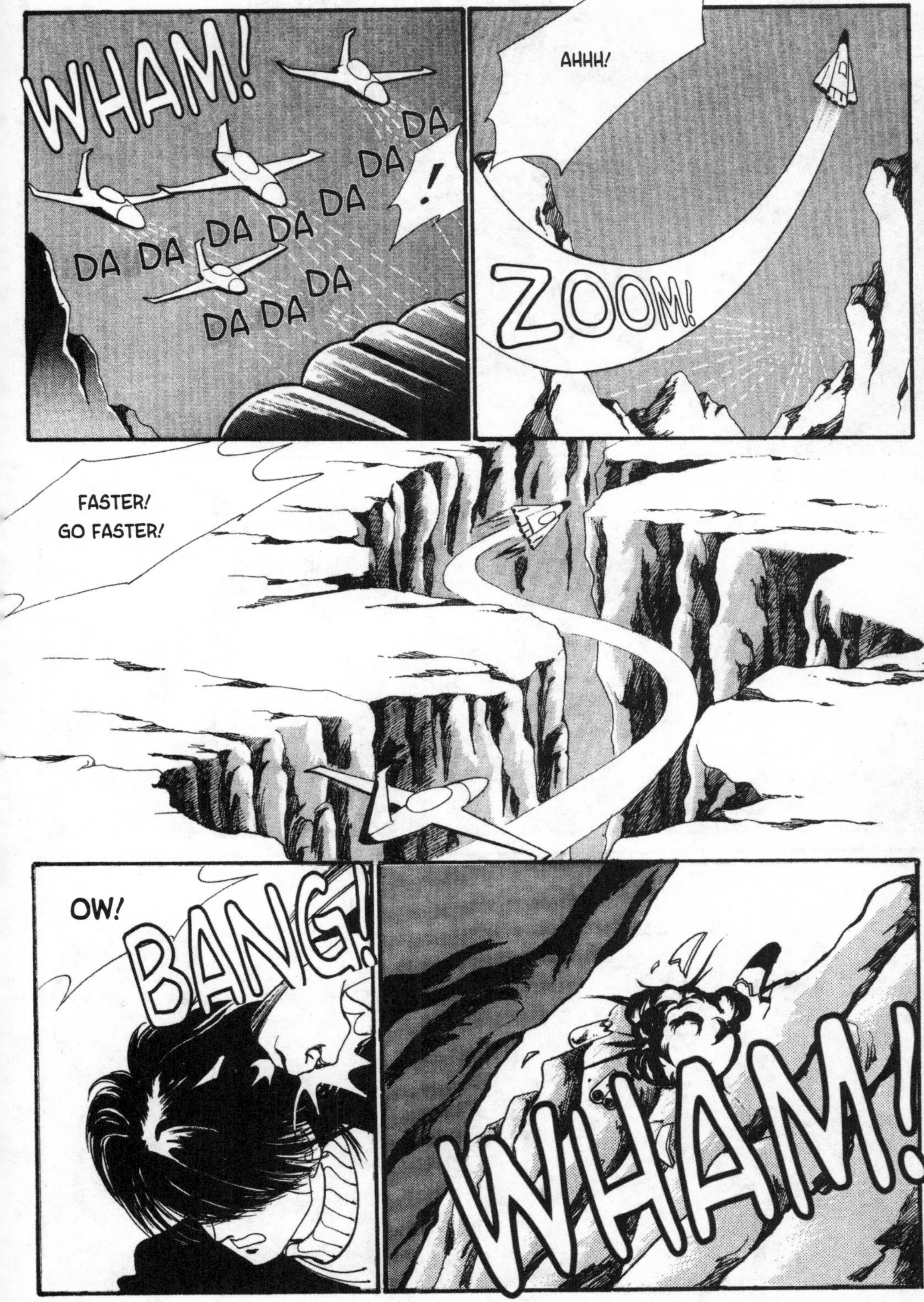

WHAM!
DA DA DA DA DA DA DA DA
DA DA DA
!
AHHH!
ZOOM!
FASTER!
GO FASTER!
OW!
BANG!
WHAM!

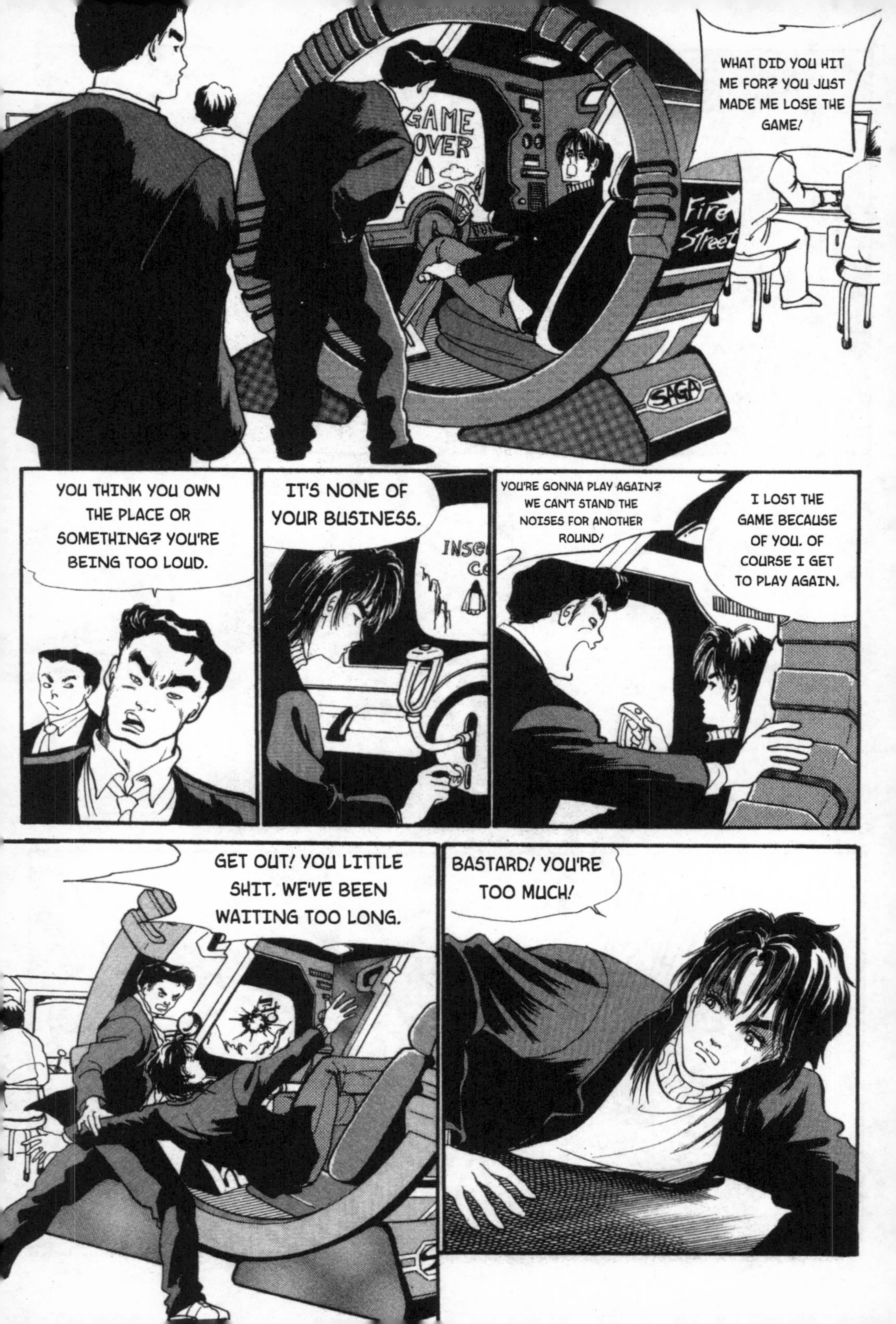
WHAT DID YOU HIT ME FOR? YOU JUST MADE ME LOSE THE GAME!
GAME OVER
Fire Street
SAGA
YOU THINK YOU OWN THE PLACE OR SOMETHING? YOU'RE BEING TOO LOUD.
IT'S NONE OF YOUR BUSINESS.
YOU'RE GONNA PLAY AGAIN? WE CAN'T STAND THE NOISES FOR ANOTHER ROUND!
I LOST THE GAME BECAUSE OF YOU. OF COURSE I GET TO PLAY AGAIN.
GET OUT! YOU LITTLE SHIT. WE'VE BEEN WAITING TOO LONG.
BASTARD! YOU'RE TOO MUCH!

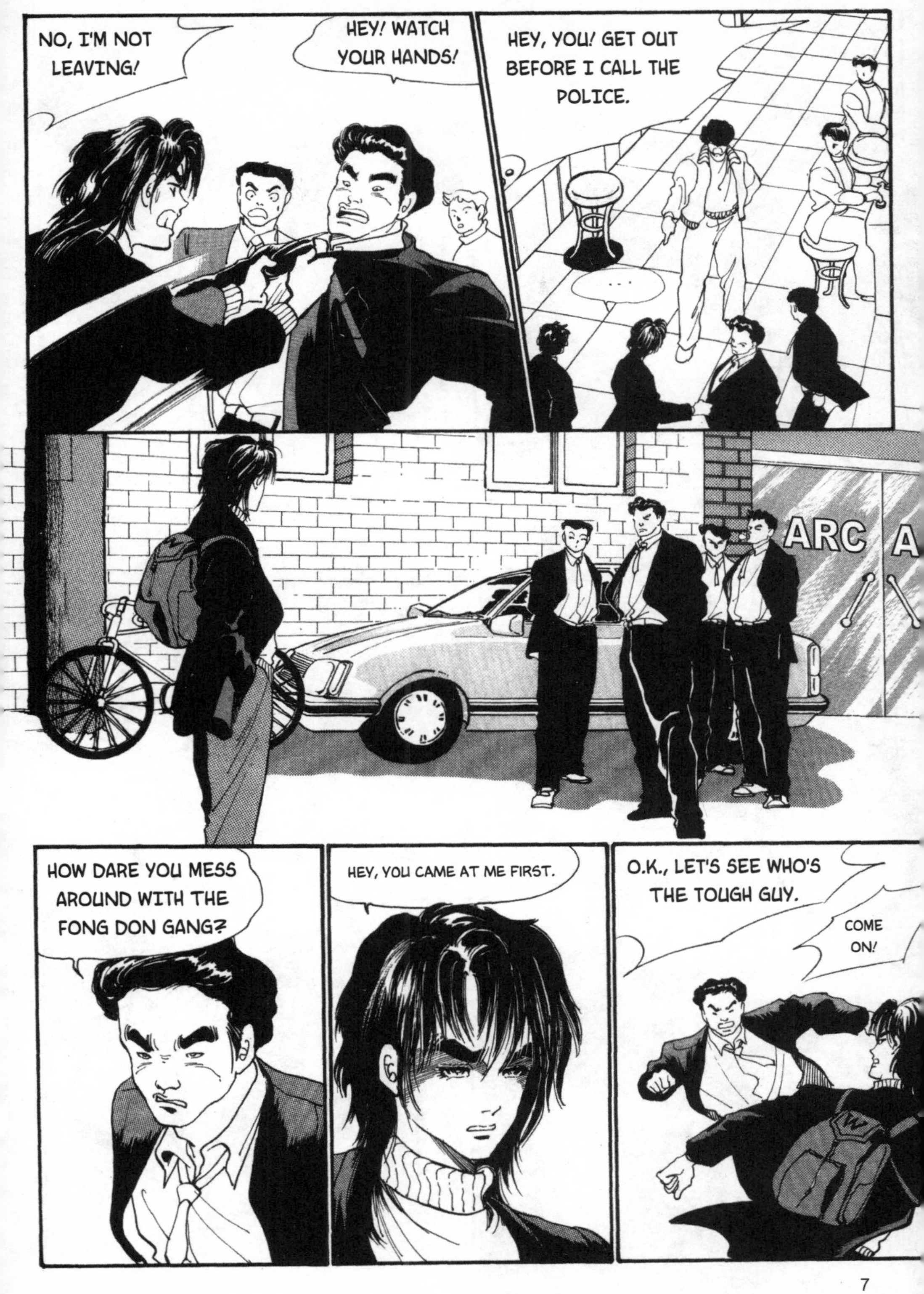
NO, I'M NOT LEAVING!
HEY! WATCH YOUR HANDS!
HEY, YOU! GET OUT BEFORE I CALL THE POLICE.
...
ARC A
HOW DARE YOU MESS AROUND WITH THE FONG DON GANG?
HEY, YOU CAME AT ME FIRST.
O.K., LET'S SEE WHO'S THE TOUGH GUY.
COME ON!

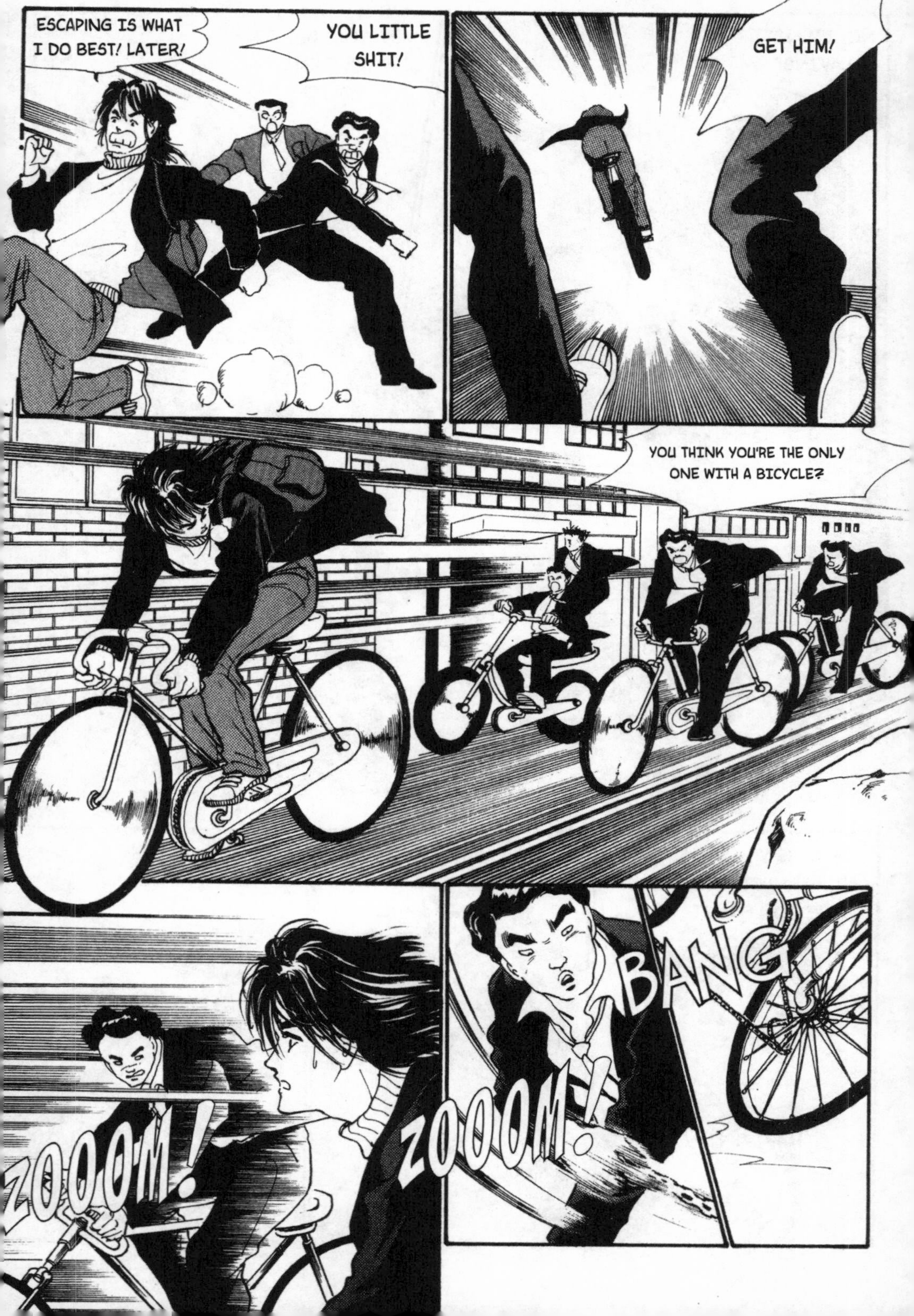
ESCAPING IS WHAT I DO BEST! LATER!
YOU LITTLE SHIT!
GET HIM!
YOU THINK YOU'RE THE ONLY ONE WITH A BICYCLE?
BANG
ZOOOM!
ZOOOM!

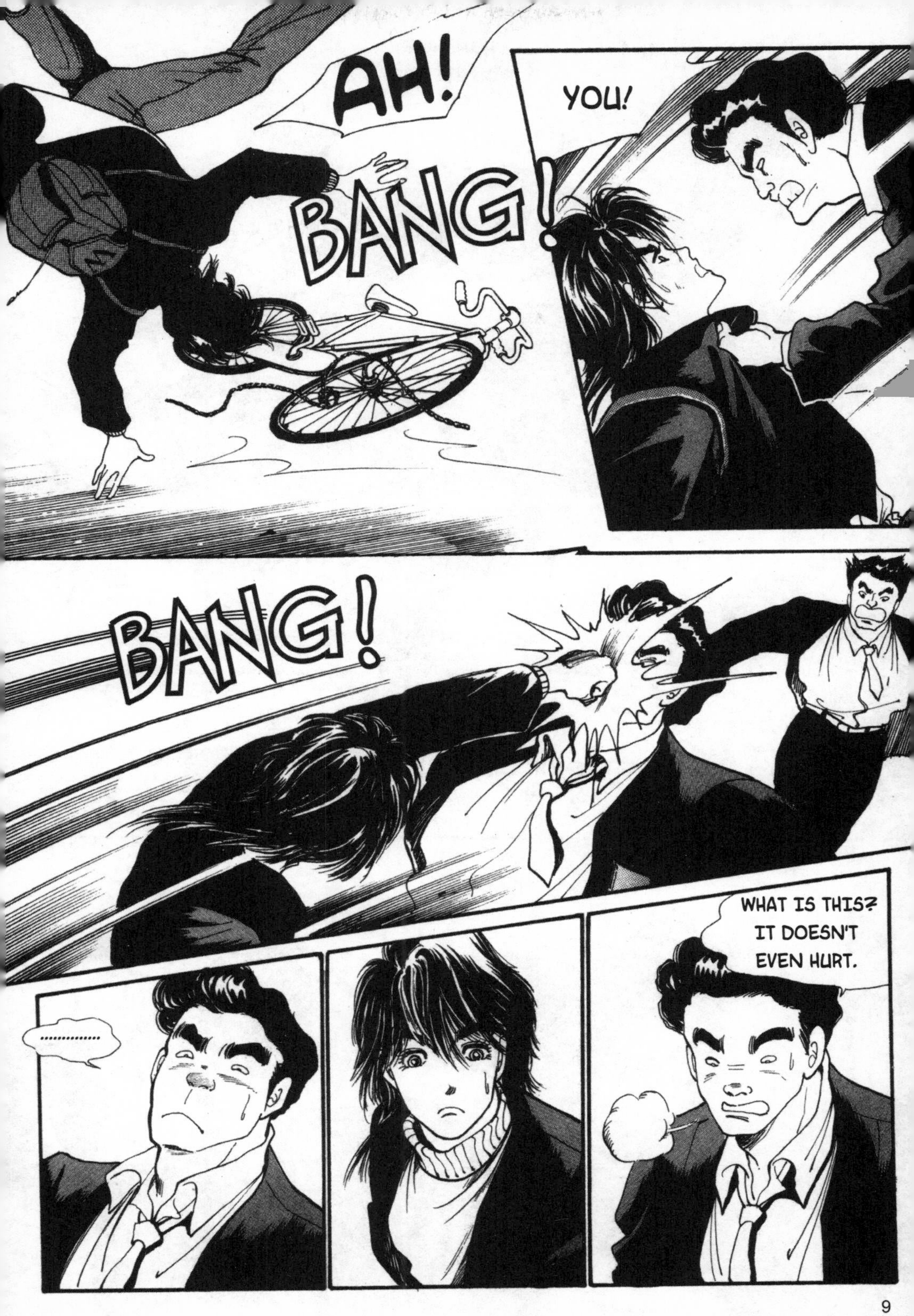
YOU!
AH!
BANG!
BANG!
....
WHAT IS THIS? IT DOESN'T EVEN HURT.

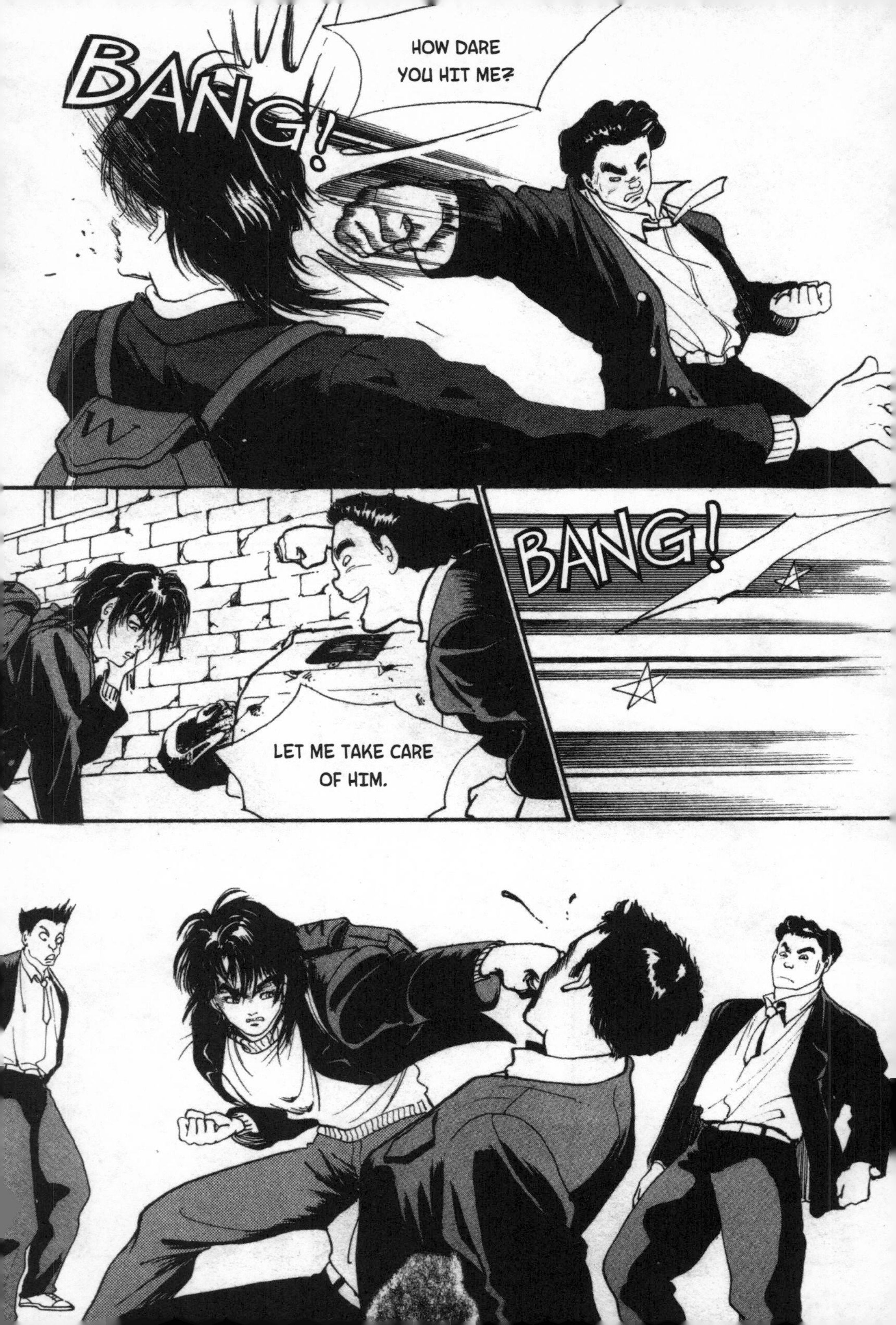

BANG!
HOW DARE YOU HIT ME?
BANG!
LET ME TAKE CARE OF HIM.

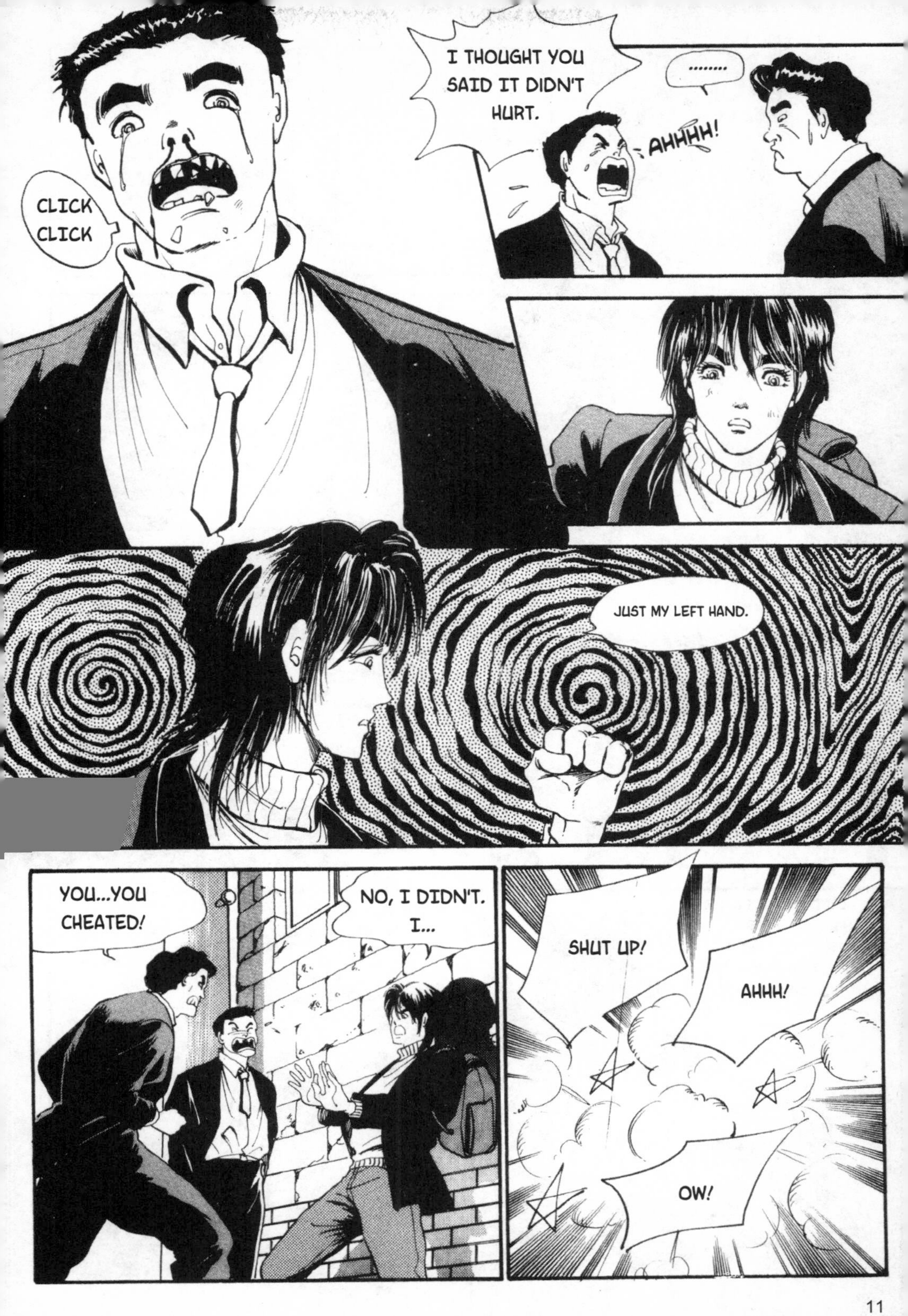
CLICK CLICK
I THOUGHT YOU SAID IT DIDN'T HURT.
....
AHHHH!
JUST MY LEFT HAND.
YOU...YOU CHEATED!
NO, I DIDN'T. I...
SHUT UP!
AHHH!
OW!

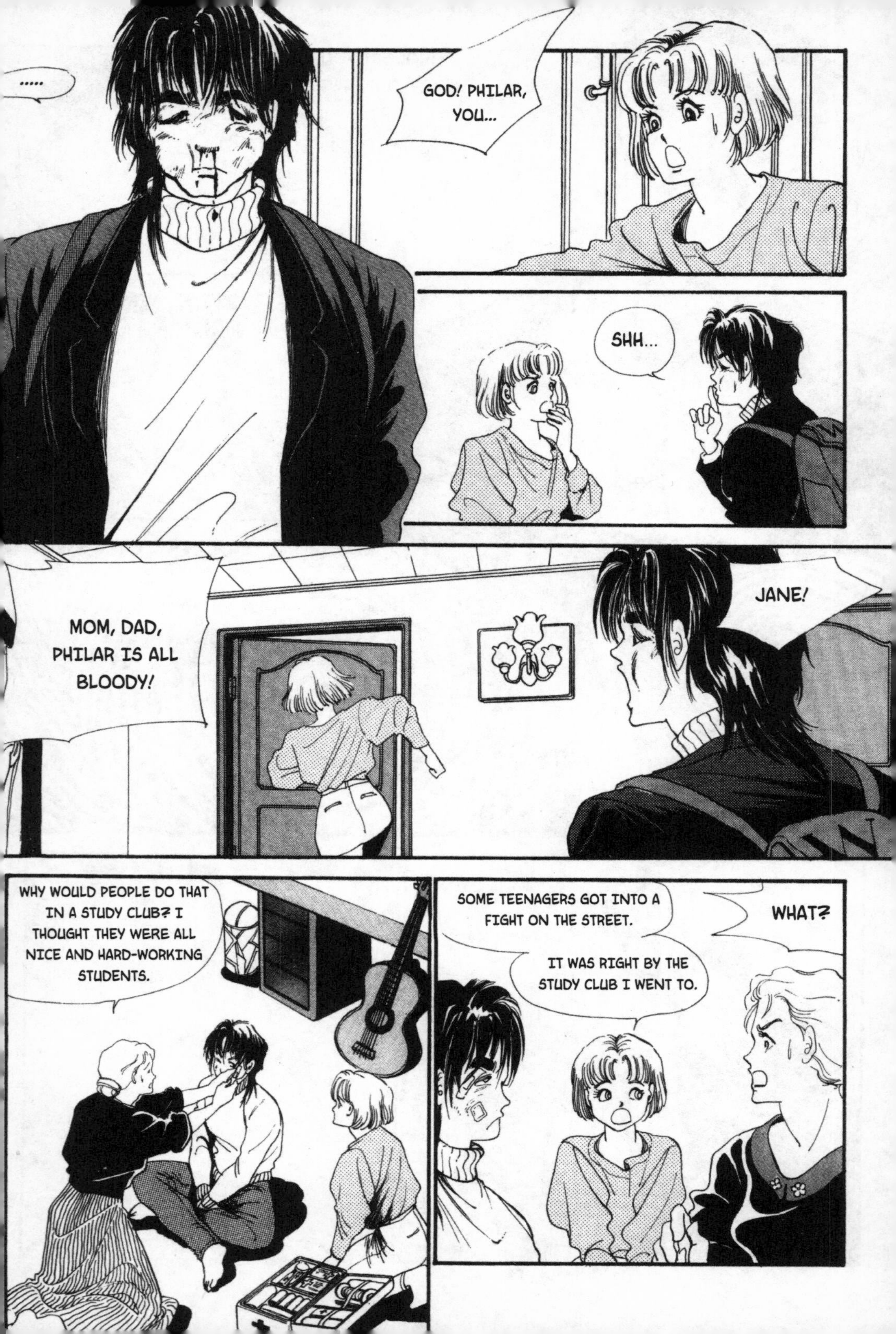
......
GOD! PHILAR, YOU...
SHH...
MOM, DAD, PHILAR IS ALL BLOODY!
JANE!
WHY WOULD PEOPLE DO THAT IN A STUDY CLUB? I THOUGHT THEY WERE ALL NICE AND HARD-WORKING STUDENTS.
SOME TEENAGERS GOT INTO A FIGHT ON THE STREET.
WHAT?
IT WAS RIGHT BY THE STUDY CLUB I WENT TO.

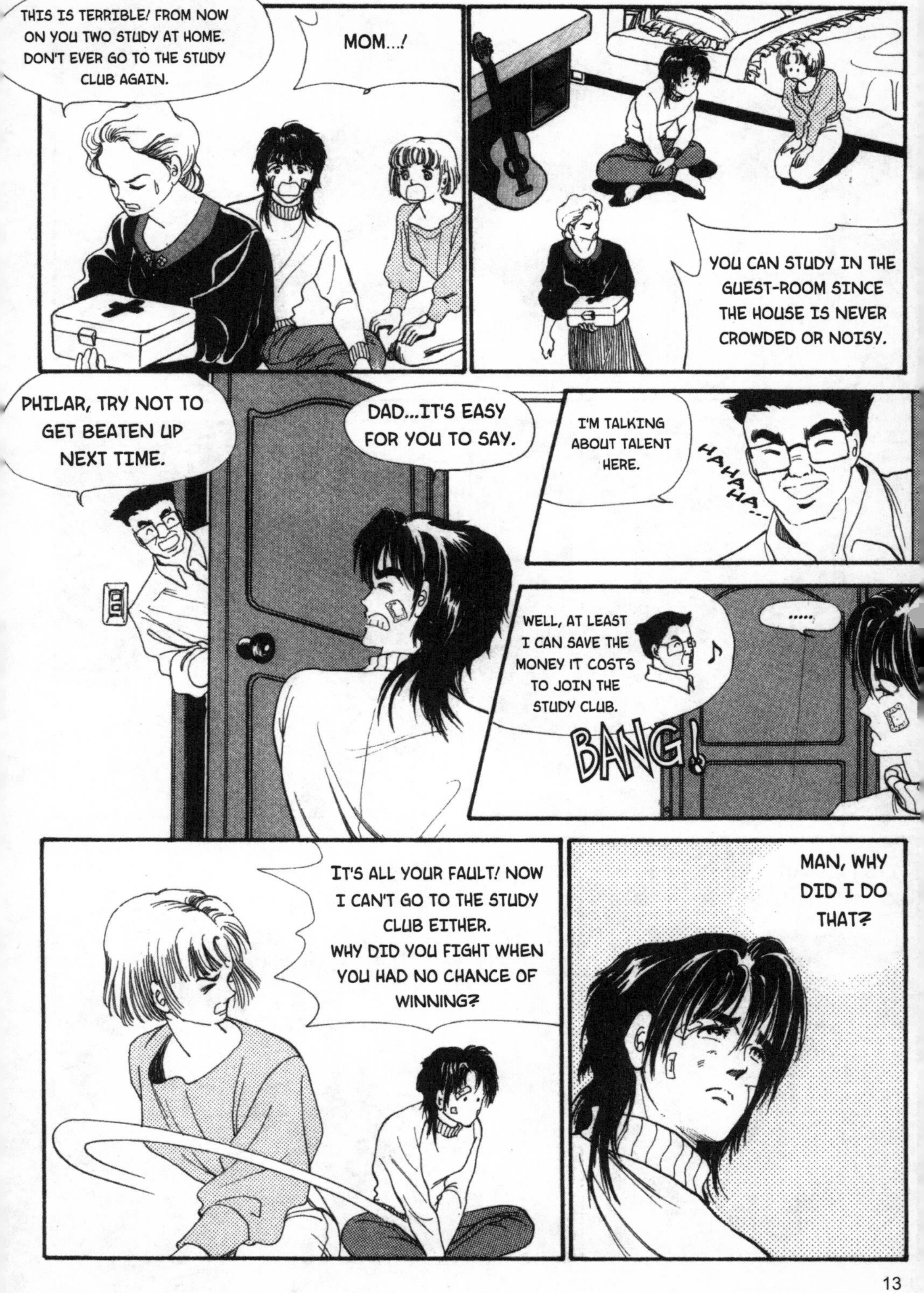
THIS IS TERRIBLE! FROM NOW ON YOU TWO STUDY AT HOME. DON'T EVER GO TO THE STUDY CLUB AGAIN.
MOM...!
YOU CAN STUDY IN THE GUEST-ROOM SINCE THE HOUSE IS NEVER CROWDED OR NOISY.
PHILAR, TRY NOT TO GET BEATEN UP NEXT TIME.
DAD...IT'S EASY FOR YOU TO SAY.
I'M TALKING ABOUT TALENT HERE.
HAHAHA...
WELL, AT LEAST I CAN SAVE THE MONEY IT COSTS TO JOIN THE STUDY CLUB.
.....
BANG!
IT'S ALL YOUR FAULT! NOW I CAN'T GO TO THE STUDY CLUB EITHER. WHY DID YOU FIGHT WHEN YOU HAD NO CHANCE OF WINNING?
MAN, WHY DID I DO THAT?

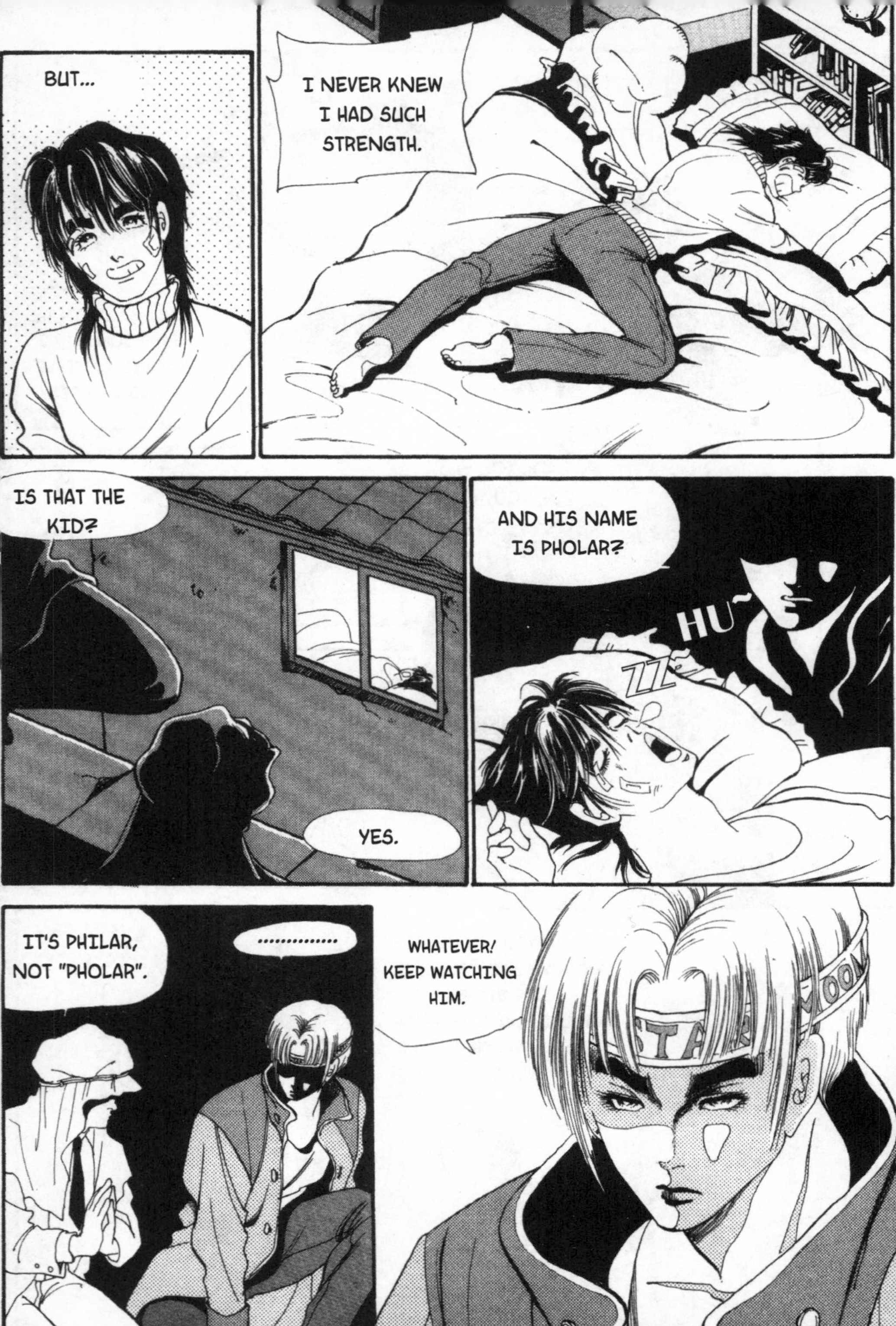
BUT...
I NEVER KNEW I HAD SUCH STRENGTH.
IS THAT THE KID?
YES.
AND HIS NAME IS PHOLAR?
HU~
ZZ
IT'S PHILAR, NOT "PHOLAR".
....
WHATEVER! KEEP WATCHING HIM.
STAR MOON

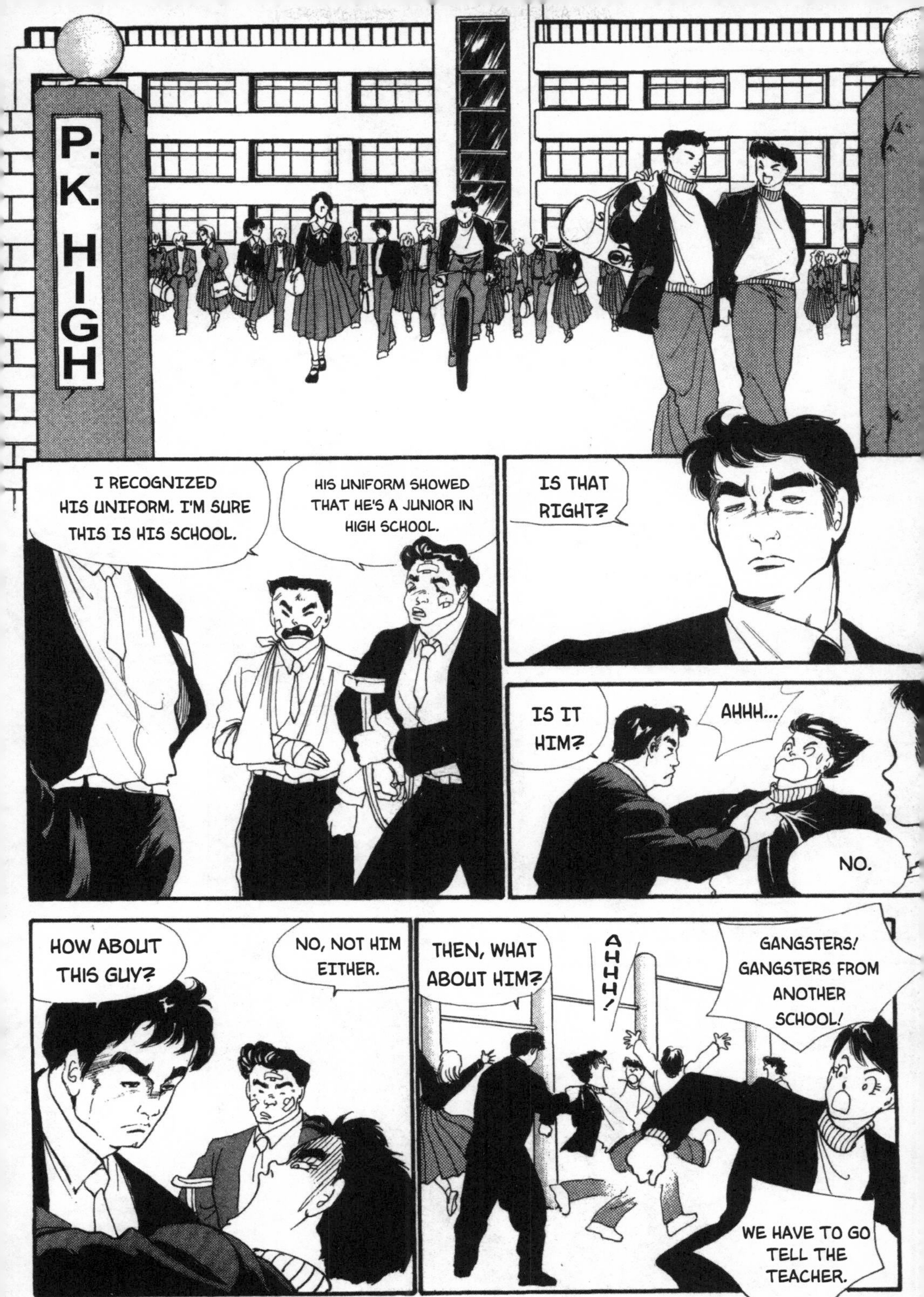
P.K. HIGH
I RECOGNIZED HIS UNIFORM. I'M SURE THIS IS HIS SCHOOL.
HIS UNIFORM SHOWED THAT HE'S A JUNIOR IN HIGH SCHOOL.
IS THAT RIGHT?
IS IT HIM?
AHHH...
NO.
HOW ABOUT THIS GUY?
NO, NOT HIM EITHER.
THEN, WHAT ABOUT HIM?
AHHH!
GANGSTERS! GANGSTERS FROM ANOTHER SCHOOL!
WE HAVE TO GO TELL THE TEACHER.

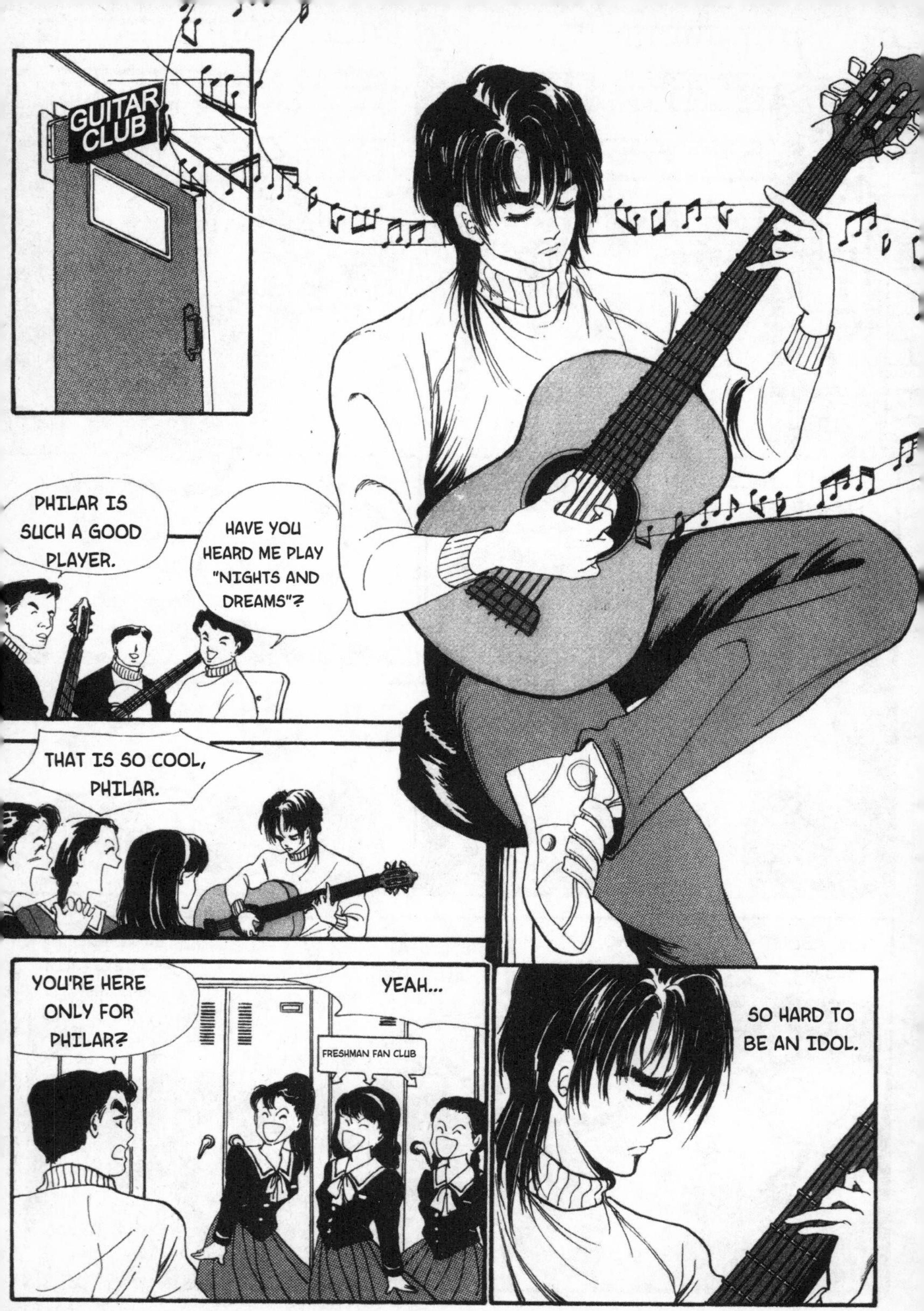

GUITAR CLUB
PHILAR IS SUCH A GOOD PLAYER.
HAVE YOU HEARD ME PLAY "NIGHTS AND DREAMS"?
THAT IS SO COOL, PHILAR.
YOU'RE HERE ONLY FOR PHILAR?
YEAH...
FRESHMAN FAN CLUB
SO HARD TO BE AN IDOL.

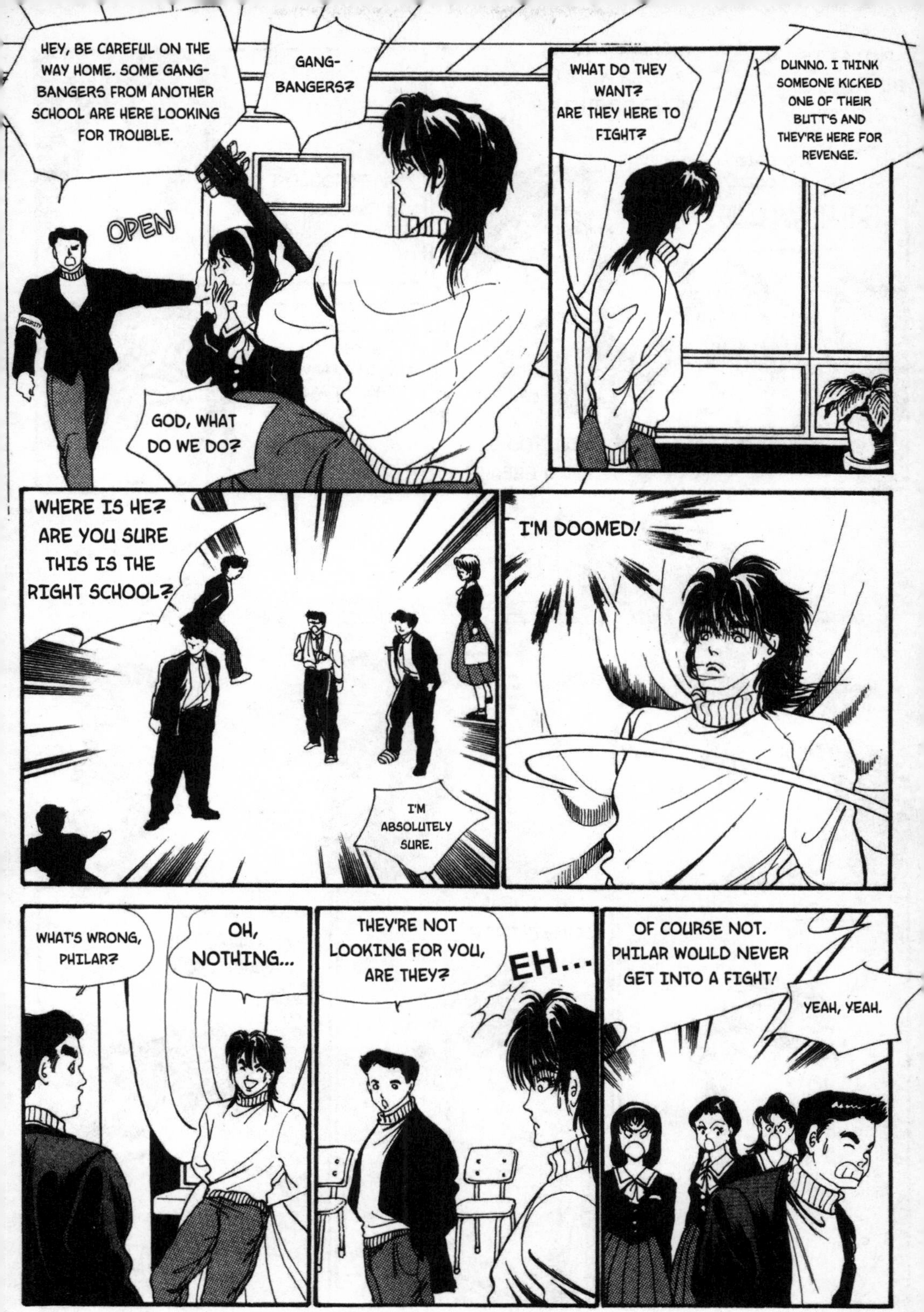
HEY, BE CAREFUL ON THE WAY HOME. SOME GANG-BANGERS FROM ANOTHER SCHOOL ARE HERE LOOKING FOR TROUBLE.
GANG-BANGERS?
OPEN
GOD, WHAT DO WE DO?
WHAT DO THEY WANT? ARE THEY HERE TO FIGHT?
DUNNO. I THINK SOMEONE KICKED ONE OF THEIR BUTT'S AND THEY'RE HERE FOR REVENGE.
WHERE IS HE? ARE YOU SURE THIS IS THE RIGHT SCHOOL?
I'M ABSOLUTELY SURE.
I'M DOOMED!
WHAT'S WRONG, PHILAR?
OH, NOTHING...
THEY'RE NOT LOOKING FOR YOU, ARE THEY?
EH...
OF COURSE NOT. PHILAR WOULD NEVER GET INTO A FIGHT!
YEAH, YEAH.

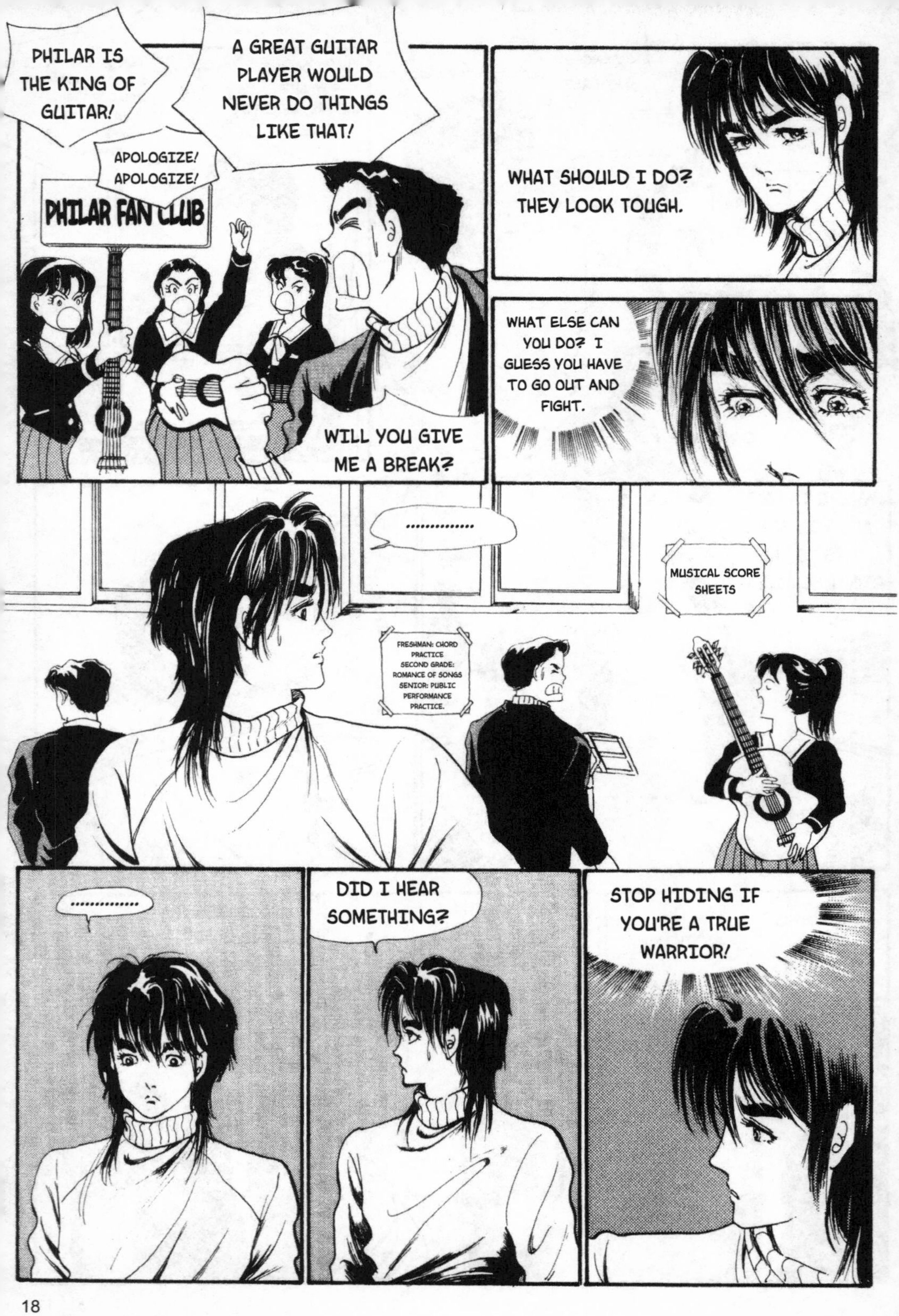
PHILAR IS THE KING OF GUITAR!
A GREAT GUITAR PLAYER WOULD NEVER DO THINGS LIKE THAT!
APOLOGIZE! APOLOGIZE!
PHILAR FAN CLUB
WILL YOU GIVE ME A BREAK?
WHAT SHOULD I DO? THEY LOOK TOUGH.
WHAT ELSE CAN YOU DO? I GUESS YOU HAVE TO GO OUT AND FIGHT.
....
MUSICAL SCORE SHEETS
FRESHMAN: CHORD PRACTICE SECOND GRADE: ROMANCE OF SONGS SENIOR: PUBLIC PERFORMANCE PRACTICE.
....
DID I HEAR SOMETHING?
STOP HIDING IF YOU'RE A TRUE WARRIOR!

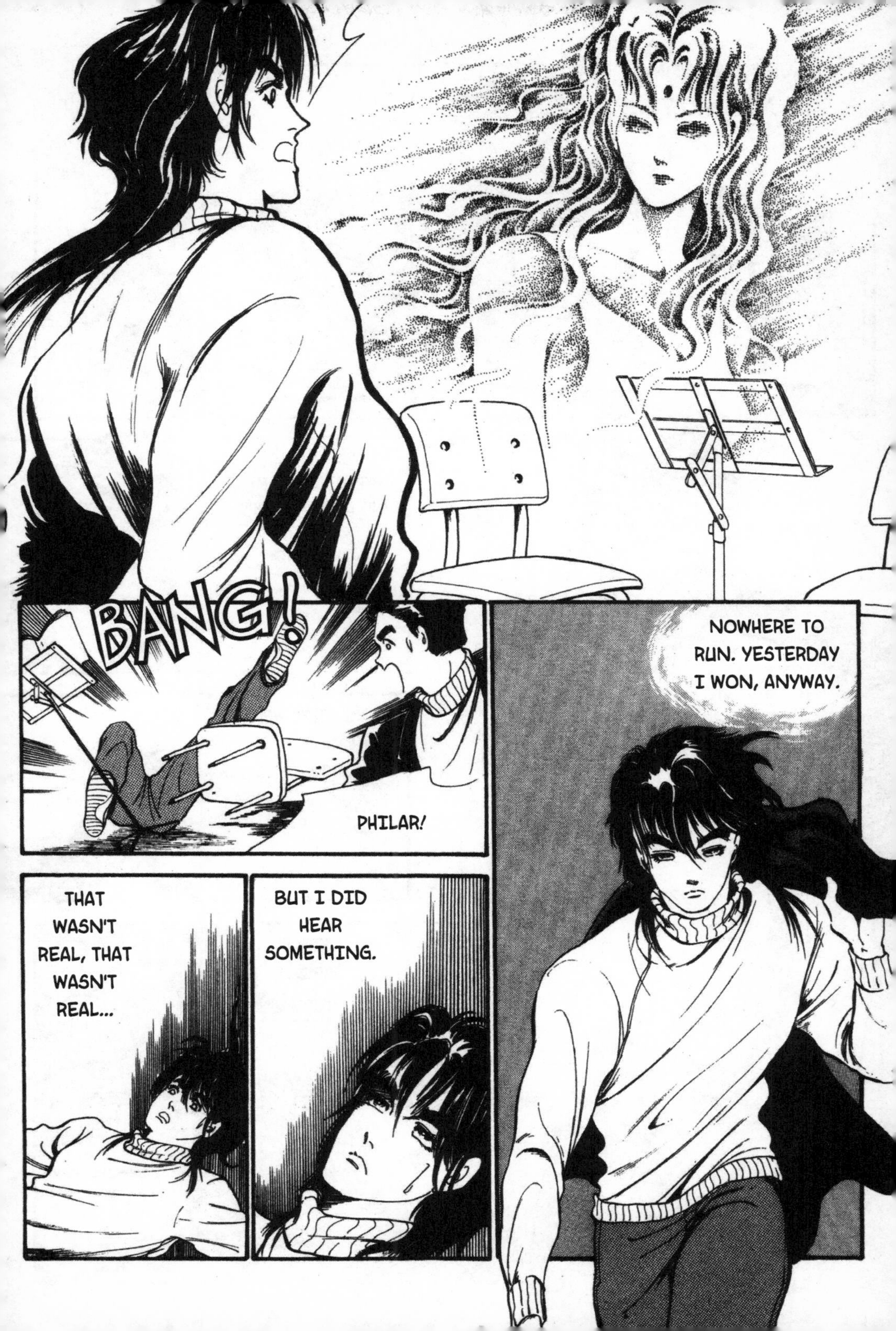
BANG!
PHILAR!
NOWHERE TO RUN. YESTERDAY I WON, ANYWAY.
THAT WASN'T REAL, THAT WASN'T REAL...
BUT I DID HEAR SOMETHING.

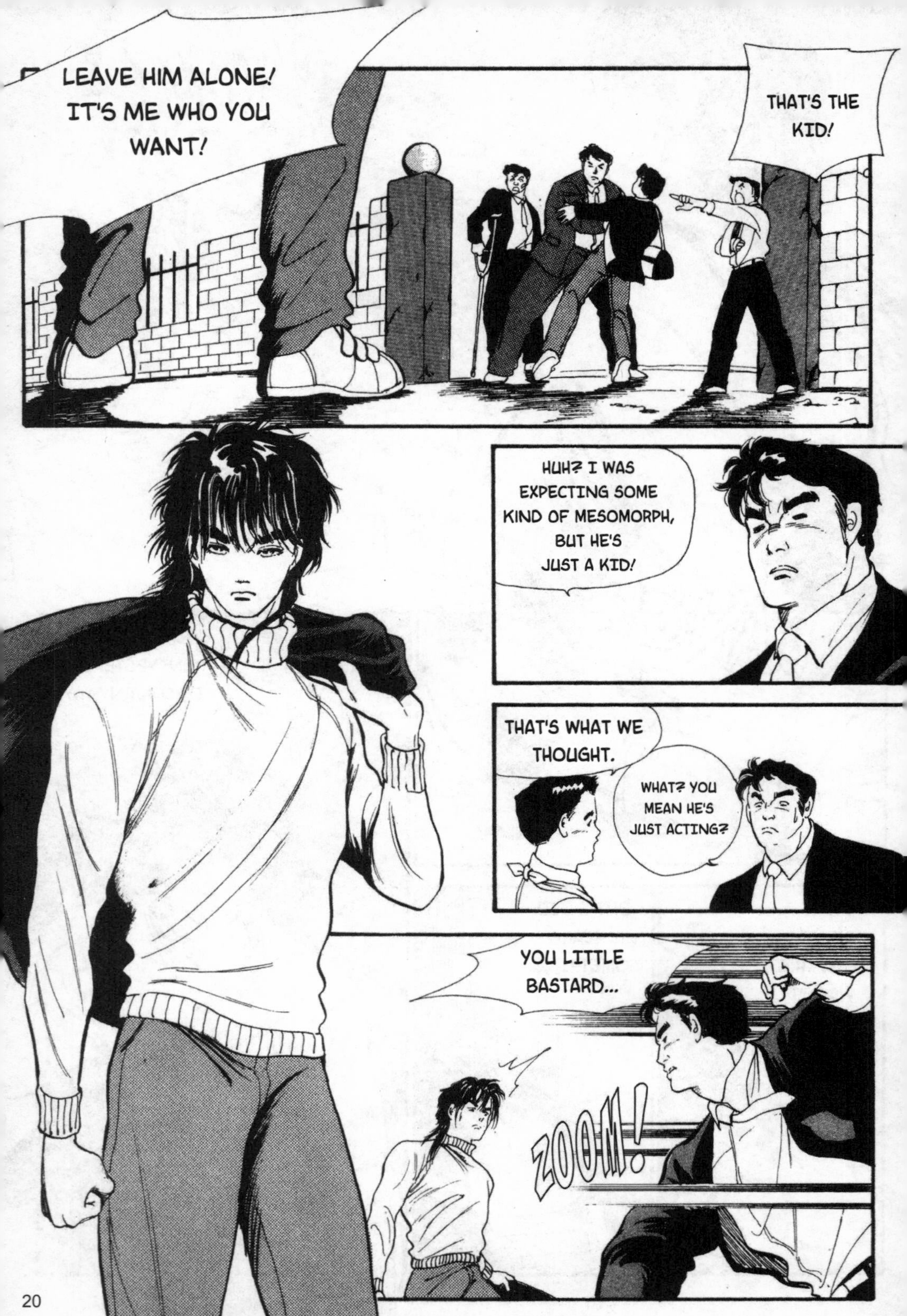
LEAVE HIM ALONE! IT'S ME WHO YOU WANT!
THAT'S THE KID!
HUH? I WAS EXPECTING SOME KIND OF MESOMORPH, BUT HE'S JUST A KID!
THAT'S WHAT WE THOUGHT.
WHAT? YOU MEAN HE'S JUST ACTING?
YOU LITTLE BASTARD...
ZOOM!

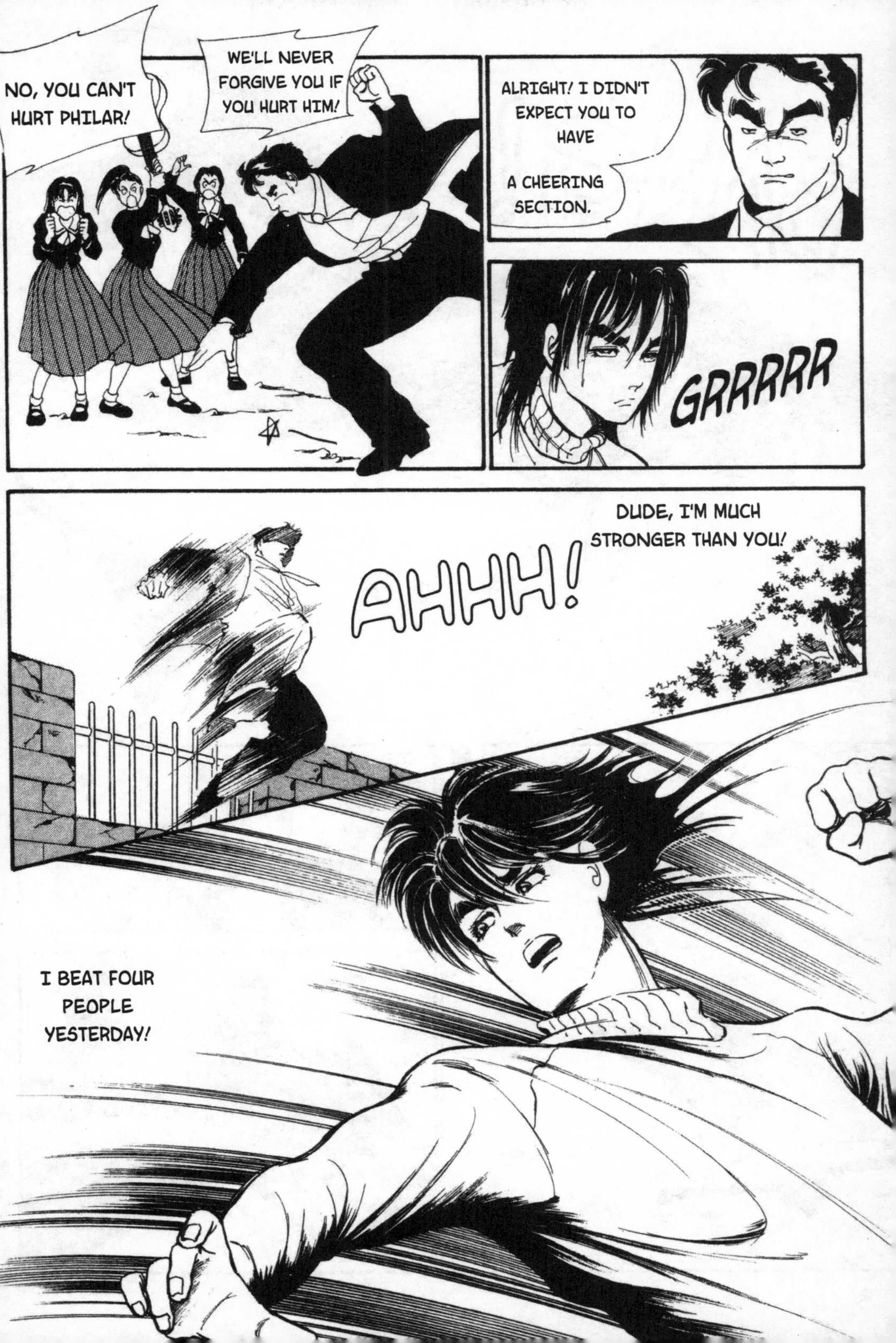
NO, YOU CAN'T HURT PHILAR!
WE'LL NEVER FORGIVE YOU IF YOU HURT HIM!
ALRIGHT! I DIDN'T EXPECT YOU TO HAVE
A CHEERING SECTION.
GRRRRR
DUDE, I'M MUCH STRONGER THAN YOU!
AHHH!
I BEAT FOUR PEOPLE YESTERDAY!

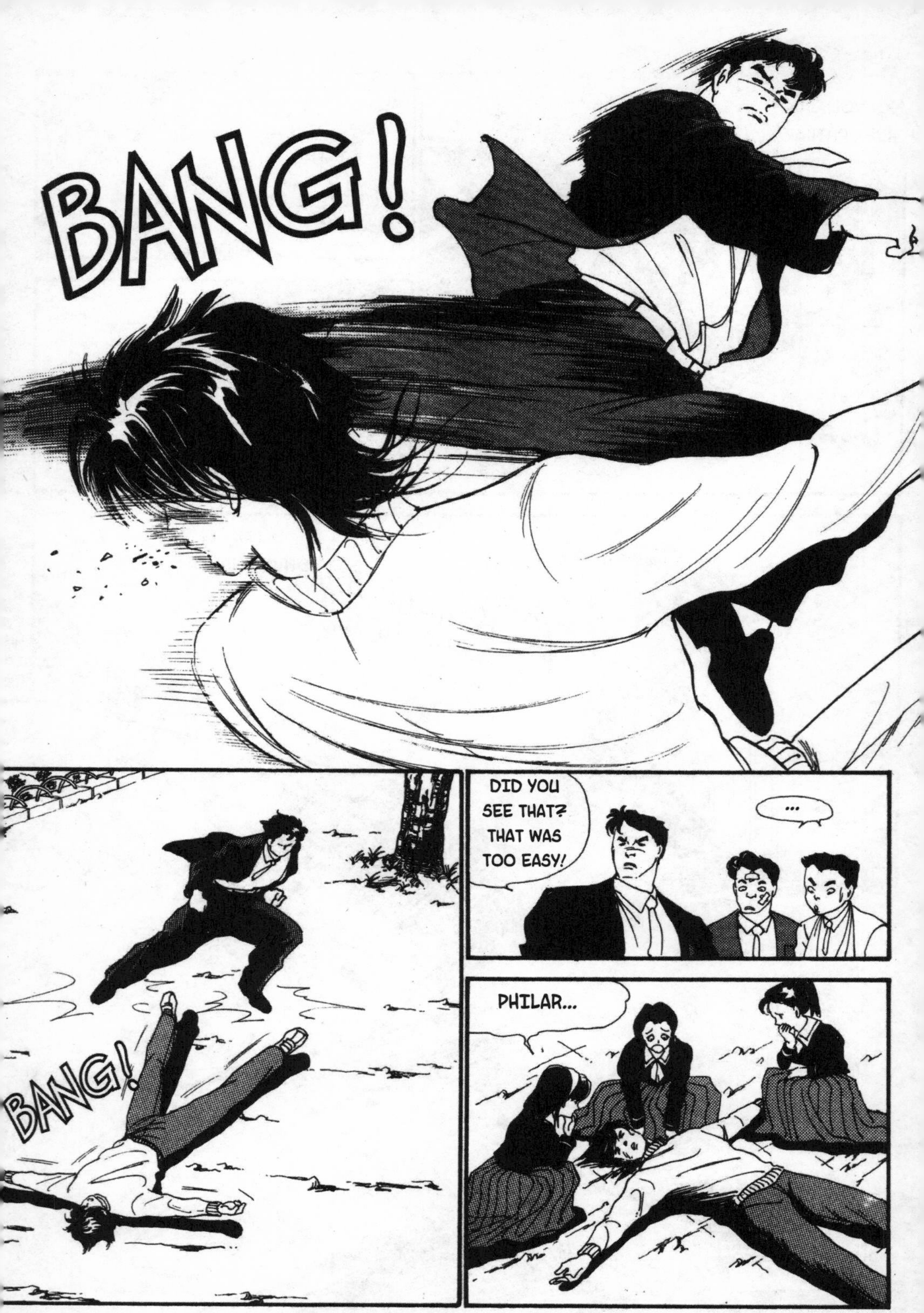
BANG!
BANG!
DID YOU SEE THAT? THAT WAS TOO EASY!
...
PHILAR...

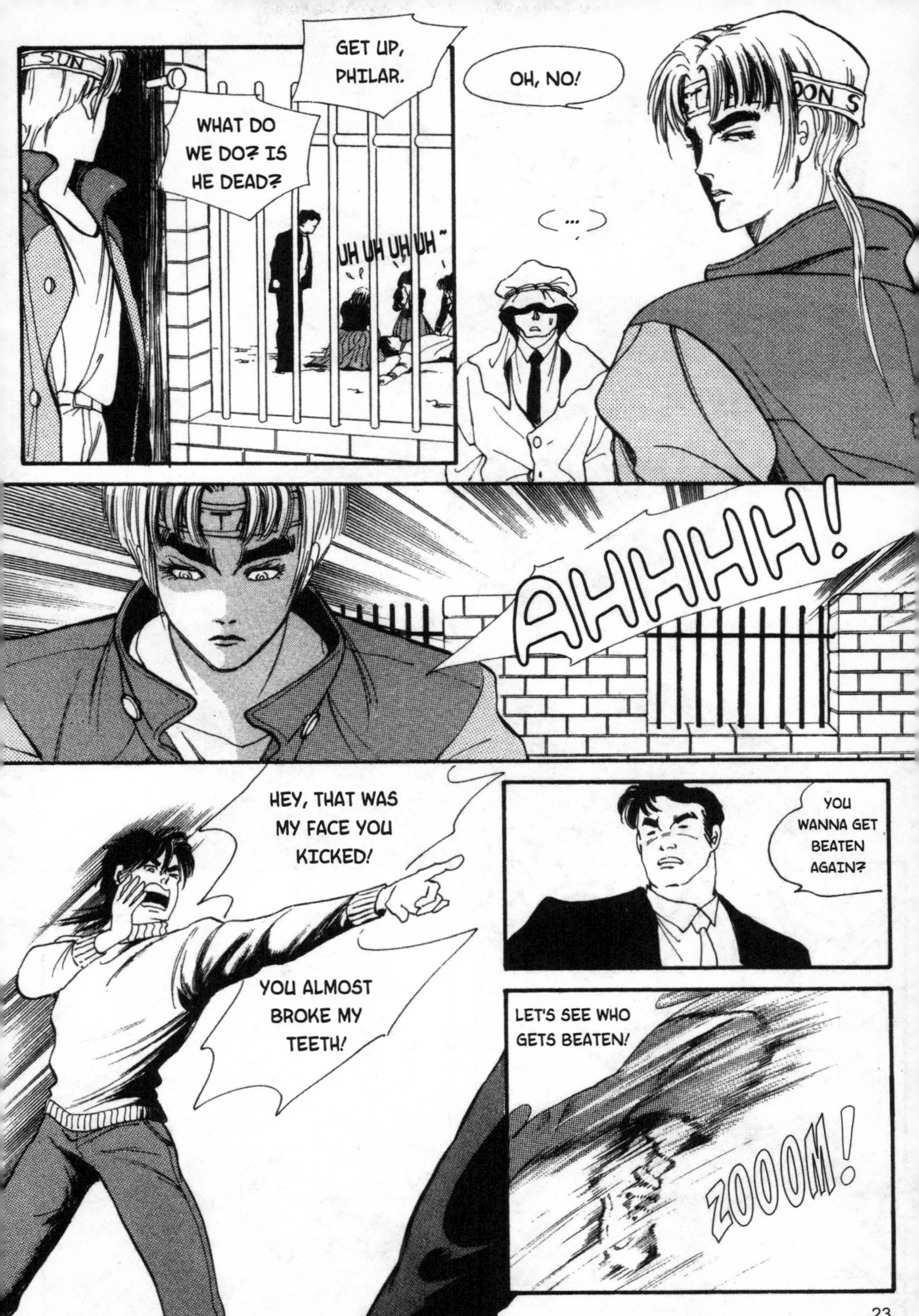
GET UP, PHILAR.
WHAT DO WE DO? IS HE DEAD?
UH UH UH UH
OH, NO!
...
AHHHH!
HEY, THAT WAS MY FACE YOU KICKED!
YOU ALMOST BROKE MY TEETH!
YOU WANNA GET BEATEN AGAIN?
LET'S SEE WHO GETS BEATEN!
ZOOOM!

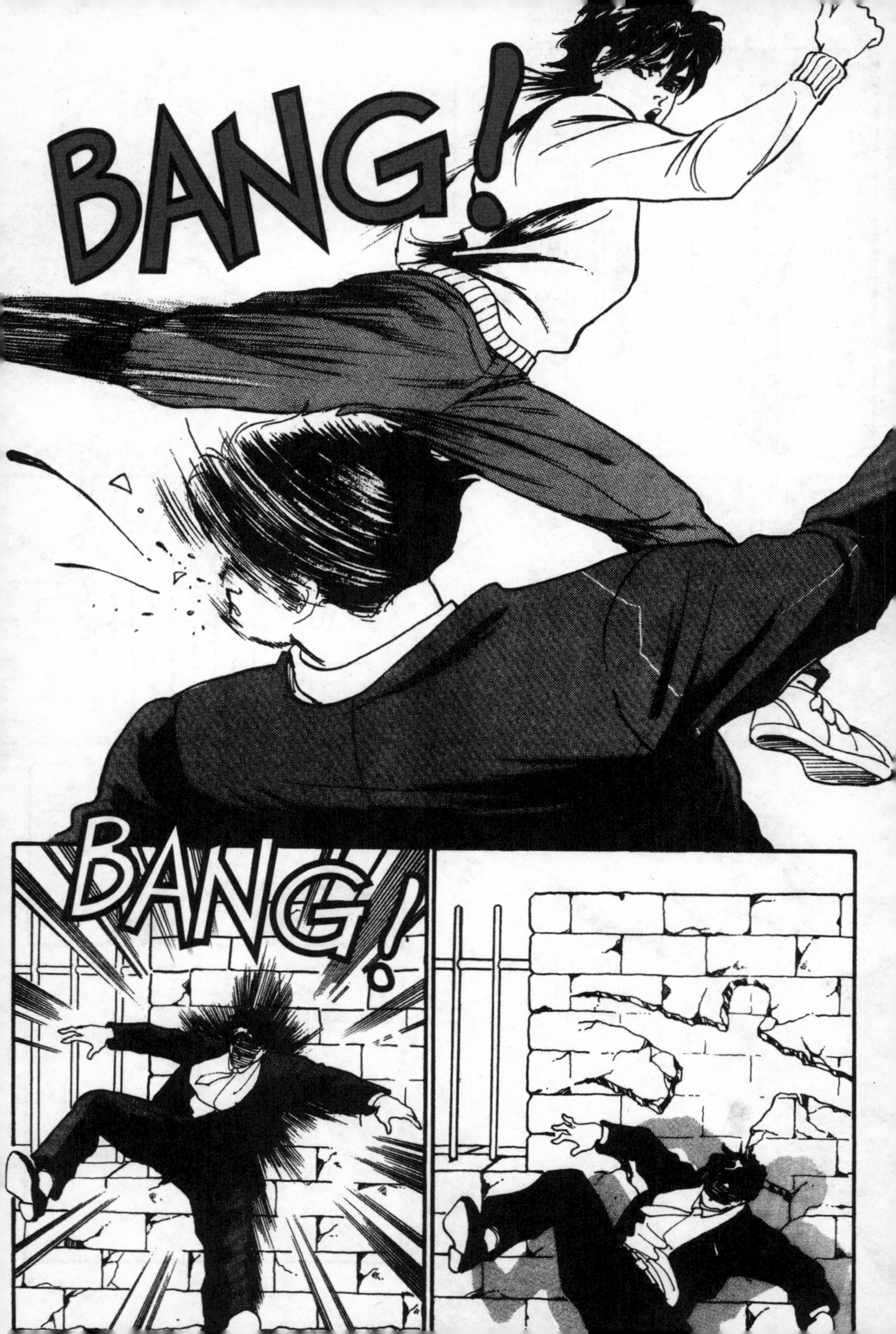
BANG!
BANG!

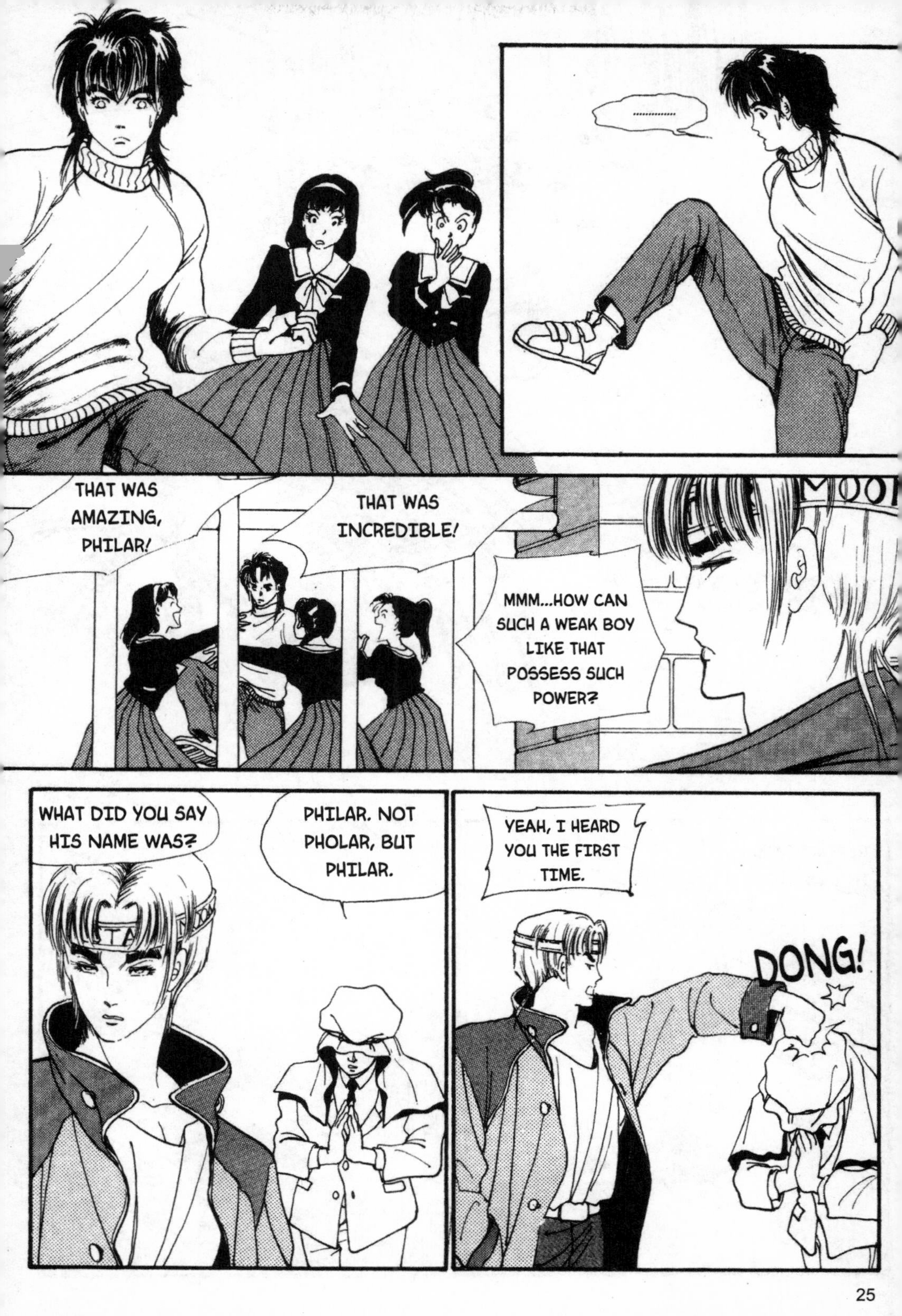
....
THAT WAS AMAZING, PHILAR!
THAT WAS INCREDIBLE!
MMM...HOW CAN SUCH A WEAK BOY LIKE THAT POSSESS SUCH POWER?
WHAT DID YOU SAY HIS NAME WAS?
PHILAR. NOT PHOLAR, BUT PHILAR.
YEAH, I HEARD YOU THE FIRST TIME.
DONG!

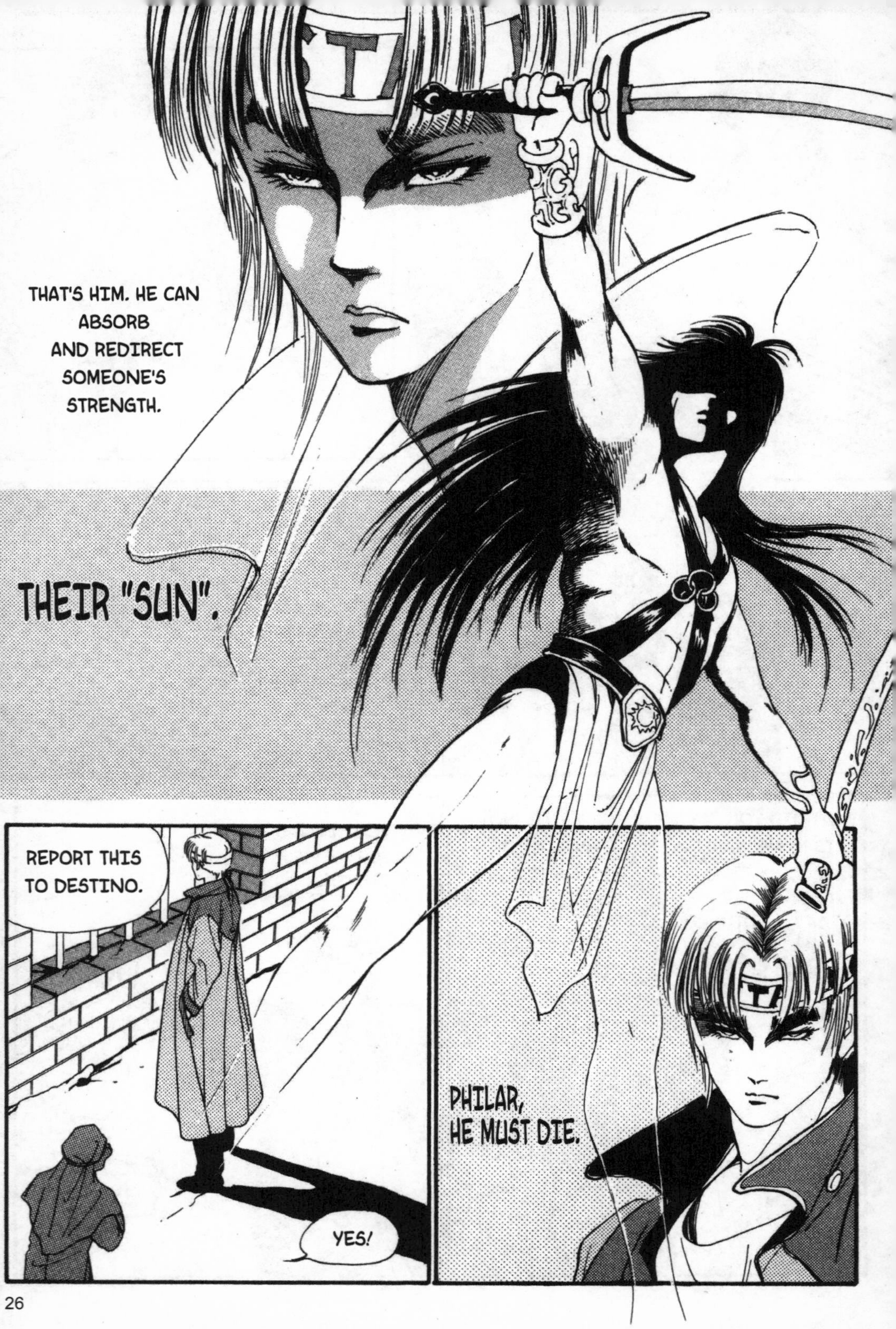
THAT'S HIM. HE CAN ABSORB AND REDIRECT SOMEONE'S STRENGTH.
THEIR "SUN".
REPORT THIS TO DESTINO.
YES!
PHILAR, HE MUST DIE.

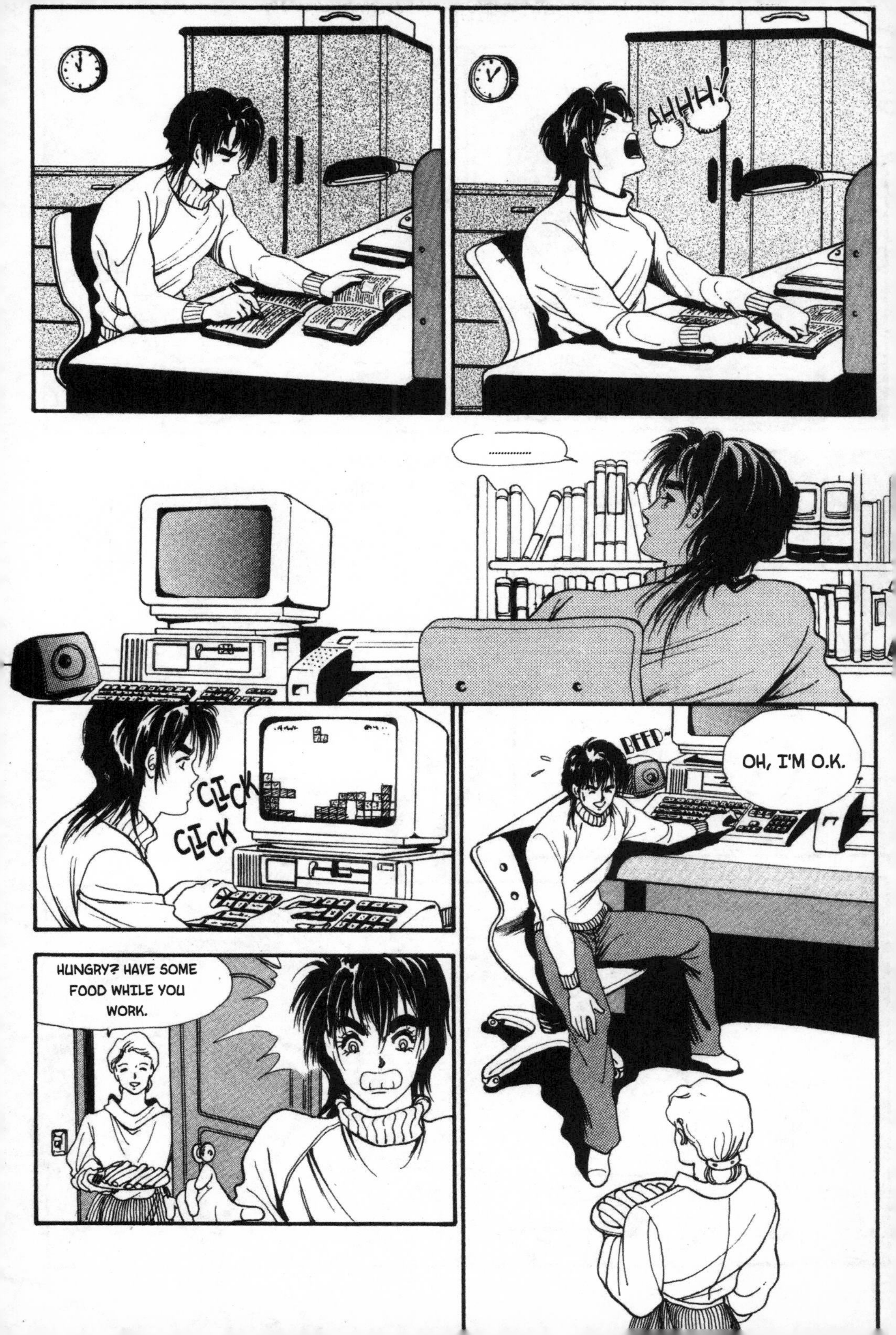
AHHH!
....
CLICK
CLICK
BEEP~
OH, I'M O.K.
HUNGRY? HAVE SOME FOOD WHILE YOU WORK.

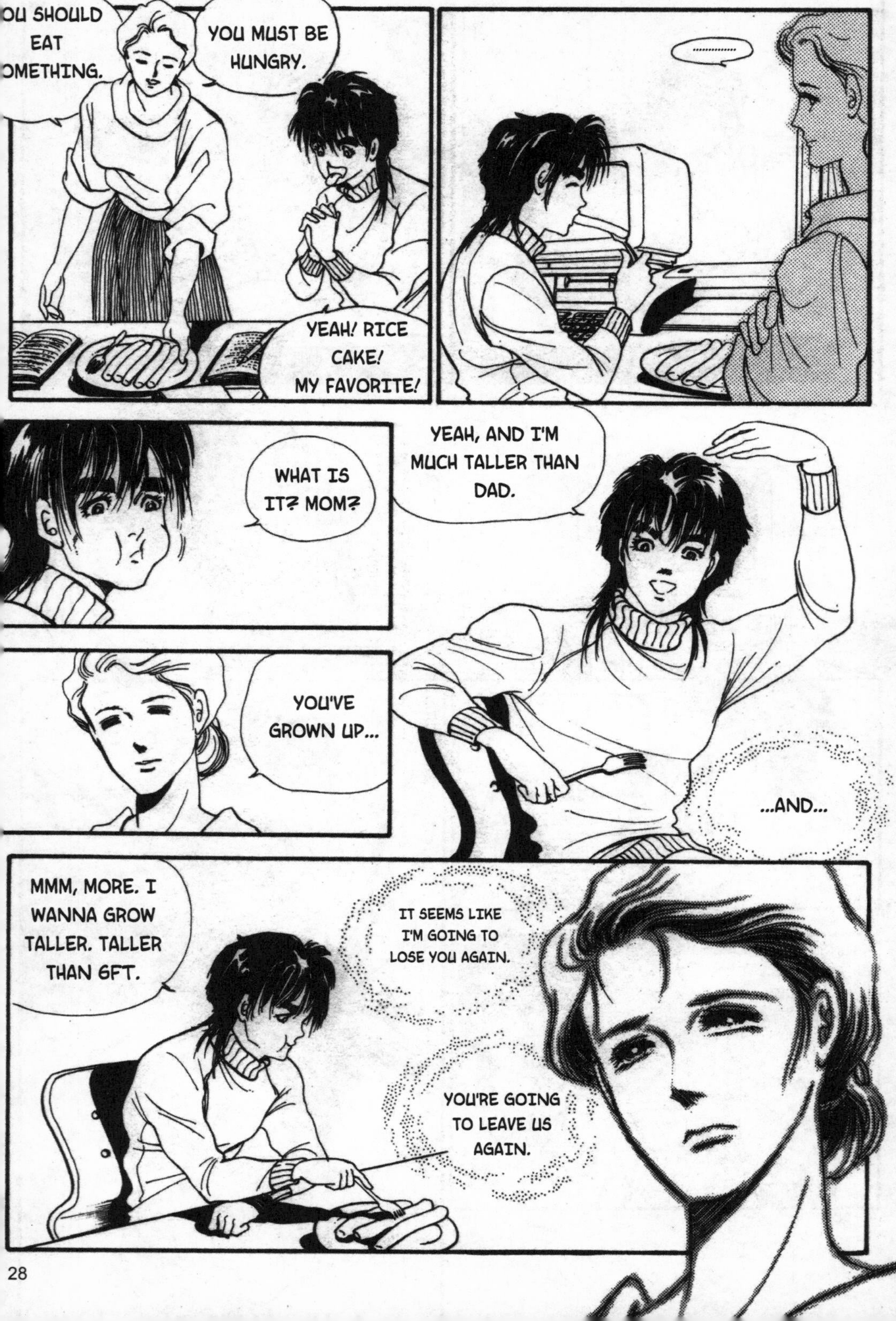
OU SHOULD EAT OMETHING.
YOU MUST BE HUNGRY.
YEAH! RICE CAKE! MY FAVORITE!
....
WHAT IS IT? MOM?
YEAH, AND I'M MUCH TALLER THAN DAD.
YOU'VE GROWN UP...
...AND...
MMM, MORE. I WANNA GROW TALLER. TALLER THAN 6FT.
IT SEEMS LIKE I'M GOING TO LOSE YOU AGAIN.
YOU'RE GOING TO LEAVE US AGAIN.

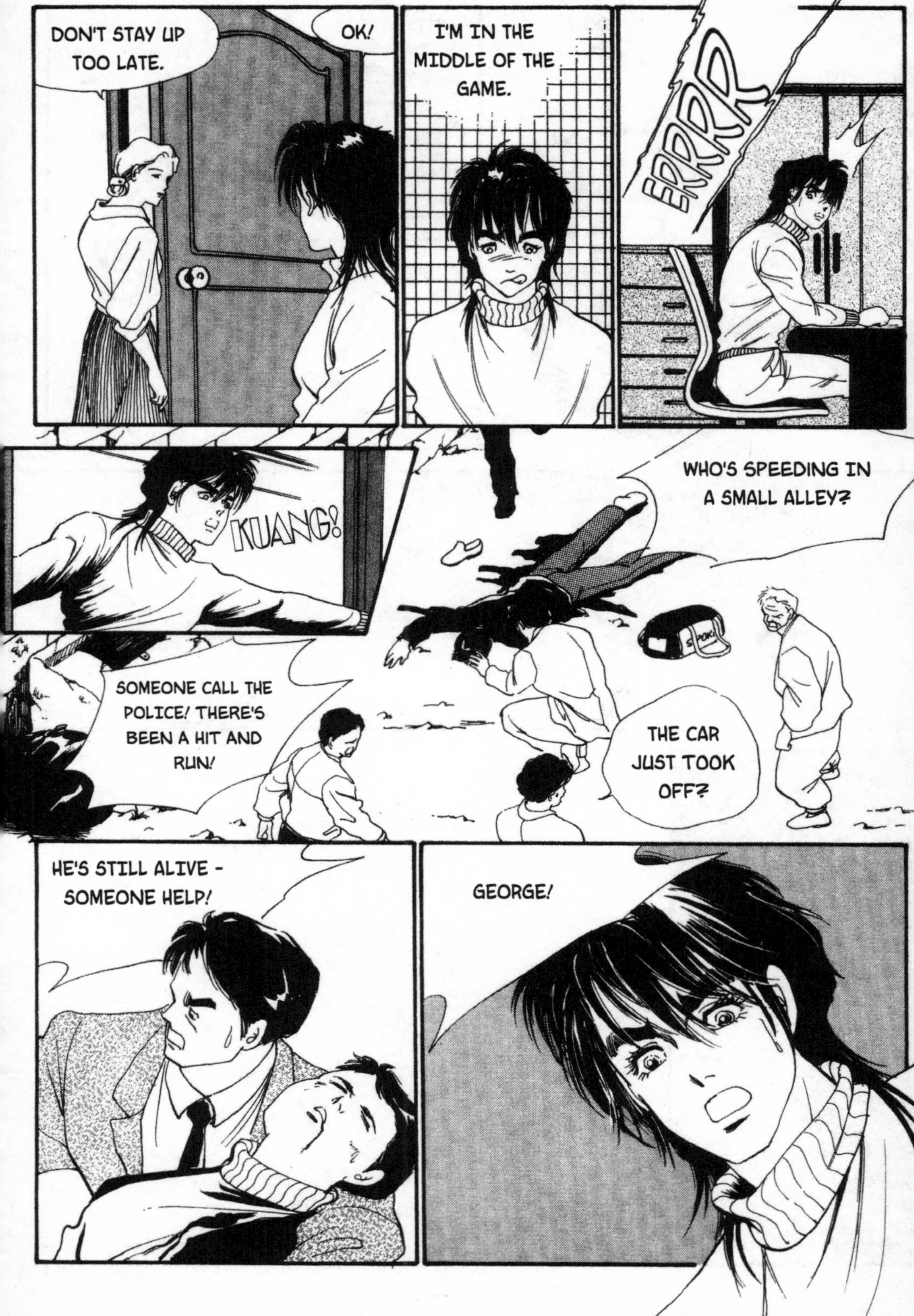
DON'T STAY UP TOO LATE.
OK!
I'M IN THE MIDDLE OF THE GAME.
ERRRR
KUANG!
WHO'S SPEEDING IN A SMALL ALLEY?
SOMEONE CALL THE POLICE! THERE'S BEEN A HIT AND RUN!
THE CAR JUST TOOK OFF?
HE'S STILL ALIVE - SOMEONE HELP!
GEORGE!

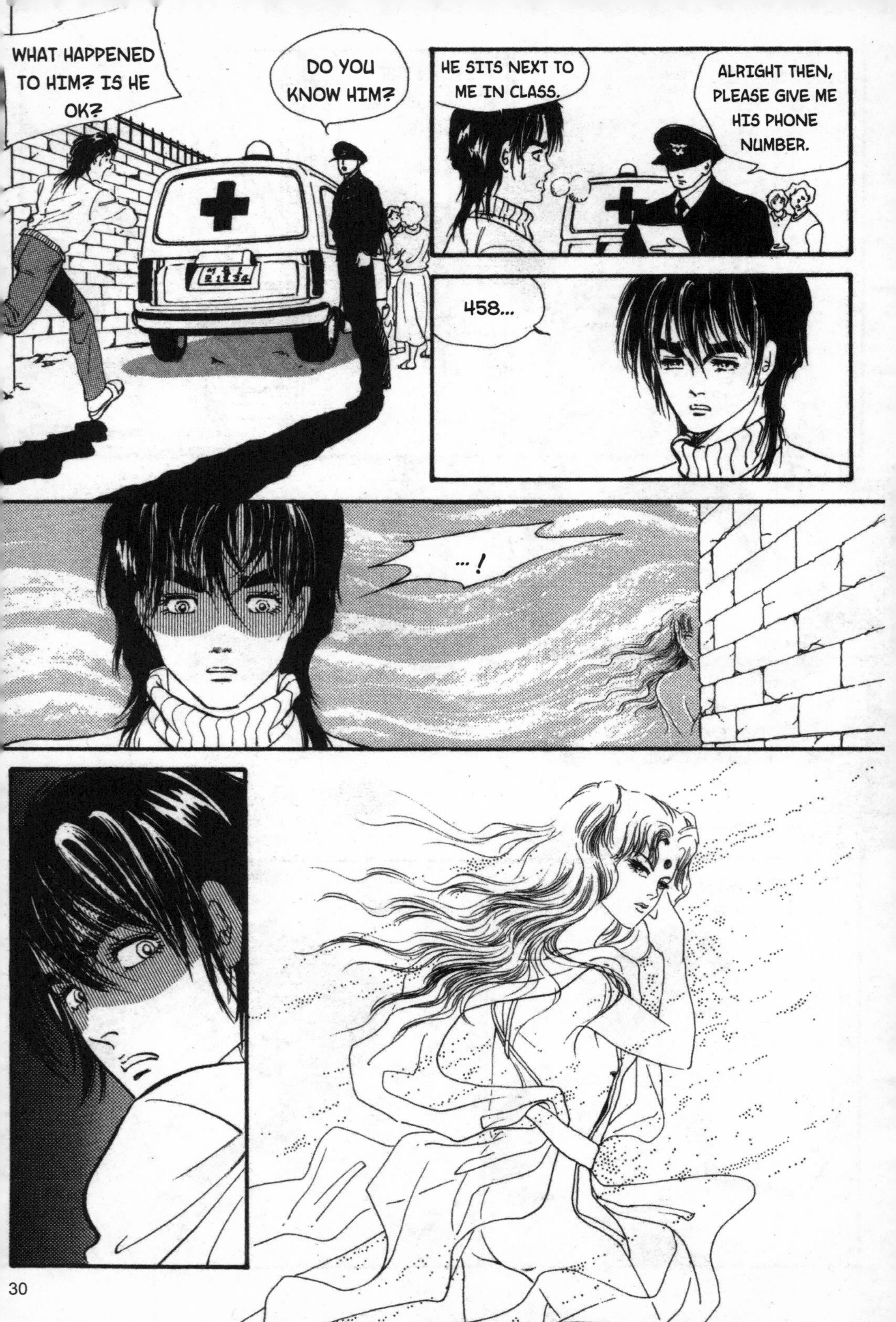
WHAT HAPPENED TO HIM? IS HE OK?
DO YOU KNOW HIM?
HE SITS NEXT TO ME IN CLASS.
ALRIGHT THEN, PLEASE GIVE ME HIS PHONE NUMBER.
458...
...!

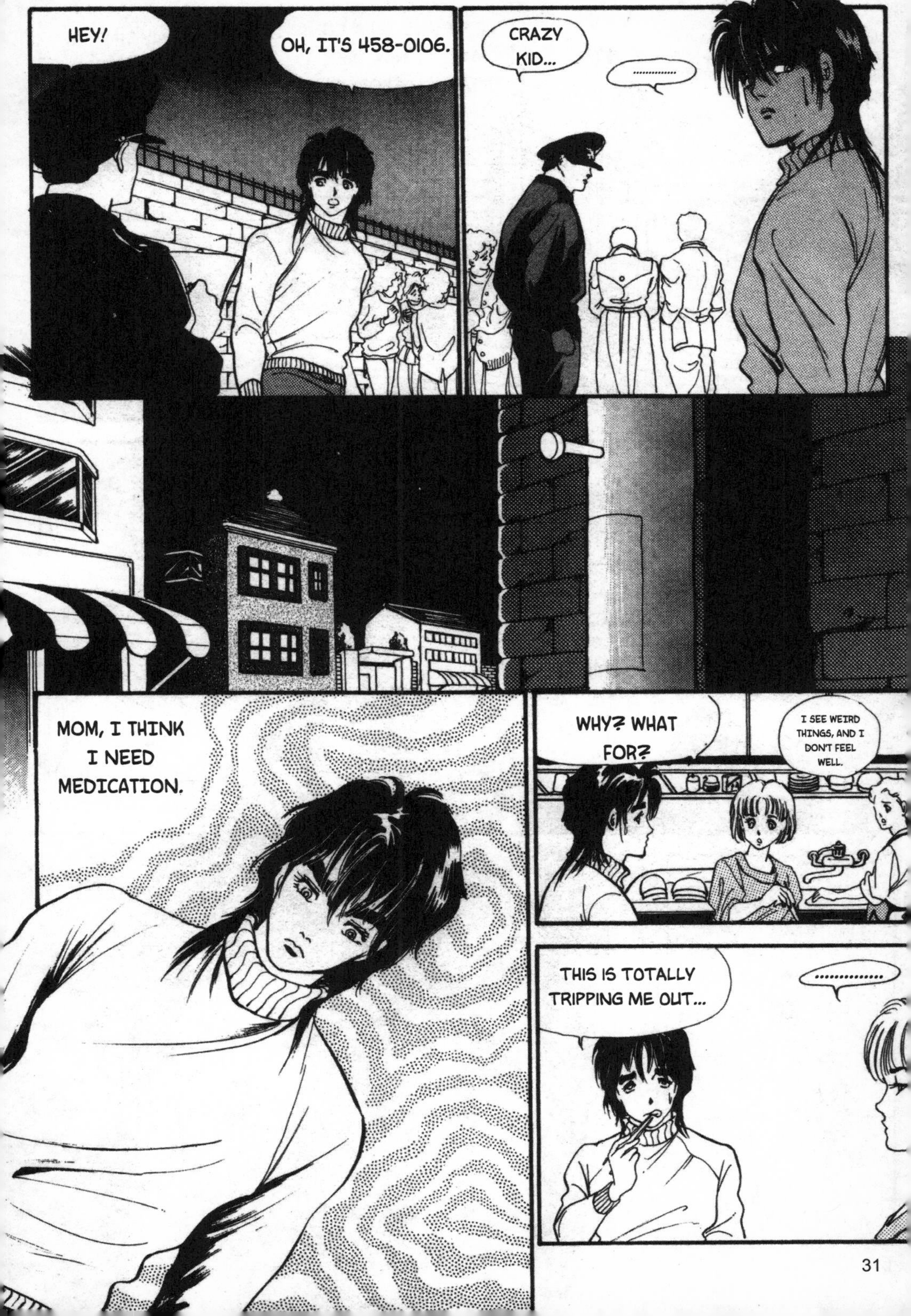
HEY!
OH, IT'S 458-0106.
CRAZY KID...
....
MOM, I THINK I NEED MEDICATION.
WHY? WHAT FOR?
I SEE WEIRD THINGS, AND I DON'T FEEL WELL.
THIS IS TOTALLY TRIPPING ME OUT...
....

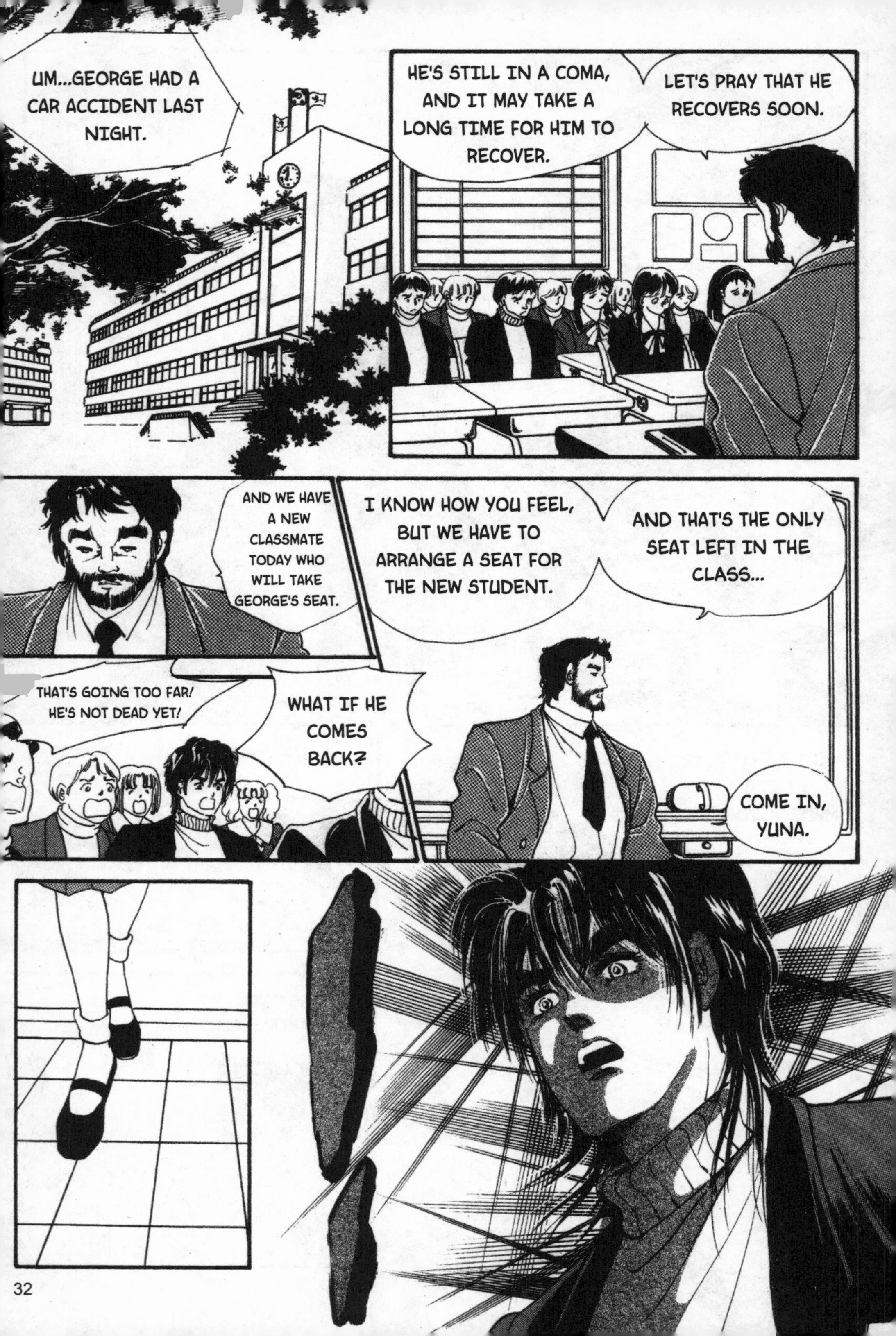
UM...GEORGE HAD A CAR ACCIDENT LAST NIGHT.
HE'S STILL IN A COMA, AND IT MAY TAKE A LONG TIME FOR HIM TO RECOVER.
LET'S PRAY THAT HE RECOVERS SOON.
AND WE HAVE A NEW CLASSMATE TODAY WHO WILL TAKE GEORGE'S SEAT.
I KNOW HOW YOU FEEL, BUT WE HAVE TO ARRANGE A SEAT FOR THE NEW STUDENT.
AND THAT'S THE ONLY SEAT LEFT IN THE CLASS...
THAT'S GOING TOO FAR! HE'S NOT DEAD YET!
WHAT IF HE COMES BACK?
COME IN, YUNA.

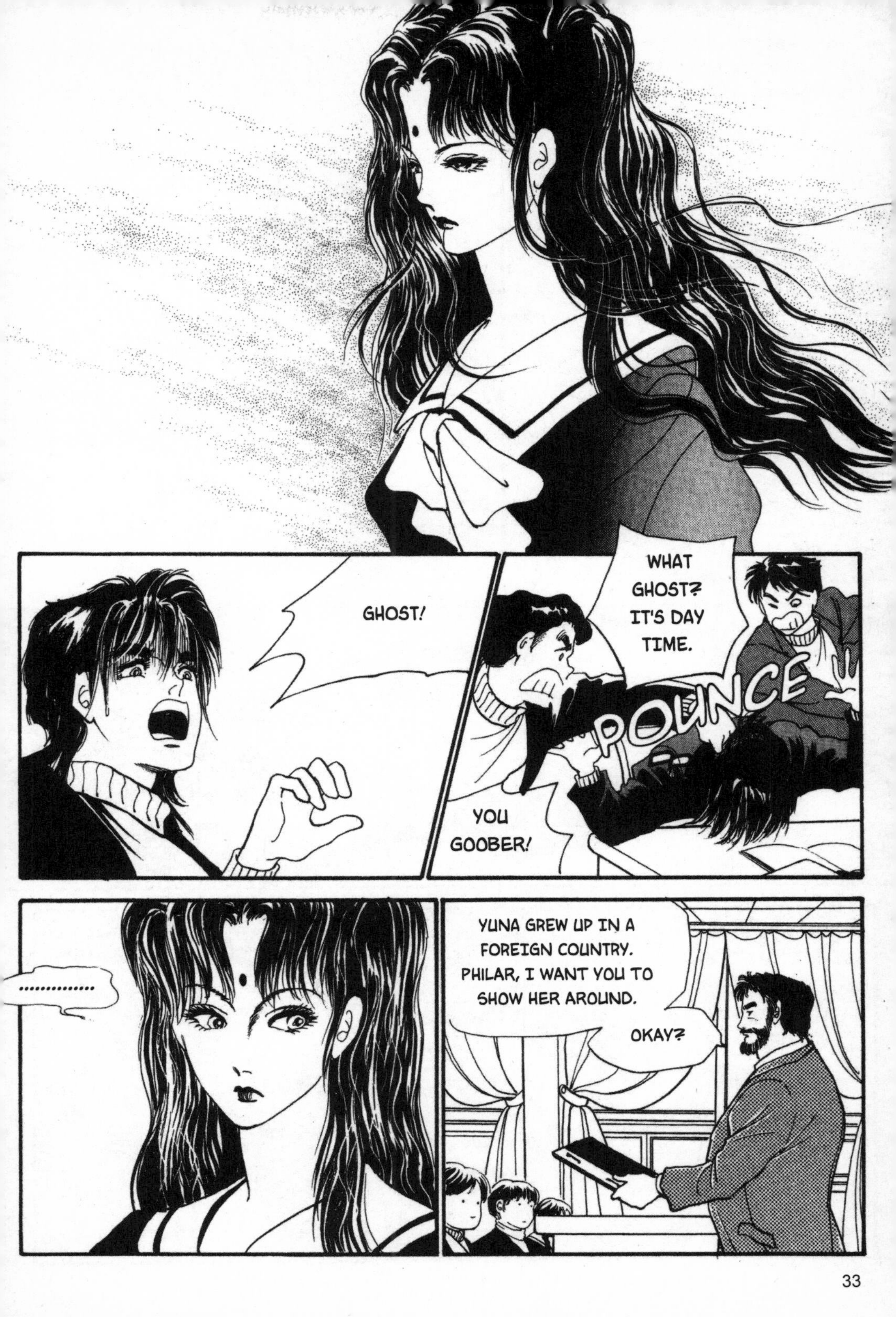
GHOST!
WHAT GHOST? IT'S DAY TIME.
POUNCE
YOU GOOBER!
....
YUNA GREW UP IN A FOREIGN COUNTRY. PHILAR, I WANT YOU TO SHOW HER AROUND.
OKAY?

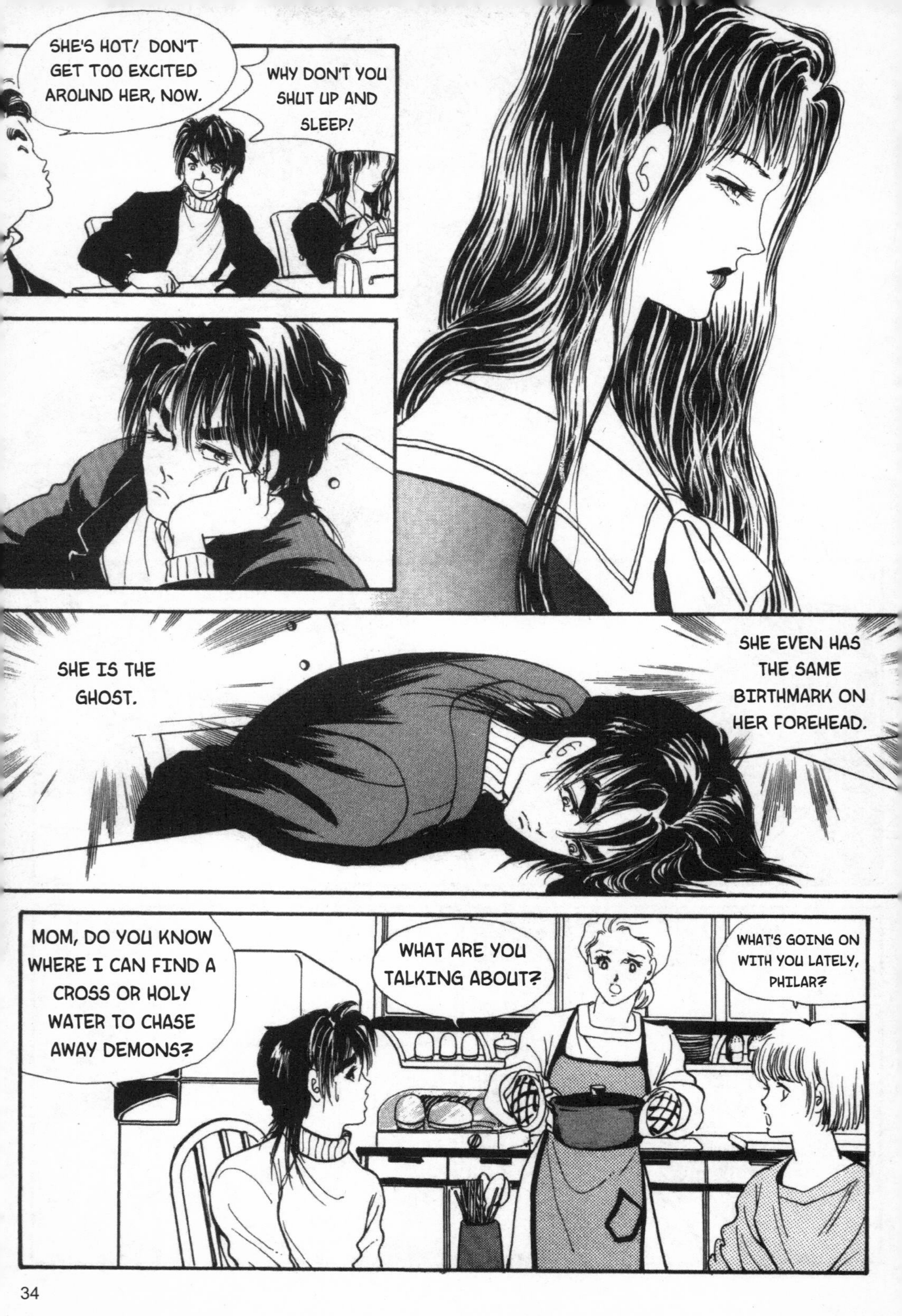

SHE'S HOT! DON'T GET TOO EXCITED AROUND HER, NOW.
WHY DON'T YOU SHUT UP AND SLEEP!
SHE IS THE GHOST.
SHE EVEN HAS THE SAME BIRTHMARK ON HER FOREHEAD.
MOM, DO YOU KNOW WHERE I CAN FIND A CROSS OR HOLY WATER TO CHASE AWAY DEMONS?
WHAT ARE YOU TALKING ABOUT?
WHAT'S GOING ON WITH YOU LATELY, PHILAR?

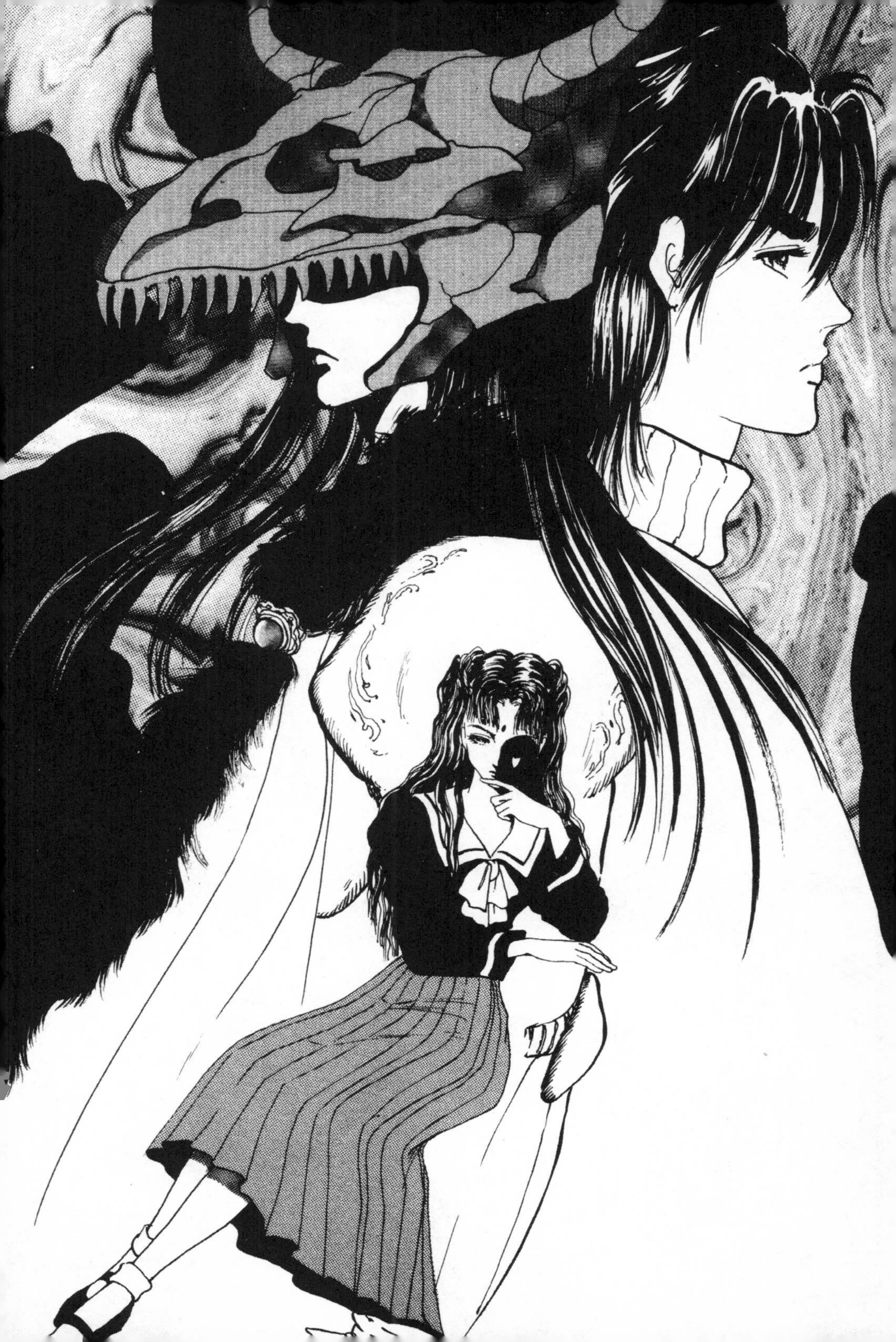

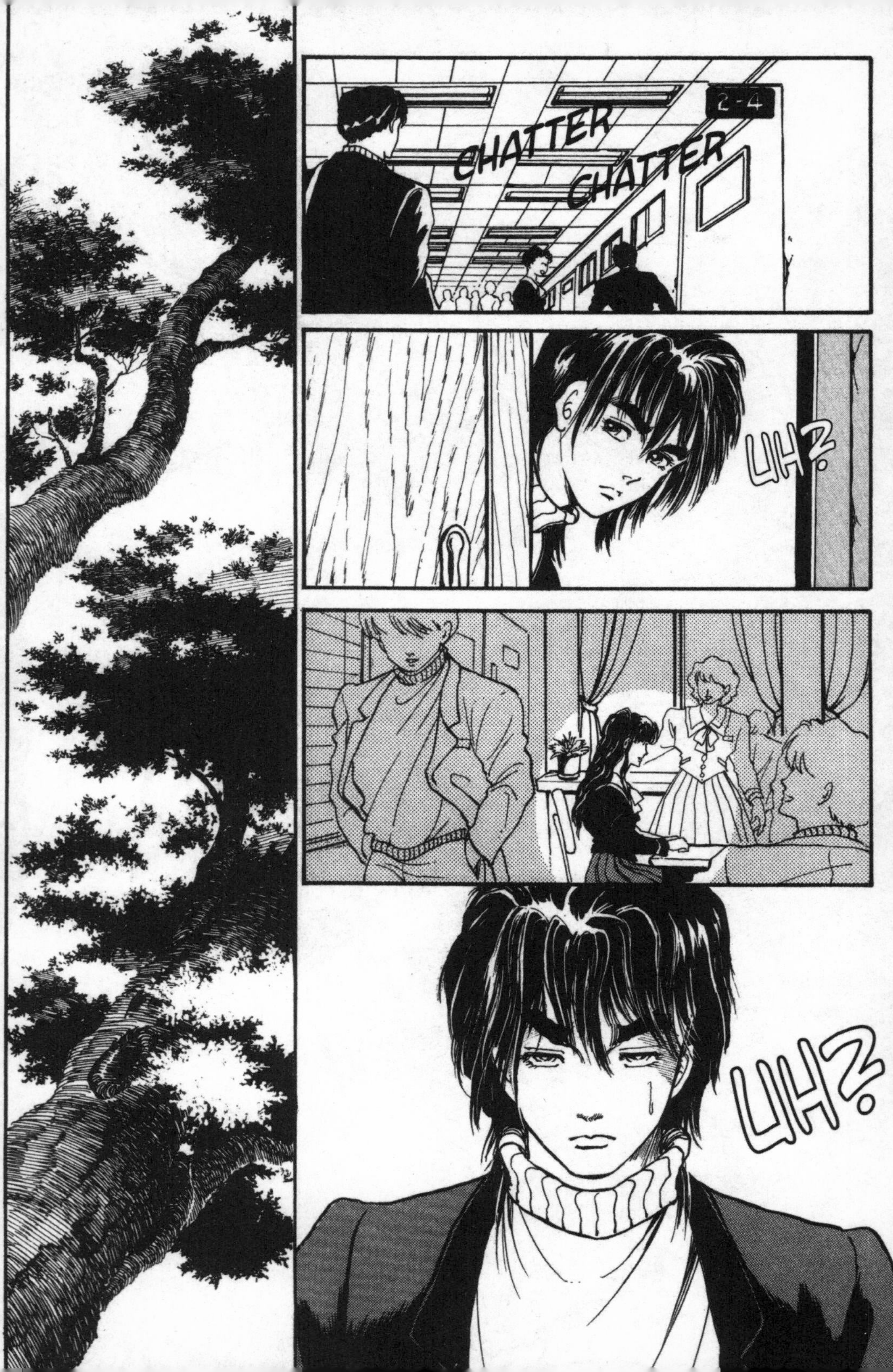
2-4
CHATTER
CHATTER
UH?
UH?

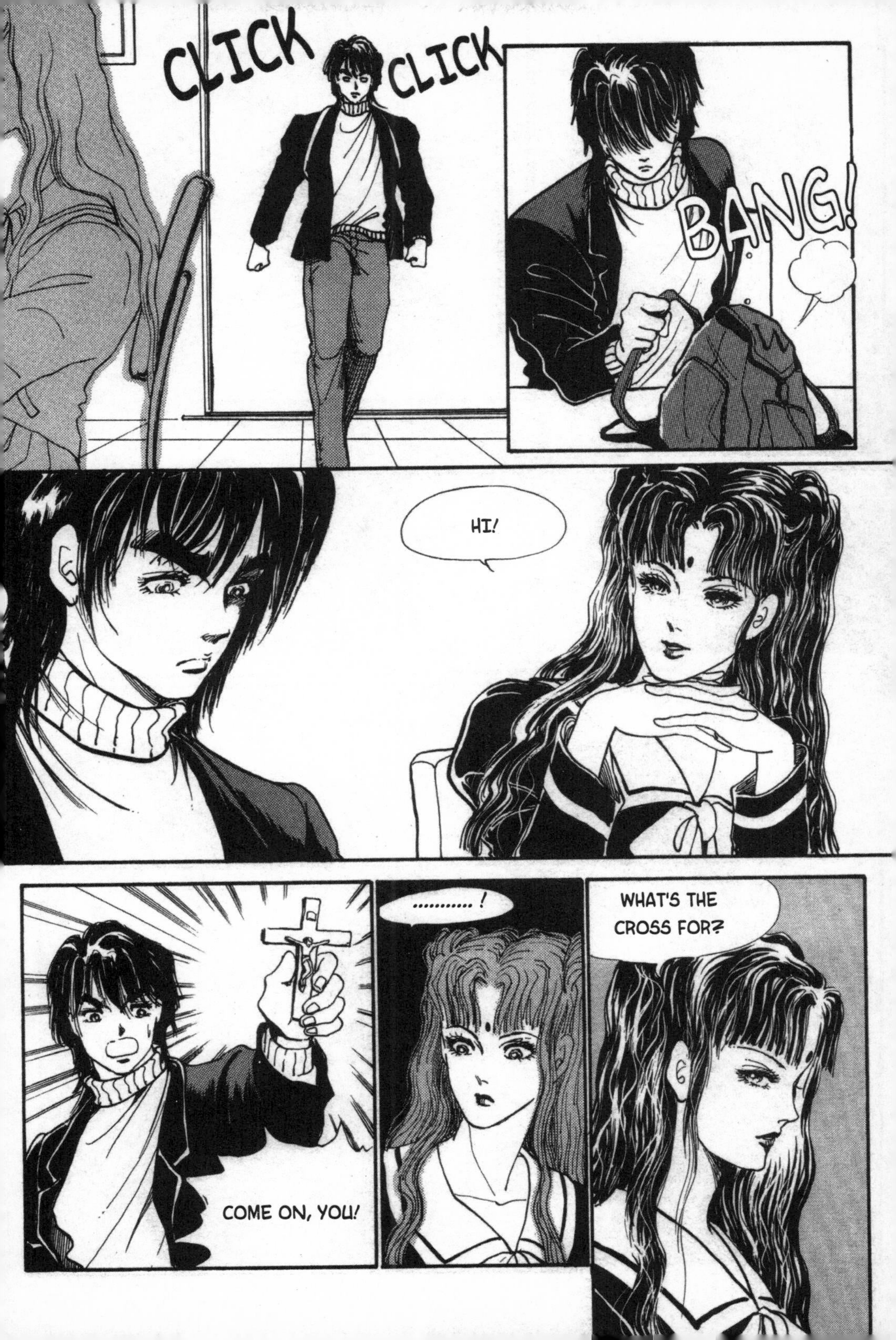
CLICK
CLICK
BANG!
HI!
COME ON, YOU!
............!
WHAT'S THE CROSS FOR?

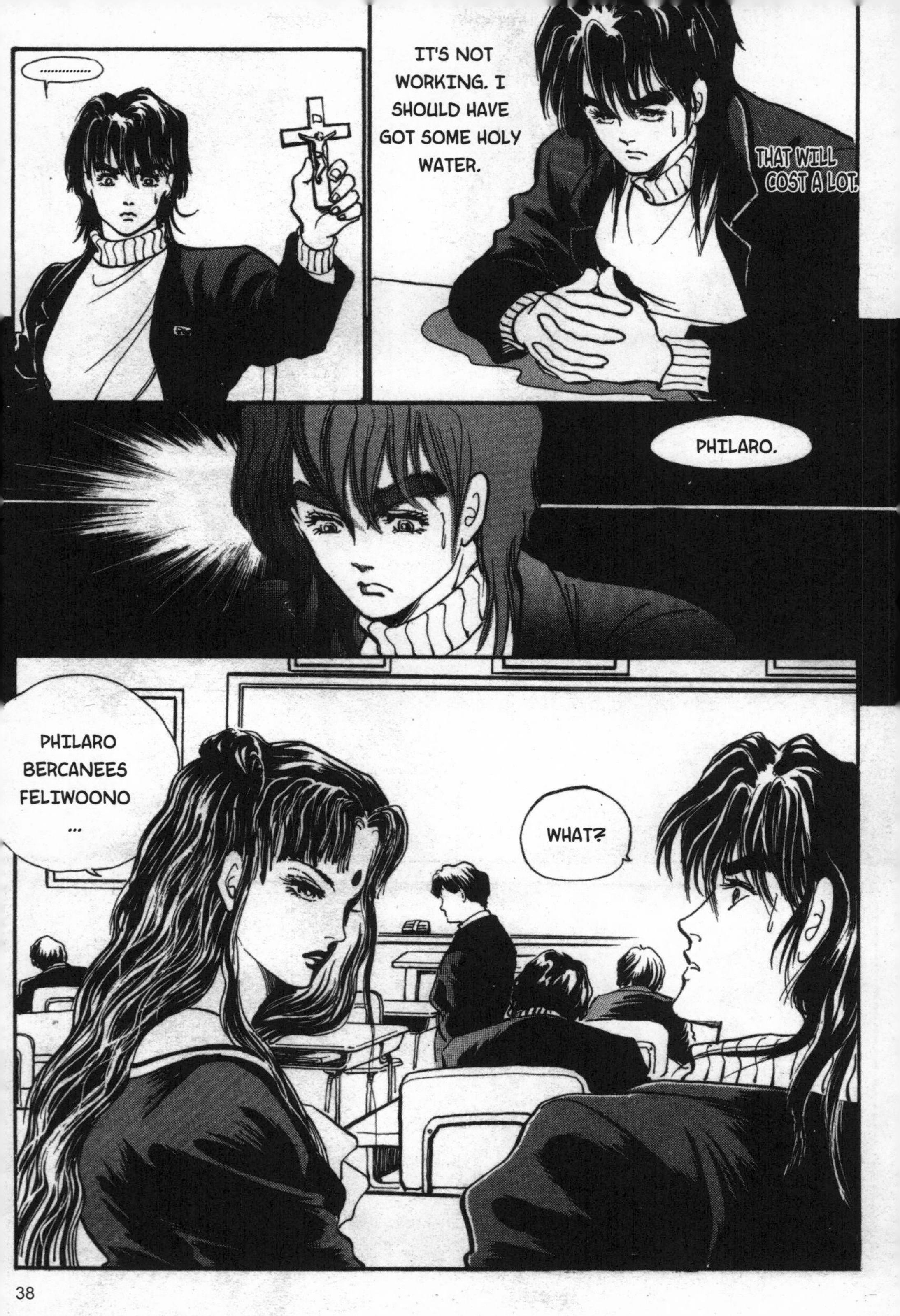
....
IT'S NOT WORKING. I SHOULD HAVE GOT SOME HOLY WATER.
THAT WILL COST A LOT.
PHILARO.
PHILARO BERCANEES FELIWOONO ...
WHAT?

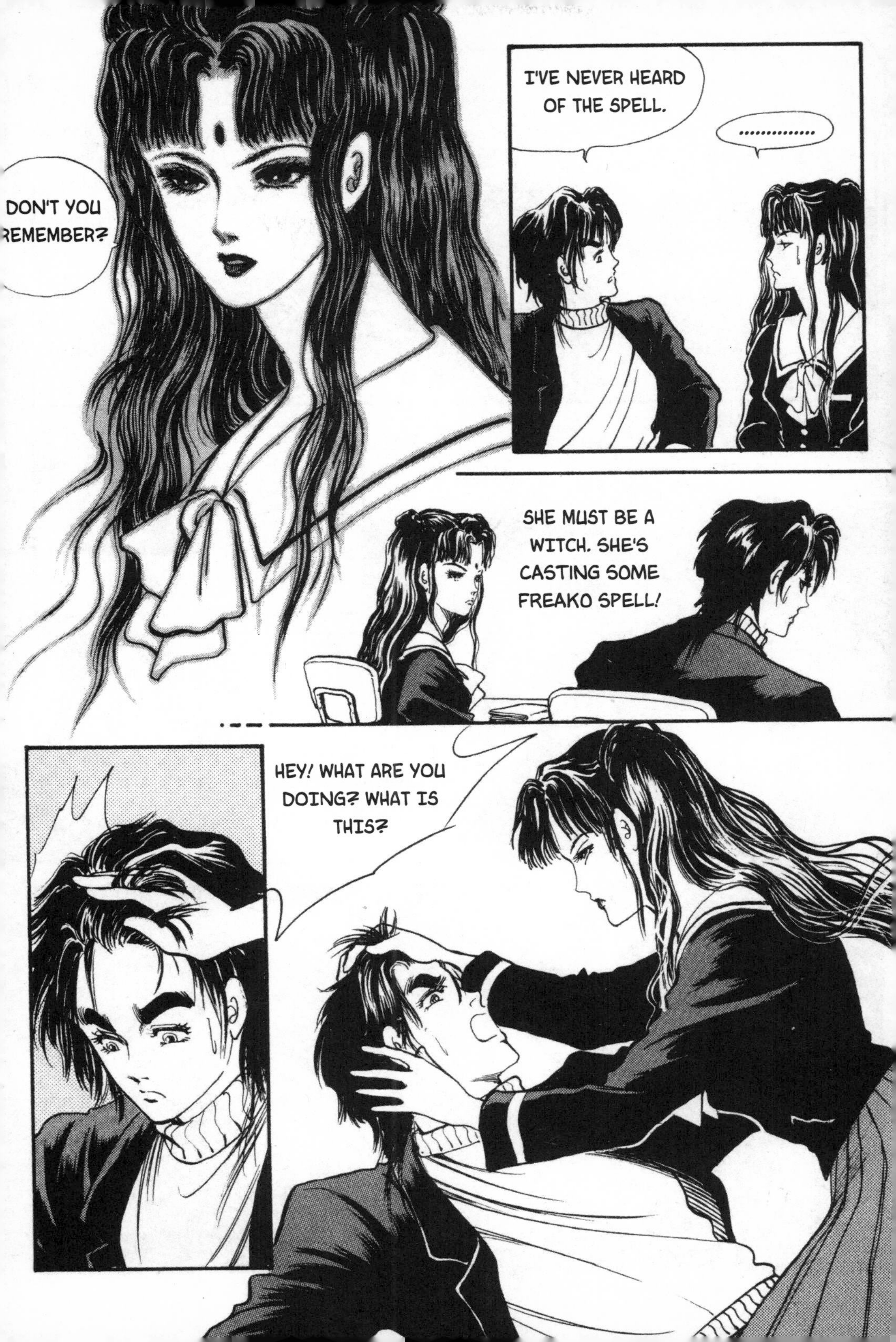
DON'T YOU REMEMBER?
I'VE NEVER HEARD OF THE SPELL.
....
SHE MUST BE A WITCH. SHE'S CASTING SOME FREAKO SPELL!
HEY! WHAT ARE YOU DOING? WHAT IS THIS?

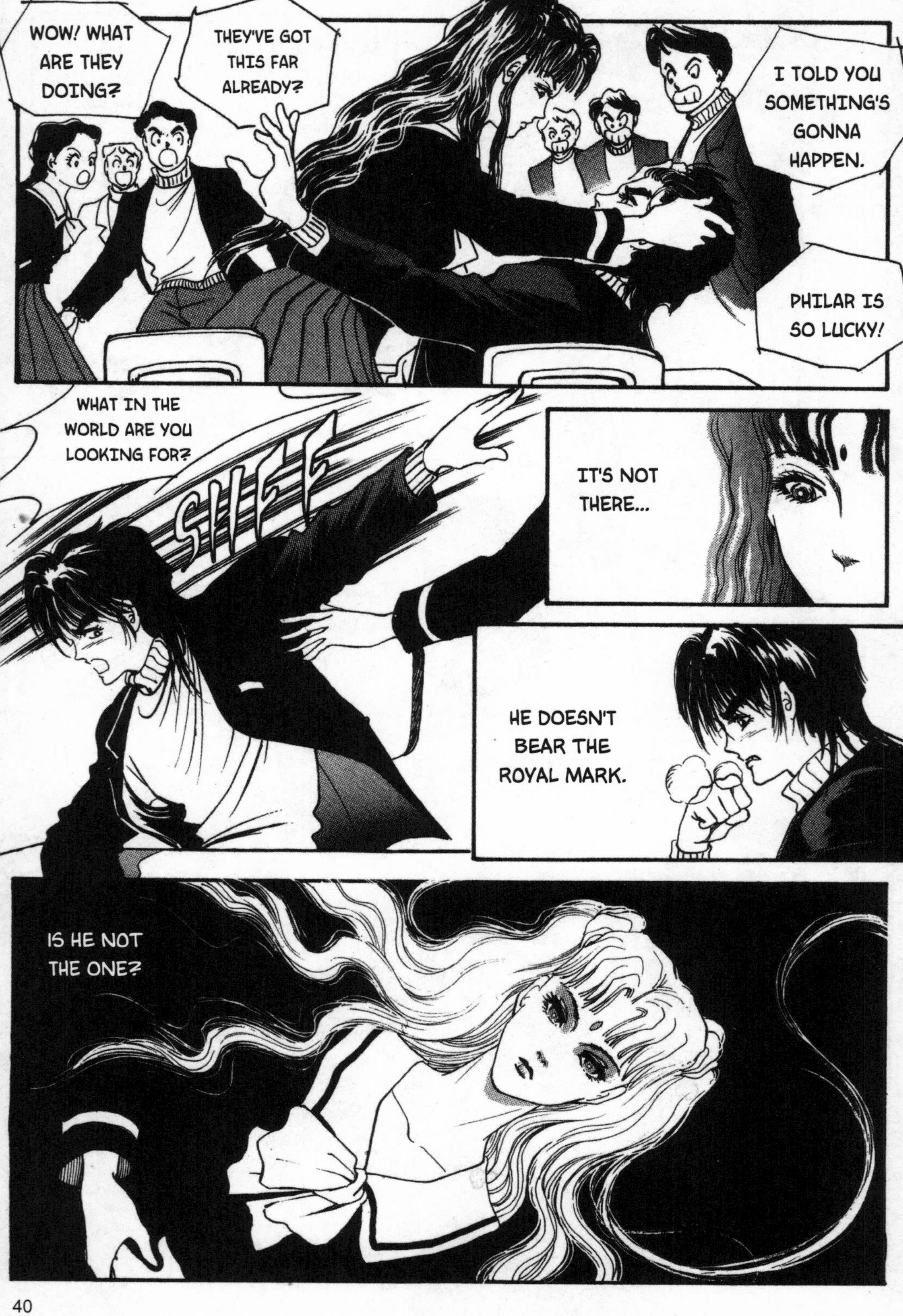
WOW! WHAT ARE THEY DOING?
THEY'VE GOT THIS FAR ALREADY?
I TOLD YOU SOMETHING'S GONNA HAPPEN.
PHILAR IS SO LUCKY!
WHAT IN THE WORLD ARE YOU LOOKING FOR?
SHFF
IT'S NOT THERE...
HE DOESN'T BEAR THE ROYAL MARK.
IS HE NOT THE ONE?

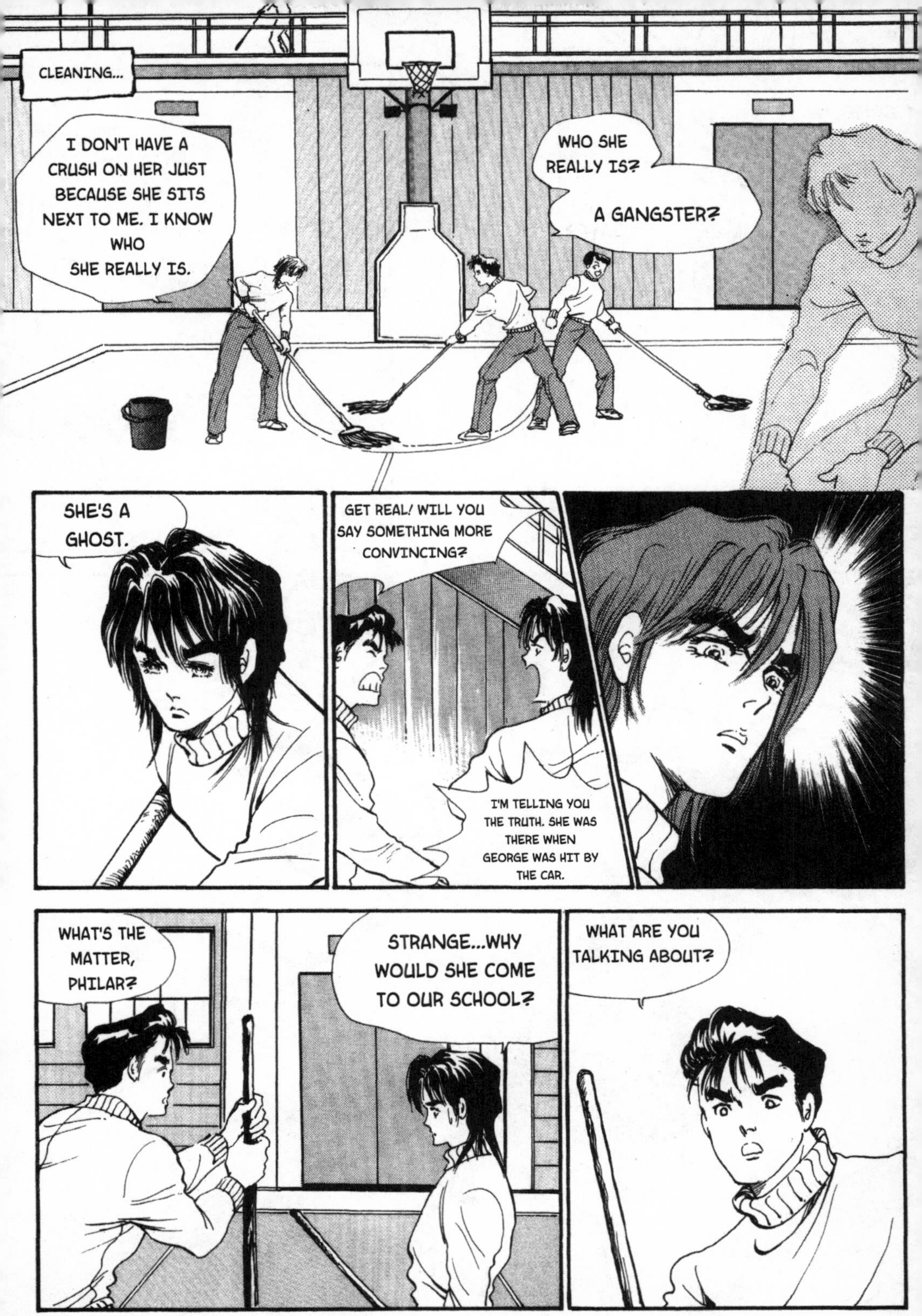
CLEANING...
I DON'T HAVE A CRUSH ON HER JUST BECAUSE SHE SITS NEXT TO ME. I KNOW WHO SHE REALLY IS.
WHO SHE REALLY IS?
A GANGSTER?
SHE'S A GHOST.
GET REAL! WILL YOU SAY SOMETHING MORE CONVINCING?
I'M TELLING YOU THE TRUTH. SHE WAS THERE WHEN GEORGE WAS HIT BY THE CAR.
WHAT'S THE MATTER, PHILAR?
STRANGE...WHY WOULD SHE COME TO OUR SCHOOL?
WHAT ARE YOU TALKING ABOUT?

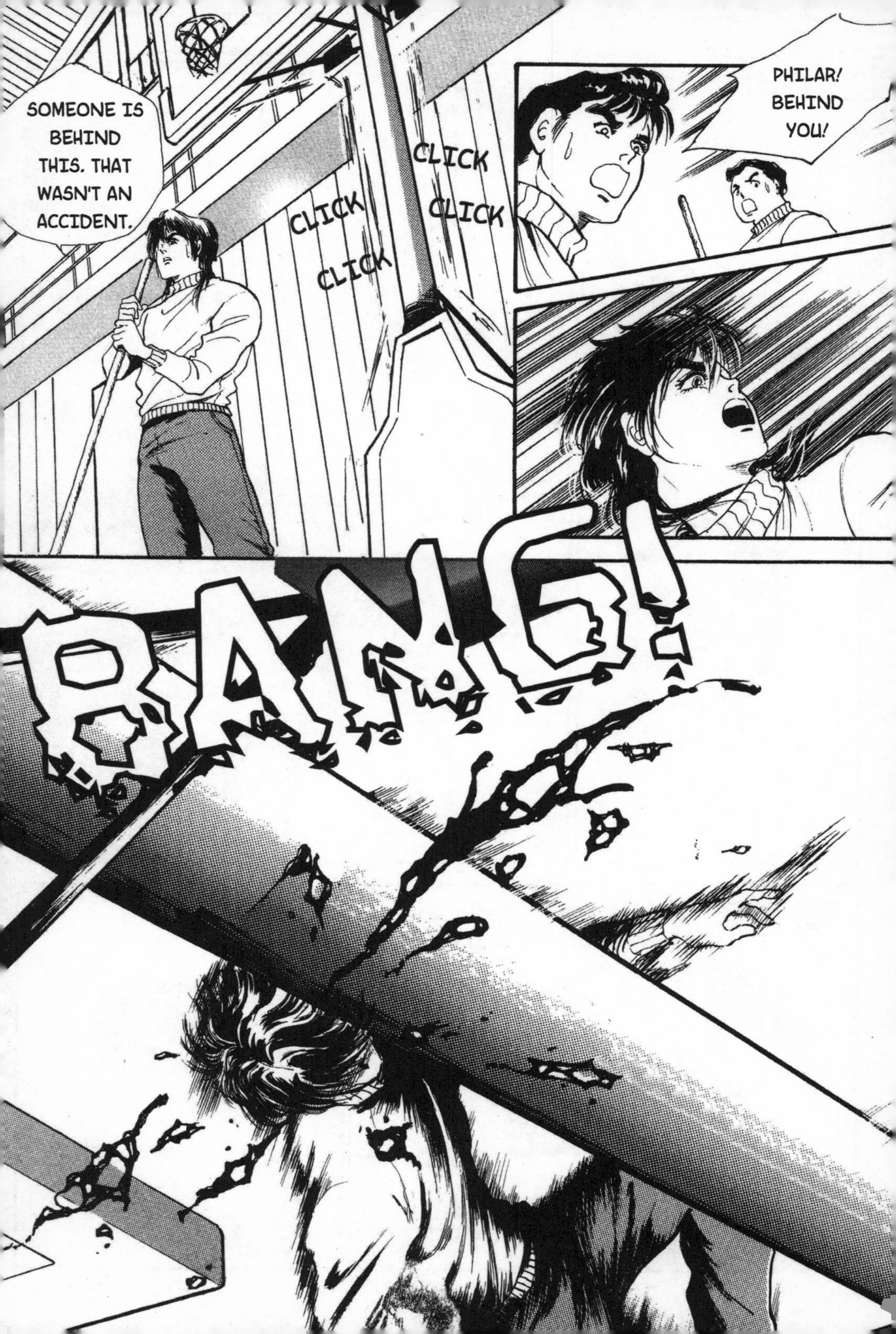
SOMEONE IS BEHIND THIS. THAT WASN'T AN ACCIDENT.
CLICK
CLICK
CLICK
CLICK
PHILAR! BEHIND YOU!
BANG!

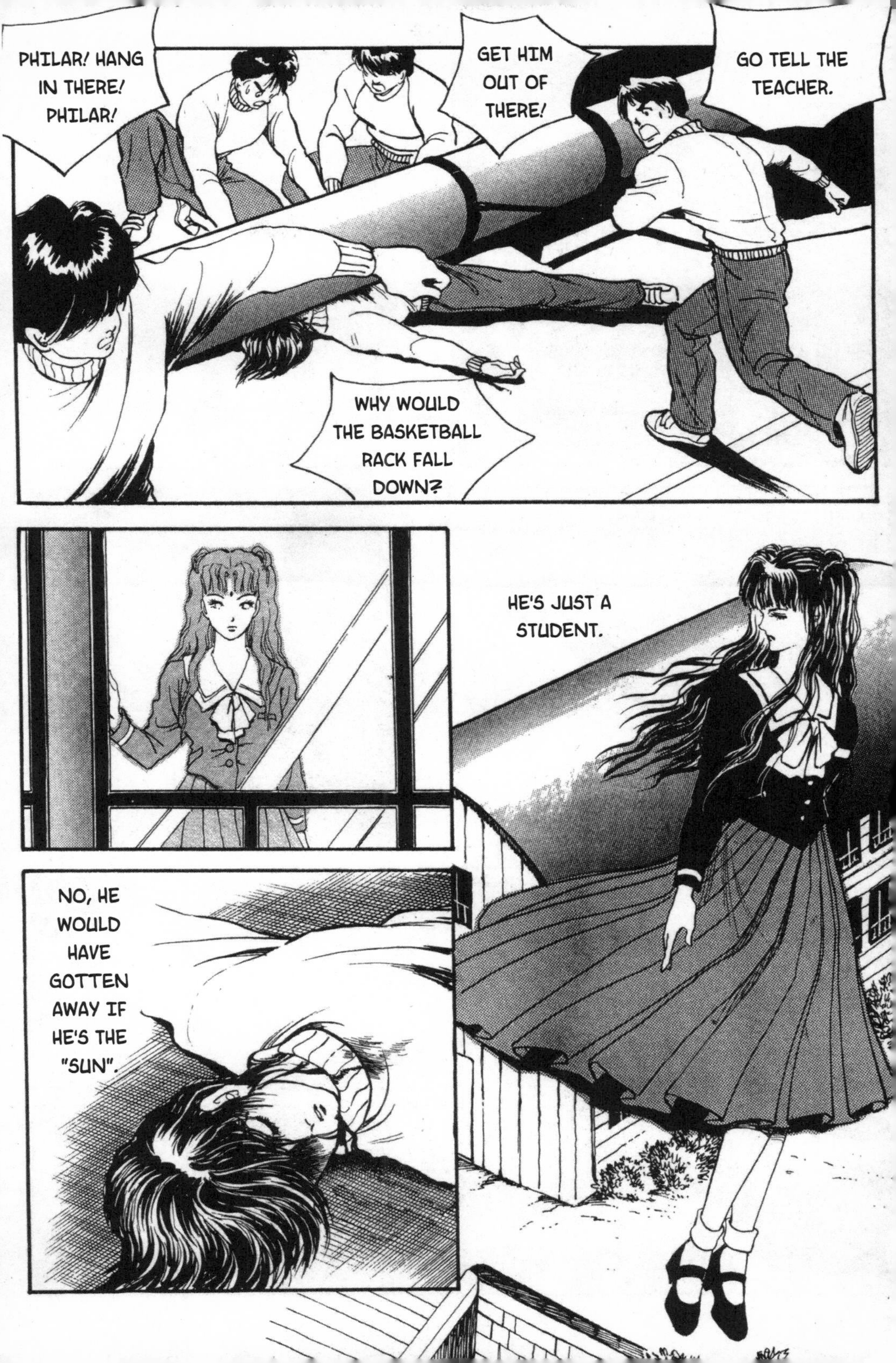
PHILAR! HANG IN THERE! PHILAR!
GET HIM OUT OF THERE!
GO TELL THE TEACHER.
WHY WOULD THE BASKETBALL RACK FALL DOWN?
HE'S JUST A STUDENT.
NO, HE WOULD HAVE GOTTEN AWAY IF HE'S THE "SUN".

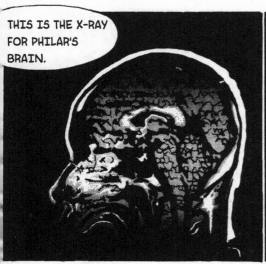

THIS IS THE X-RAY FOR PHILAR'S BRAIN.

AS YOU CAN SEE, WE MIGHT HAVE TO HAVE AN OPERATION TO REMOVE THE BLOOD CLOT IN HIS LEFT BRAIN.

WOULDN'T THAT BE DANGEROUS?

IT'S HARD TO SAY.

MRS. YOON?

FAINT

HOW DID IT HAPPEN? WHY PHILAR AGAIN?

PLEASE BE CALM. JUST GO SEE HIM. EVERYTHING'S GOING TO BE FINE.

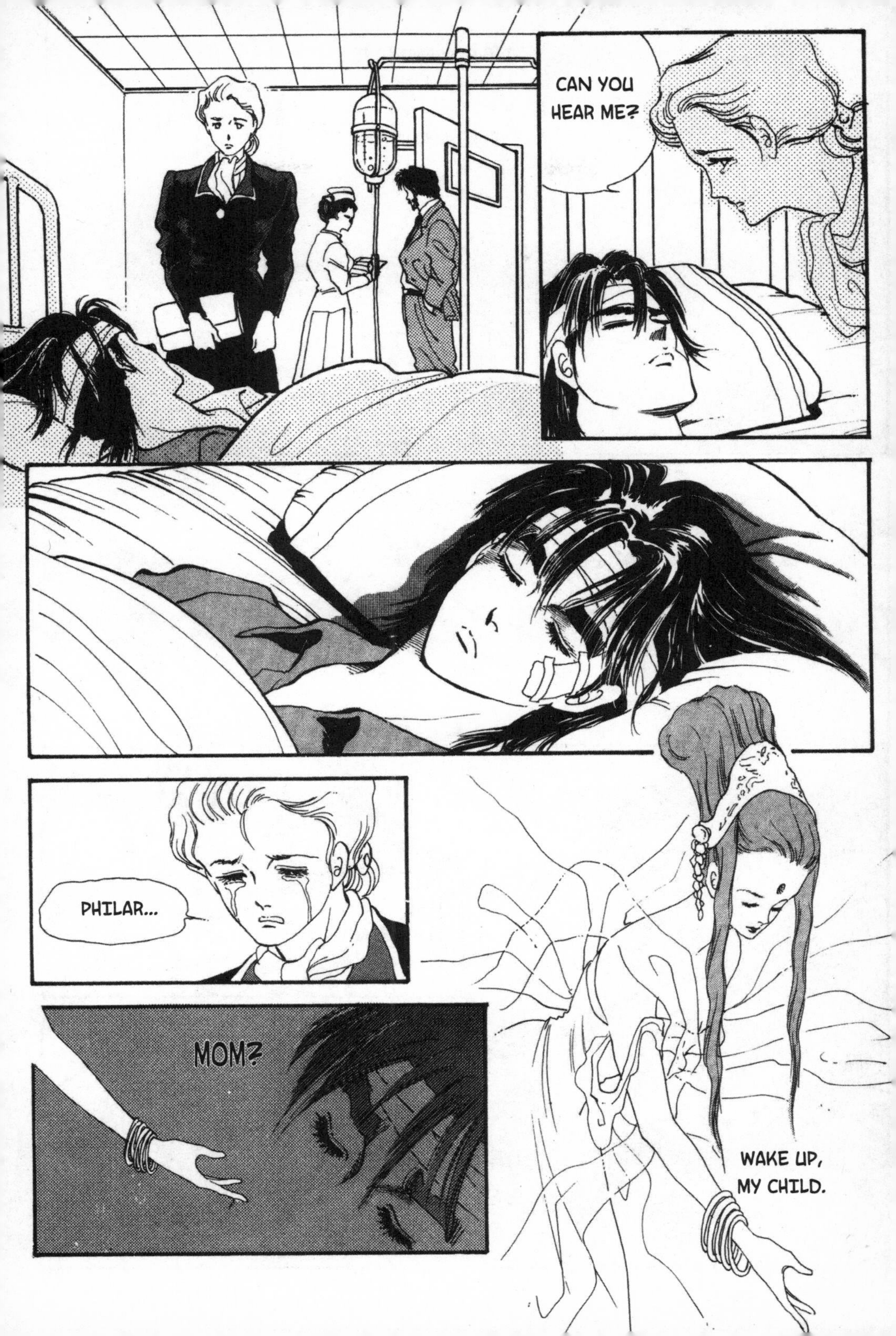
CAN YOU HEAR ME?
PHILAR...
MOM?
WAKE UP, MY CHILD.

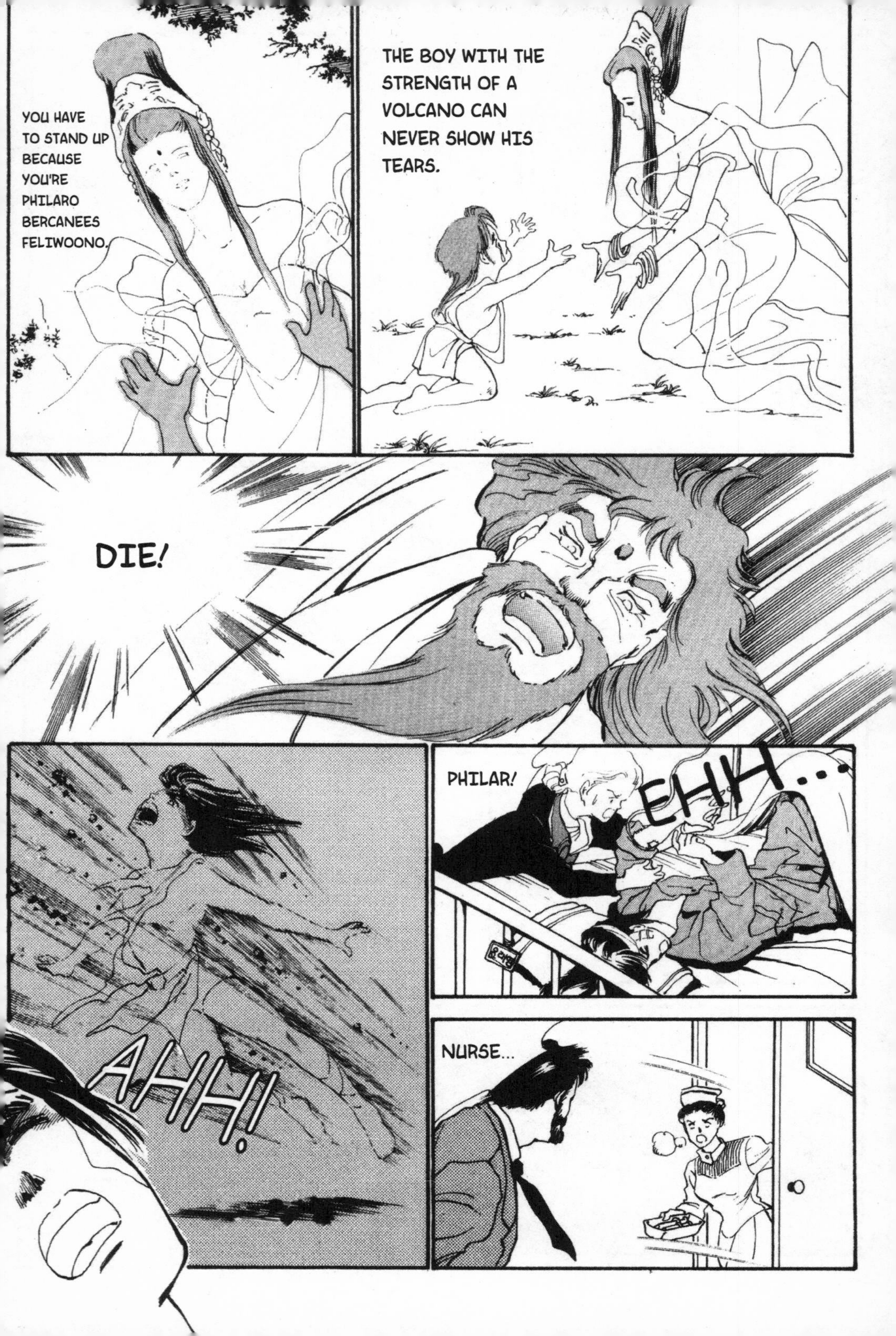
YOU HAVE TO STAND UP BECAUSE YOU'RE PHILARO BERCANEES FELIWOONO.
THE BOY WITH THE STRENGTH OF A VOLCANO CAN NEVER SHOW HIS TEARS.
DIE!
PHILAR!
EHH...
AHH!
NURSE...

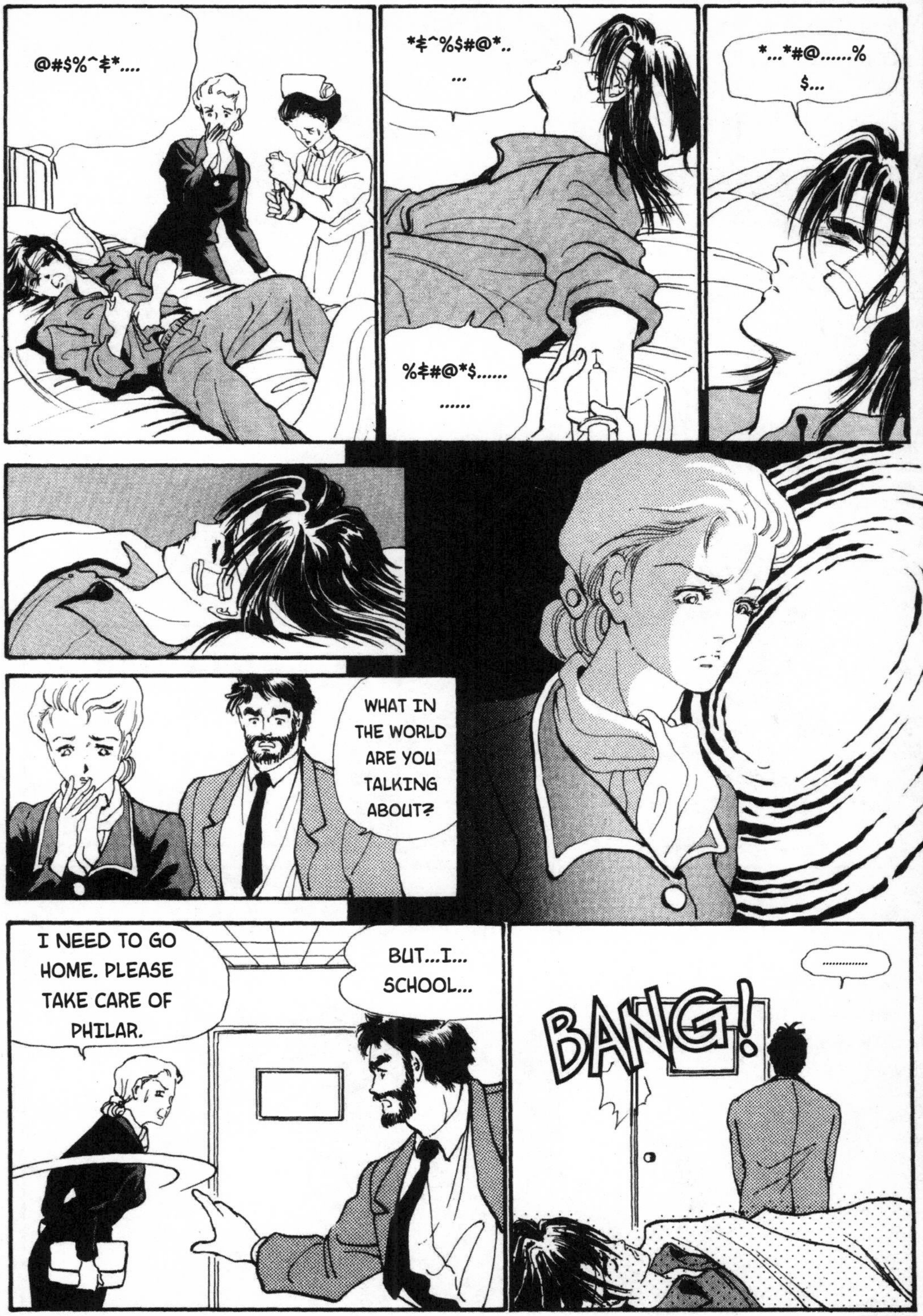

@#$%^≢*....
≢^%$#@..
...
%≢#@*$......
......
...#@......%
$...
WHAT IN THE WORLD ARE YOU TALKING ABOUT?
I NEED TO GO HOME. PLEASE TAKE CARE OF PHILAR.
BUT...I... SCHOOL...
BANG!
....

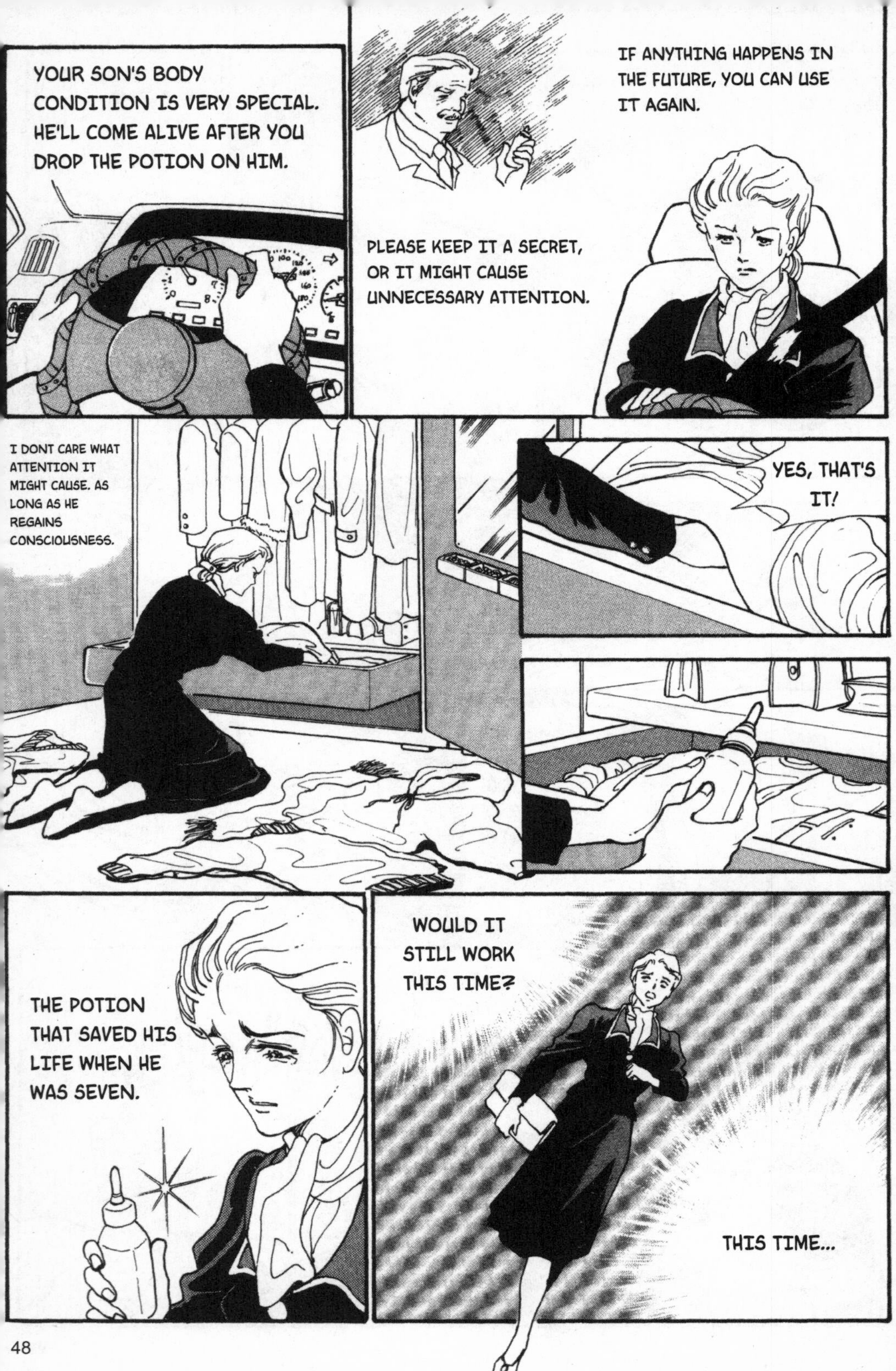
YOUR SON'S BODY CONDITION IS VERY SPECIAL. HE'LL COME ALIVE AFTER YOU DROP THE POTION ON HIM.
IF ANYTHING HAPPENS IN THE FUTURE, YOU CAN USE IT AGAIN.
PLEASE KEEP IT A SECRET, OR IT MIGHT CAUSE UNNECESSARY ATTENTION.
I DONT CARE WHAT ATTENTION IT MIGHT CAUSE. AS LONG AS HE REGAINS CONSCIOUSNESS.
YES, THAT'S IT!
THE POTION THAT SAVED HIS LIFE WHEN HE WAS SEVEN.
WOULD IT STILL WORK THIS TIME?
THIS TIME...

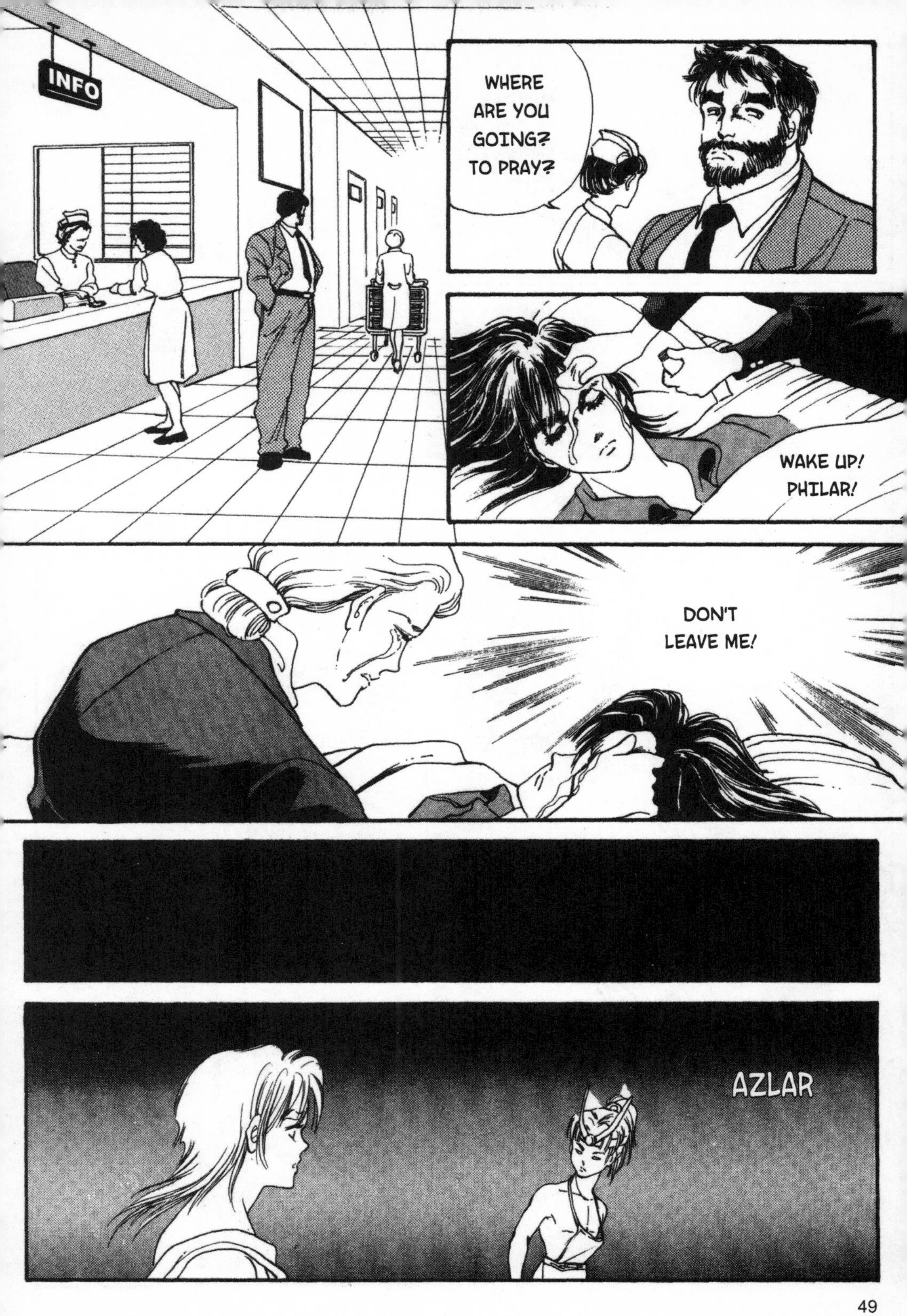
INFO
WHERE ARE YOU GOING? TO PRAY?
WAKE UP! PHILAR!
DON'T LEAVE ME!
AZLAR

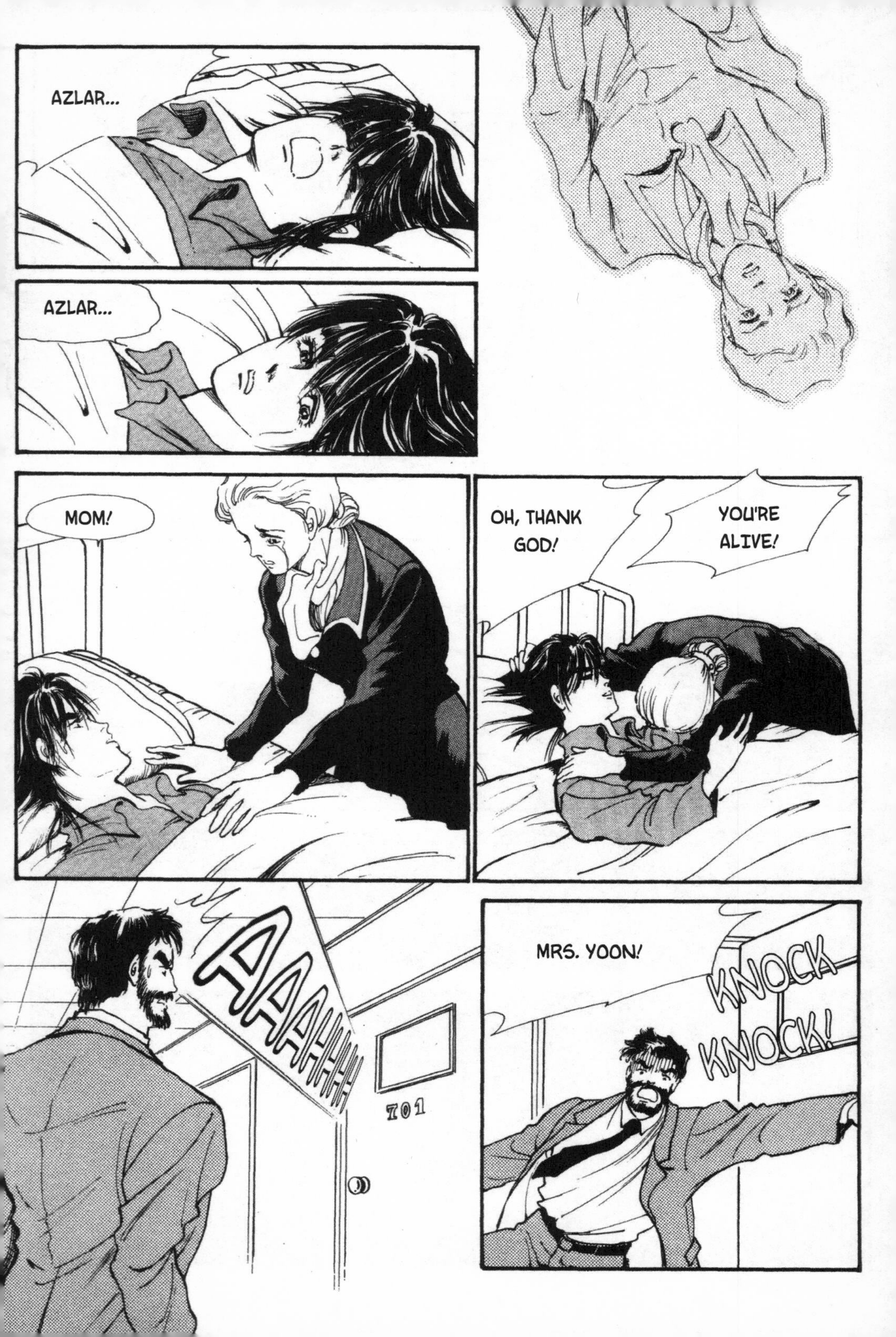
AZLAR...
AZLAR...
MOM!
OH, THANK GOD!
YOU'RE ALIVE!
AAAHHH
701
MRS. YOON!
KNOCK KNOCK!

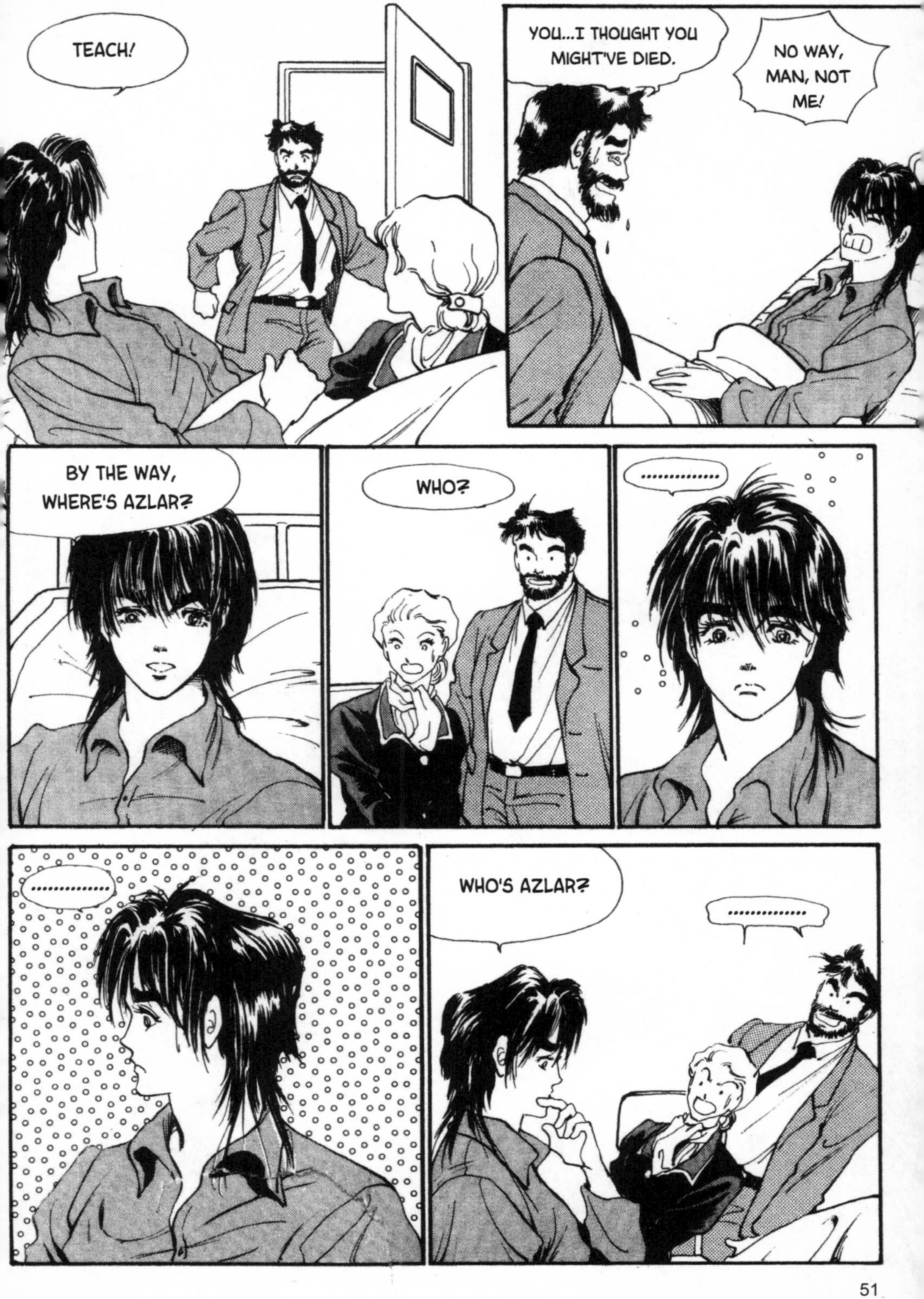
TEACH!
YOU...I THOUGHT YOU MIGHT'VE DIED.
NO WAY, MAN, NOT ME!
BY THE WAY, WHERE'S AZLAR?
WHO?
....
....
WHO'S AZLAR?
....

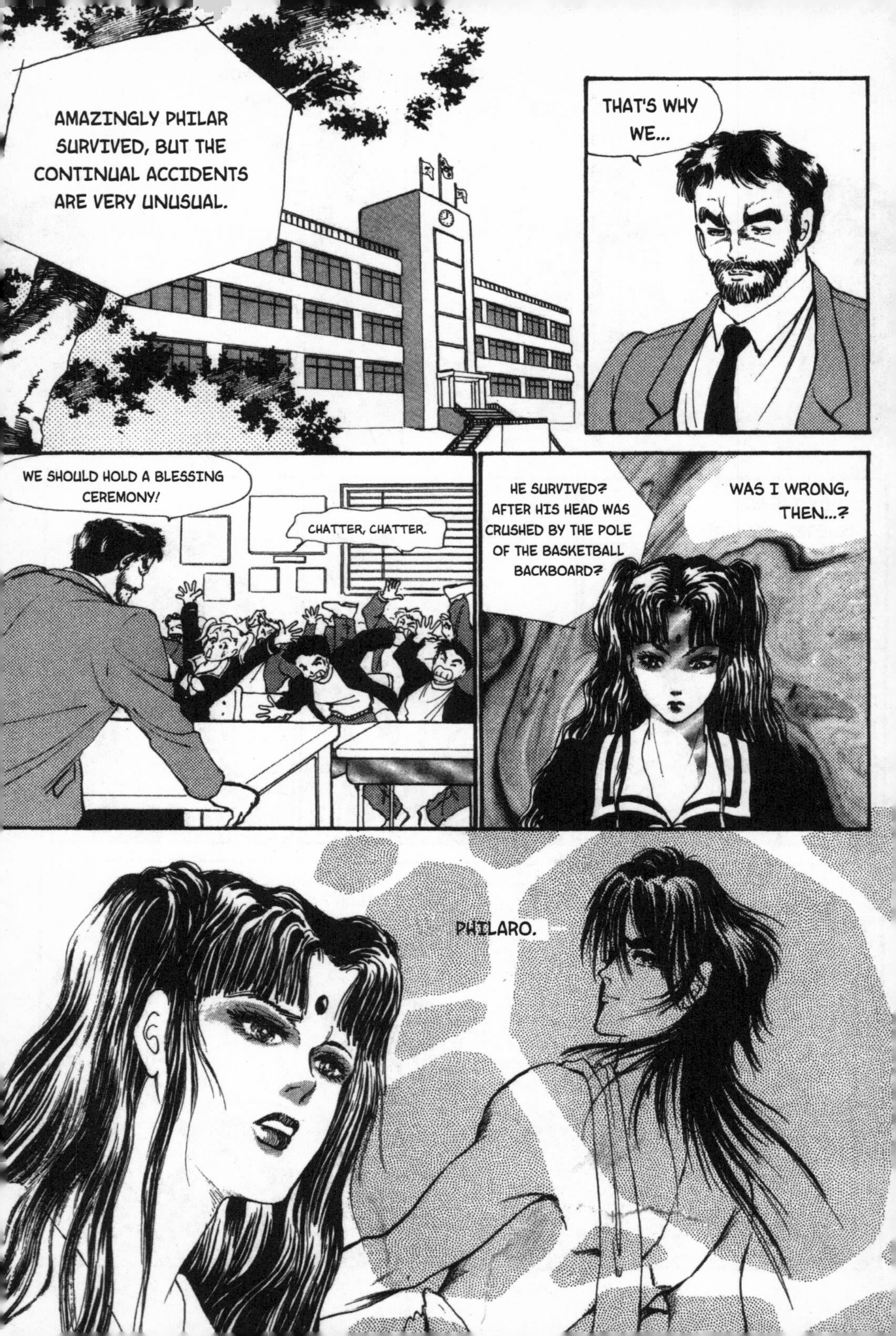
AMAZINGLY PHILAR SURVIVED, BUT THE CONTINUAL ACCIDENTS ARE VERY UNUSUAL.
THAT'S WHY WE...
WE SHOULD HOLD A BLESSING CEREMONY!
CHATTER, CHATTER.
HE SURVIVED? AFTER HIS HEAD WAS CRUSHED BY THE POLE OF THE BASKETBALL BACKBOARD?
WAS I WRONG, THEN...?
PHILARO.

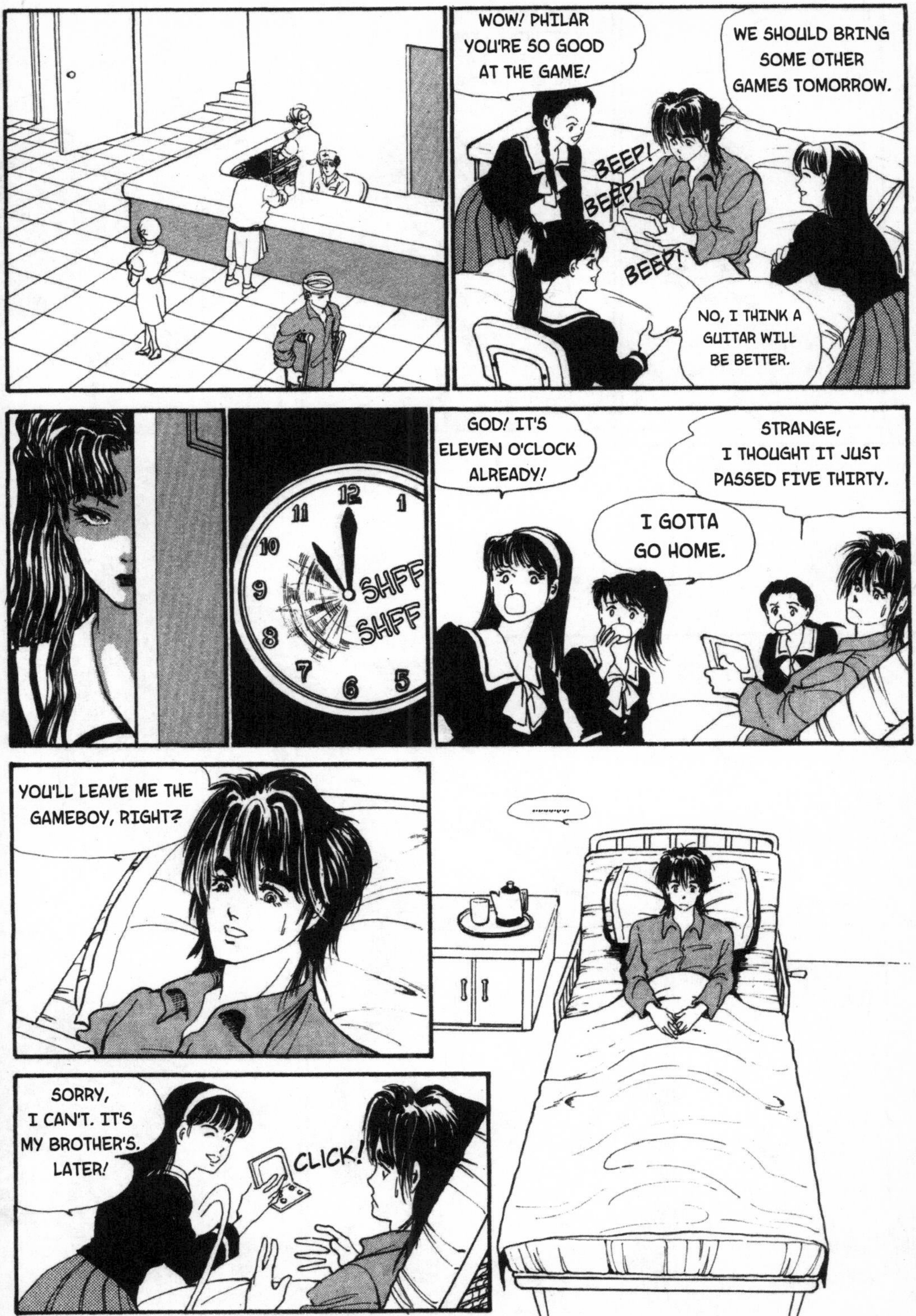
WOW! PHILAR YOU'RE SO GOOD AT THE GAME!
WE SHOULD BRING SOME OTHER GAMES TOMORROW.
BEEP! BEEP!
BEEP!
NO, I THINK A GUITAR WILL BE BETTER.
12
1
11
10
9
8
7
6
5
SHFF SHFF
GOD! IT'S ELEVEN O'CLOCK ALREADY!
STRANGE, I THOUGHT IT JUST PASSED FIVE THIRTY.
I GOTTA GO HOME.
YOU'LL LEAVE ME THE GAMEBOY, RIGHT?
SORRY, I CAN'T. IT'S MY BROTHER'S. LATER!
CLICK!
......

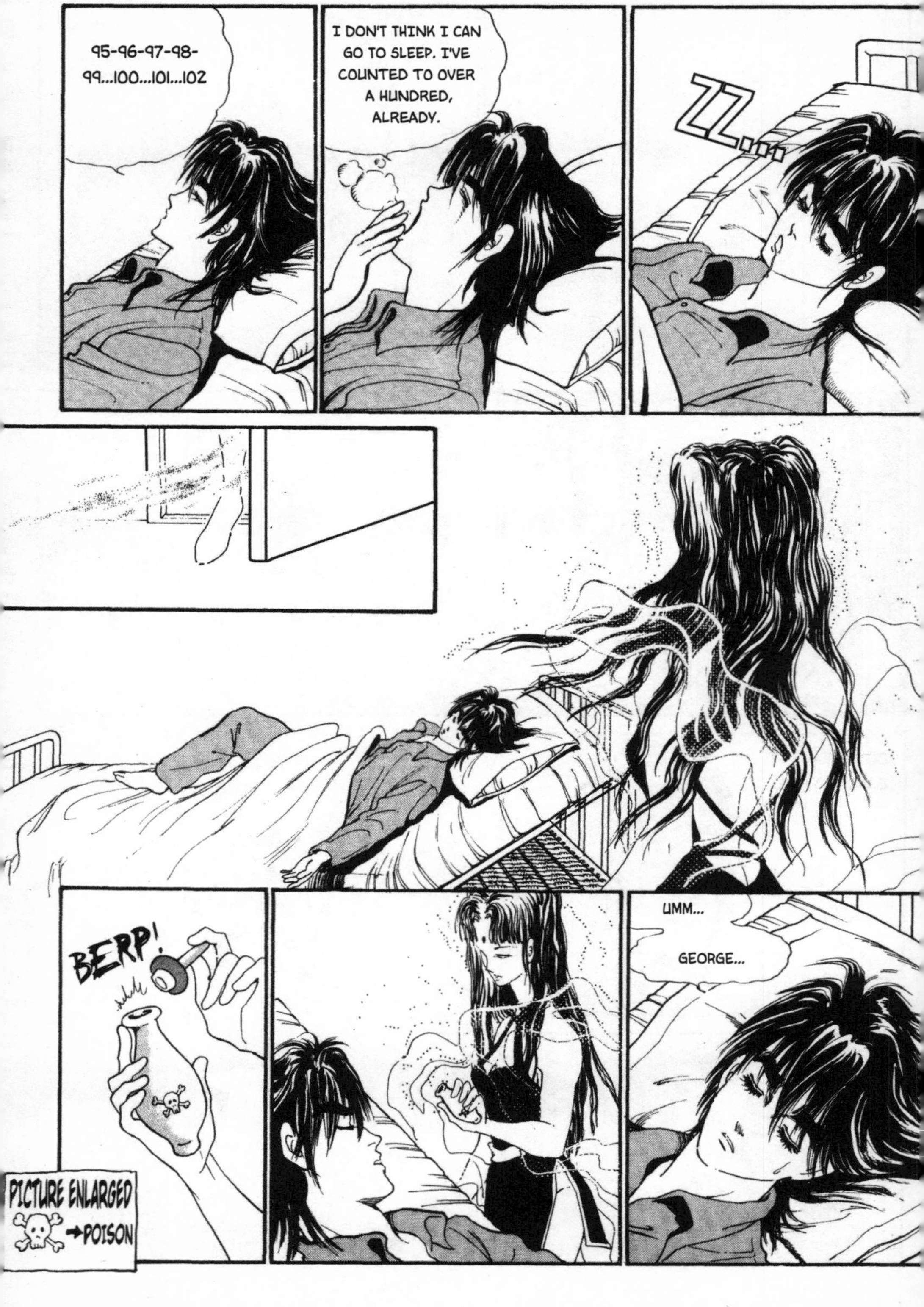
95-96-97-98-
99...100...101...102
I DON'T THINK I CAN GO TO SLEEP. I'VE COUNTED TO OVER A HUNDRED, ALREADY.
ZZ...
BERP!
PICTURE ENLARGED
→POISON
UMM...
GEORGE...

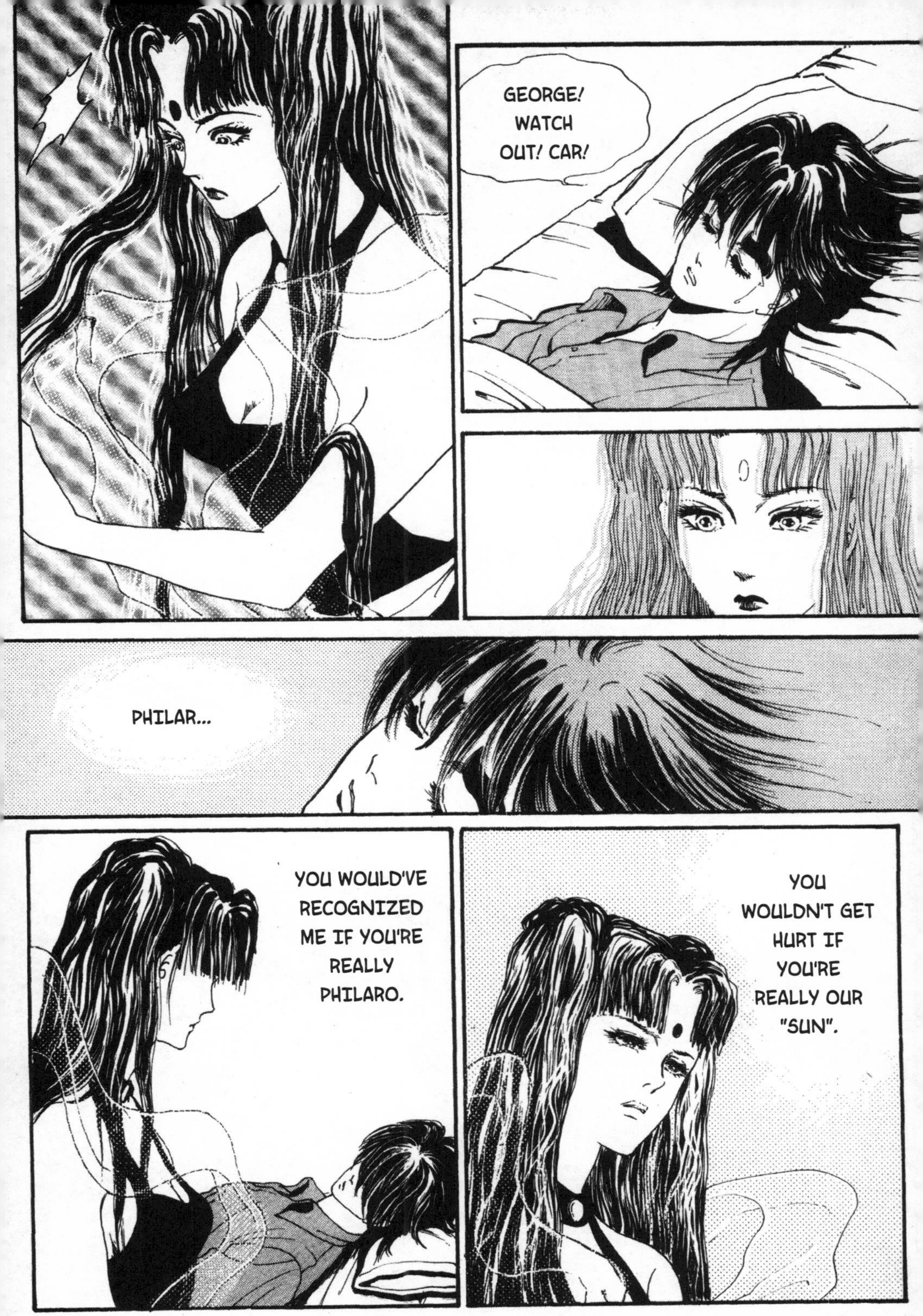
GEORGE! WATCH OUT! CAR!
PHILAR...
YOU WOULD'VE RECOGNIZED ME IF YOU'RE REALLY PHILARO.
YOU WOULDN'T GET HURT IF YOU'RE REALLY OUR "SUN".

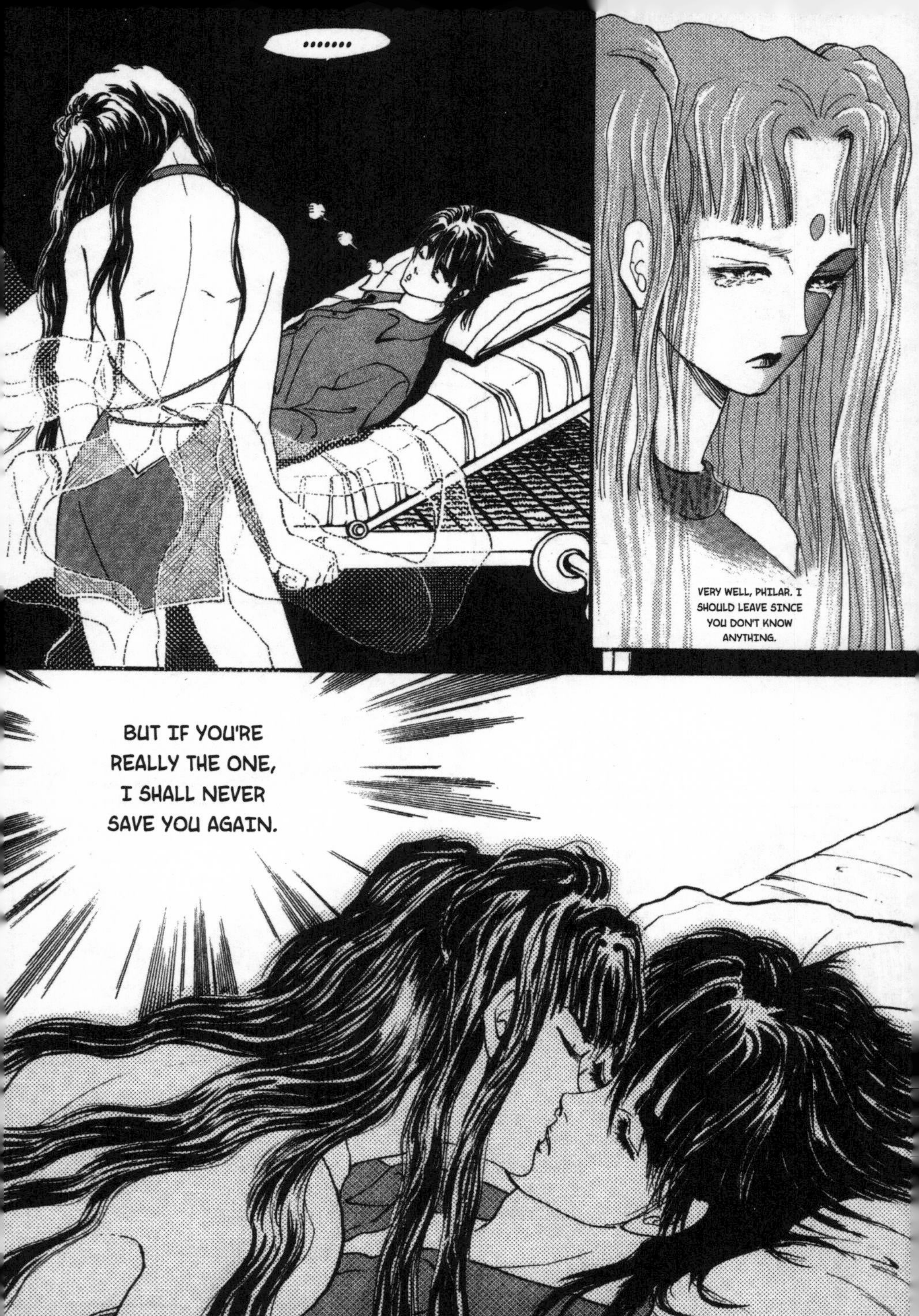
....
VERY WELL, PHILAR. I SHOULD LEAVE SINCE YOU DON'T KNOW ANYTHING.
BUT IF YOU'RE REALLY THE ONE, I SHALL NEVER SAVE YOU AGAIN.

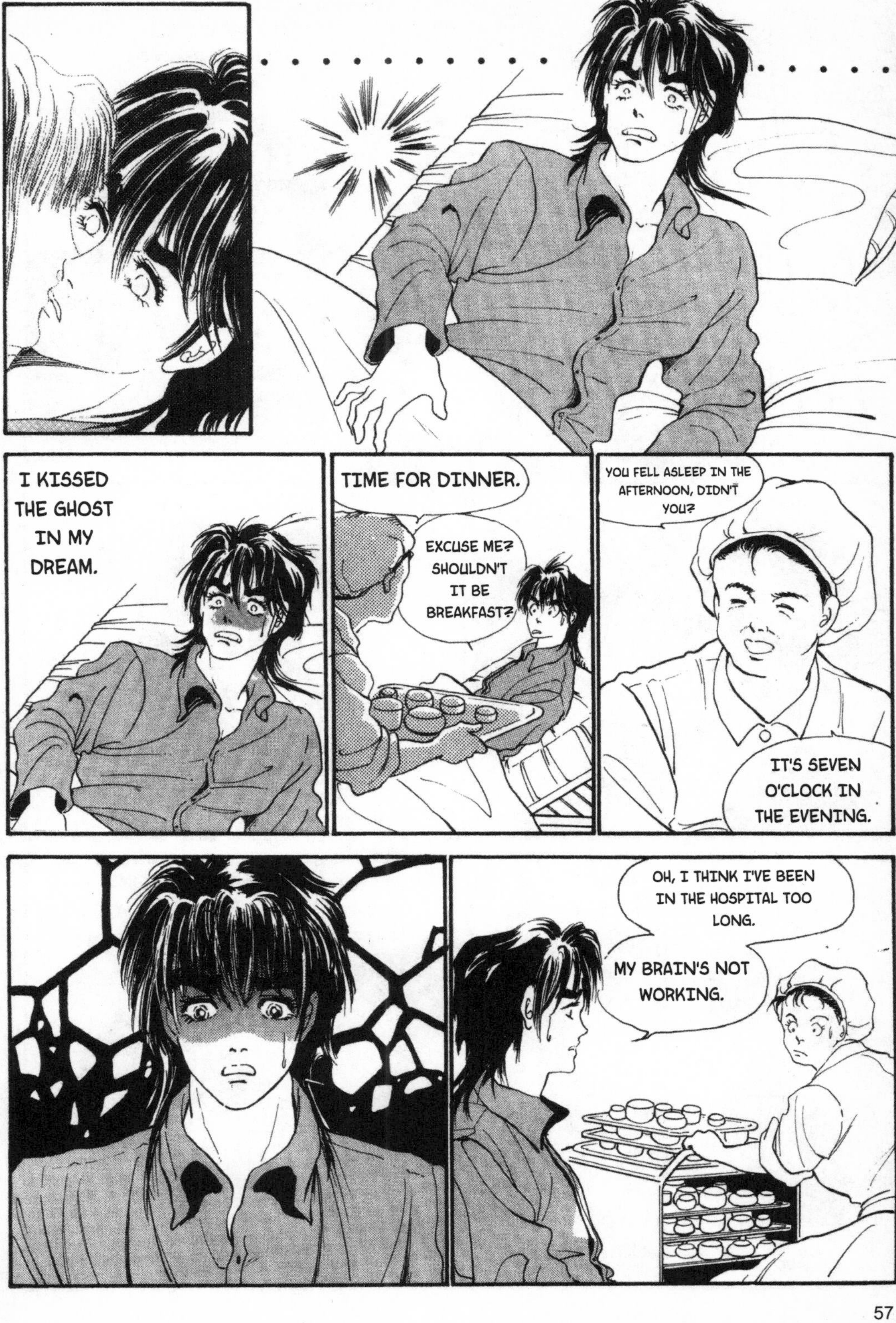
I KISSED THE GHOST IN MY DREAM.
TIME FOR DINNER.
EXCUSE ME? SHOULDN'T IT BE BREAKFAST?
YOU FELL ASLEEP IN THE AFTERNOON, DIDN'T YOU?
IT'S SEVEN O'CLOCK IN THE EVENING.
OH, I THINK I'VE BEEN IN THE HOSPITAL TOO LONG.
MY BRAIN'S NOT WORKING.

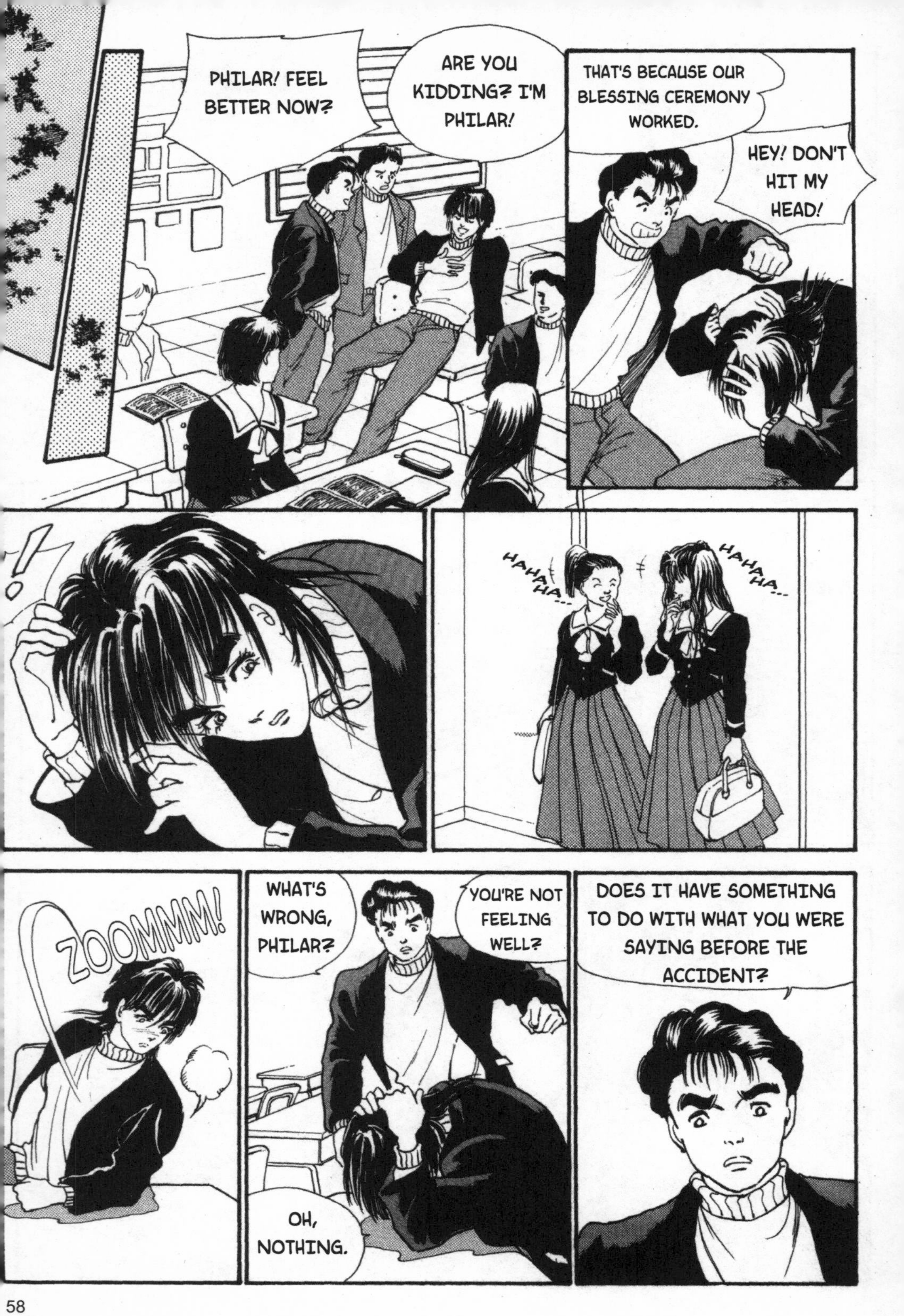
PHILAR! FEEL BETTER NOW?
ARE YOU KIDDING? I'M PHILAR!
THAT'S BECAUSE OUR BLESSING CEREMONY WORKED.
HEY! DON'T HIT MY HEAD!
!
HAHAHA...
HAHAHA...
ZOOMMM!
WHAT'S WRONG, PHILAR?
YOU'RE NOT FEELING WELL?
OH, NOTHING.
DOES IT HAVE SOMETHING TO DO WITH WHAT YOU WERE SAYING BEFORE THE ACCIDENT?

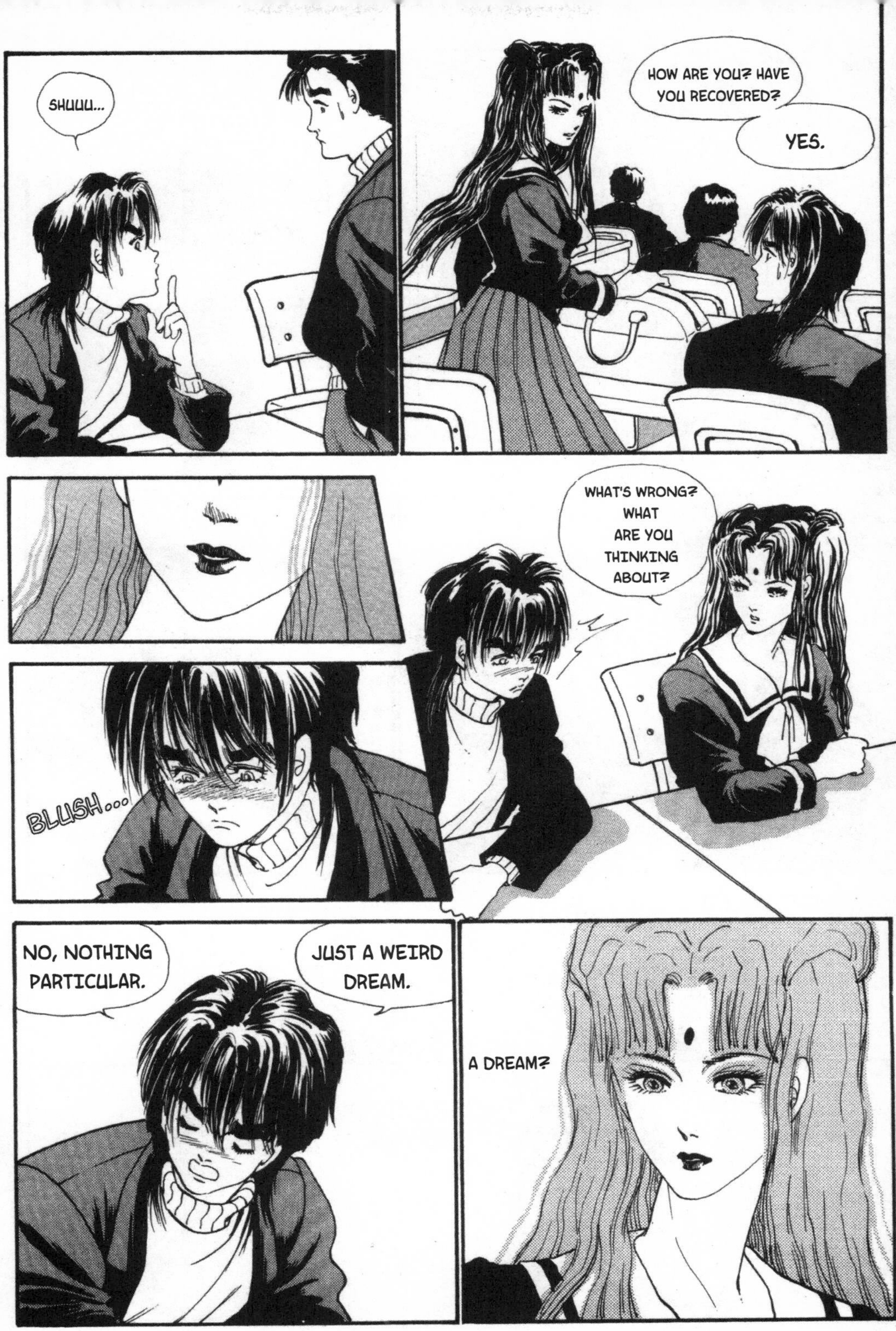

SHUUU...
HOW ARE YOU? HAVE YOU RECOVERED?
YES.
WHAT'S WRONG? WHAT ARE YOU THINKING ABOUT?
BLUSH...
NO, NOTHING PARTICULAR.
JUST A WEIRD DREAM.
A DREAM?

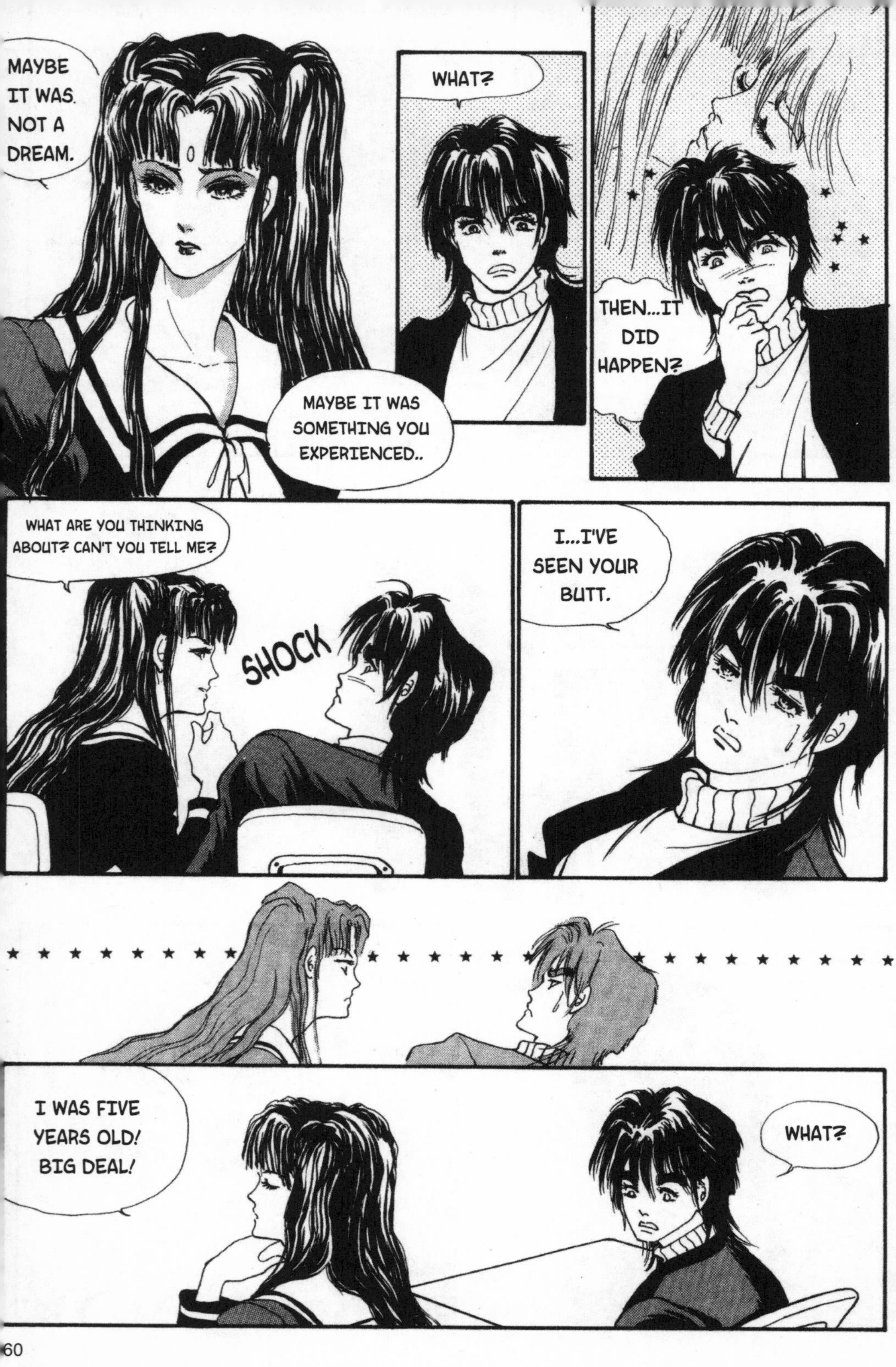

MAYBE IT WAS. NOT A DREAM.
WHAT?
MAYBE IT WAS SOMETHING YOU EXPERIENCED..
THEN...IT DID HAPPEN?
WHAT ARE YOU THINKING ABOUT? CAN'T YOU TELL ME?
SHOCK
I...I'VE SEEN YOUR BUTT.
I WAS FIVE YEARS OLD! BIG DEAL!
WHAT?

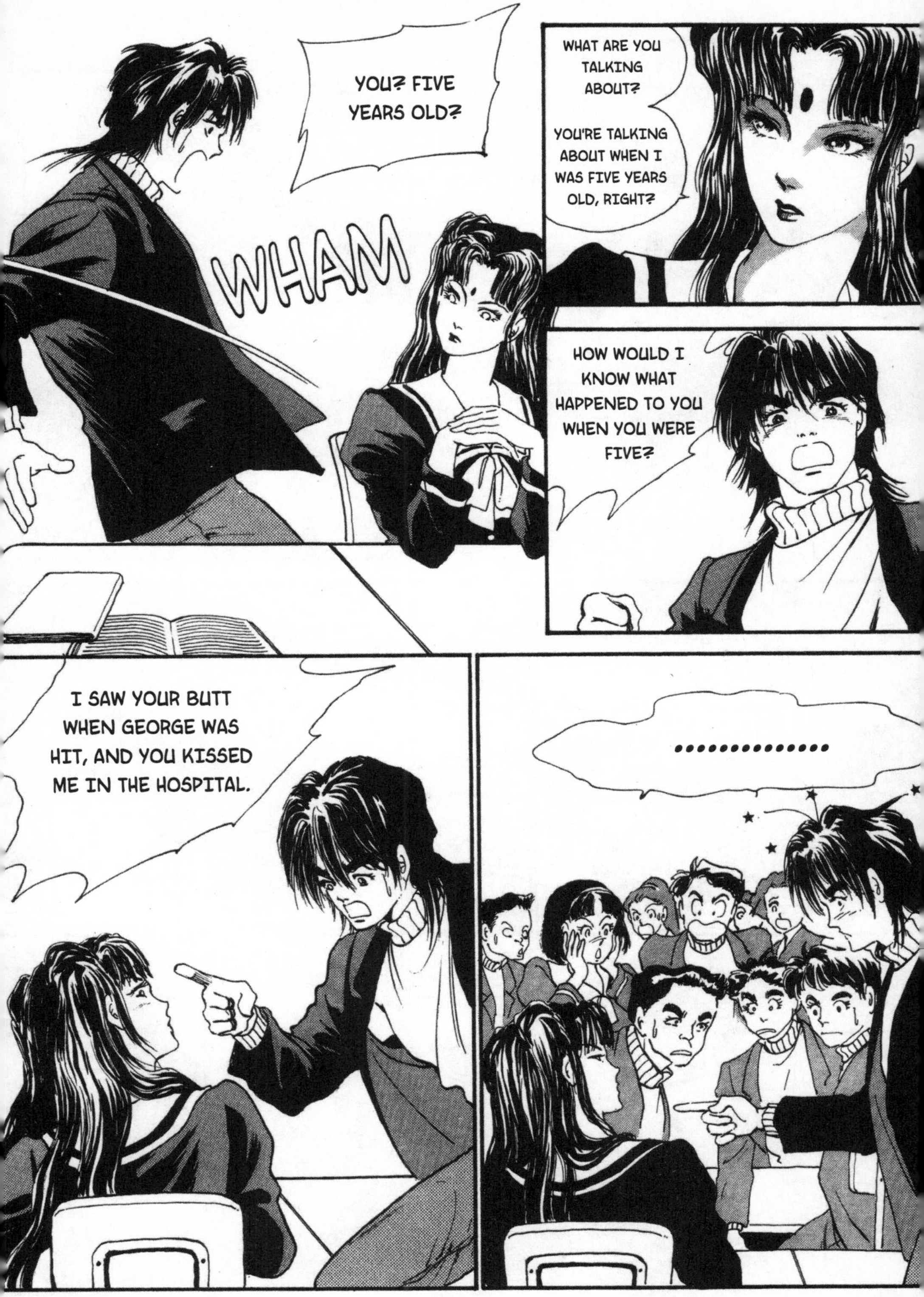

WHAT ARE YOU TALKING ABOUT?
YOU'RE TALKING ABOUT WHEN I WAS FIVE YEARS OLD, RIGHT?
YOU? FIVE YEARS OLD?
WHAM
HOW WOULD I KNOW WHAT HAPPENED TO YOU WHEN YOU WERE FIVE?
I SAW YOUR BUTT WHEN GEORGE WAS HIT, AND YOU KISSED ME IN THE HOSPITAL.
....

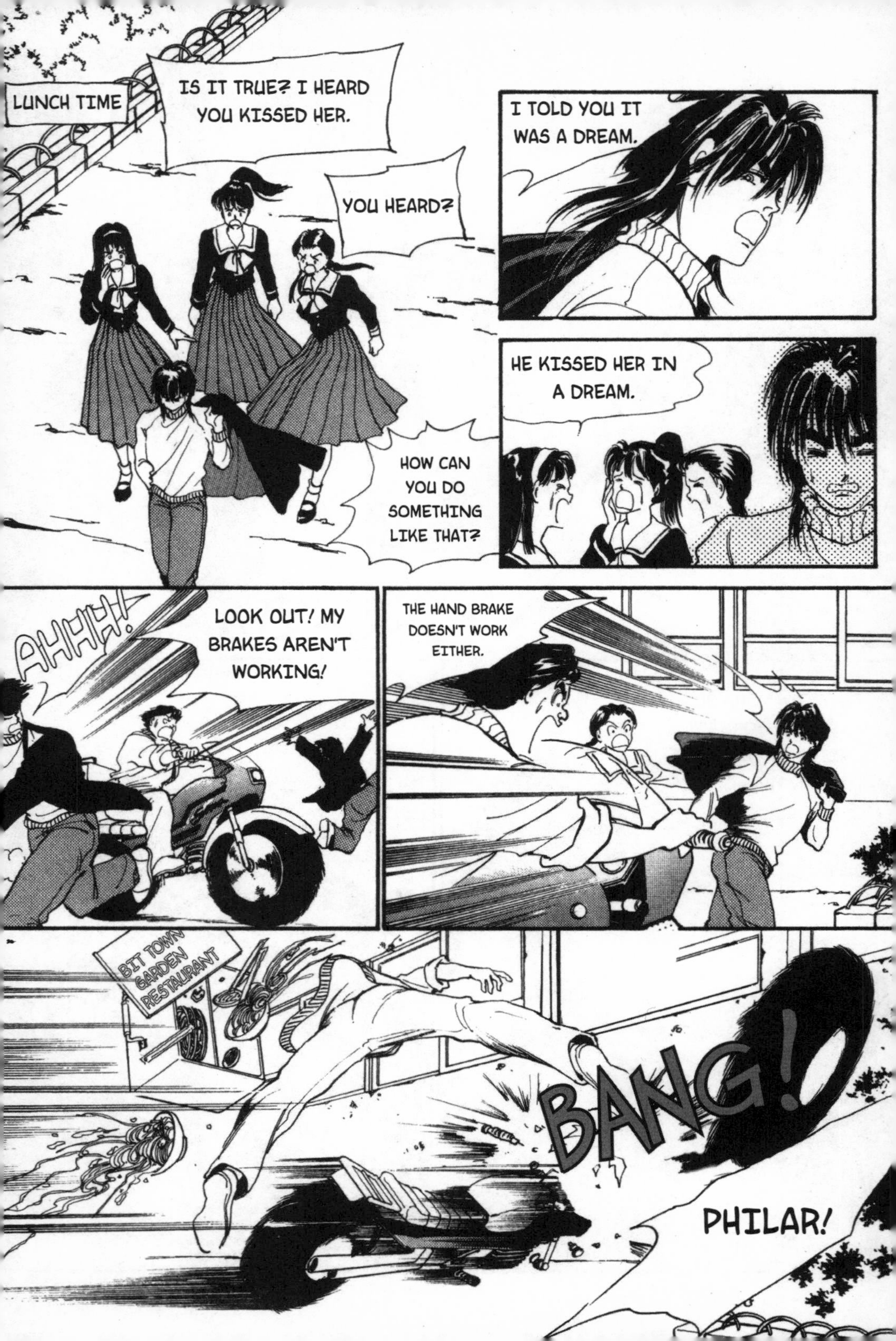
LUNCH TIME
IS IT TRUE? I HEARD YOU KISSED HER.
YOU HEARD?
I TOLD YOU IT WAS A DREAM.
HE KISSED HER IN A DREAM.
HOW CAN YOU DO SOMETHING LIKE THAT?
AHHH!
LOOK OUT! MY BRAKES AREN'T WORKING!
THE HAND BRAKE DOESN'T WORK EITHER.
BIT TOWN GARDEN RESTAURANT
BANG!
PHILAR!

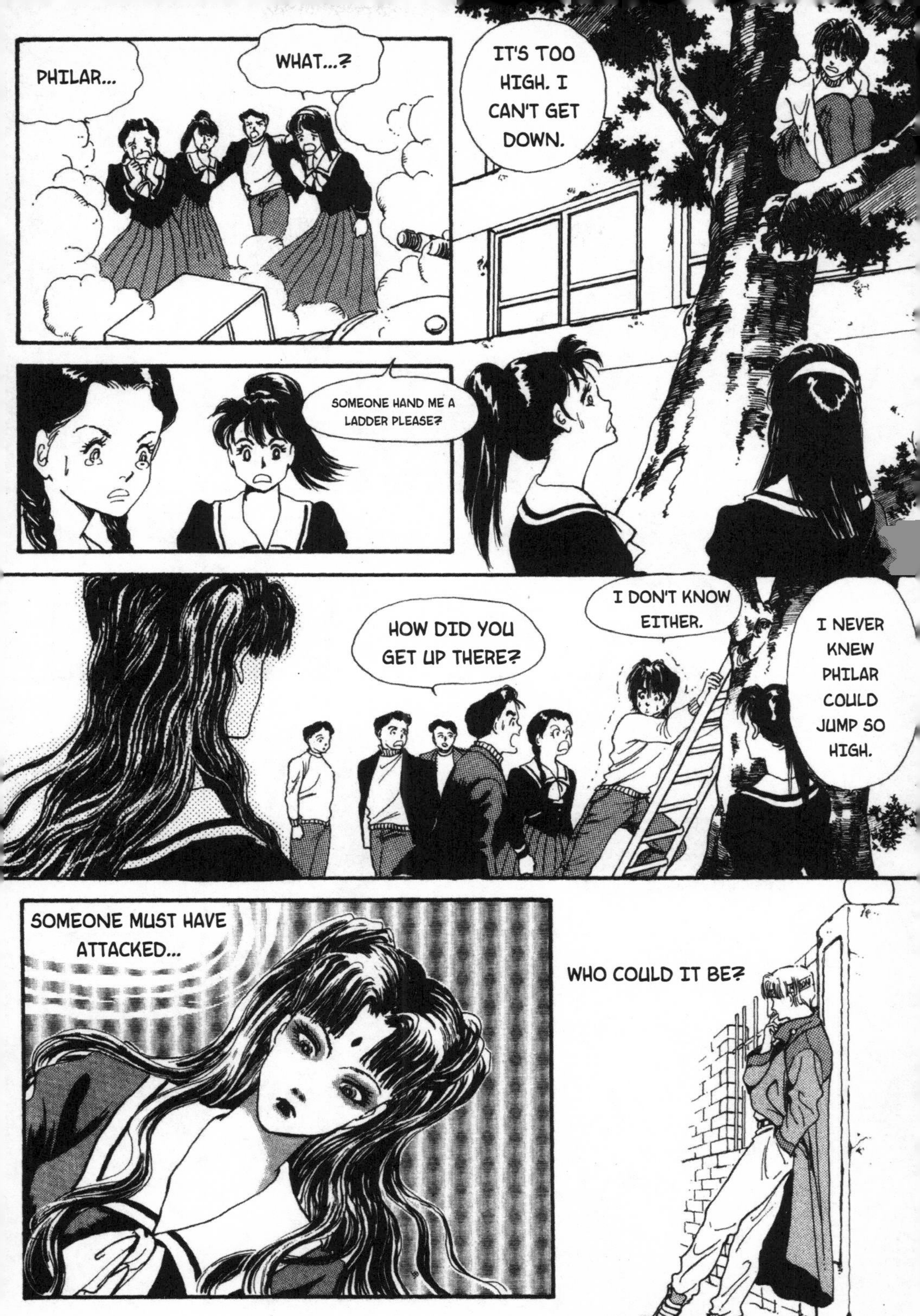
PHILAR...
WHAT...?
IT'S TOO HIGH. I CAN'T GET DOWN.
SOMEONE HAND ME A LADDER PLEASE?
HOW DID YOU GET UP THERE?
I DON'T KNOW EITHER.
I NEVER KNEW PHILAR COULD JUMP SO HIGH.
SOMEONE MUST HAVE ATTACKED...
WHO COULD IT BE?

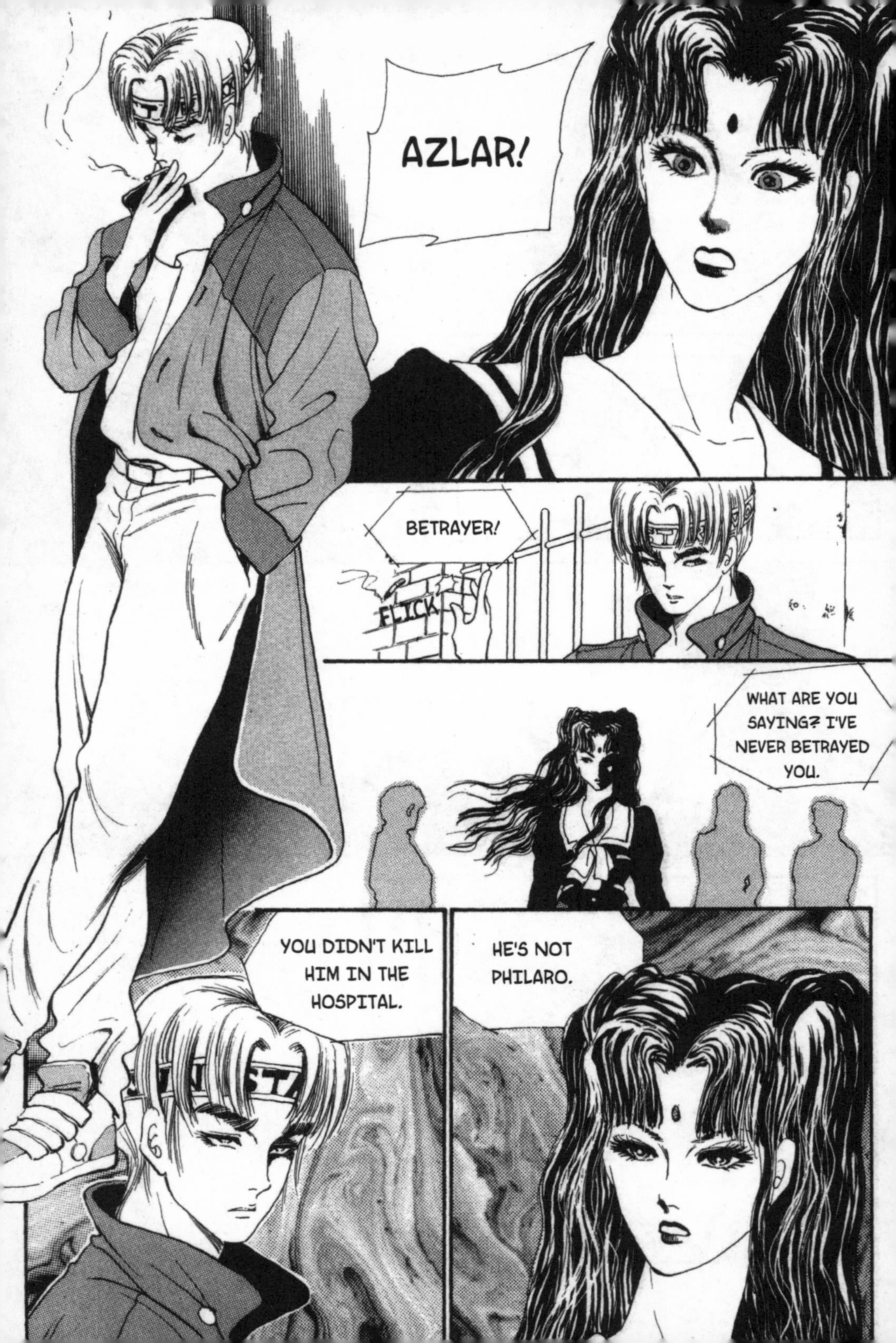
AZLAR!
BETRAYER!
FLICK
WHAT ARE YOU SAYING? I'VE NEVER BETRAYED YOU.
YOU DIDN'T KILL HIM IN THE HOSPITAL.
HE'S NOT PHILARO.

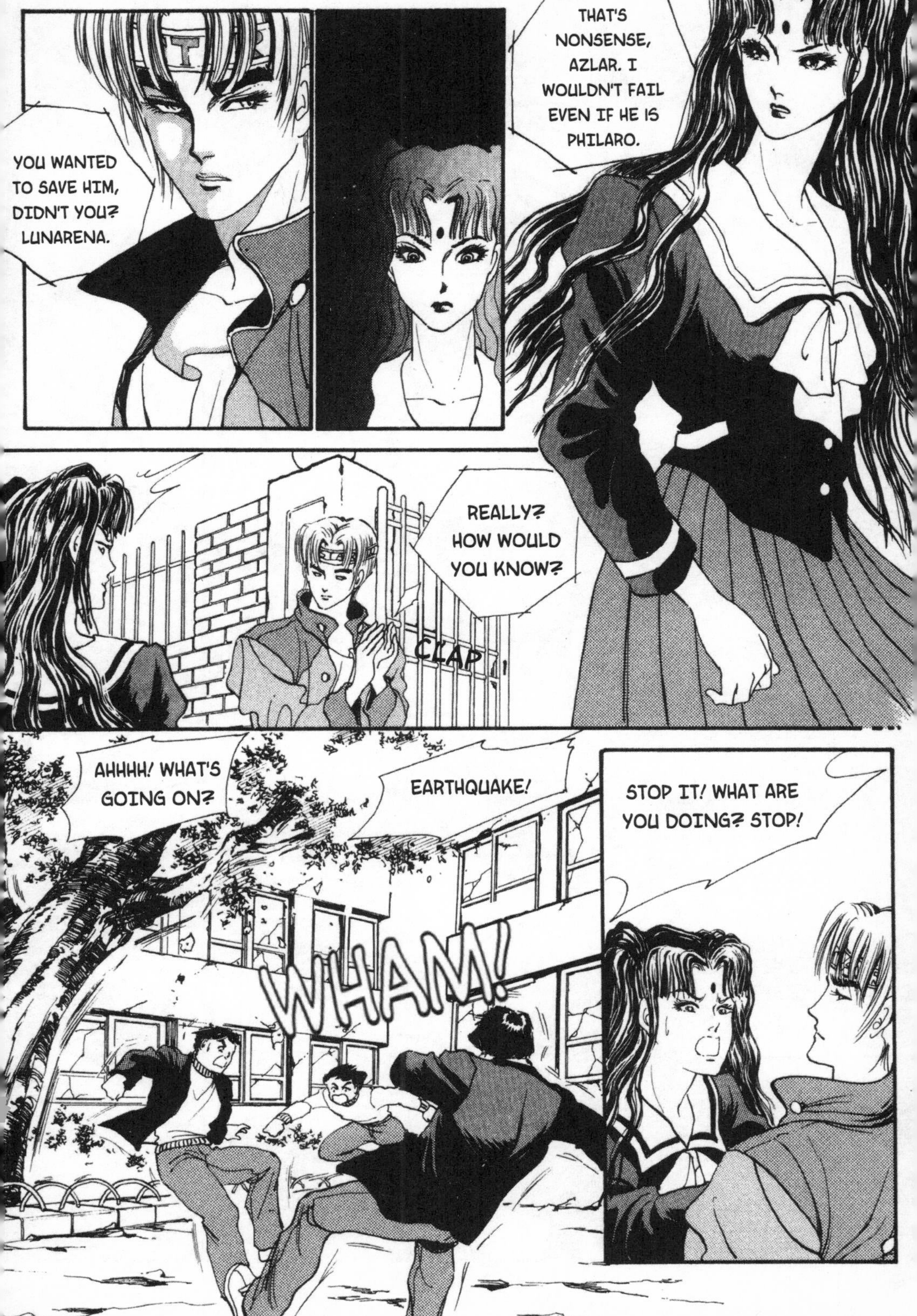
YOU WANTED TO SAVE HIM, DIDN'T YOU? LUNARENA.
THAT'S NONSENSE, AZLAR. I WOULDN'T FAIL EVEN IF HE IS PHILARO.
REALLY? HOW WOULD YOU KNOW?
CLAP
AHHHH! WHAT'S GOING ON?
EARTHQUAKE!
STOP IT! WHAT ARE YOU DOING? STOP!
WHAM!

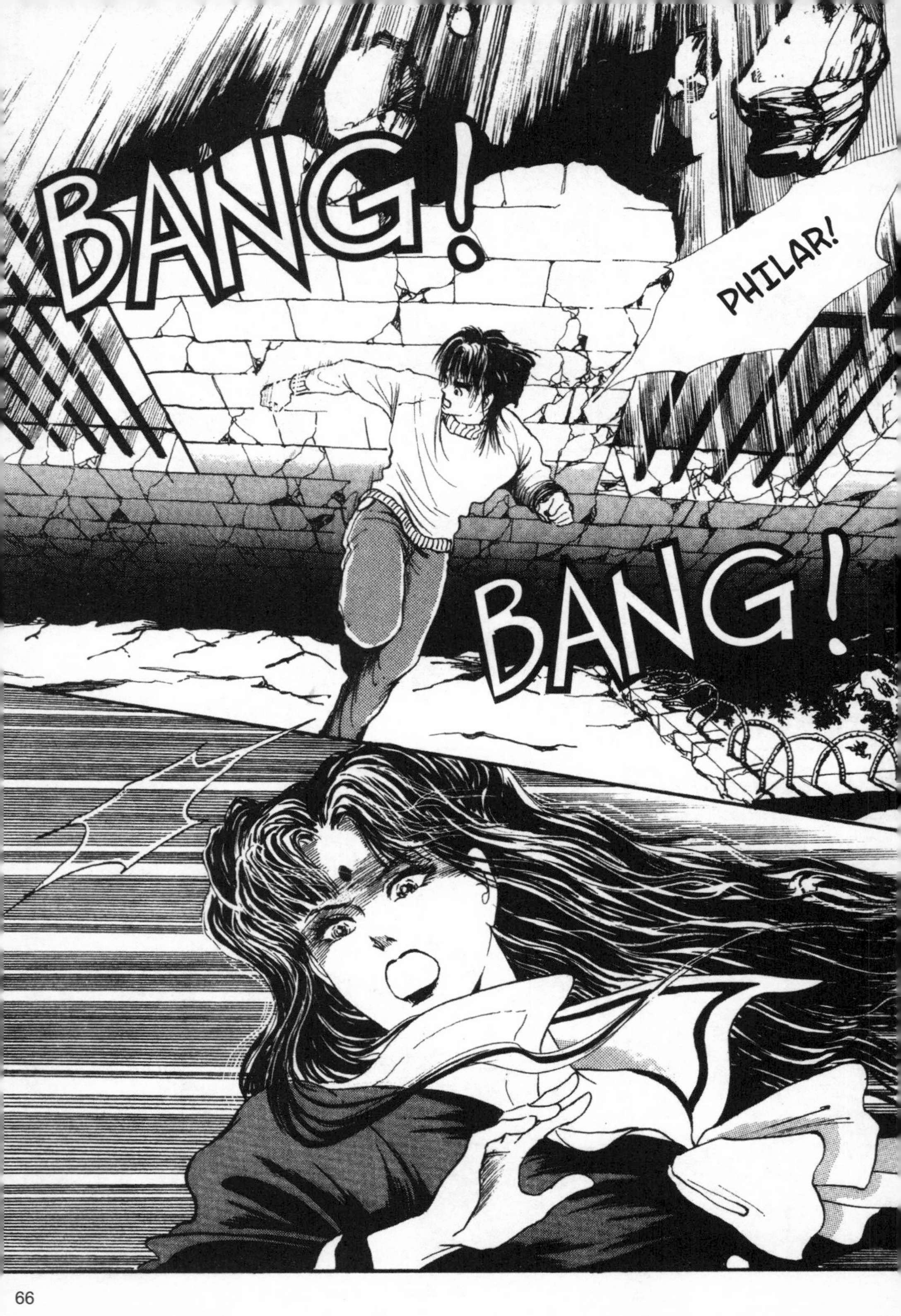
BANG!
PHILAR!
BANG!

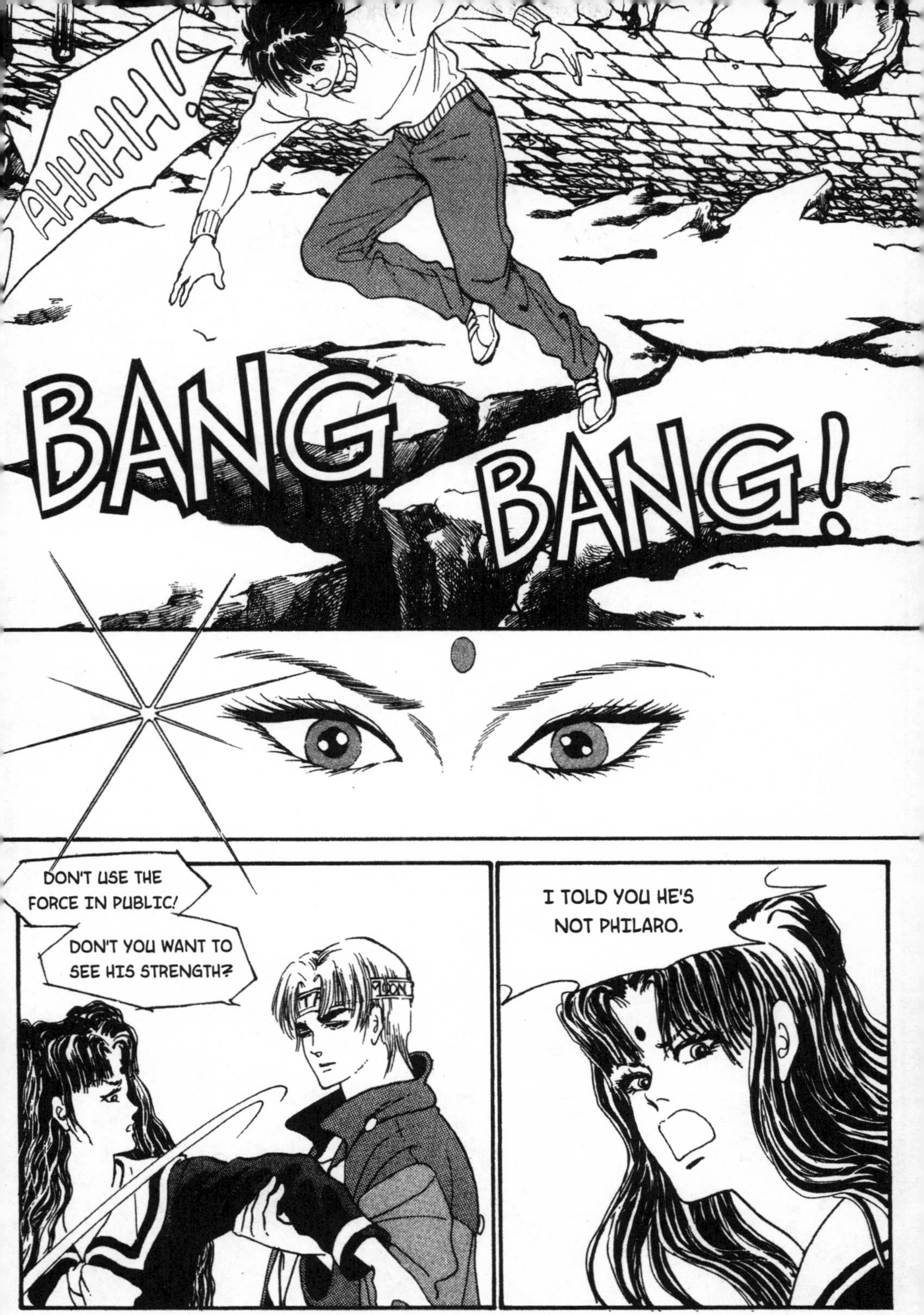
AHHHH!
BANG BANG!
DON'T USE THE FORCE IN PUBLIC!
DON'T YOU WANT TO SEE HIS STRENGTH?
I TOLD YOU HE'S NOT PHILARO.

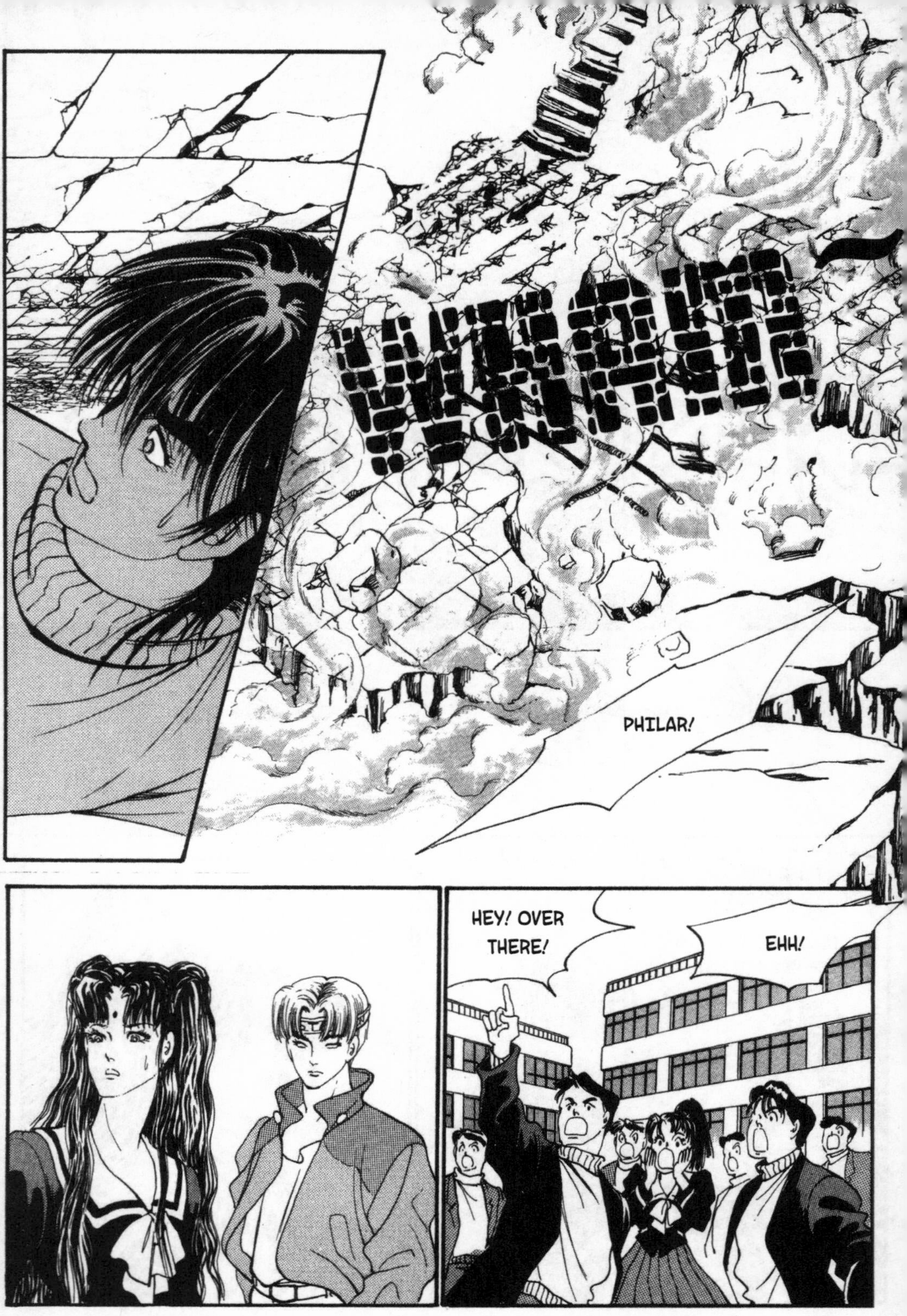
PHILAR!
HEY! OVER THERE!
EHH!

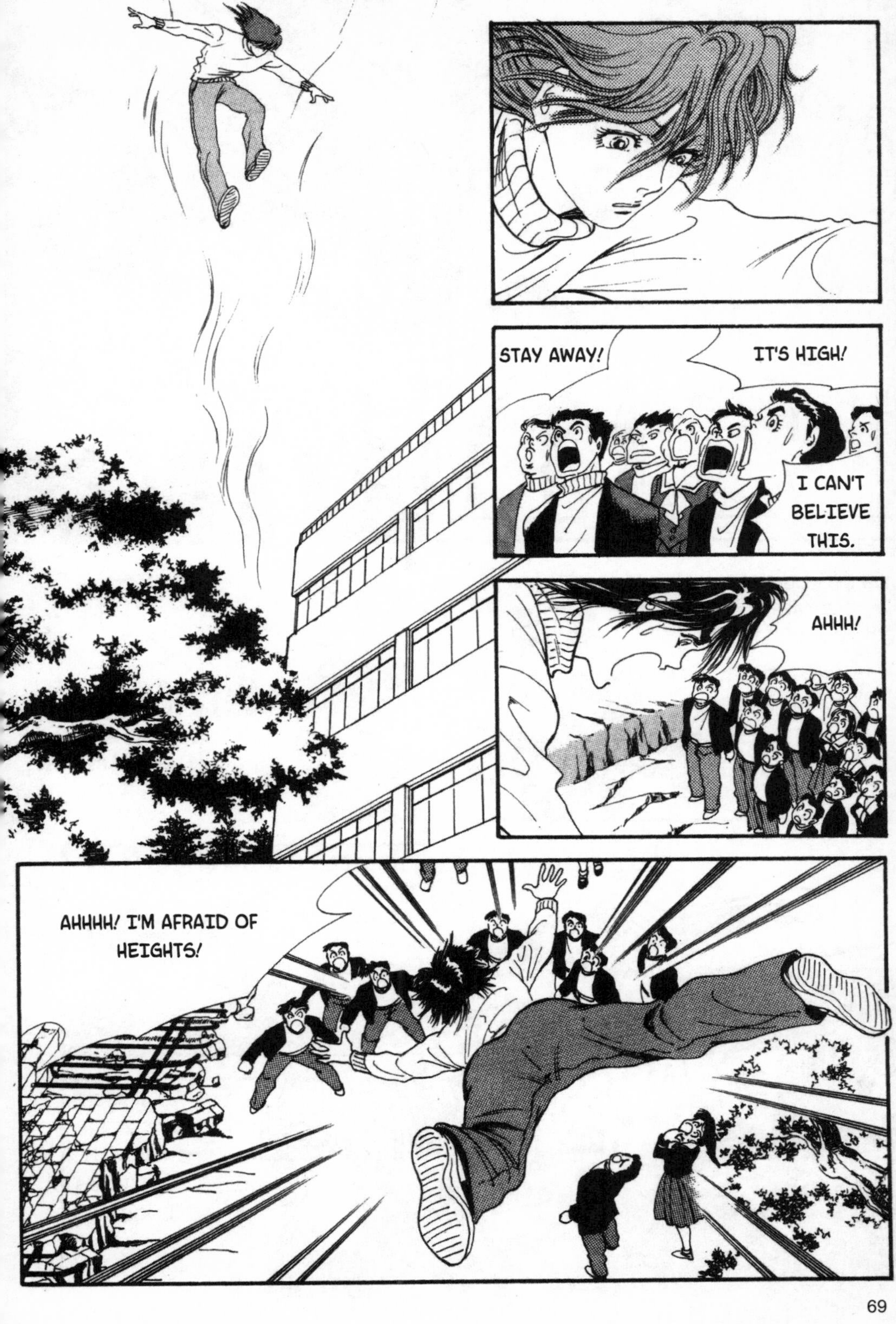
STAY AWAY!
IT'S HIGH!
I CAN'T BELIEVE THIS.
AHHH!
AHHHH! I'M AFRAID OF HEIGHTS!

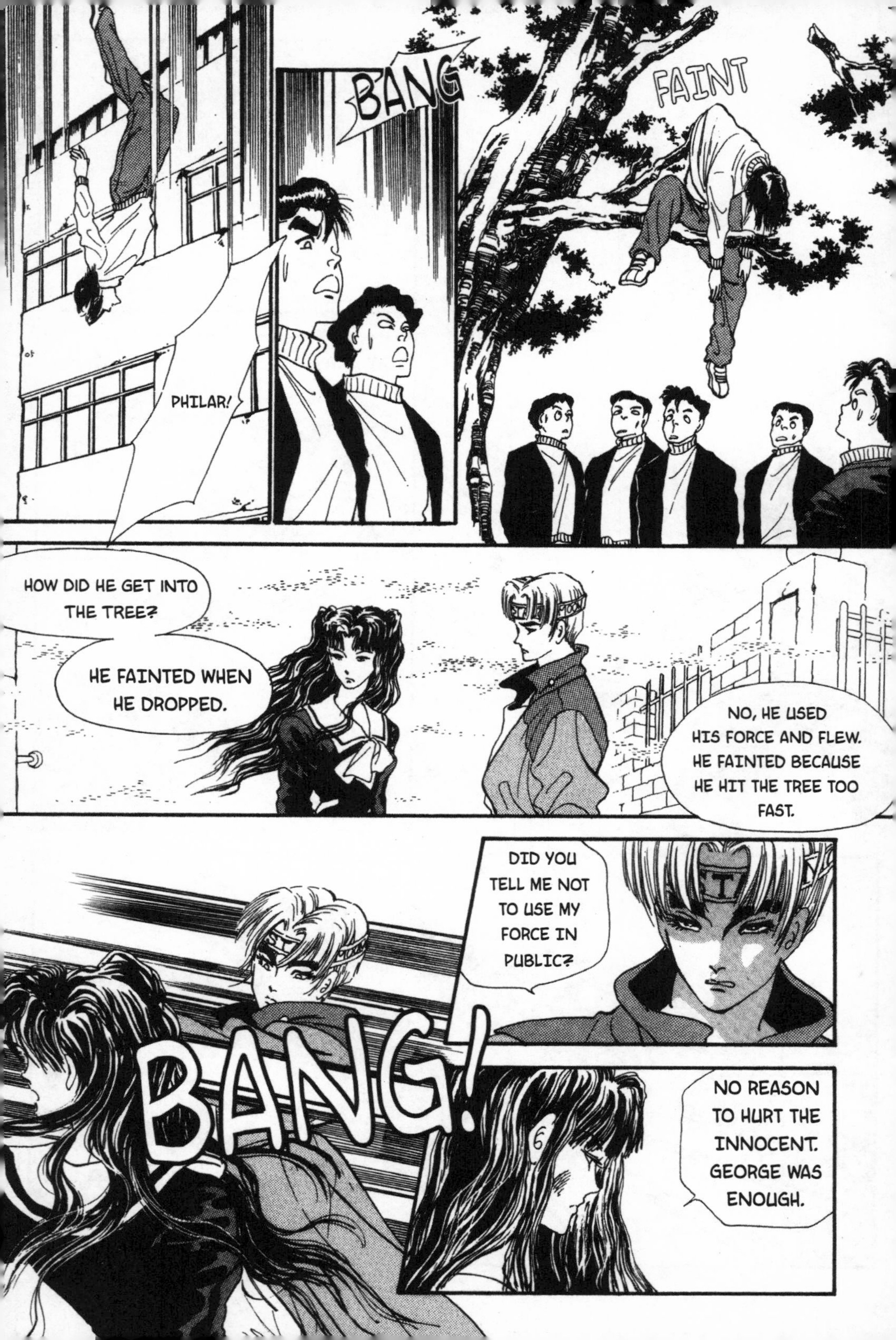
BANG
FAINT
PHILAR!
HOW DID HE GET INTO THE TREE?
HE FAINTED WHEN HE DROPPED.
NO, HE USED HIS FORCE AND FLEW. HE FAINTED BECAUSE HE HIT THE TREE TOO FAST.
DID YOU TELL ME NOT TO USE MY FORCE IN PUBLIC?
BANG!
NO REASON TO HURT THE INNOCENT. GEORGE WAS ENOUGH.

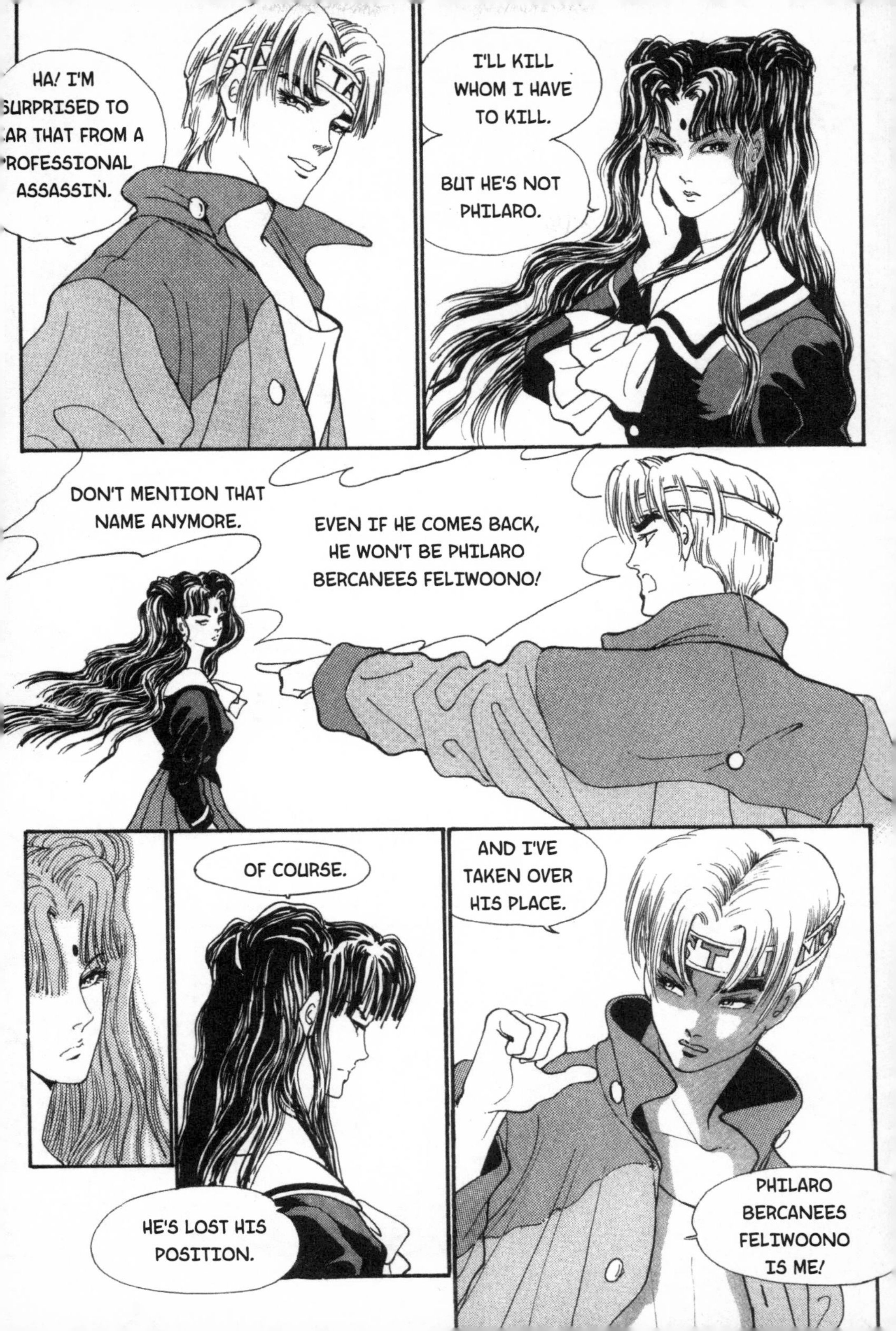
HA! I'M SURPRISED TO AR THAT FROM A ROFESSIONAL ASSASSIN.
I'LL KILL WHOM I HAVE TO KILL.
BUT HE'S NOT PHILARO.
DON'T MENTION THAT NAME ANYMORE.
EVEN IF HE COMES BACK, HE WON'T BE PHILARO BERCANEES FELIWOONO!
OF COURSE.
HE'S LOST HIS POSITION.
AND I'VE TAKEN OVER HIS PLACE.
PHILARO BERCANEES FELIWOONO IS ME!

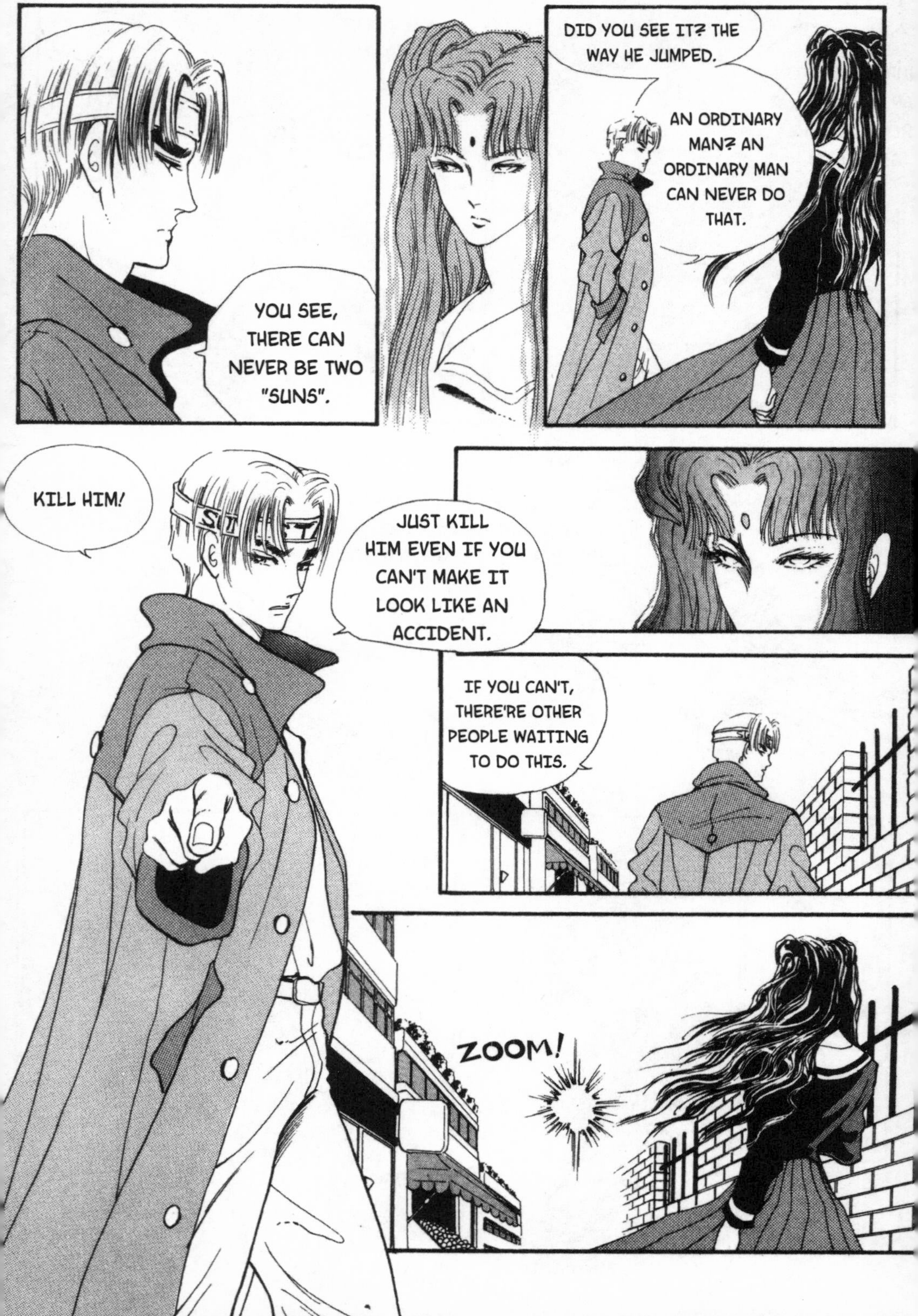
YOU SEE, THERE CAN NEVER BE TWO "SUNS".
DID YOU SEE IT? THE WAY HE JUMPED.
AN ORDINARY MAN? AN ORDINARY MAN CAN NEVER DO THAT.
KILL HIM!
JUST KILL HIM EVEN IF YOU CAN'T MAKE IT LOOK LIKE AN ACCIDENT.
IF YOU CAN'T, THERE'RE OTHER PEOPLE WAITING TO DO THIS.
ZOOM!

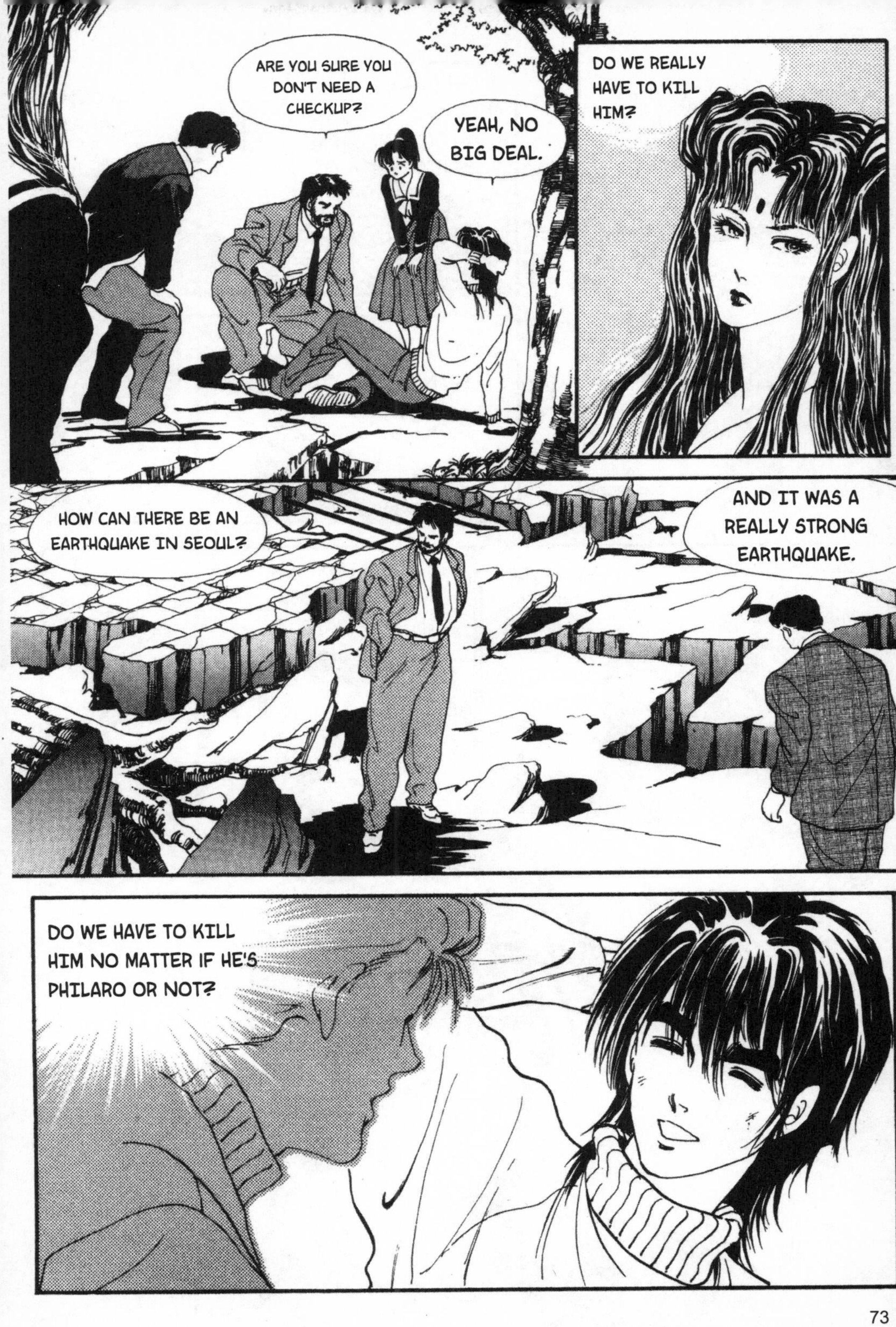
ARE YOU SURE YOU DON'T NEED A CHECKUP?
YEAH, NO BIG DEAL.
DO WE REALLY HAVE TO KILL HIM?
HOW CAN THERE BE AN EARTHQUAKE IN SEOUL?
AND IT WAS A REALLY STRONG EARTHQUAKE.
DO WE HAVE TO KILL HIM NO MATTER IF HE'S PHILARO OR NOT?

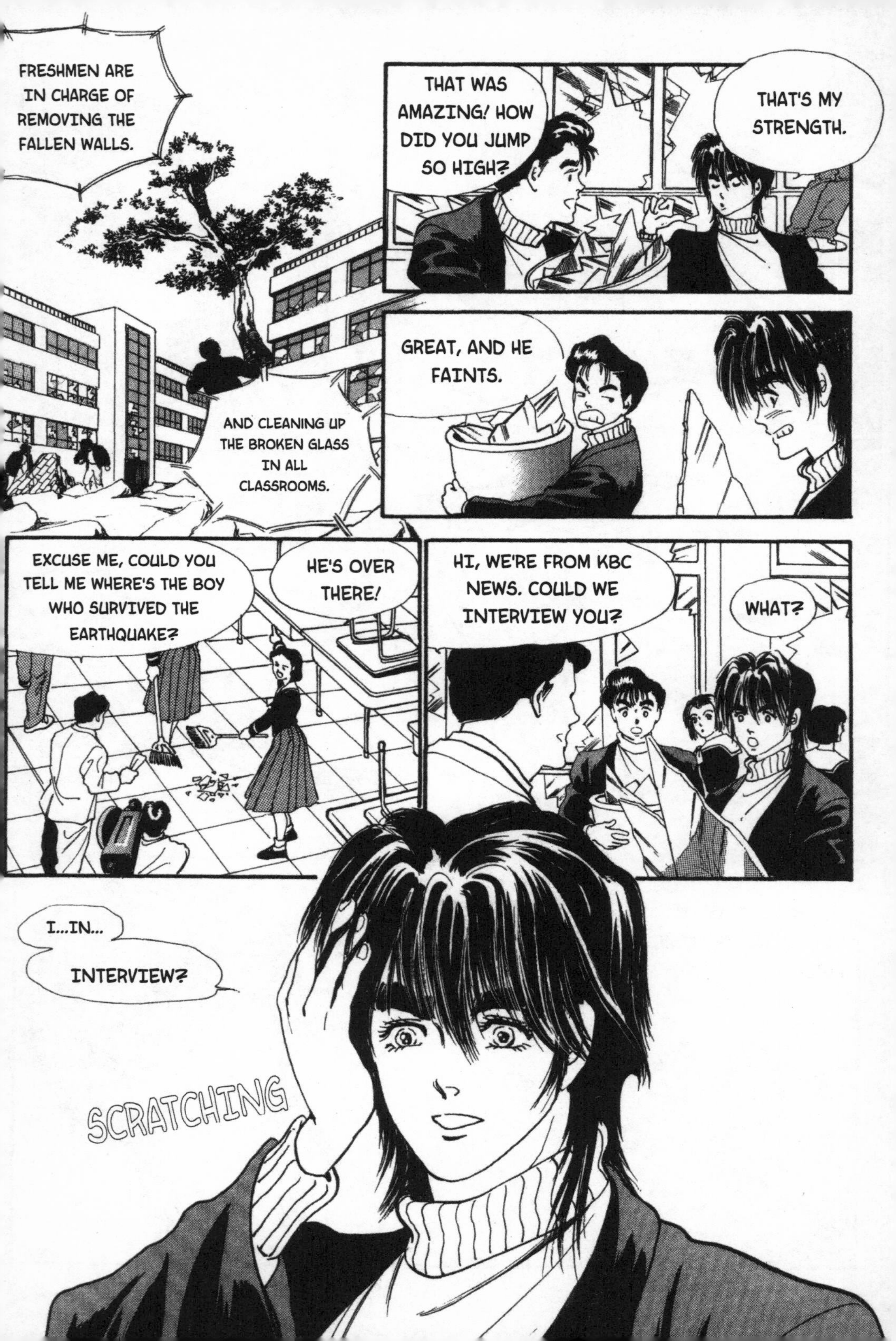
FRESHMEN ARE IN CHARGE OF REMOVING THE FALLEN WALLS.
THAT WAS AMAZING! HOW DID YOU JUMP SO HIGH?
THAT'S MY STRENGTH.
GREAT, AND HE FAINTS.
AND CLEANING UP THE BROKEN GLASS IN ALL CLASSROOMS.
EXCUSE ME, COULD YOU TELL ME WHERE'S THE BOY WHO SURVIVED THE EARTHQUAKE?
HE'S OVER THERE!
HI, WE'RE FROM KBC NEWS. COULD WE INTERVIEW YOU?
WHAT?
I...IN...
INTERVIEW?
SCRATCHING

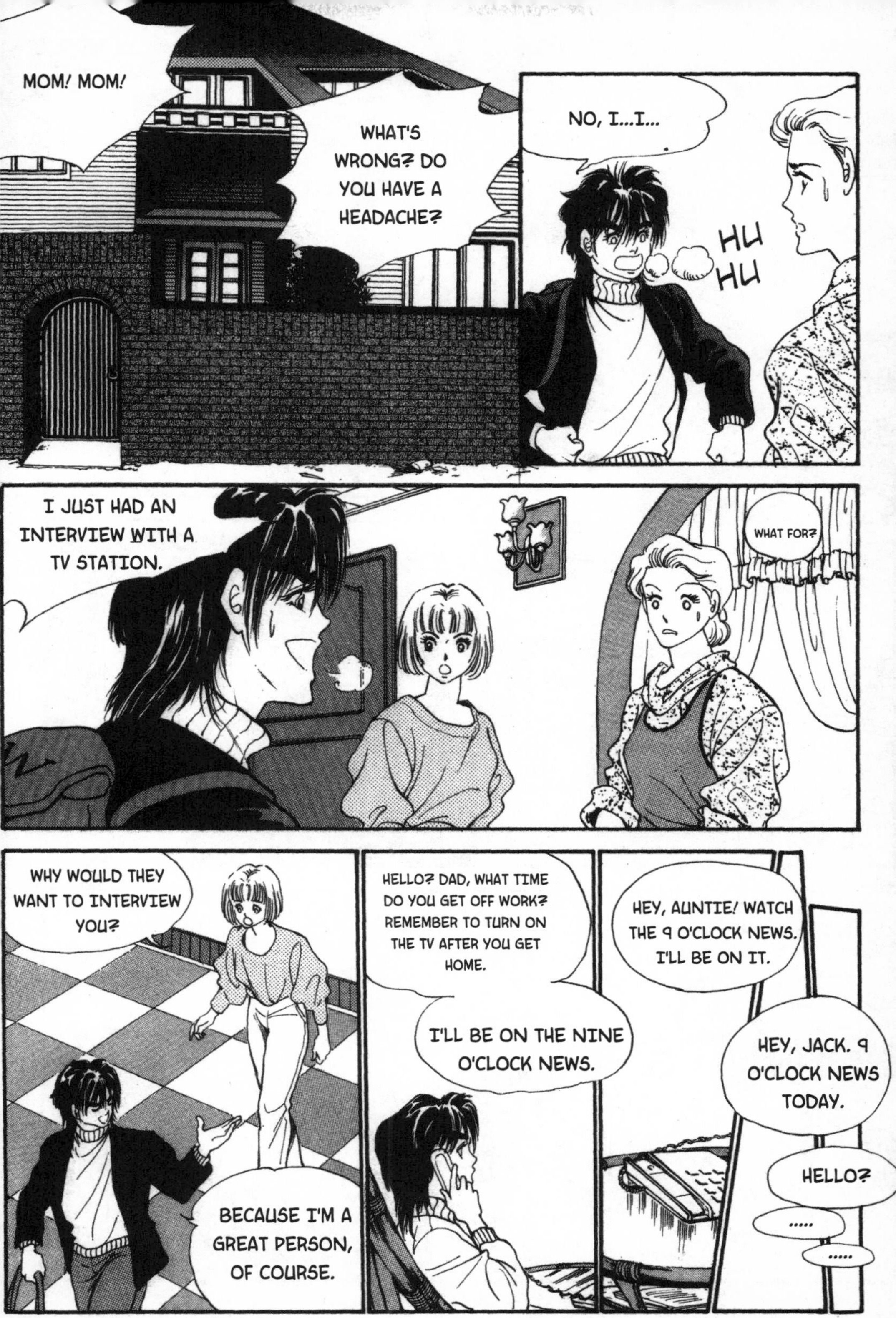
MOM! MOM!
WHAT'S WRONG? DO YOU HAVE A HEADACHE?
NO, I...I...
HU HU
I JUST HAD AN INTERVIEW WITH A TV STATION.
WHAT FOR?
WHY WOULD THEY WANT TO INTERVIEW YOU?
BECAUSE I'M A GREAT PERSON, OF COURSE.
HELLO? DAD, WHAT TIME DO YOU GET OFF WORK? REMEMBER TO TURN ON THE TV AFTER YOU GET HOME.
I'LL BE ON THE NINE O'CLOCK NEWS.
HEY, AUNTIE! WATCH THE 9 O'CLOCK NEWS. I'LL BE ON IT.
HEY, JACK. 9 O'CLOCK NEWS TODAY.
HELLO?
.....
.....

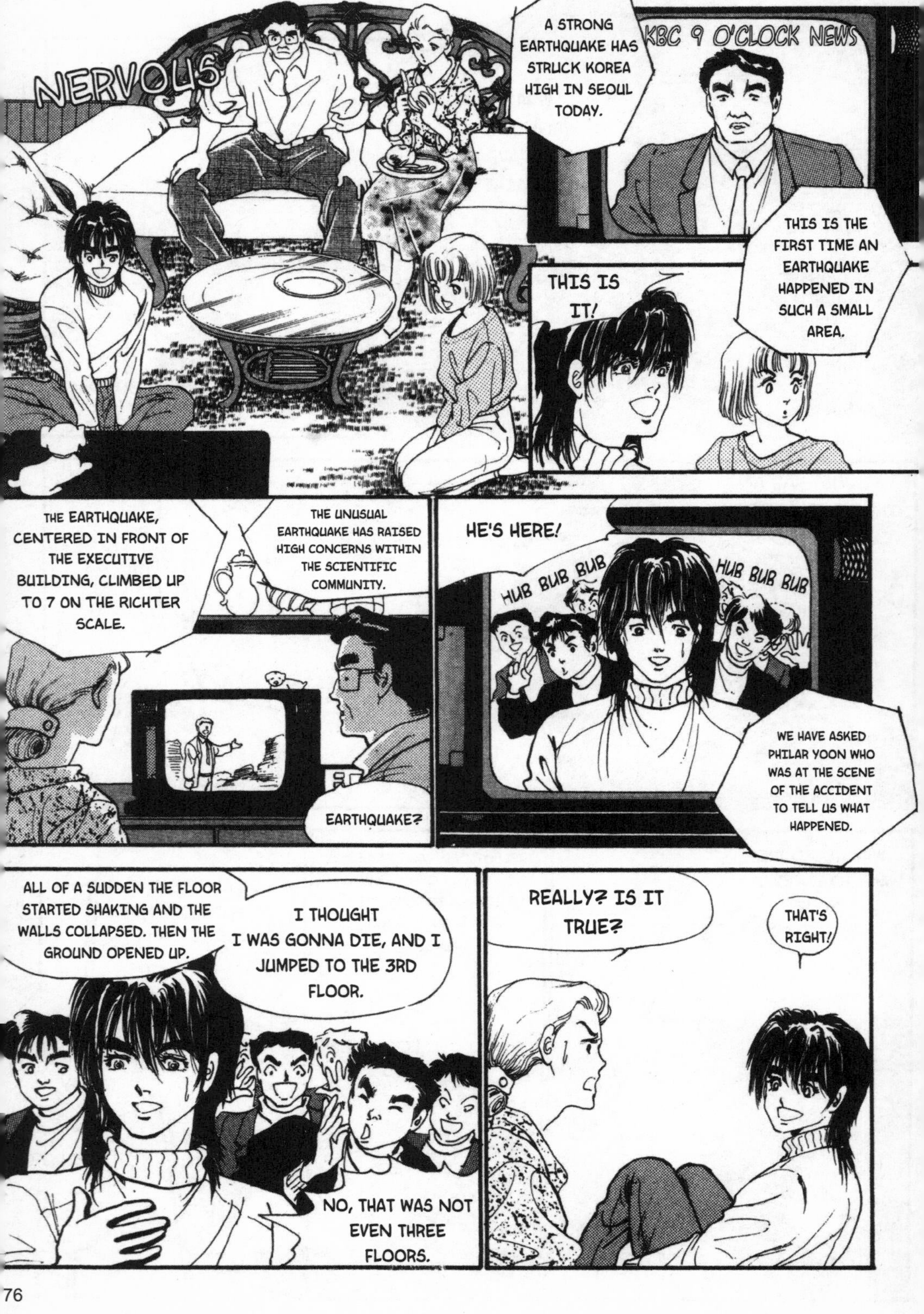
NERVOUS
A STRONG EARTHQUAKE HAS STRUCK KOREA HIGH IN SEOUL TODAY.
KBC 9 O'CLOCK NEWS
THIS IS THE FIRST TIME AN EARTHQUAKE HAPPENED IN SUCH A SMALL AREA.
THIS IS IT!
THE EARTHQUAKE, CENTERED IN FRONT OF THE EXECUTIVE BUILDING, CLIMBED UP TO 7 ON THE RICHTER SCALE.
THE UNUSUAL EARTHQUAKE HAS RAISED HIGH CONCERNS WITHIN THE SCIENTIFIC COMMUNITY.
EARTHQUAKE?
HE'S HERE!
HUB BUB BUB
HUB BUB BUB
WE HAVE ASKED PHILAR YOON WHO WAS AT THE SCENE OF THE ACCIDENT TO TELL US WHAT HAPPENED.
ALL OF A SUDDEN THE FLOOR STARTED SHAKING AND THE WALLS COLLAPSED. THEN THE GROUND OPENED UP.
I THOUGHT I WAS GONNA DIE, AND I JUMPED TO THE 3RD FLOOR.
NO, THAT WAS NOT EVEN THREE FLOORS.
REALLY? IS IT TRUE?
THAT'S RIGHT!

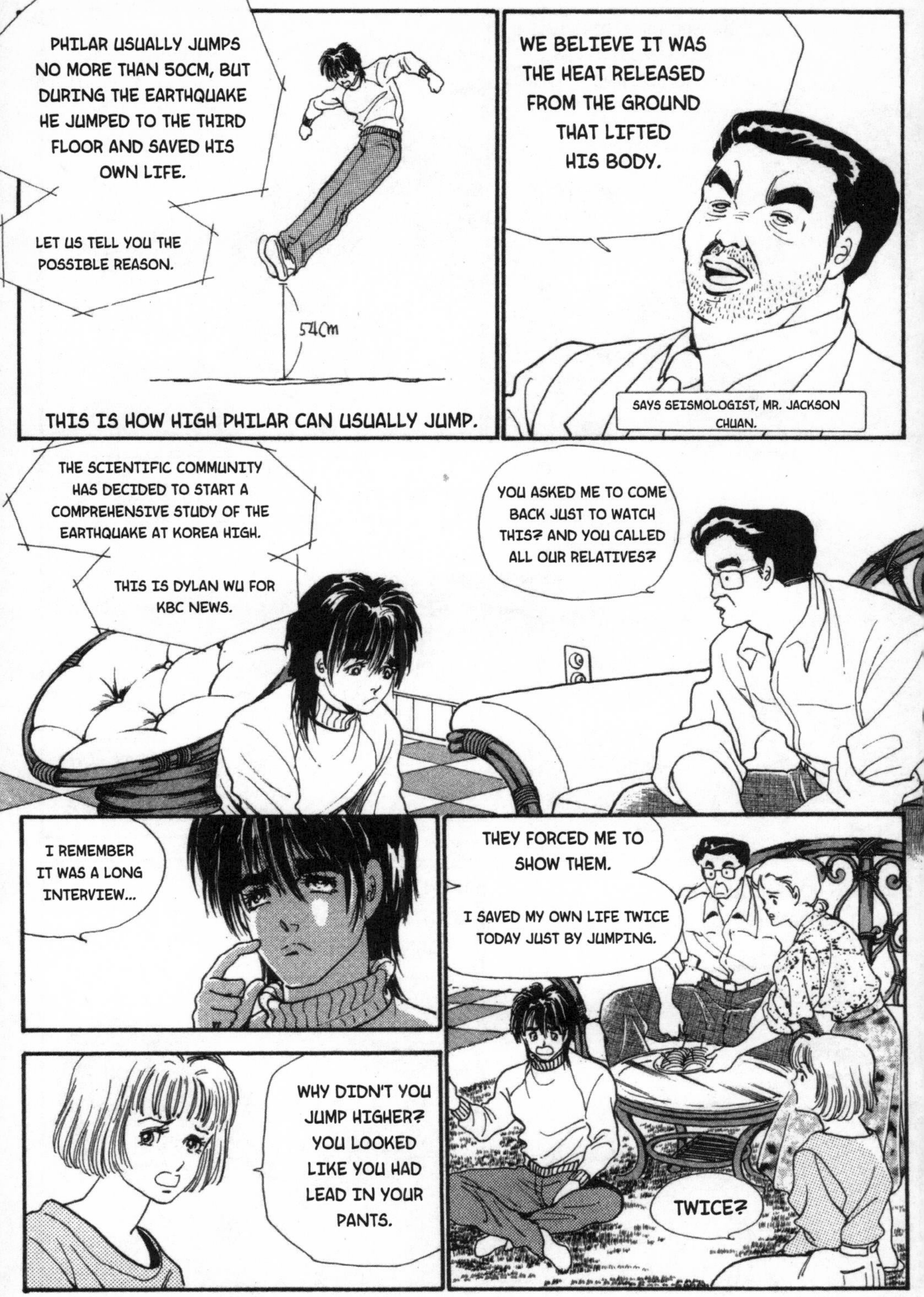

PHILAR USUALLY JUMPS NO MORE THAN 50CM, BUT DURING THE EARTHQUAKE HE JUMPED TO THE THIRD FLOOR AND SAVED HIS OWN LIFE.
LET US TELL YOU THE POSSIBLE REASON.
54cm
THIS IS HOW HIGH PHILAR CAN USUALLY JUMP.
WE BELIEVE IT WAS THE HEAT RELEASED FROM THE GROUND THAT LIFTED HIS BODY.
SAYS SEISMOLOGIST, MR. JACKSON CHUAN.
THE SCIENTIFIC COMMUNITY HAS DECIDED TO START A COMPREHENSIVE STUDY OF THE EARTHQUAKE AT KOREA HIGH.
THIS IS DYLAN WU FOR KBC NEWS.
YOU ASKED ME TO COME BACK JUST TO WATCH THIS? AND YOU CALLED ALL OUR RELATIVES?
I REMEMBER IT WAS A LONG INTERVIEW...
THEY FORCED ME TO SHOW THEM.
I SAVED MY OWN LIFE TWICE TODAY JUST BY JUMPING.
WHY DIDN'T YOU JUMP HIGHER? YOU LOOKED LIKE YOU HAD LEAD IN YOUR PANTS.
TWICE?

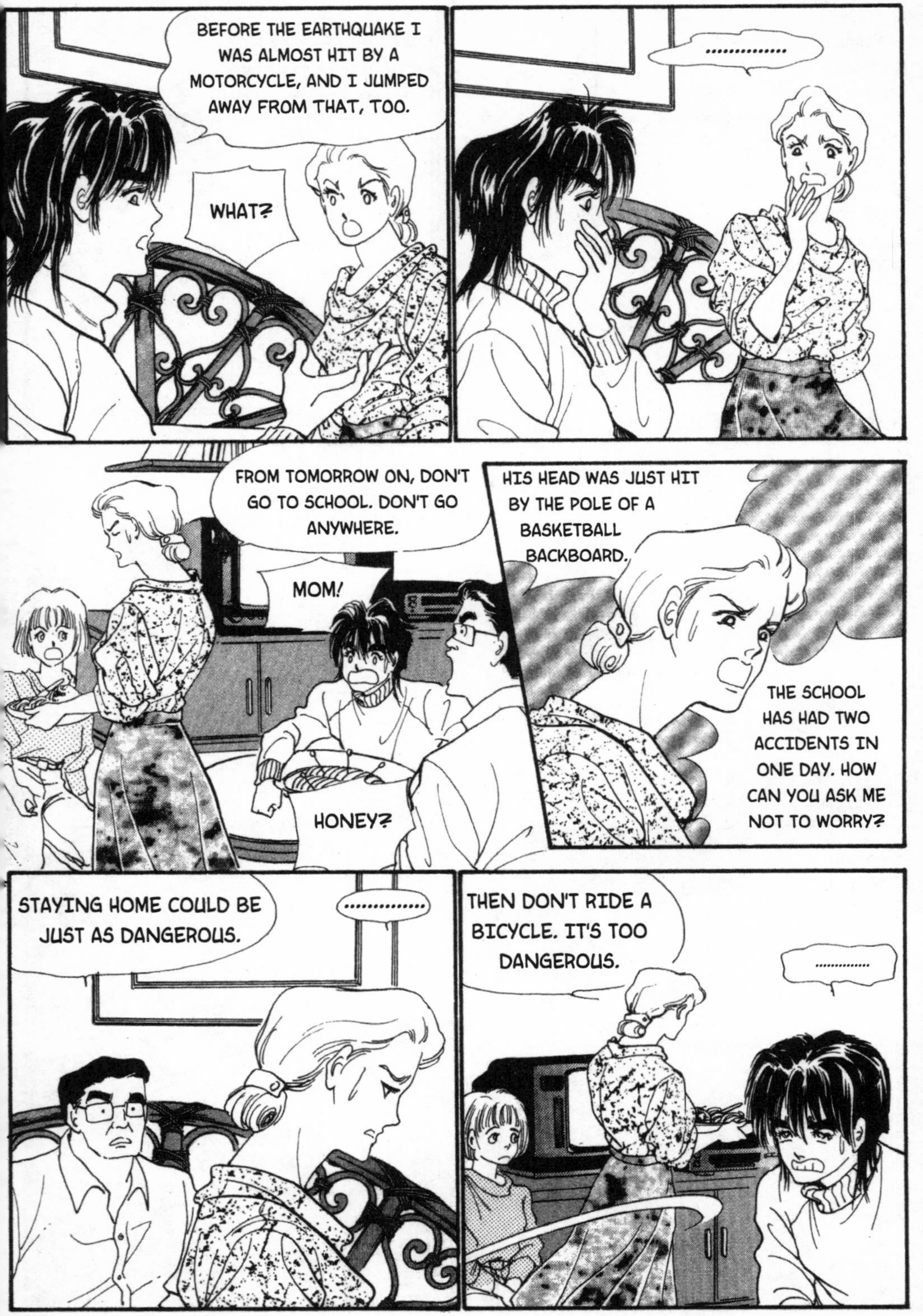
BEFORE THE EARTHQUAKE I WAS ALMOST HIT BY A MOTORCYCLE, AND I JUMPED AWAY FROM THAT, TOO.
WHAT?
....
FROM TOMORROW ON, DON'T GO TO SCHOOL. DON'T GO ANYWHERE.
MOM!
HONEY?
HIS HEAD WAS JUST HIT BY THE POLE OF A BASKETBALL BACKBOARD.
THE SCHOOL HAS HAD TWO ACCIDENTS IN ONE DAY. HOW CAN YOU ASK ME NOT TO WORRY?
STAYING HOME COULD BE JUST AS DANGEROUS.
....
THEN DON'T RIDE A BICYCLE. IT'S TOO DANGEROUS.
....

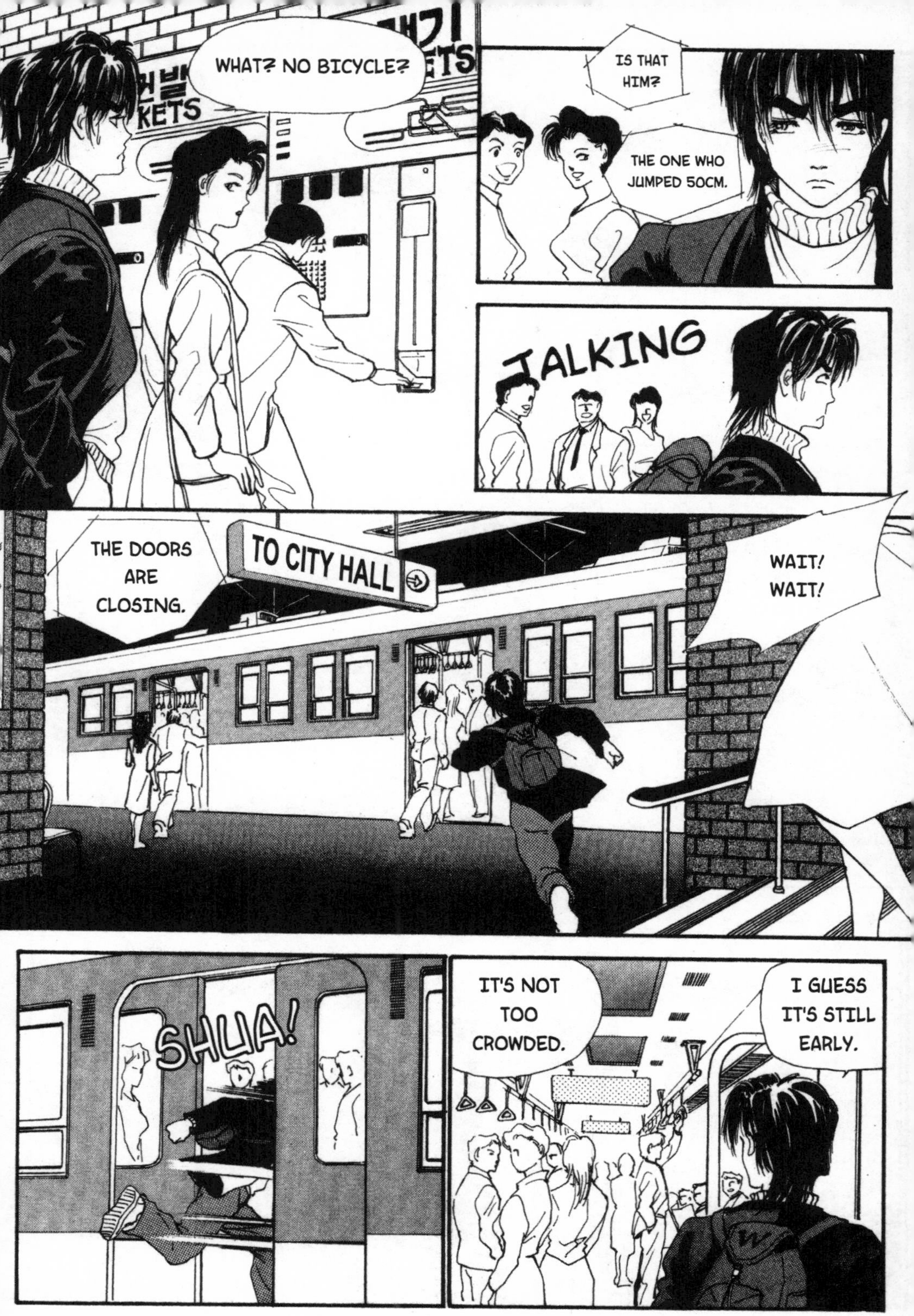
WHAT? NO BICYCLE?
IS THAT HIM?
THE ONE WHO JUMPED 50CM.
TALKING
THE DOORS ARE CLOSING.
TO CITY HALL
WAIT! WAIT!
SHUA!
IT'S NOT TOO CROWDED.
I GUESS IT'S STILL EARLY.

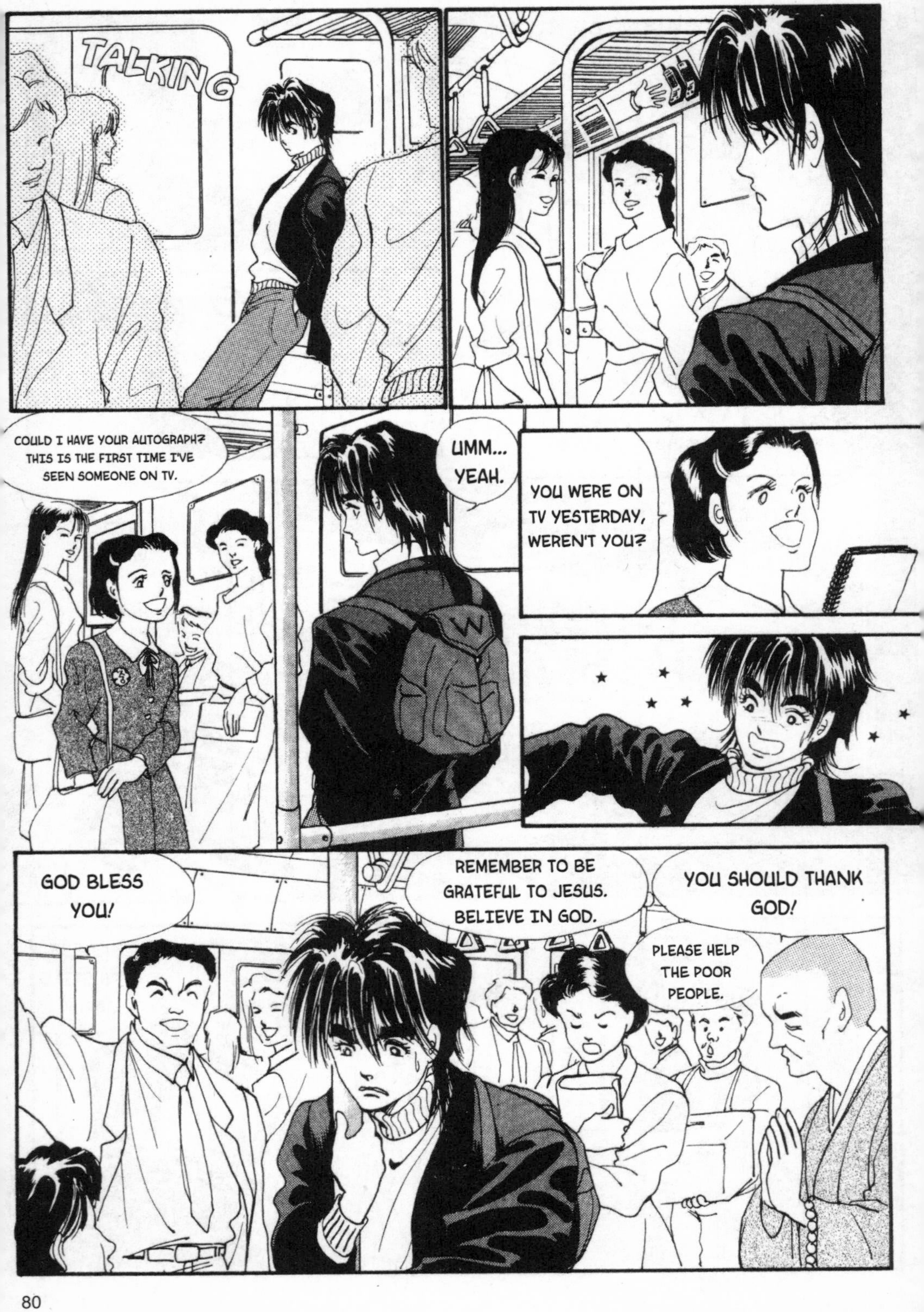
TALKING
COULD I HAVE YOUR AUTOGRAPH? THIS IS THE FIRST TIME I'VE SEEN SOMEONE ON TV.
UMM... YEAH.
YOU WERE ON TV YESTERDAY, WEREN'T YOU?
GOD BLESS YOU!
REMEMBER TO BE GRATEFUL TO JESUS. BELIEVE IN GOD.
YOU SHOULD THANK GOD!
PLEASE HELP THE POOR PEOPLE.

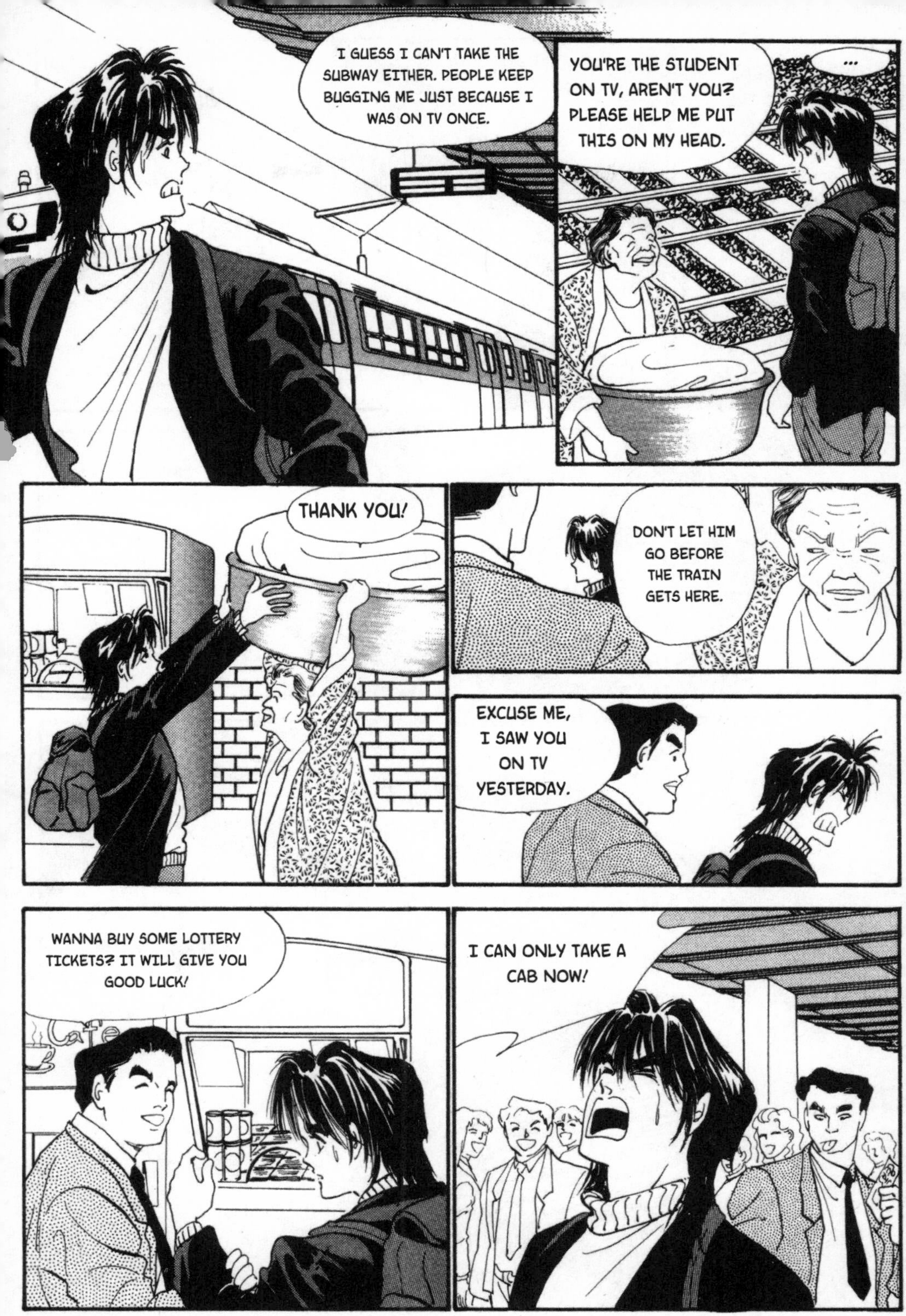
I GUESS I CAN'T TAKE THE SUBWAY EITHER. PEOPLE KEEP BUGGING ME JUST BECAUSE I WAS ON TV ONCE.
YOU'RE THE STUDENT ON TV, AREN'T YOU? PLEASE HELP ME PUT THIS ON MY HEAD.
...
THANK YOU!
DON'T LET HIM GO BEFORE THE TRAIN GETS HERE.
EXCUSE ME, I SAW YOU ON TV YESTERDAY.
WANNA BUY SOME LOTTERY TICKETS? IT WILL GIVE YOU GOOD LUCK!
I CAN ONLY TAKE A CAB NOW!

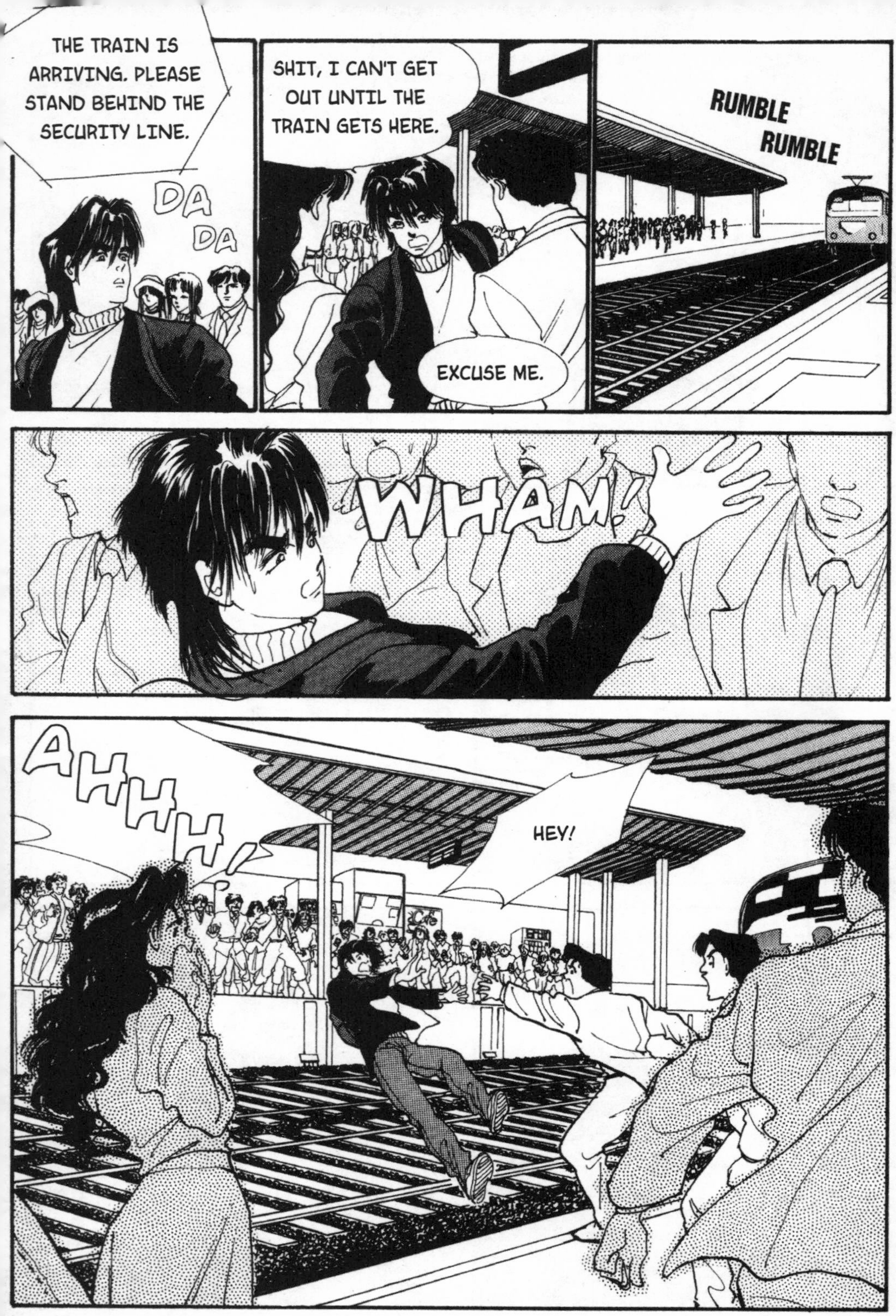
THE TRAIN IS ARRIVING. PLEASE STAND BEHIND THE SECURITY LINE.
DA DA
SHIT, I CAN'T GET OUT UNTIL THE TRAIN GETS HERE.
EXCUSE ME.
RUMBLE RUMBLE
WHAM!
AHHH!
HEY!

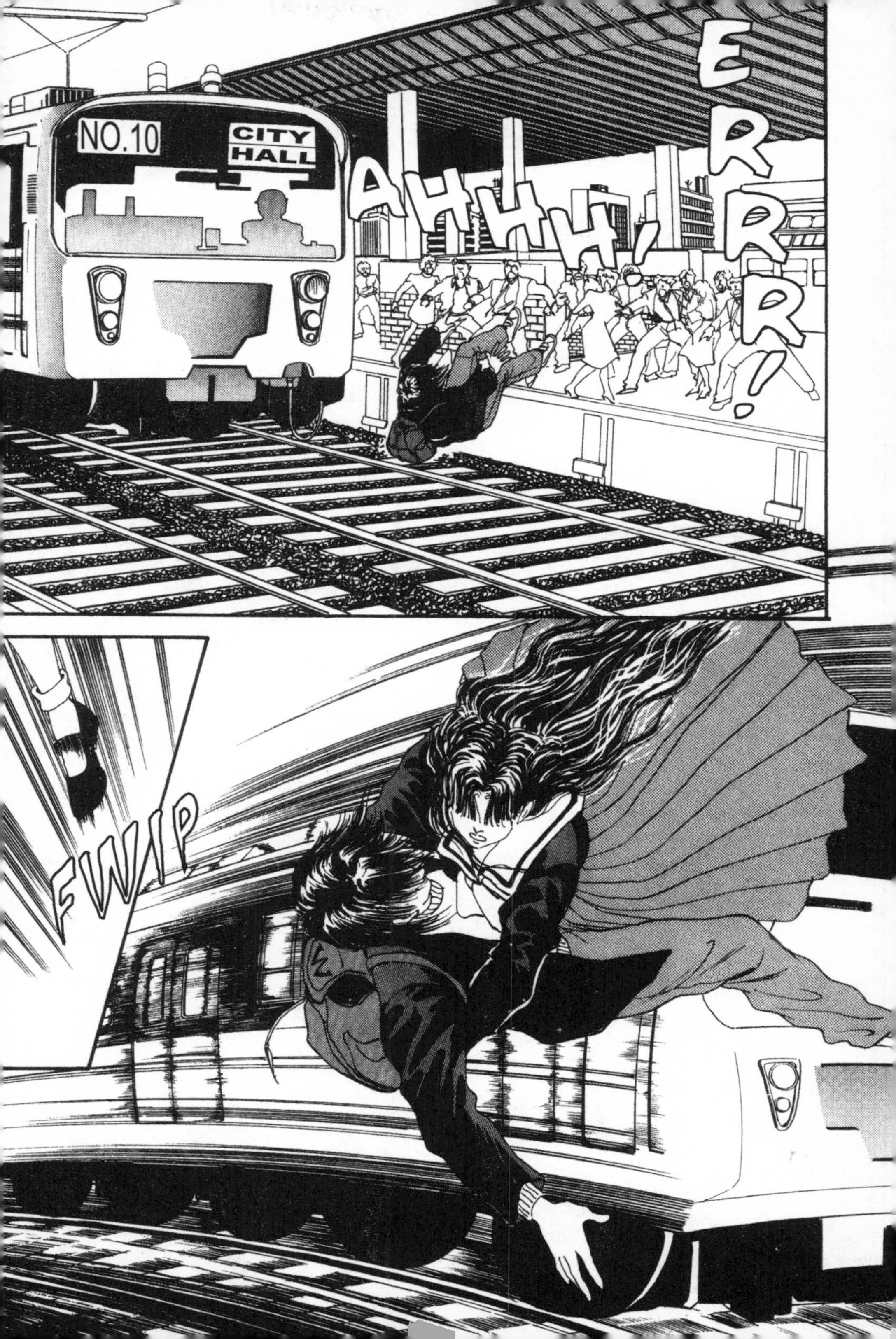
NO.10
CITY HALL
AHHH!
ERRR!
FWIP

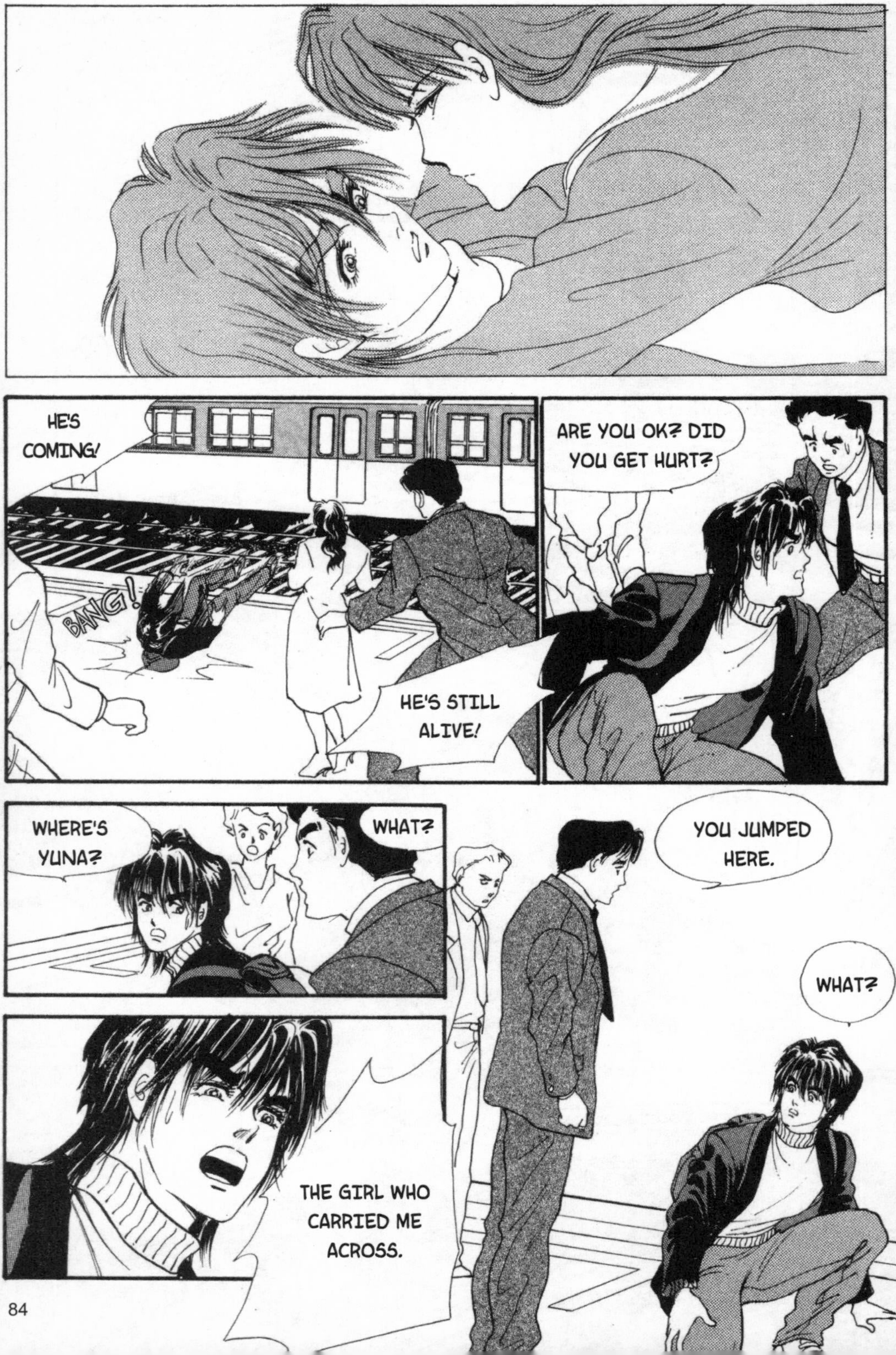
HE'S COMING!
BANG!
HE'S STILL ALIVE!
ARE YOU OK? DID YOU GET HURT?
WHERE'S YUNA?
WHAT?
YOU JUMPED HERE.
WHAT?
THE GIRL WHO CARRIED ME ACROSS.

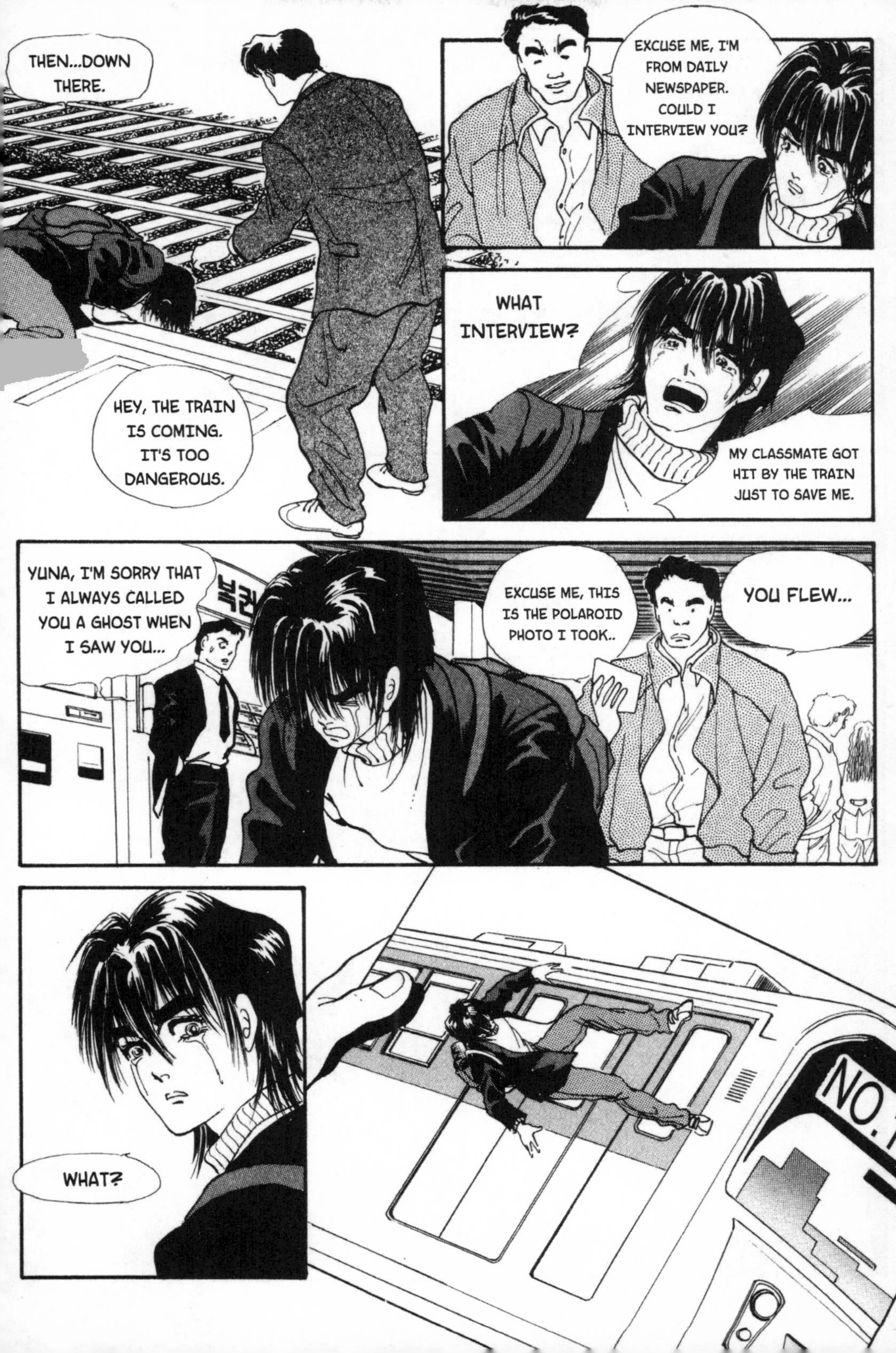

THEN...DOWN THERE.
HEY, THE TRAIN IS COMING. IT'S TOO DANGEROUS.
EXCUSE ME, I'M FROM DAILY NEWSPAPER. COULD I INTERVIEW YOU?
WHAT INTERVIEW?
MY CLASSMATE GOT HIT BY THE TRAIN JUST TO SAVE ME.
YUNA, I'M SORRY THAT I ALWAYS CALLED YOU A GHOST WHEN I SAW YOU...
EXCUSE ME, THIS IS THE POLAROID PHOTO I TOOK..
YOU FLEW...
WHAT?
NO.1

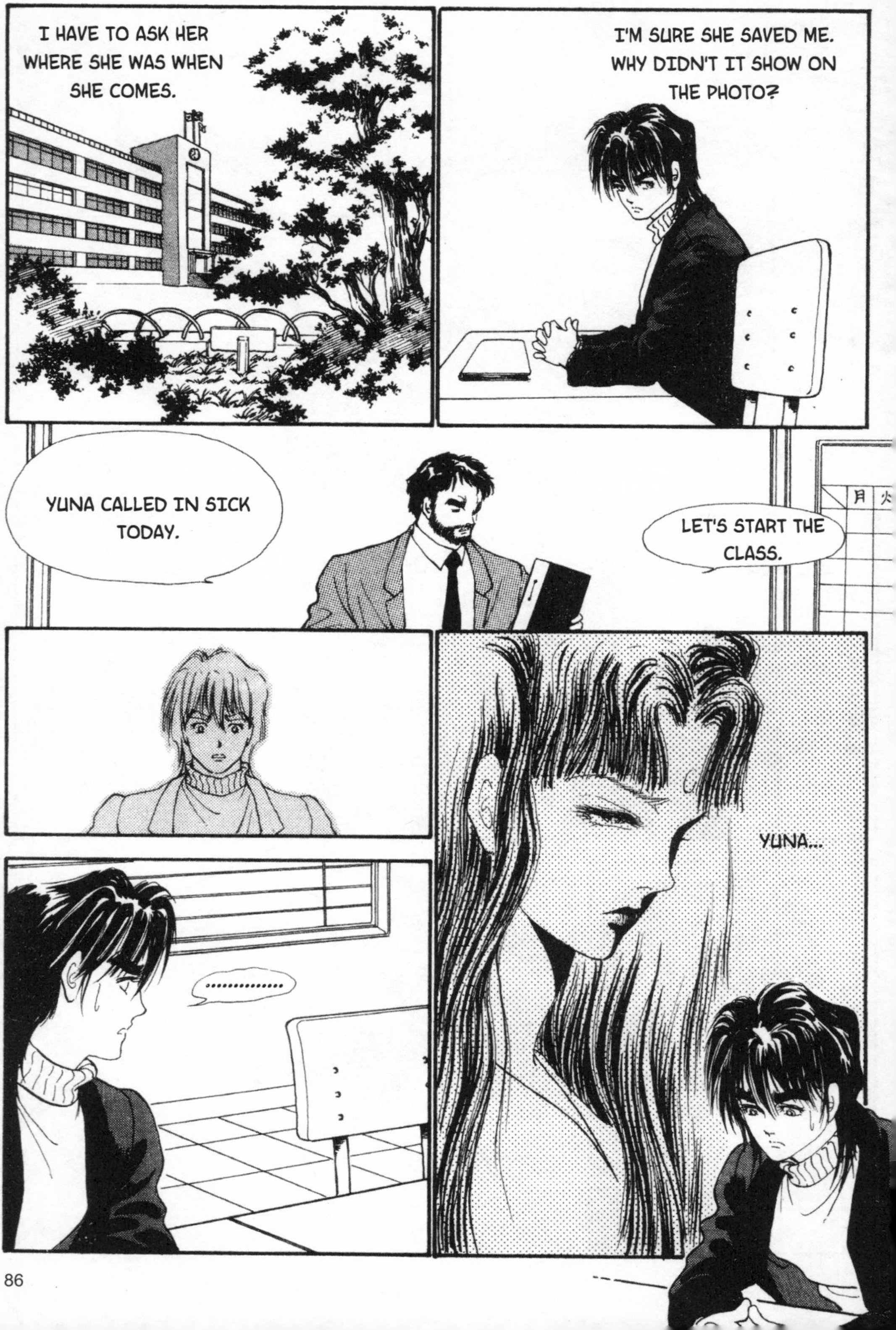
I HAVE TO ASK HER WHERE SHE WAS WHEN SHE COMES.
I'M SURE SHE SAVED ME. WHY DIDN'T IT SHOW ON THE PHOTO?
YUNA CALLED IN SICK TODAY.
LET'S START THE CLASS.
月 火
YUNA...
....

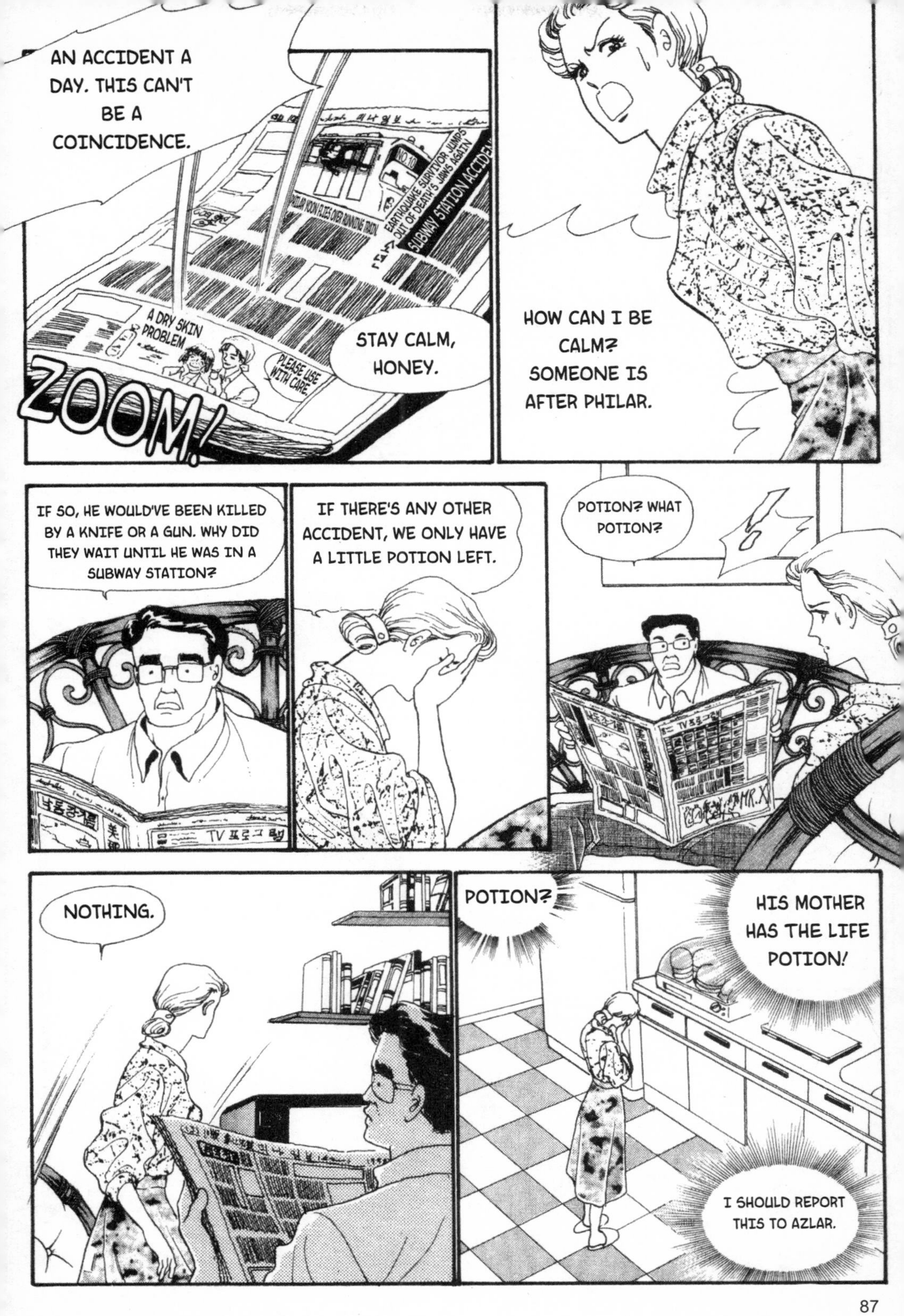
AN ACCIDENT A DAY. THIS CAN'T BE A COINCIDENCE.
EARTHQUAKE SURVIVOR JUMPS OUT OF DEATH'S JAWS AGAIN
SUBWAY STATION ACCIDENT
A DRY SKIN PROBLEM
PLEASE USE WITH CARE.
ZOOM!
STAY CALM, HONEY.
HOW CAN I BE CALM? SOMEONE IS AFTER PHILAR.
IF SO, HE WOULD'VE BEEN KILLED BY A KNIFE OR A GUN. WHY DID THEY WAIT UNTIL HE WAS IN A SUBWAY STATION?
IF THERE'S ANY OTHER ACCIDENT, WE ONLY HAVE A LITTLE POTION LEFT.
POTION? WHAT POTION?
MR. X
NOTHING.
POTION?
HIS MOTHER HAS THE LIFE POTION!
I SHOULD REPORT THIS TO AZLAR.

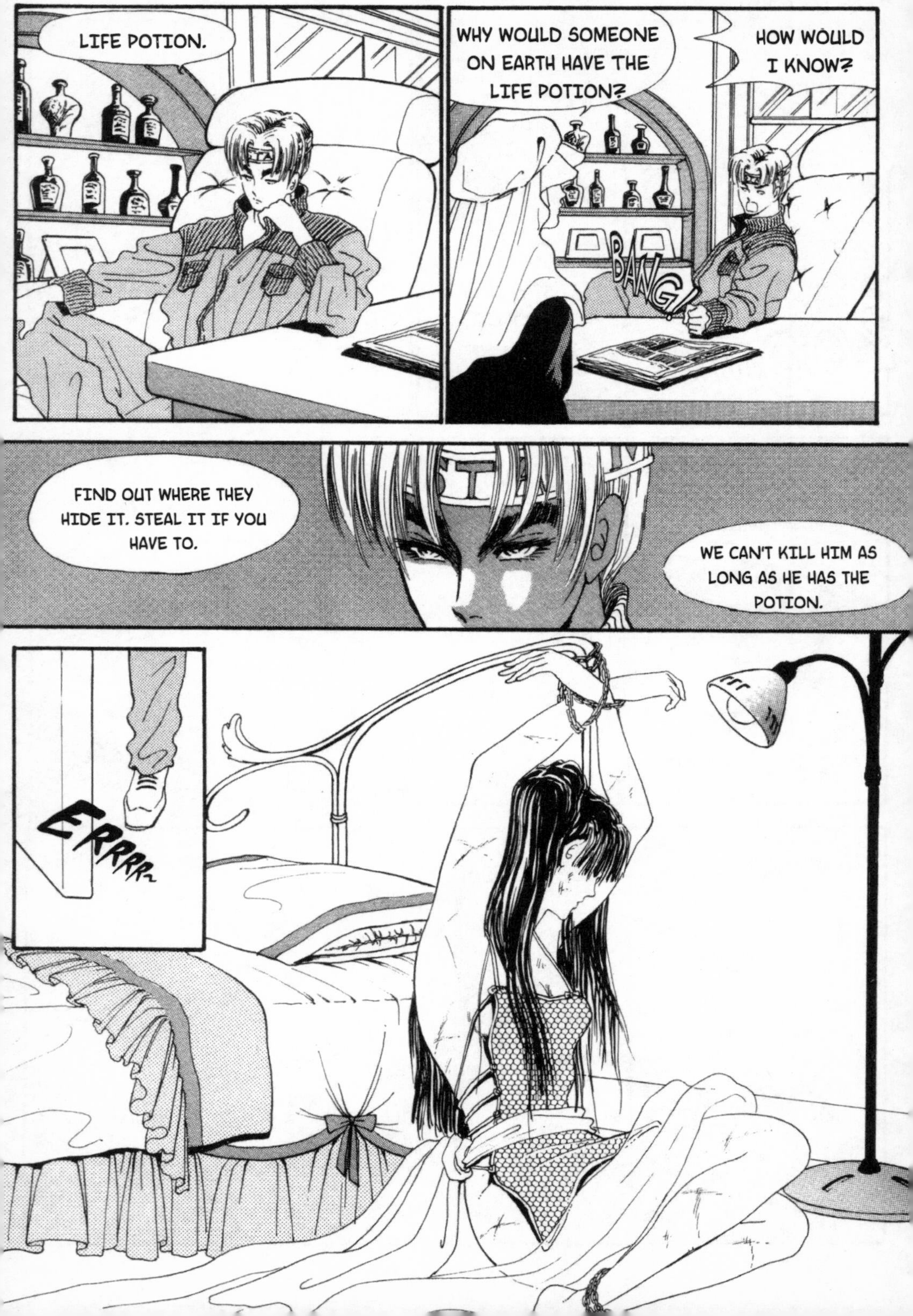
LIFE POTION.
WHY WOULD SOMEONE ON EARTH HAVE THE LIFE POTION?
HOW WOULD I KNOW?
BANG!
FIND OUT WHERE THEY HIDE IT. STEAL IT IF YOU HAVE TO.
WE CAN'T KILL HIM AS LONG AS HE HAS THE POTION.
ERRRRR

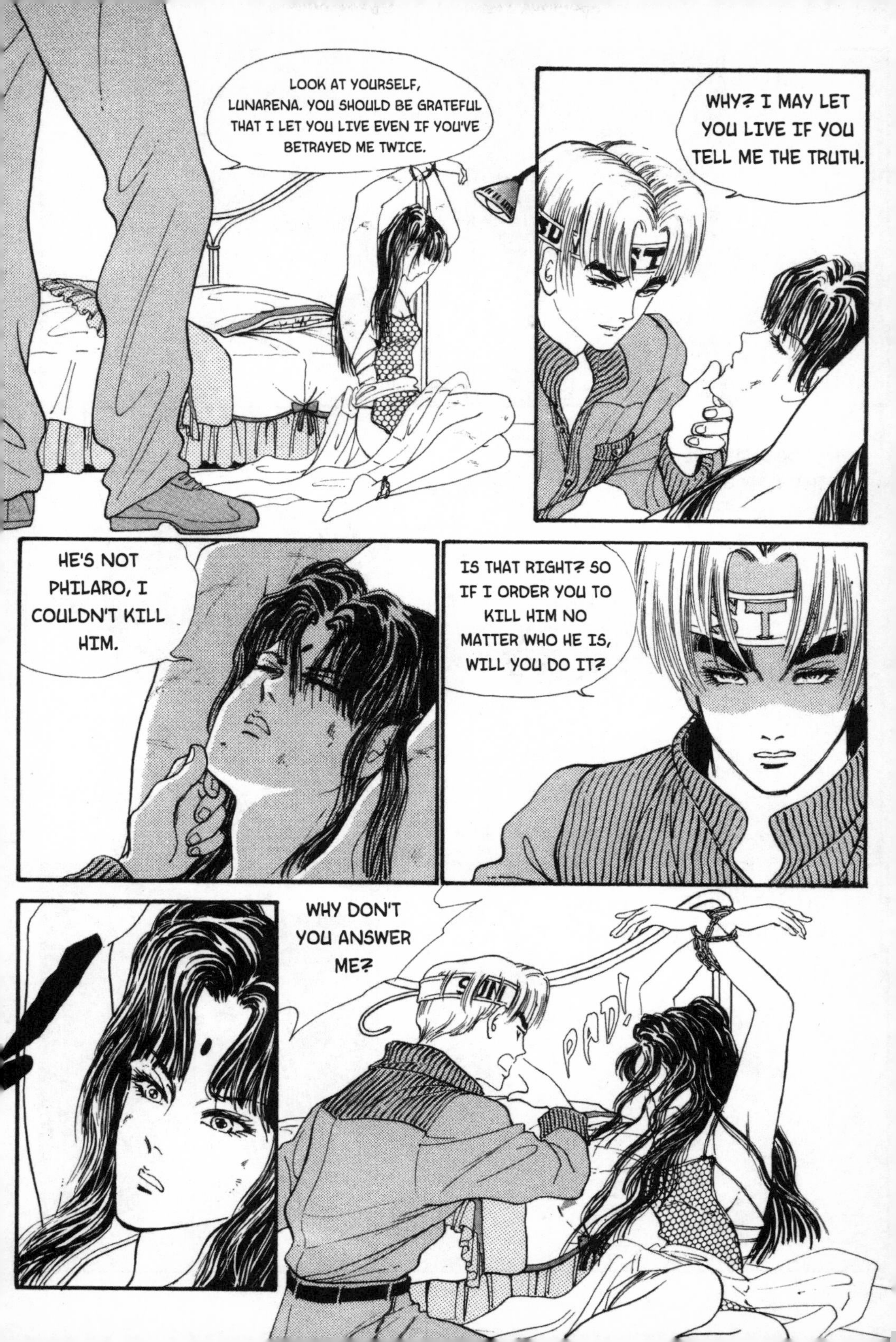
LOOK AT YOURSELF, LUNARENA. YOU SHOULD BE GRATEFUL THAT I LET YOU LIVE EVEN IF YOU'VE BETRAYED ME TWICE.
WHY? I MAY LET YOU LIVE IF YOU TELL ME THE TRUTH.
HE'S NOT PHILARO, I COULDN'T KILL HIM.
IS THAT RIGHT? SO IF I ORDER YOU TO KILL HIM NO MATTER WHO HE IS, WILL YOU DO IT?
WHY DON'T YOU ANSWER ME?
PAD!

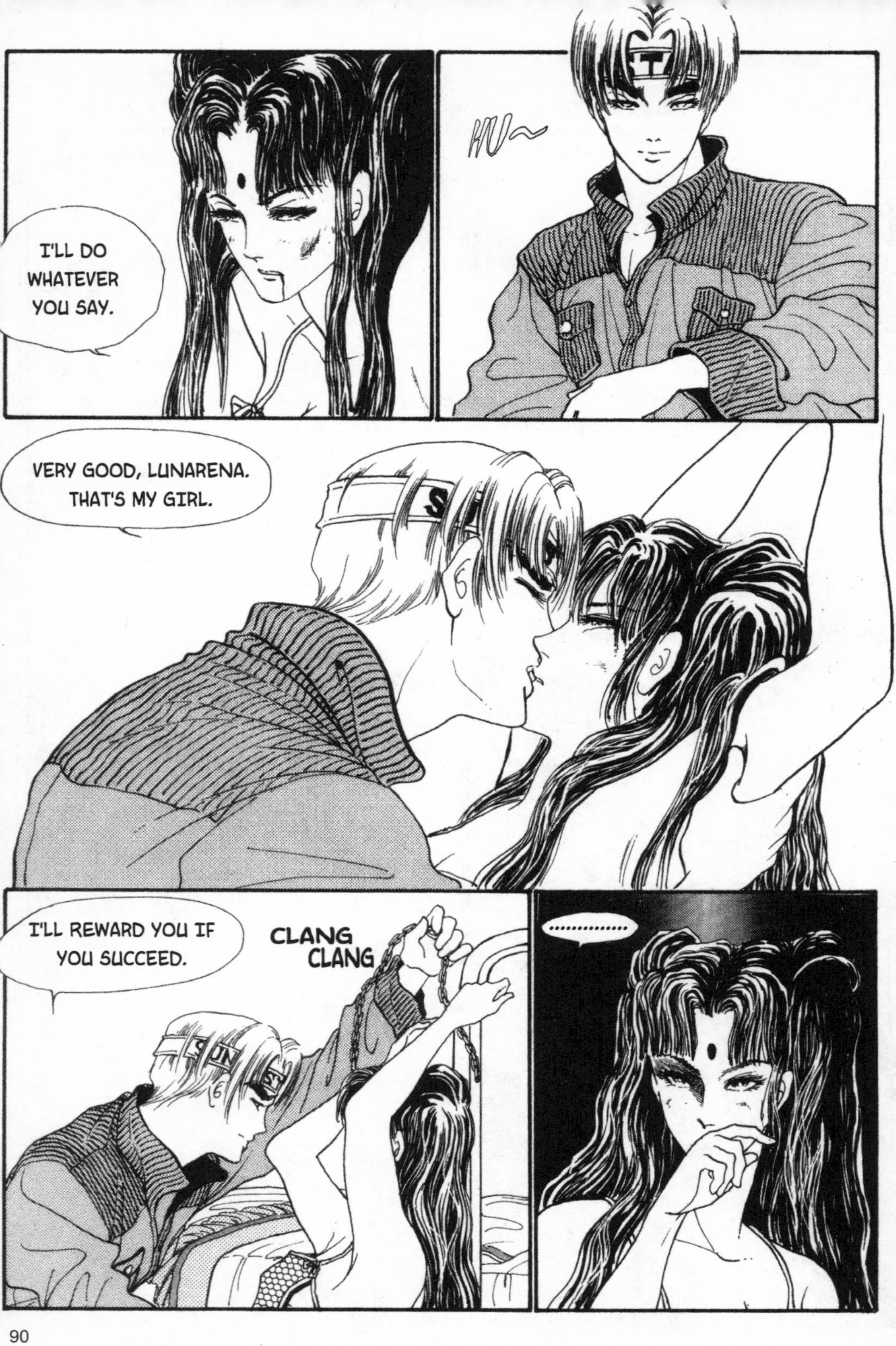
I'LL DO WHATEVER YOU SAY.
HU~
VERY GOOD, LUNARENA. THAT'S MY GIRL.
I'LL REWARD YOU IF YOU SUCCEED.
CLANG CLANG
....

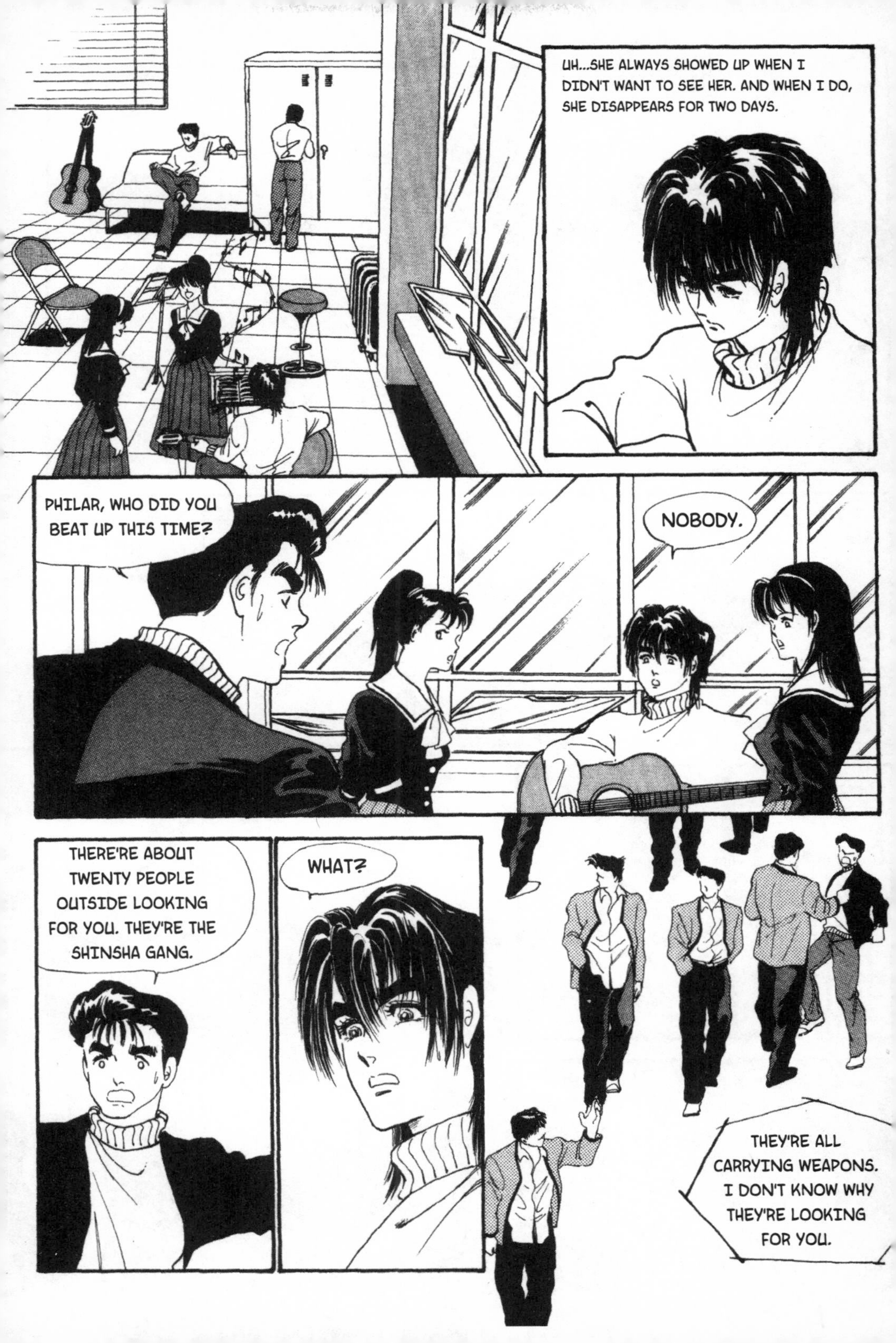

UH...SHE ALWAYS SHOWED UP WHEN I DIDN'T WANT TO SEE HER. AND WHEN I DO, SHE DISAPPEARS FOR TWO DAYS.
PHILAR, WHO DID YOU BEAT UP THIS TIME?
NOBODY.
THERE'RE ABOUT TWENTY PEOPLE OUTSIDE LOOKING FOR YOU. THEY'RE THE SHINSHA GANG.
WHAT?
THEY'RE ALL CARRYING WEAPONS. I DON'T KNOW WHY THEY'RE LOOKING FOR YOU.

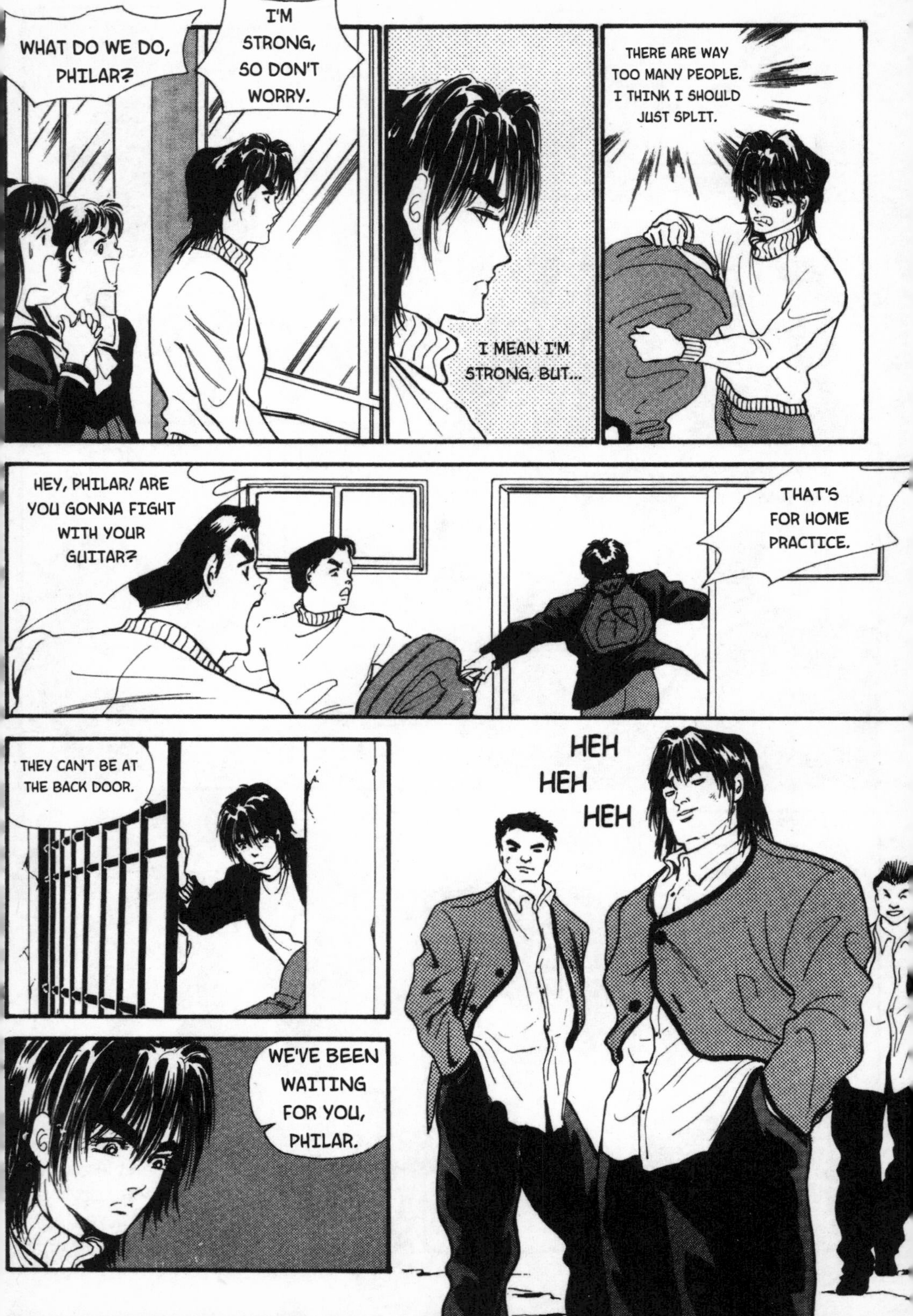

WHAT DO WE DO, PHILAR?
I'M STRONG, SO DON'T WORRY.
I MEAN I'M STRONG, BUT...
THERE ARE WAY TOO MANY PEOPLE. I THINK I SHOULD JUST SPLIT.
HEY, PHILAR! ARE YOU GONNA FIGHT WITH YOUR GUITAR?
THAT'S FOR HOME PRACTICE.
THEY CAN'T BE AT THE BACK DOOR.
WE'VE BEEN WAITING FOR YOU, PHILAR.
HEH HEH HEH

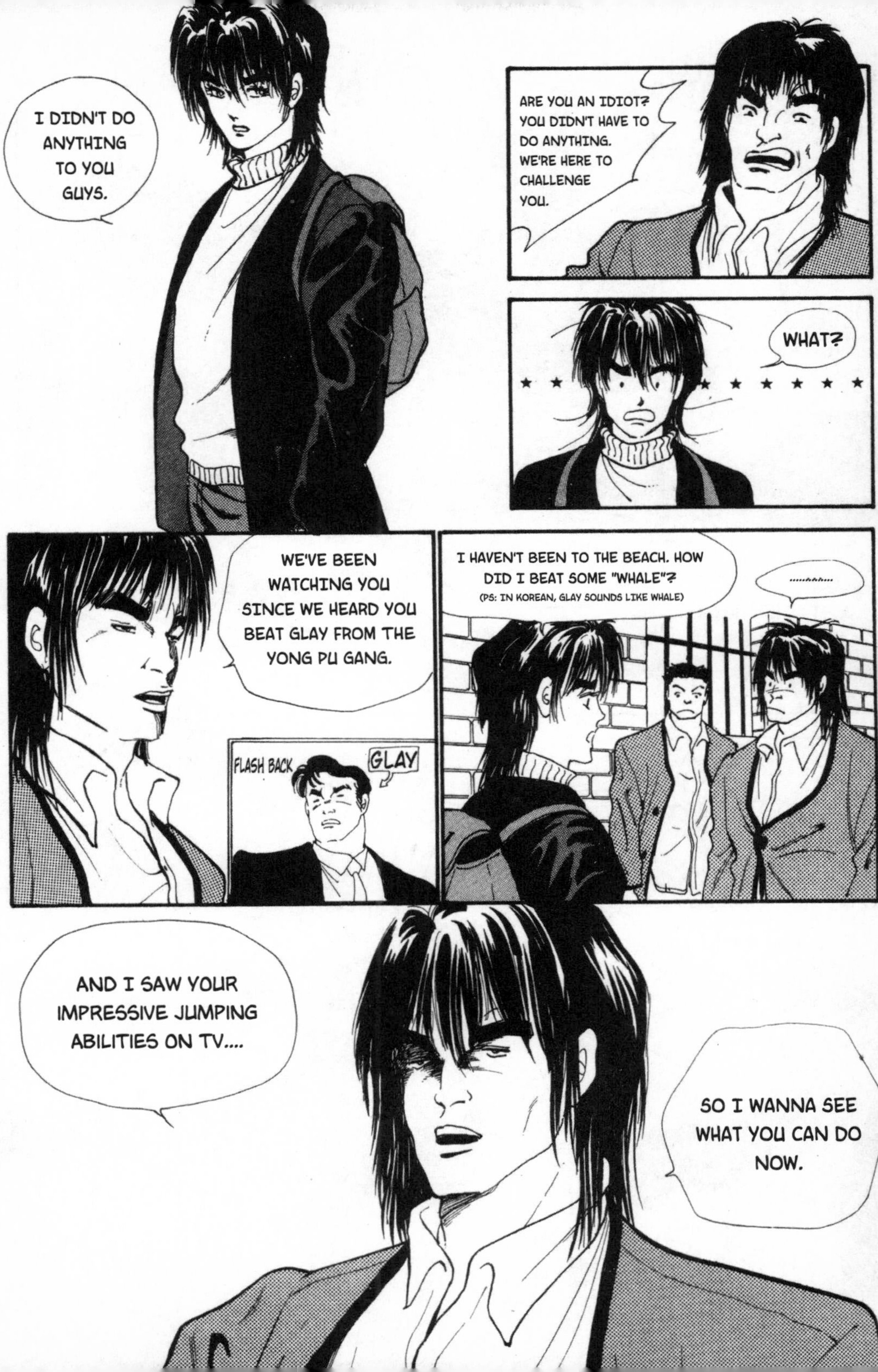
I DIDN'T DO ANYTHING TO YOU GUYS.
ARE YOU AN IDIOT? YOU DIDN'T HAVE TO DO ANYTHING. WE'RE HERE TO CHALLENGE YOU.
WHAT?
WE'VE BEEN WATCHING YOU SINCE WE HEARD YOU BEAT GLAY FROM THE YONG PU GANG.
FLASH BACK
GLAY
I HAVEN'T BEEN TO THE BEACH. HOW DID I BEAT SOME "WHALE"?
(PS: IN KOREAN, GLAY SOUNDS LIKE WHALE)
AND I SAW YOUR IMPRESSIVE JUMPING ABILITIES ON TV....
SO I WANNA SEE WHAT YOU CAN DO NOW.

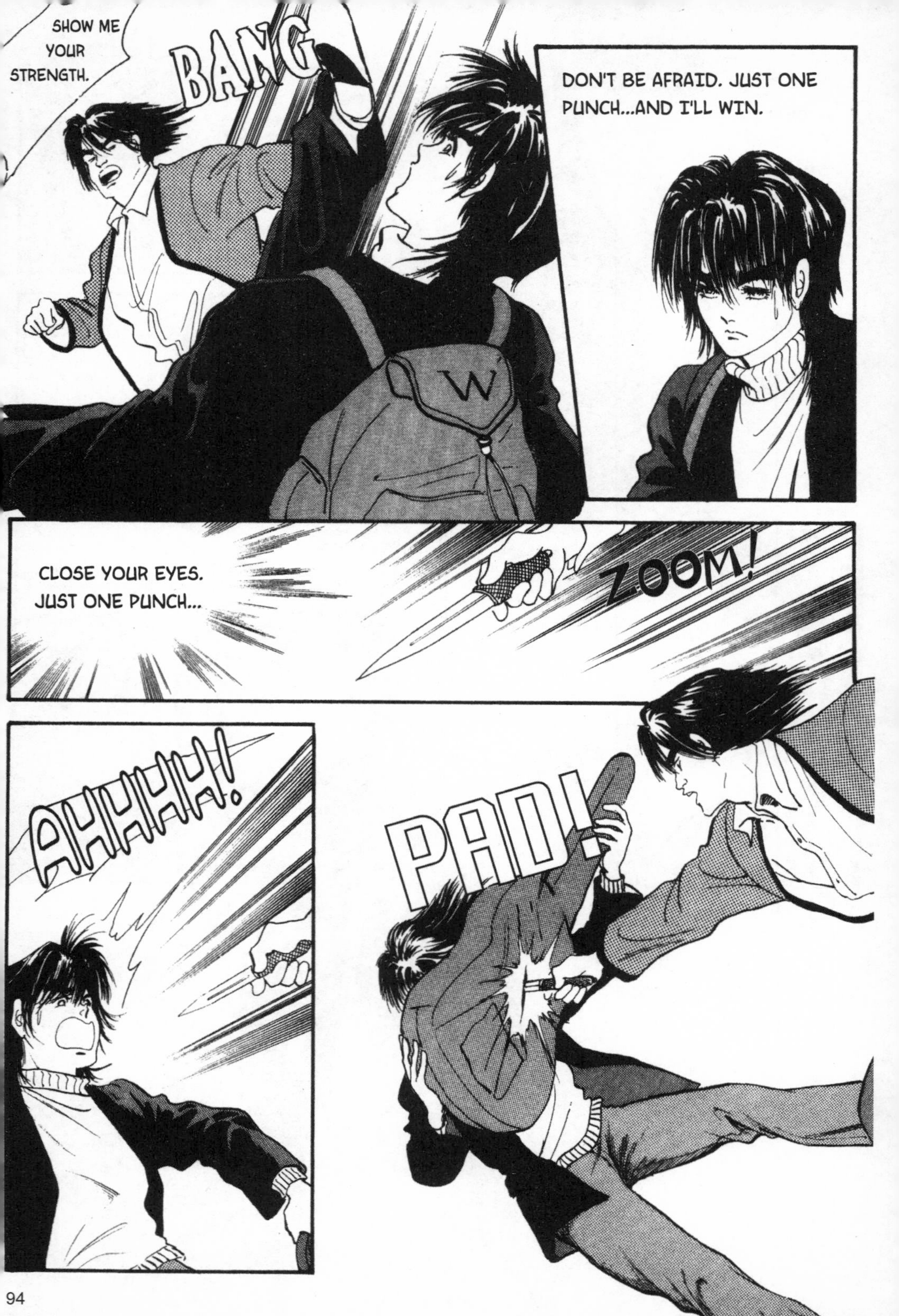
SHOW ME YOUR STRENGTH.
BANG
DON'T BE AFRAID. JUST ONE PUNCH...AND I'LL WIN.
CLOSE YOUR EYES. JUST ONE PUNCH...
ZOOM!
AHHHH!
PAD!

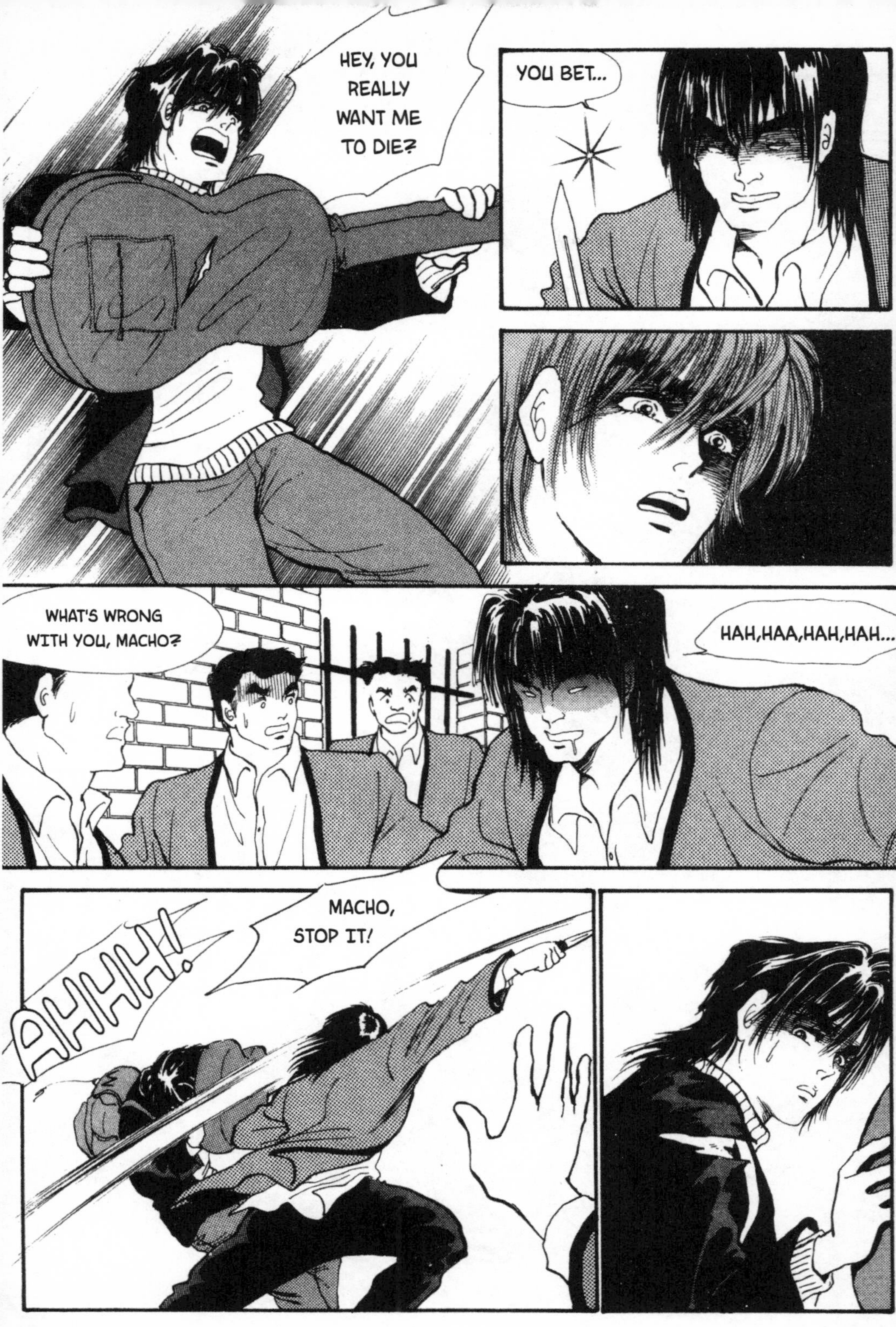
HEY, YOU REALLY WANT ME TO DIE?
YOU BET...
WHAT'S WRONG WITH YOU, MACHO?
HAH,HAA,HAH,HAH...
MACHO, STOP IT!
AHHH!

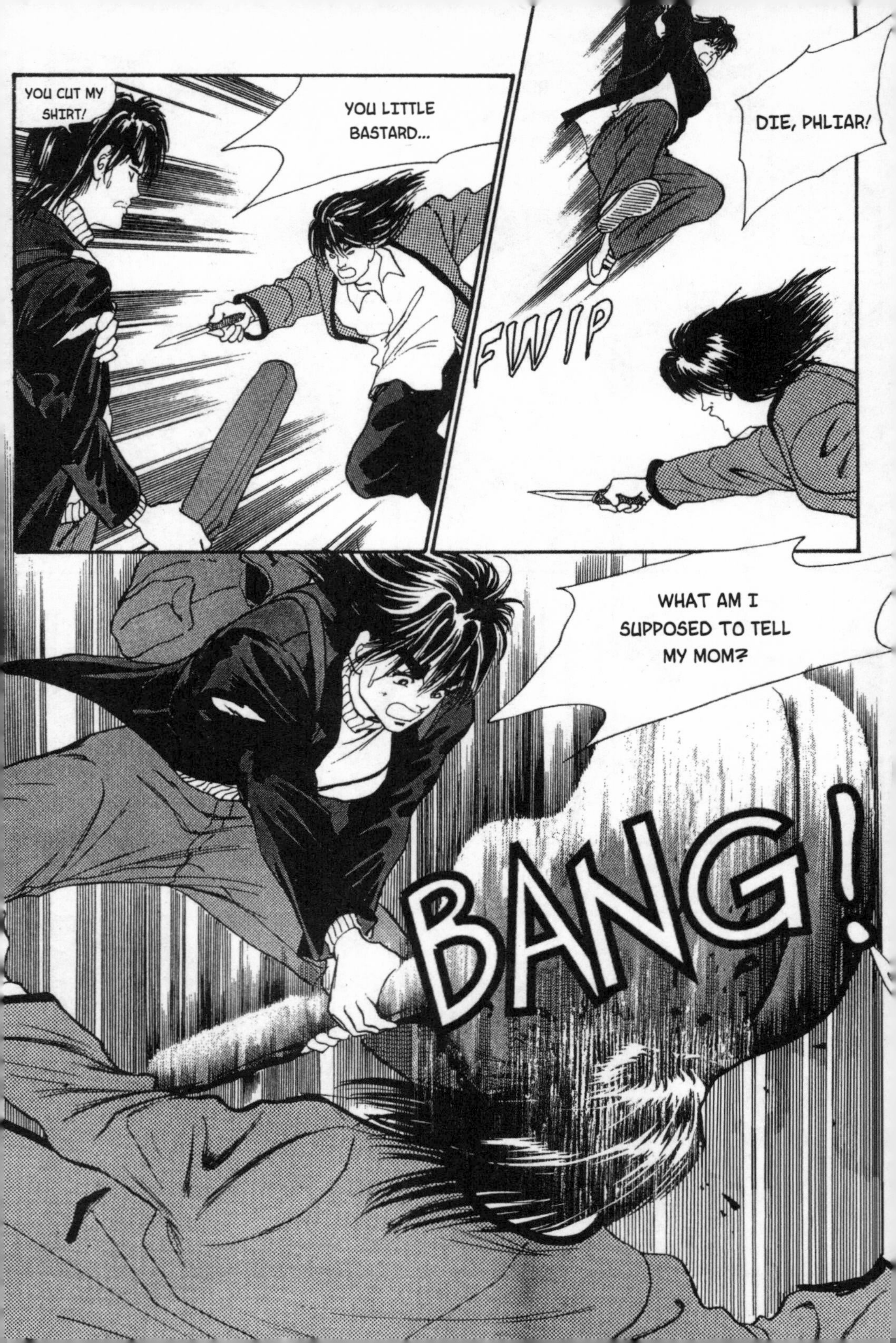
YOU CUT MY SHIRT!
YOU LITTLE BASTARD...
DIE, PHLIAR!
FWIP
WHAT AM I SUPPOSED TO TELL MY MOM?
BANG!

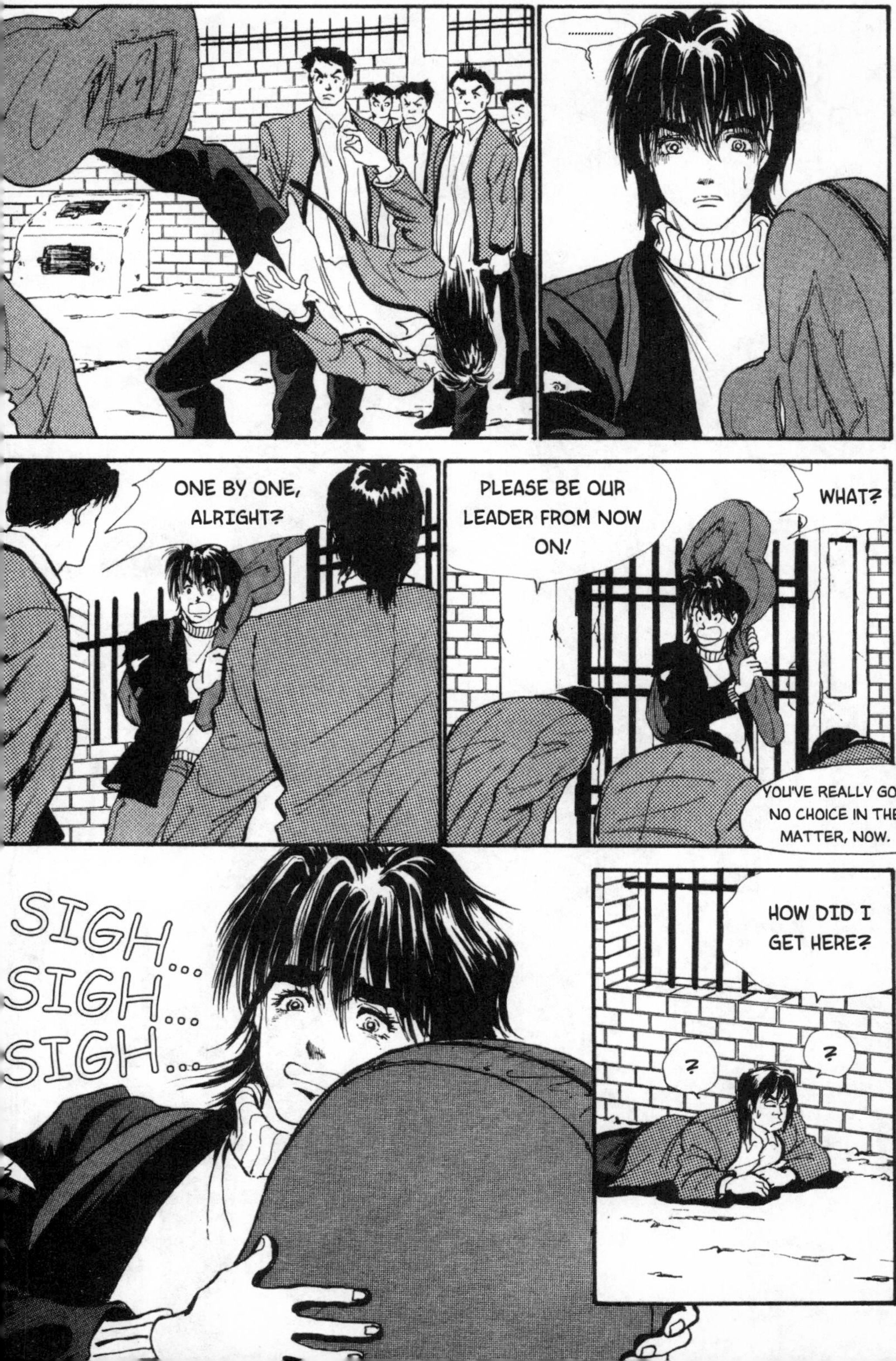
....
ONE BY ONE, ALRIGHT?
PLEASE BE OUR LEADER FROM NOW ON!
WHAT?
YOU'VE REALLY GOT NO CHOICE IN THE MATTER, NOW.
SIGH... SIGH... SIGH...
HOW DID I GET HERE?
?
?

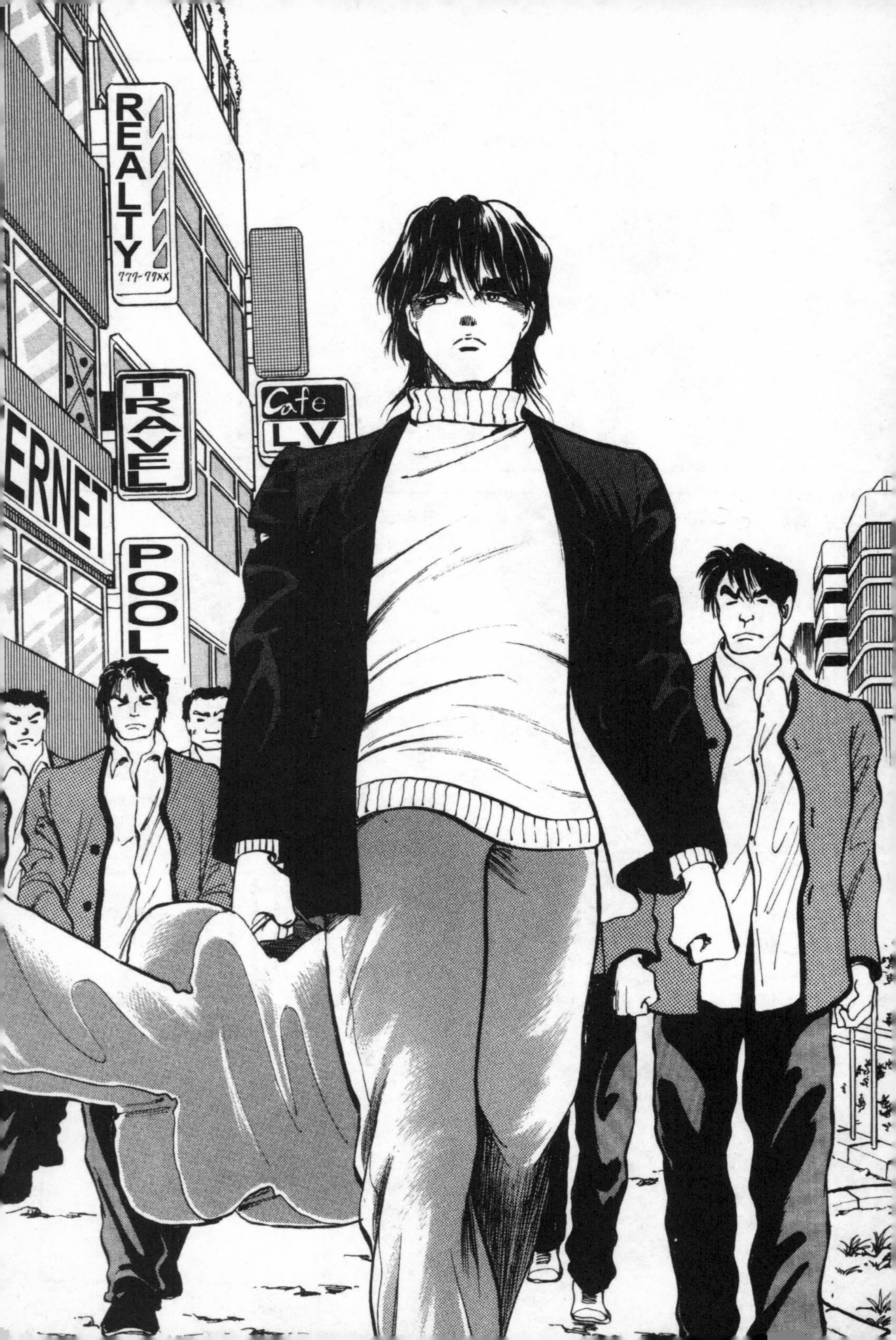
REALTY
777-77XX
TRAVEL
Cafe
LV
ERNET
POOL

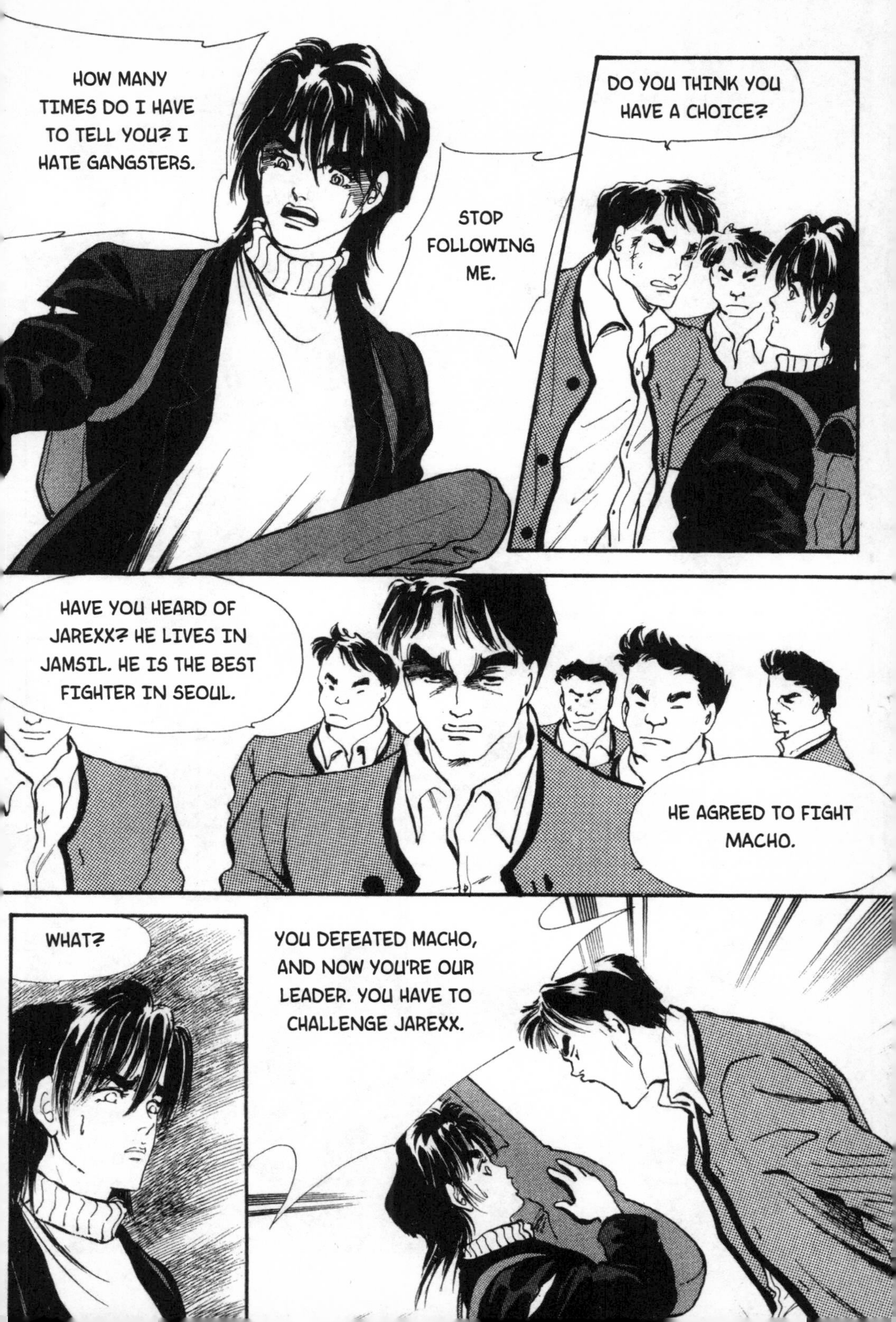
HOW MANY TIMES DO I HAVE TO TELL YOU? I HATE GANGSTERS.
STOP FOLLOWING ME.
DO YOU THINK YOU HAVE A CHOICE?
HAVE YOU HEARD OF JAREXX? HE LIVES IN JAMSIL. HE IS THE BEST FIGHTER IN SEOUL.
HE AGREED TO FIGHT MACHO.
WHAT?
YOU DEFEATED MACHO, AND NOW YOU'RE OUR LEADER. YOU HAVE TO CHALLENGE JAREXX.

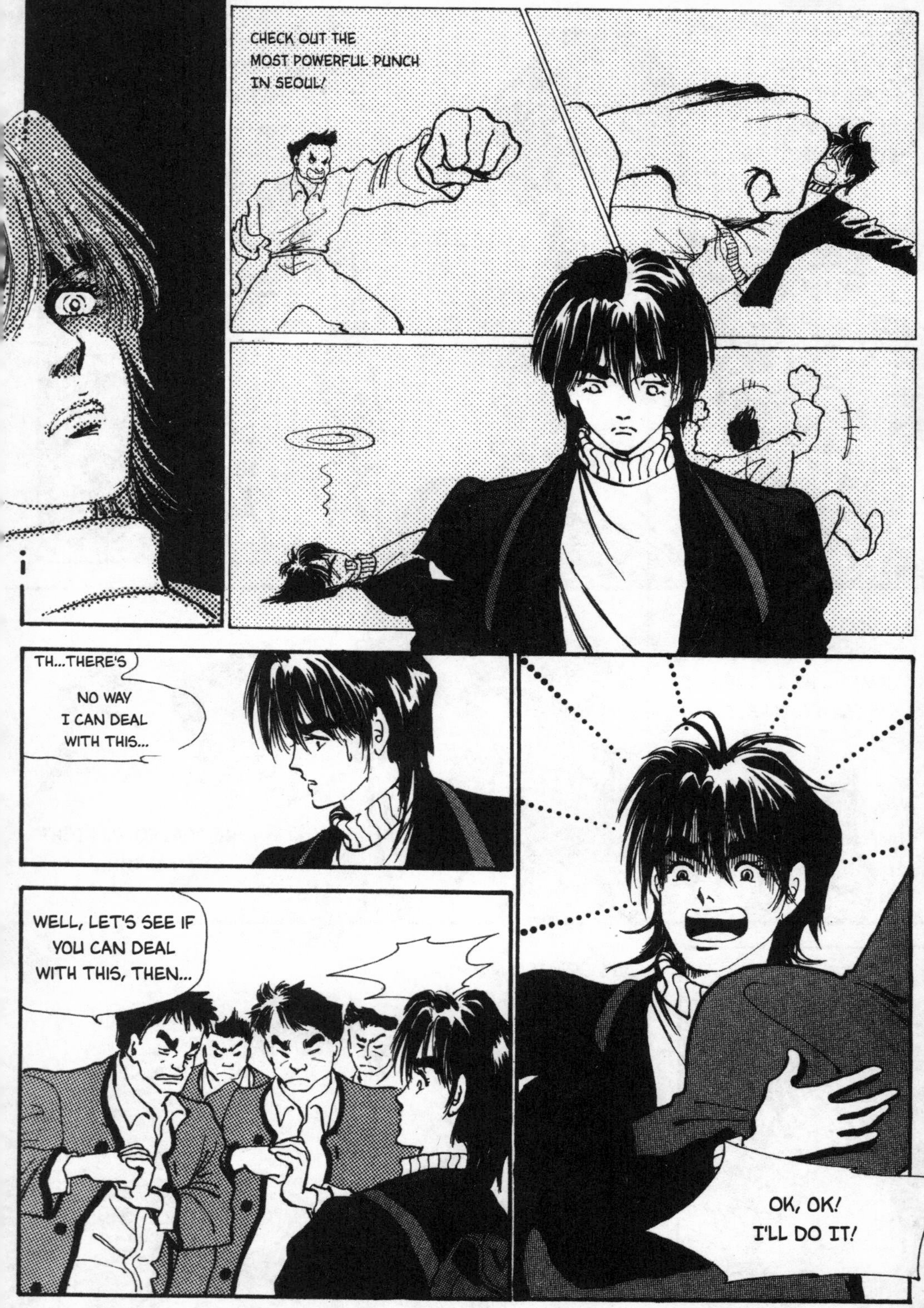
CHECK OUT THE MOST POWERFUL PUNCH IN SEOUL!
TH...THERE'S NO WAY I CAN DEAL WITH THIS...
WELL, LET'S SEE IF YOU CAN DEAL WITH THIS, THEN...
OK, OK! I'LL DO IT!

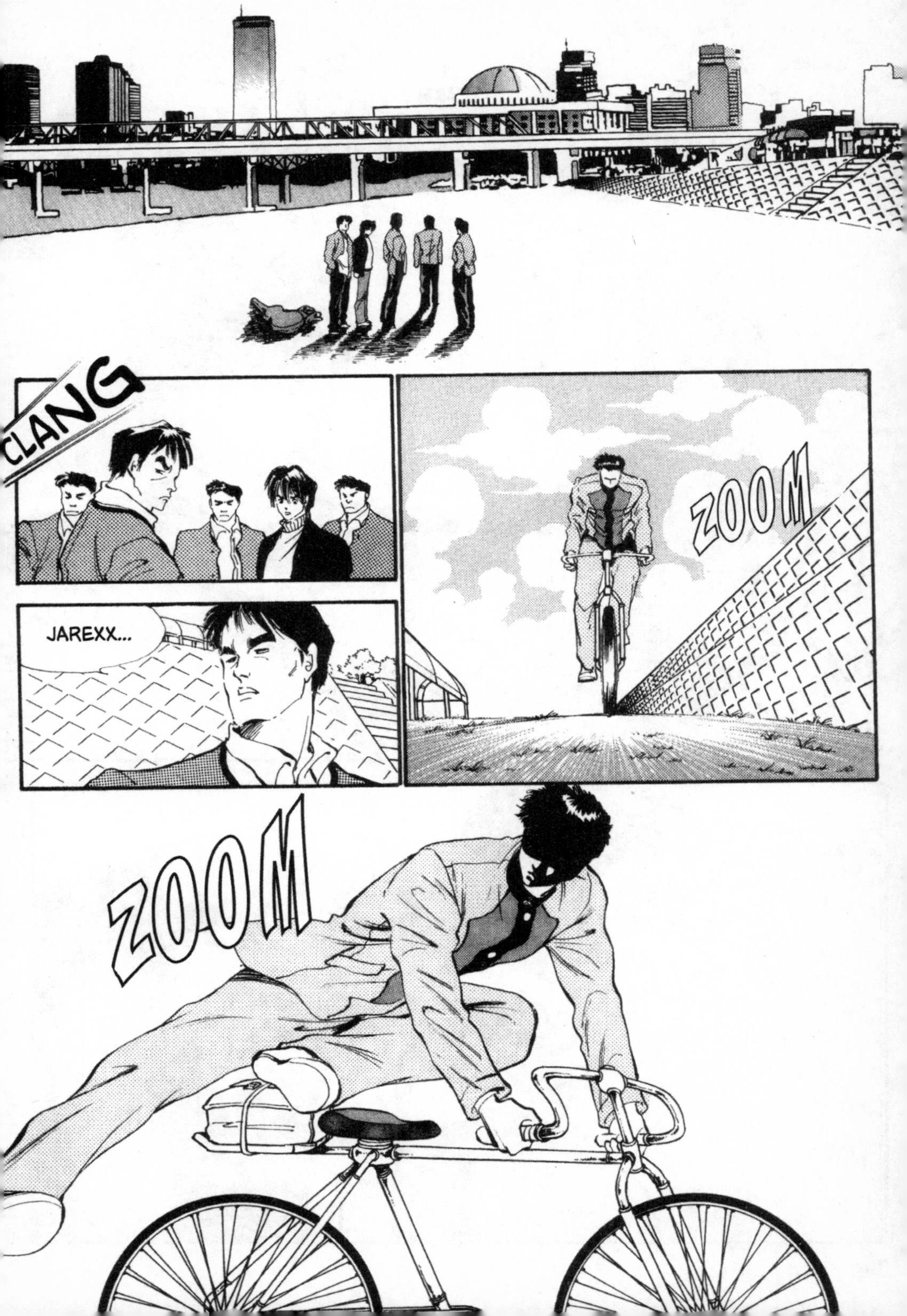
CLANG
ZOOM
JAREXX...
ZOOM

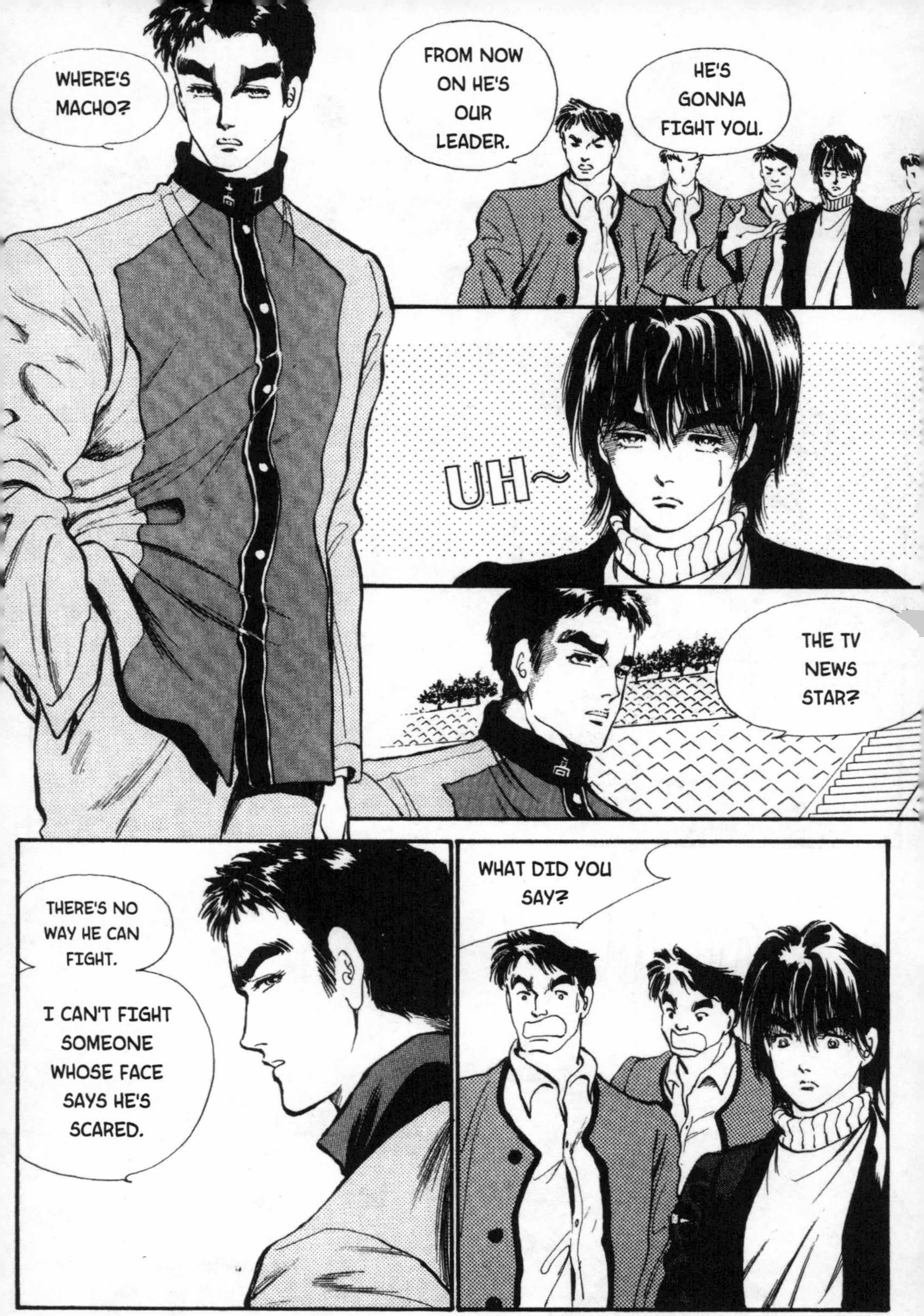
WHERE'S MACHO?
FROM NOW ON HE'S OUR LEADER.
HE'S GONNA FIGHT YOU.
UH~
THE TV NEWS STAR?
THERE'S NO WAY HE CAN FIGHT.
I CAN'T FIGHT SOMEONE WHOSE FACE SAYS HE'S SCARED.
WHAT DID YOU SAY?

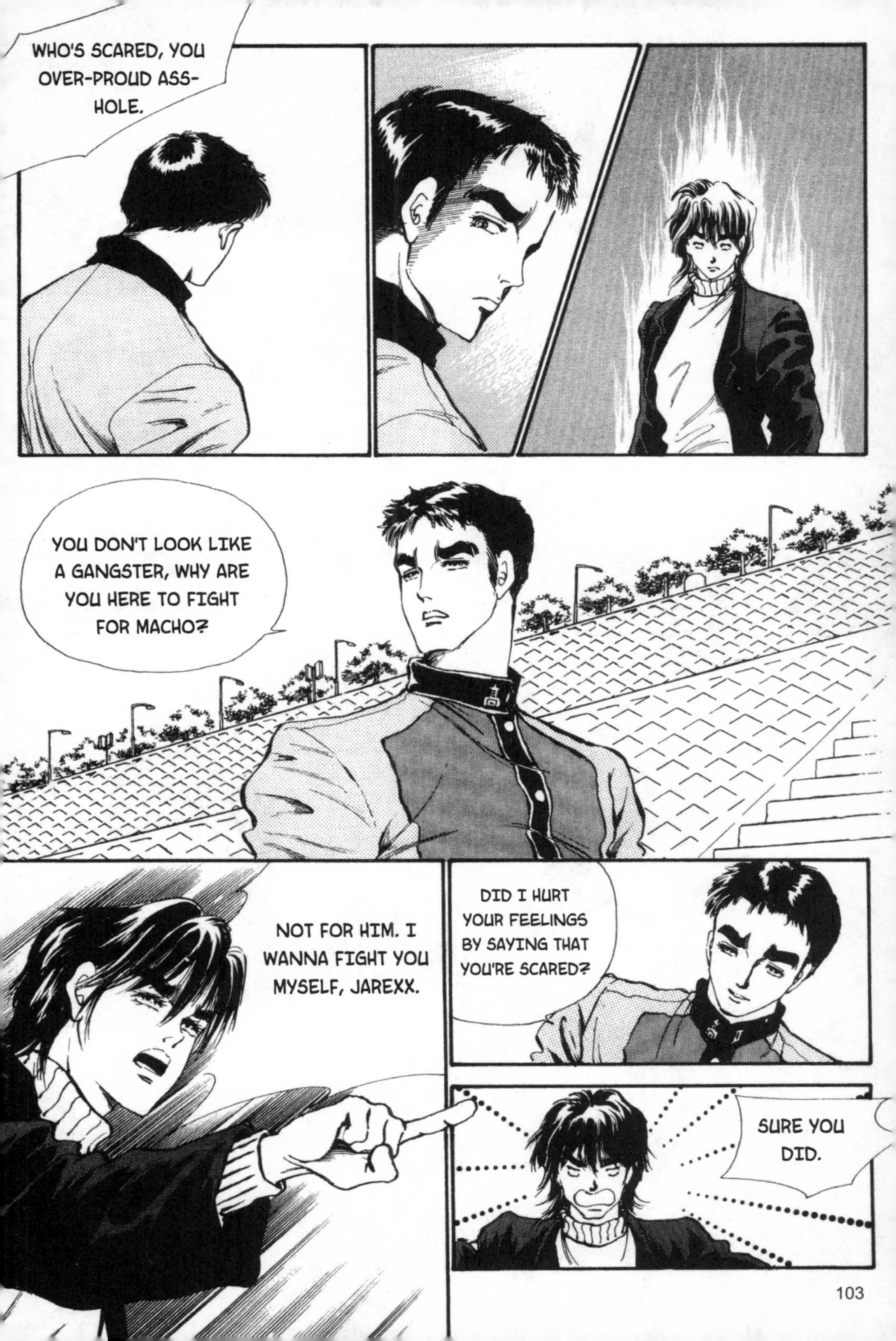
WHO'S SCARED, YOU OVER-PROUD ASS-HOLE.
YOU DON'T LOOK LIKE A GANGSTER, WHY ARE YOU HERE TO FIGHT FOR MACHO?
NOT FOR HIM. I WANNA FIGHT YOU MYSELF, JAREXX.
DID I HURT YOUR FEELINGS BY SAYING THAT YOU'RE SCARED?
SURE YOU DID.

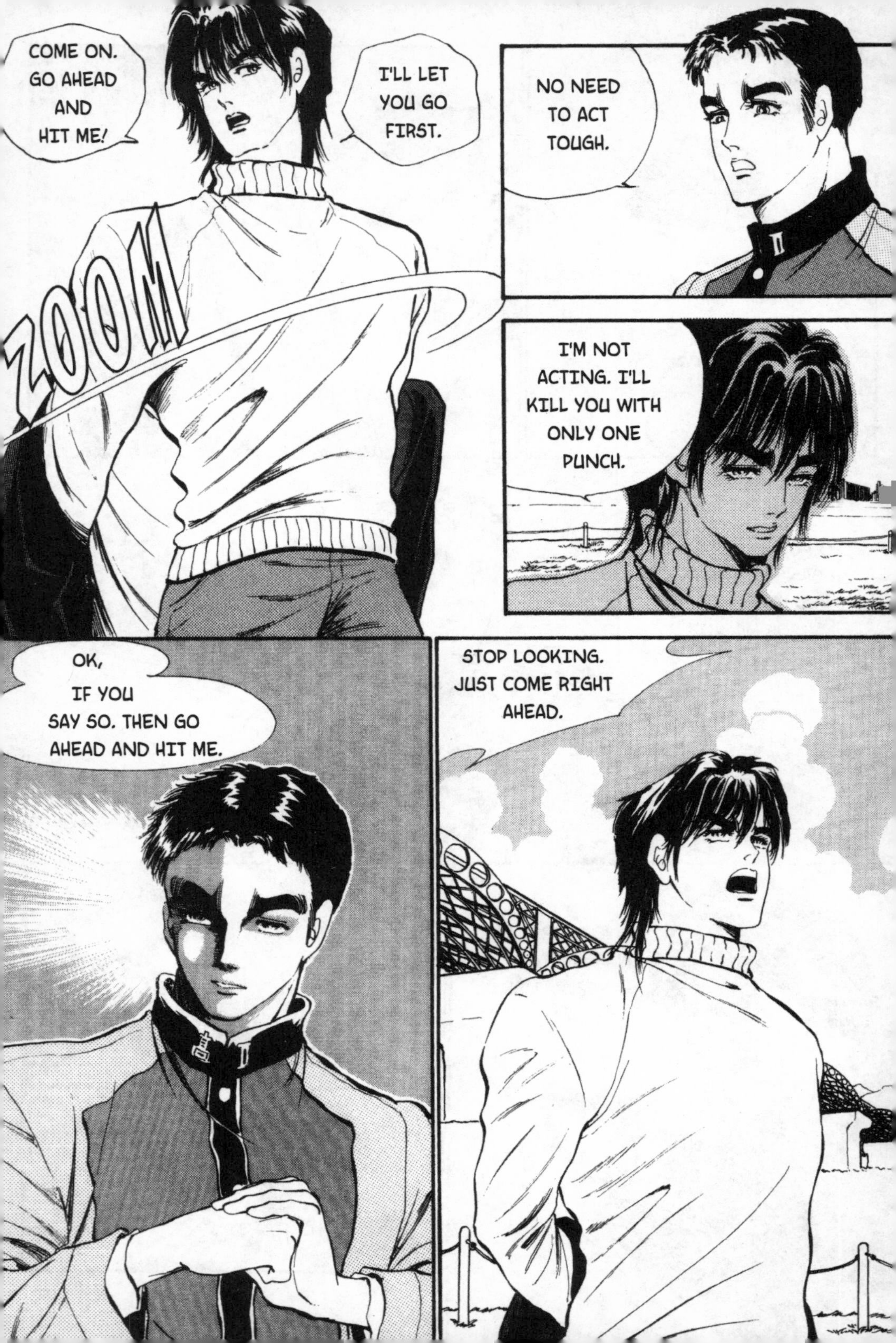
COME ON. GO AHEAD AND HIT ME!
I'LL LET YOU GO FIRST.
ZOOM
NO NEED TO ACT TOUGH.
I'M NOT ACTING. I'LL KILL YOU WITH ONLY ONE PUNCH.
OK, IF YOU SAY SO. THEN GO AHEAD AND HIT ME.
STOP LOOKING. JUST COME RIGHT AHEAD.

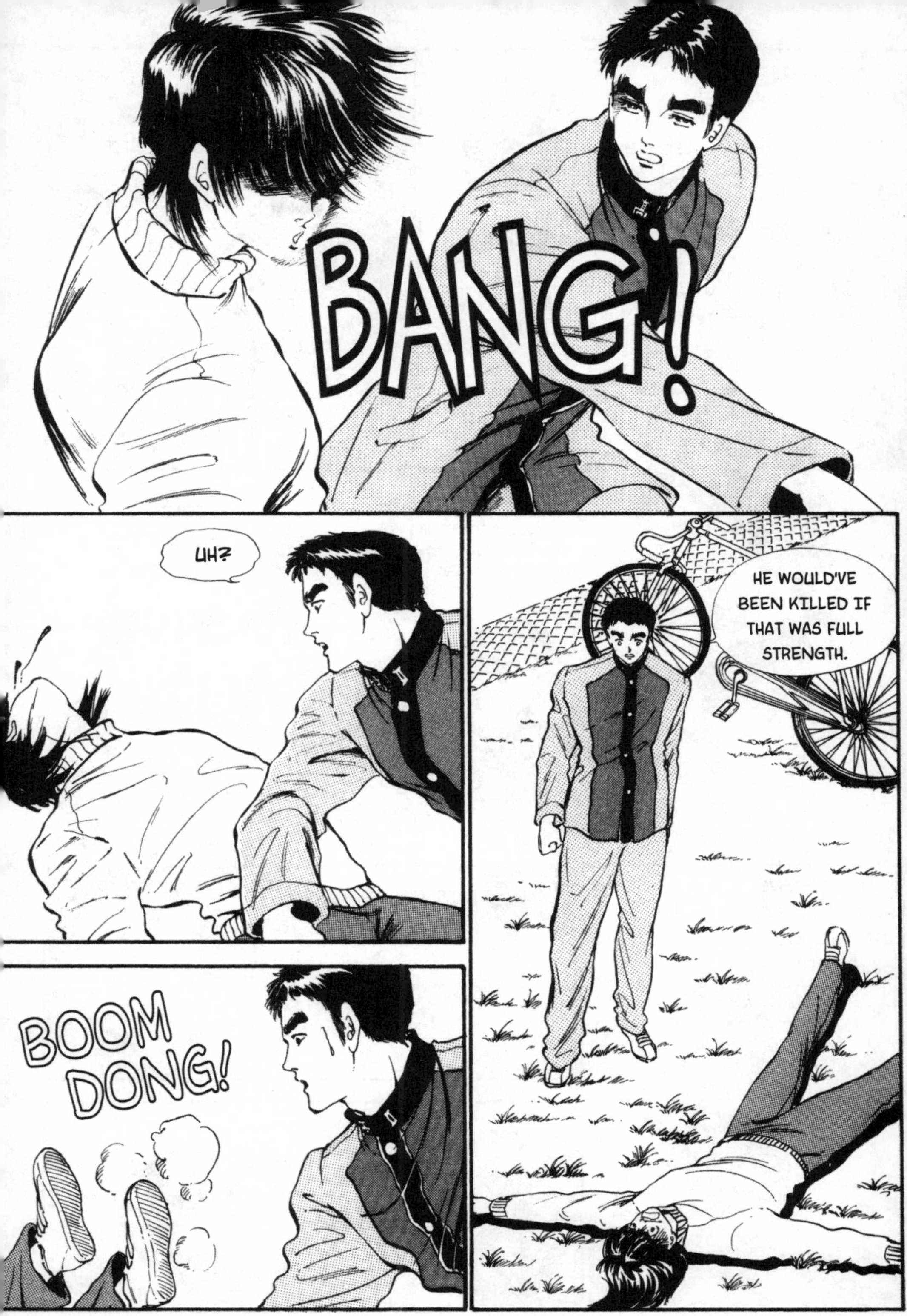
BANG!
UH?
BOOM DONG!
HE WOULD'VE BEEN KILLED IF THAT WAS FULL STRENGTH.

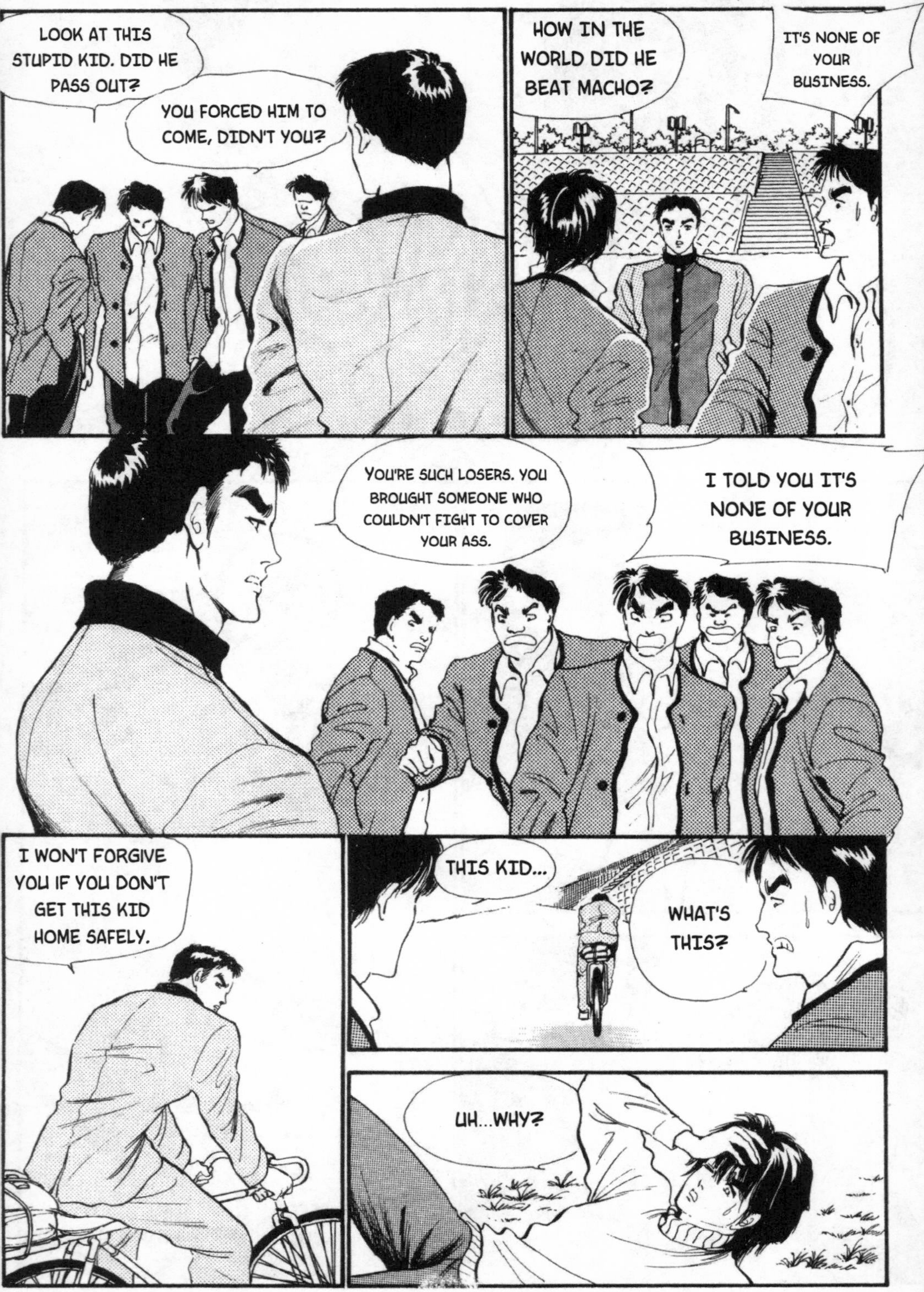
LOOK AT THIS STUPID KID. DID HE PASS OUT?
YOU FORCED HIM TO COME, DIDN'T YOU?
HOW IN THE WORLD DID HE BEAT MACHO?
IT'S NONE OF YOUR BUSINESS.
YOU'RE SUCH LOSERS. YOU BROUGHT SOMEONE WHO COULDN'T FIGHT TO COVER YOUR ASS.
I TOLD YOU IT'S NONE OF YOUR BUSINESS.
I WON'T FORGIVE YOU IF YOU DON'T GET THIS KID HOME SAFELY.
THIS KID...
WHAT'S THIS?
UH...WHY?

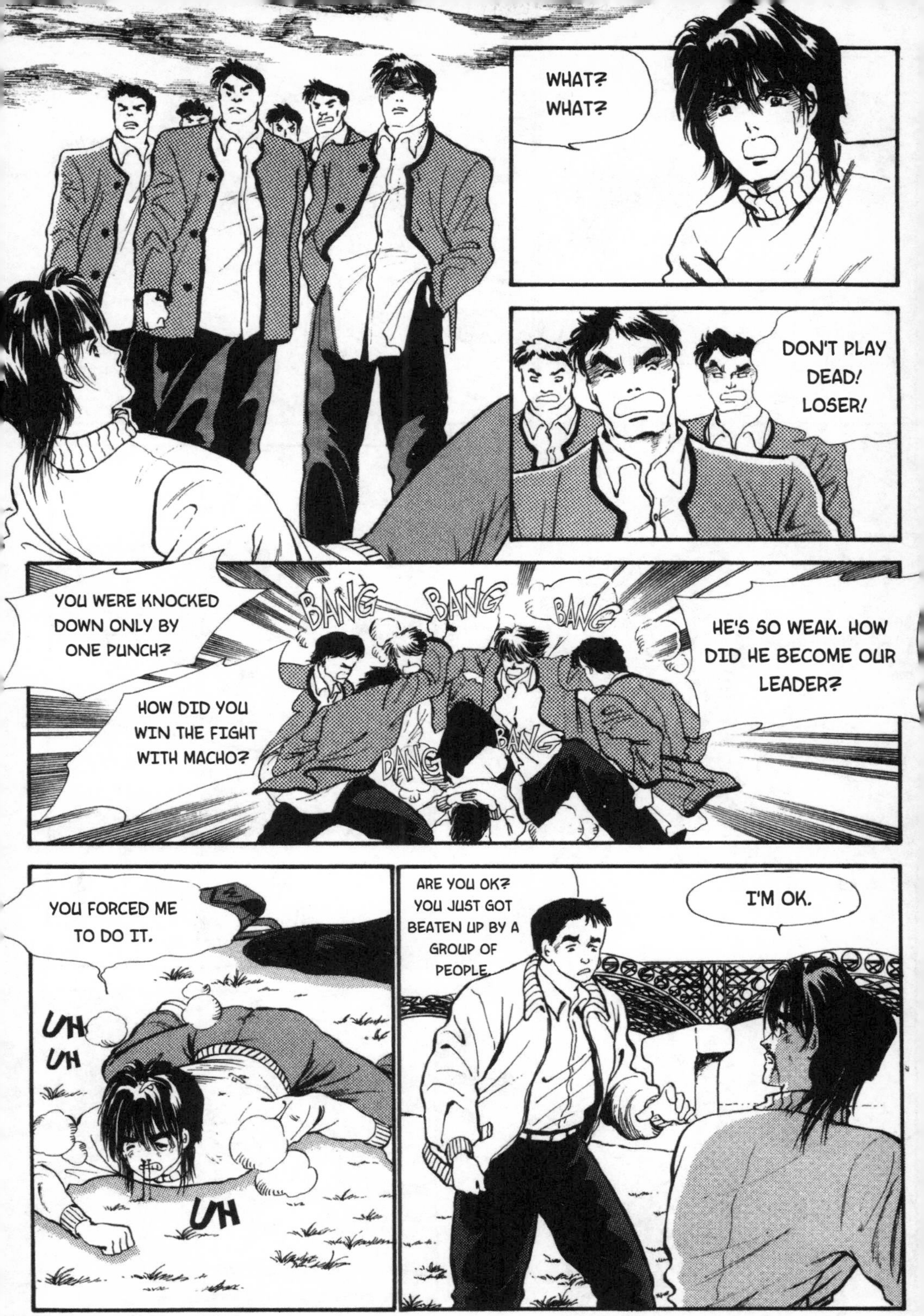
WHAT? WHAT?
DON'T PLAY DEAD! LOSER!
YOU WERE KNOCKED DOWN ONLY BY ONE PUNCH?
BANG
BANG
BANG
HE'S SO WEAK. HOW DID HE BECOME OUR LEADER?
HOW DID YOU WIN THE FIGHT WITH MACHO?
BANG
BANG
YOU FORCED ME TO DO IT.
UH
UH
UH
ARE YOU OK? YOU JUST GOT BEATEN UP BY A GROUP OF PEOPLE.
I'M OK.

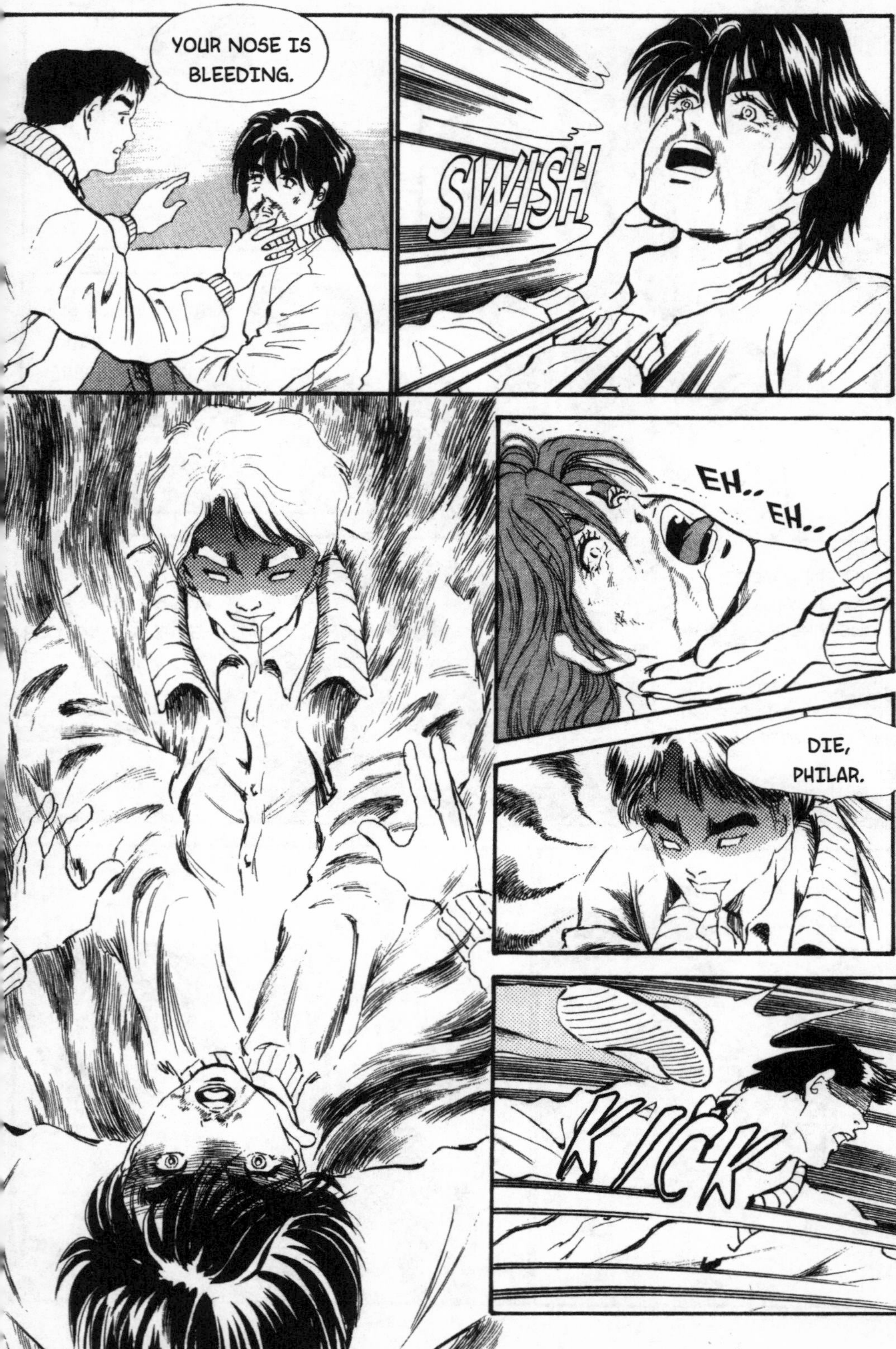
YOUR NOSE IS BLEEDING.
SWISH
EH.. EH..
DIE, PHILAR.
KICK

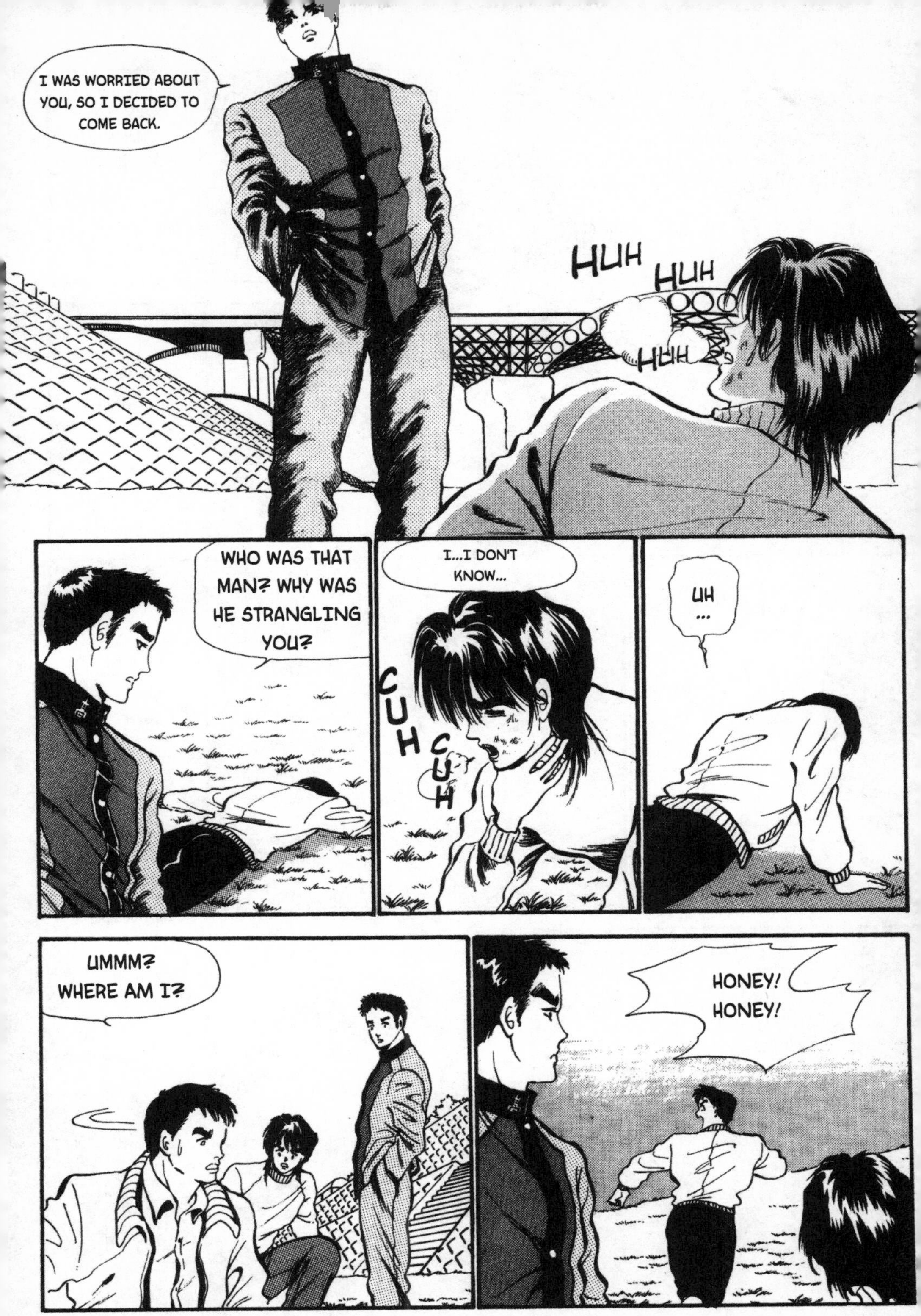
I WAS WORRIED ABOUT YOU, SO I DECIDED TO COME BACK.
HUH
HUH
HUH
WHO WAS THAT MAN? WHY WAS HE STRANGLING YOU?
I...I DON'T KNOW...
CUH
CUH
UH ...
UMMM? WHERE AM I?
HONEY! HONEY!

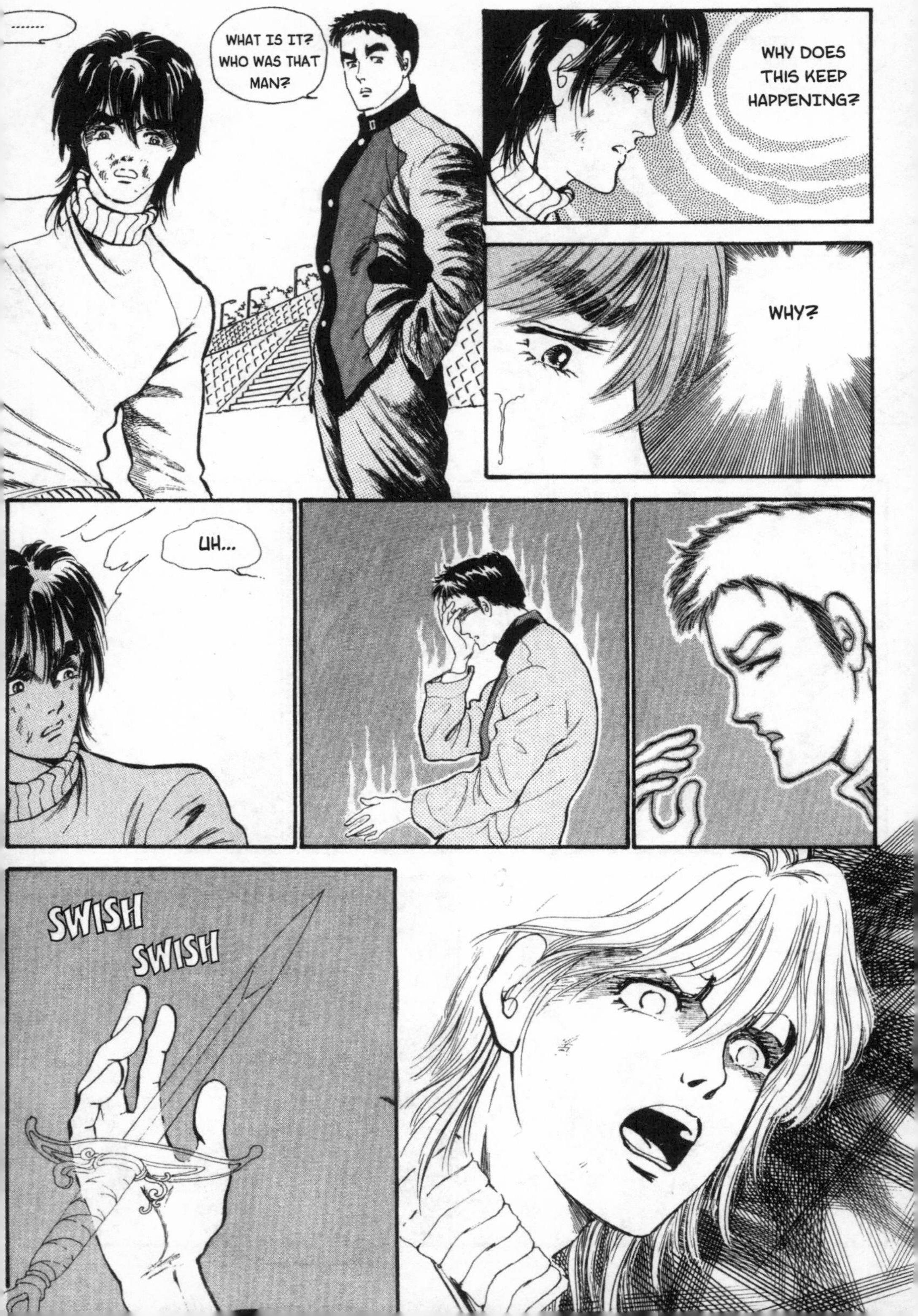

....
WHAT IS IT? WHO WAS THAT MAN?
WHY DOES THIS KEEP HAPPENING?
WHY?
UH...
SWISH
SWISH

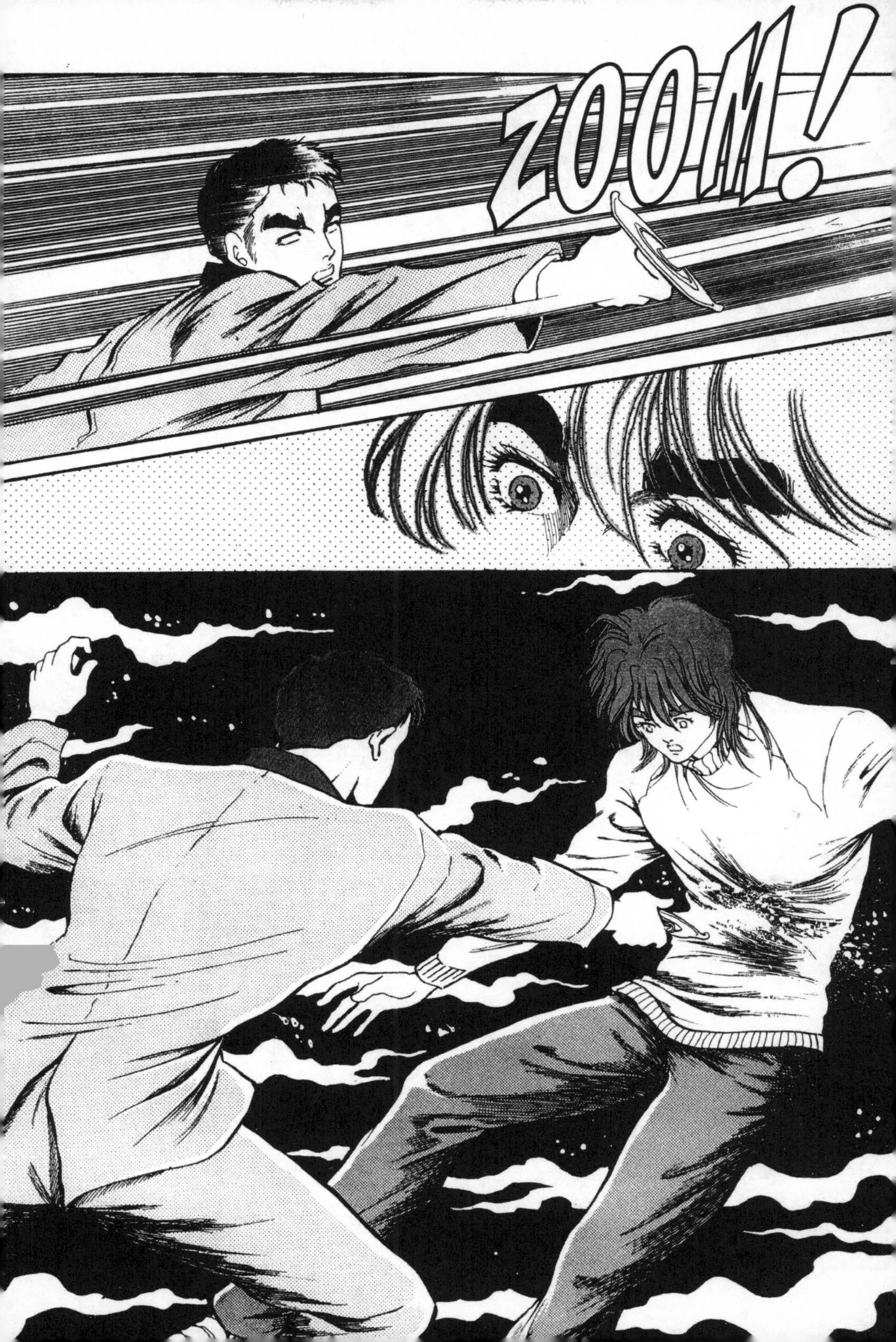
ZOOM!

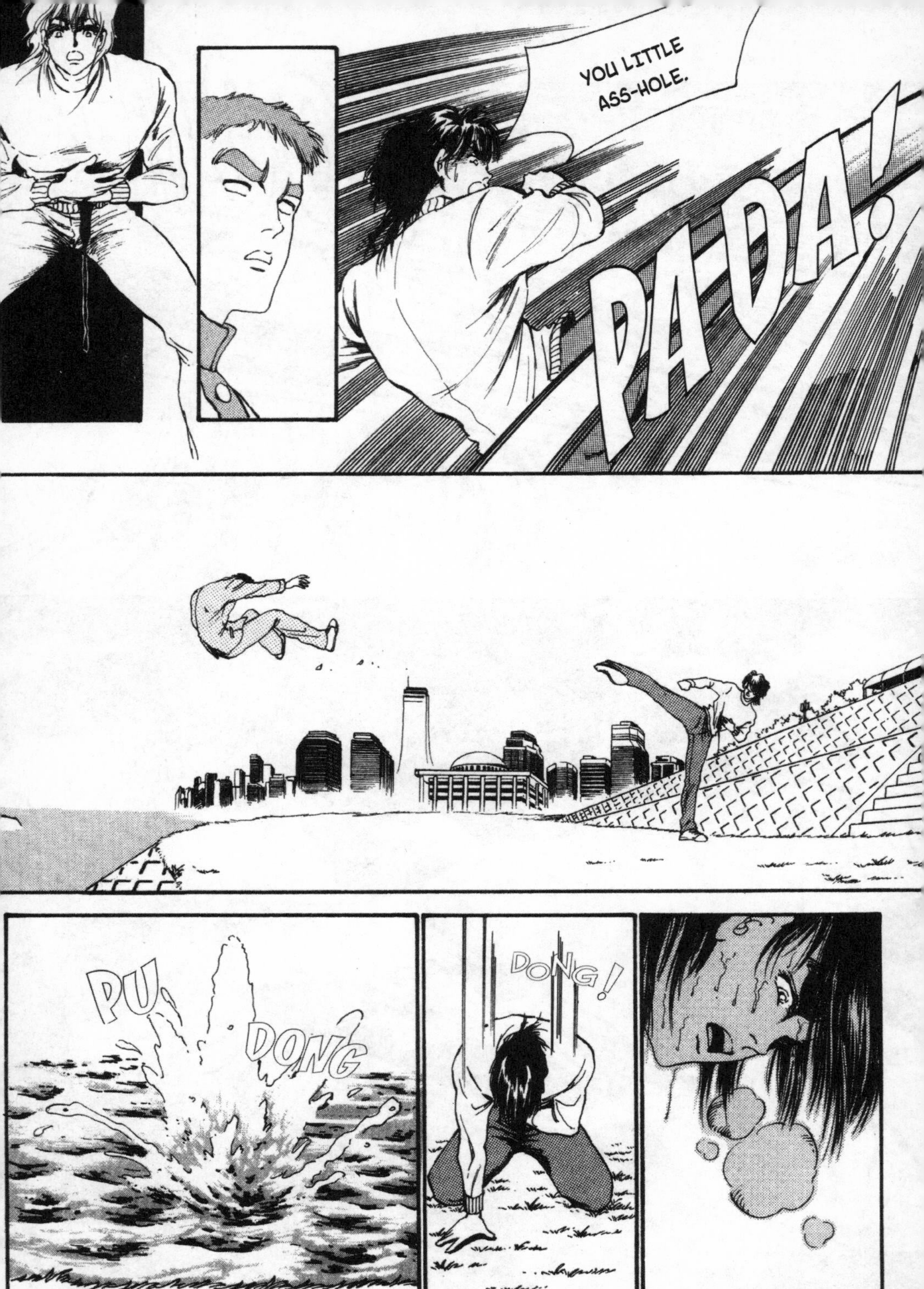
YOU LITTLE ASS-HOLE.
PA-DA!
PU
DONG
DONG!

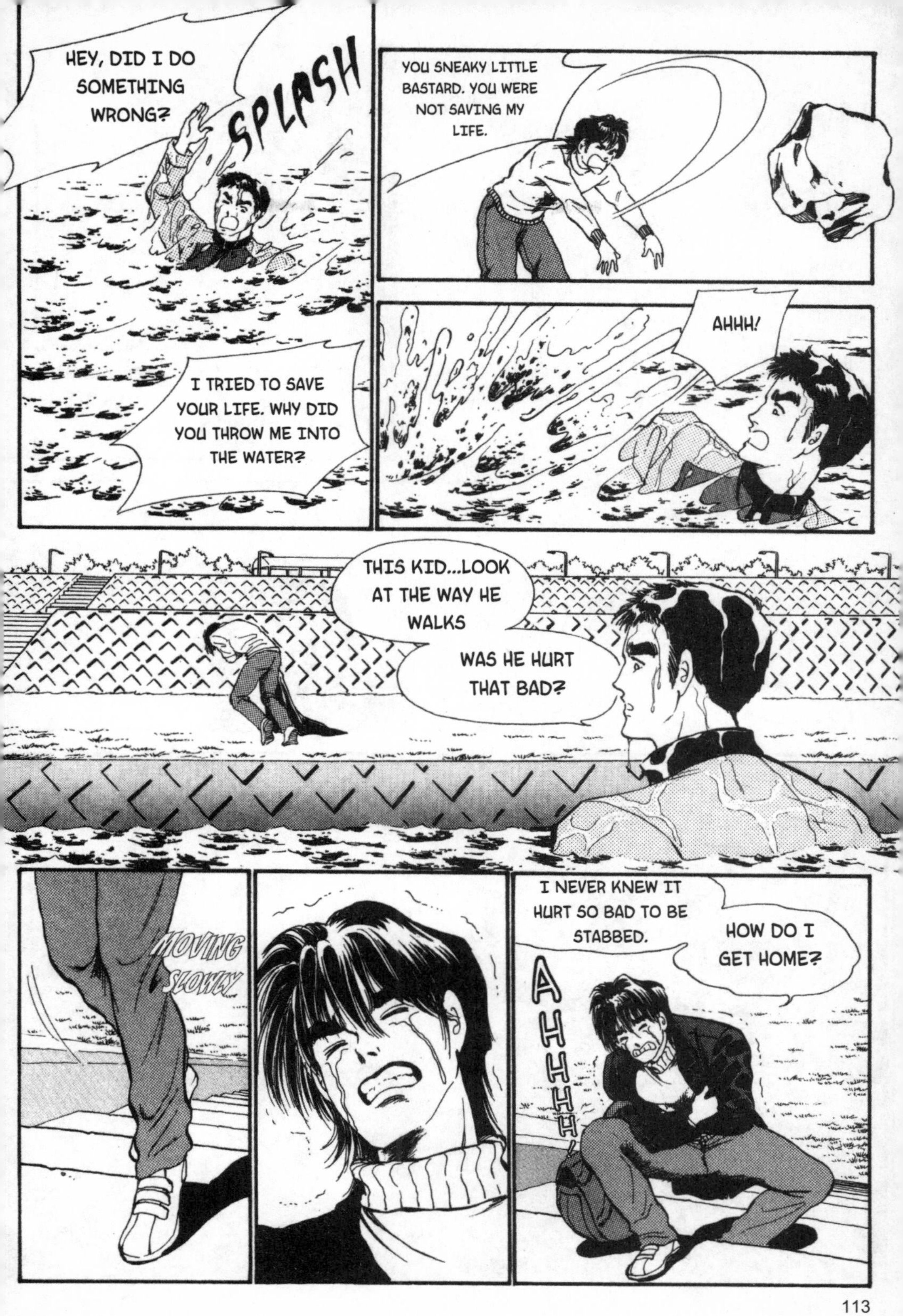
HEY, DID I DO SOMETHING WRONG?
SPLASH
I TRIED TO SAVE YOUR LIFE. WHY DID YOU THROW ME INTO THE WATER?
YOU SNEAKY LITTLE BASTARD. YOU WERE NOT SAVING MY LIFE.
AHHH!
THIS KID...LOOK AT THE WAY HE WALKS
WAS HE HURT THAT BAD?
MOVING SLOWLY
I NEVER KNEW IT HURT SO BAD TO BE STABBED.
HOW DO I GET HOME?
AHHHH!

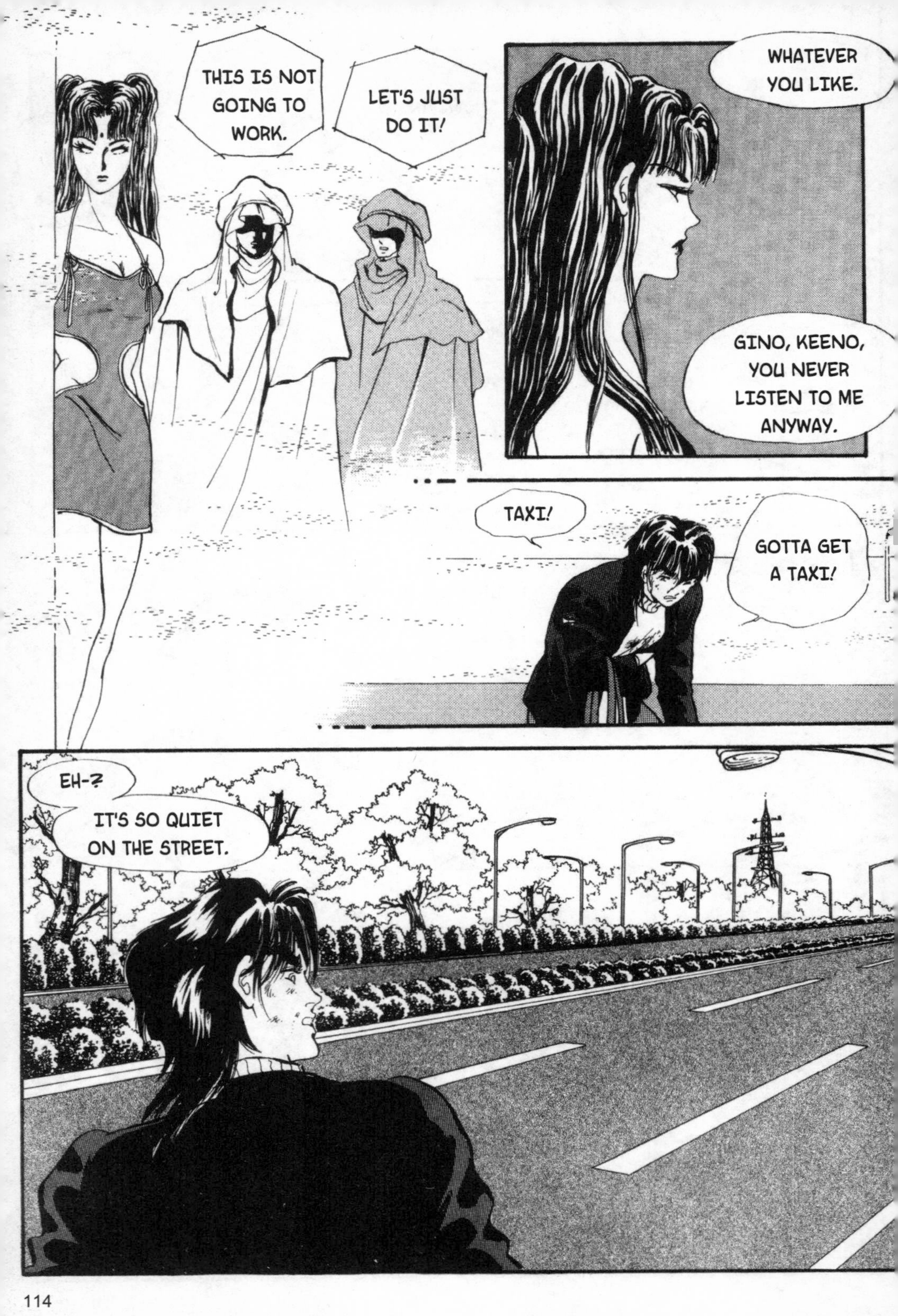
THIS IS NOT GOING TO WORK.
LET'S JUST DO IT!
WHATEVER YOU LIKE.
GINO, KEENO, YOU NEVER LISTEN TO ME ANYWAY.
TAXI!
GOTTA GET A TAXI!
EH-?
IT'S SO QUIET ON THE STREET.

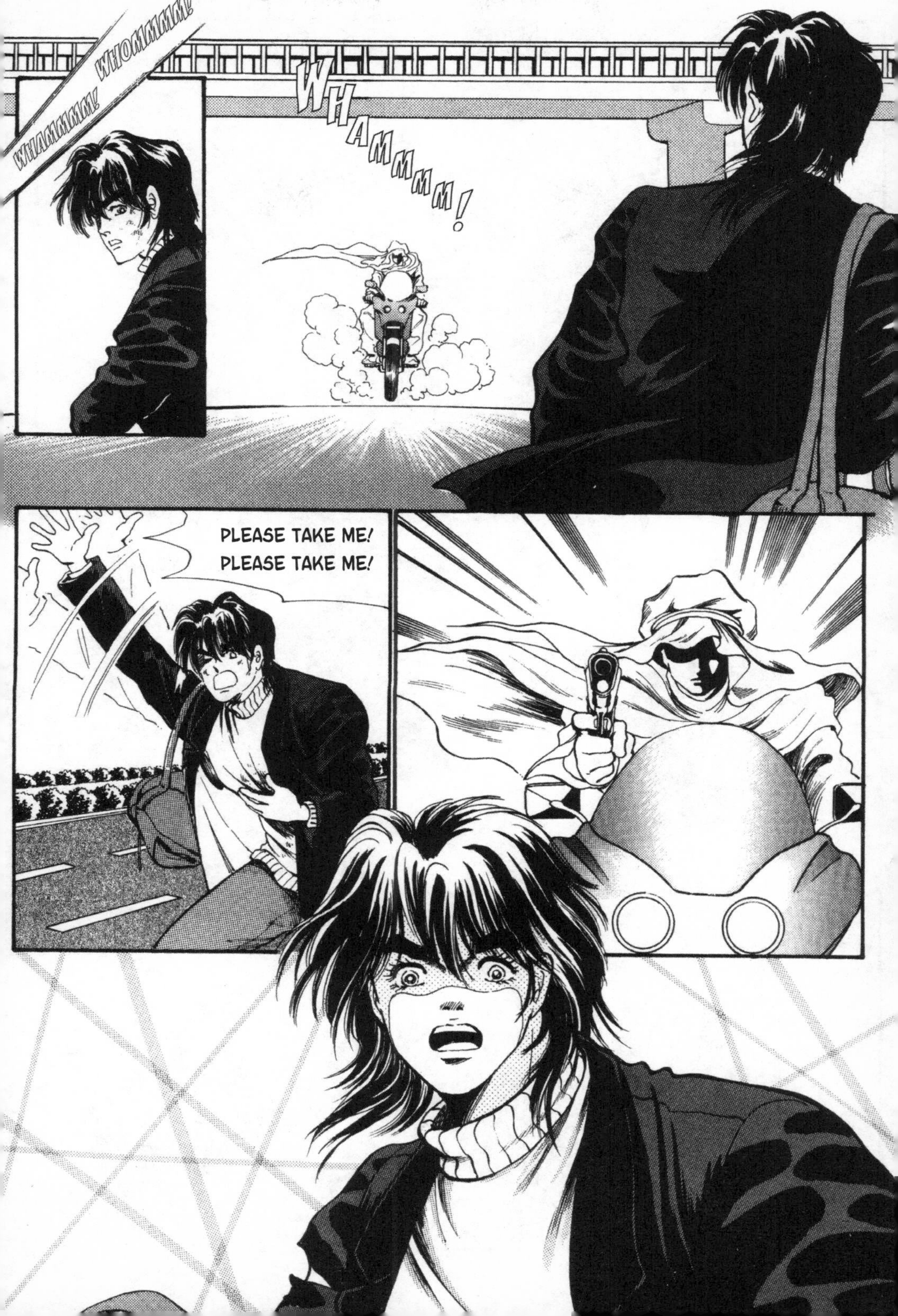
WHAMMMM! WHOMMMM!
WHAMMMMM!
PLEASE TAKE ME!
PLEASE TAKE ME!

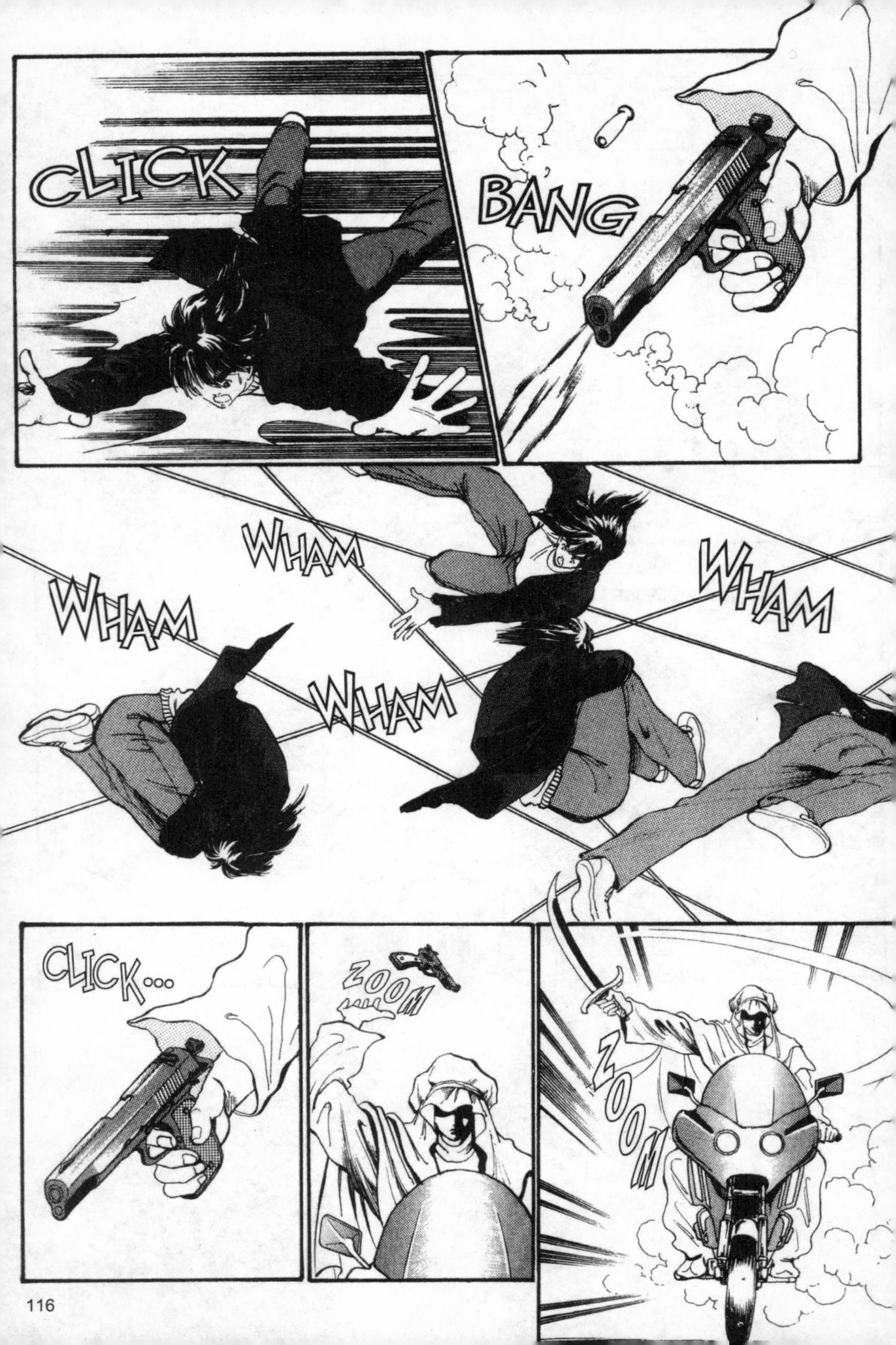
CLICK
BANG
WHAM
WHAM
WHAM
WHAM
CLICK...
ZOOM
ZOOM

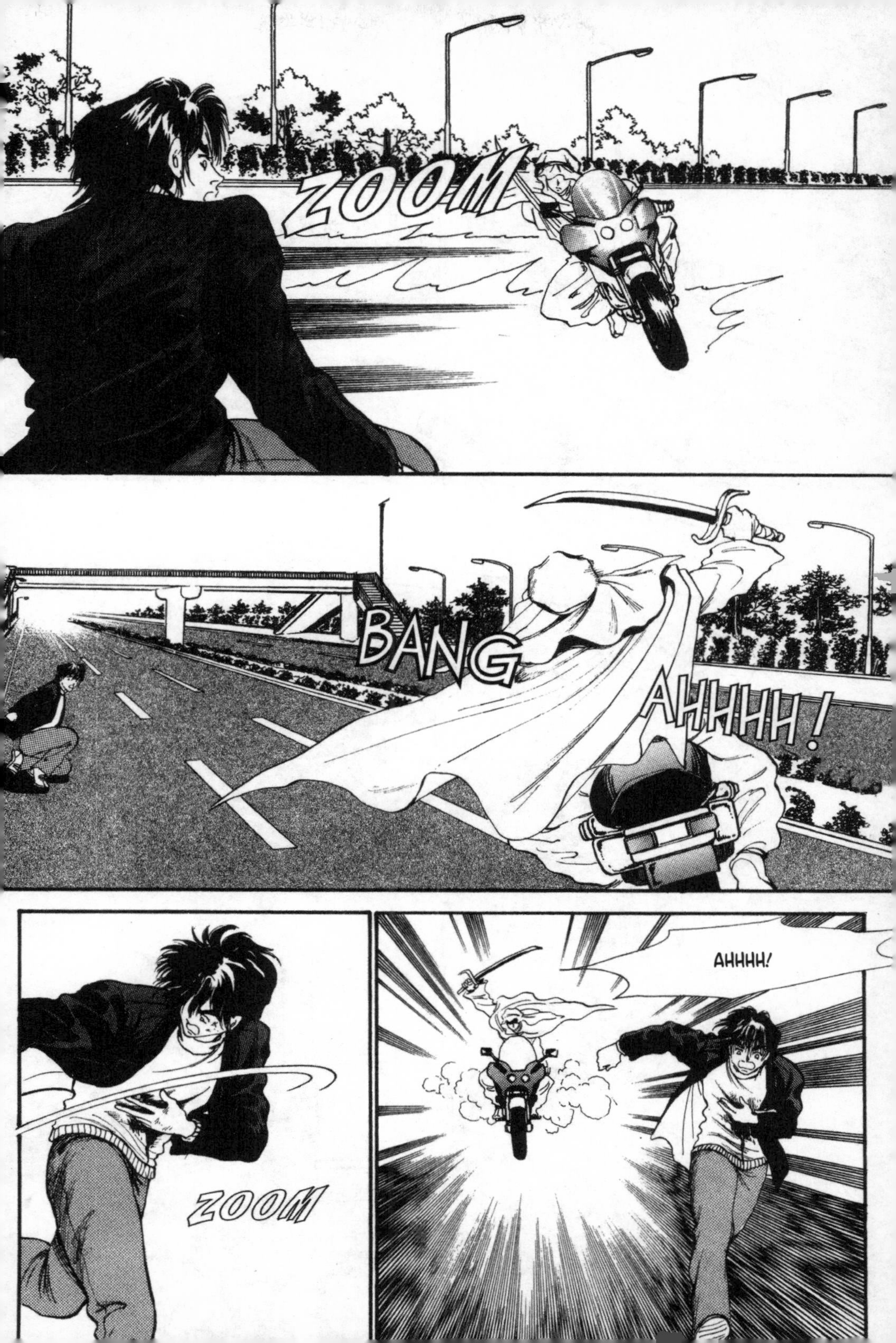
ZOOM
BANG
AHHHH!
ZOOM
AHHHH!

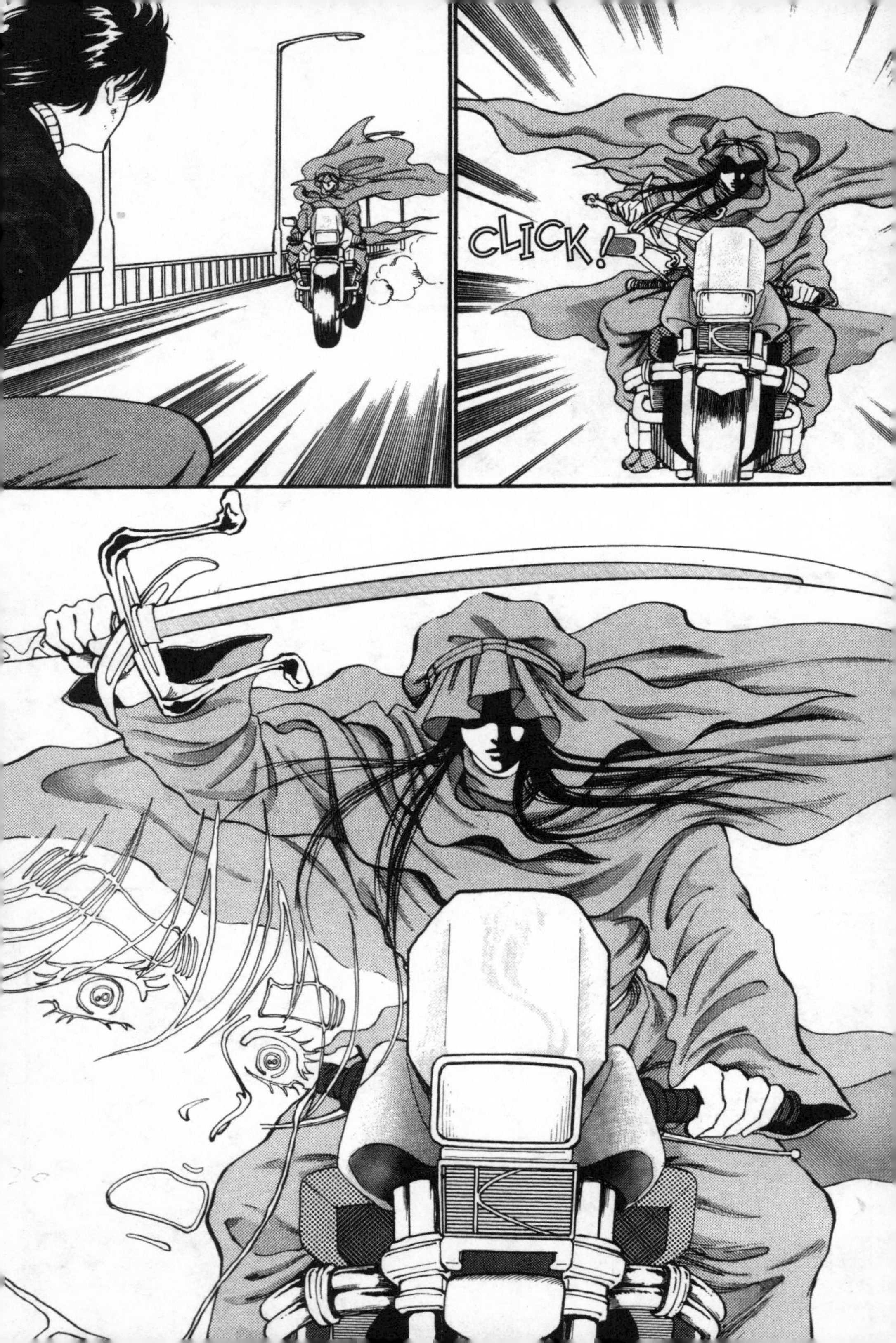
CLICK!

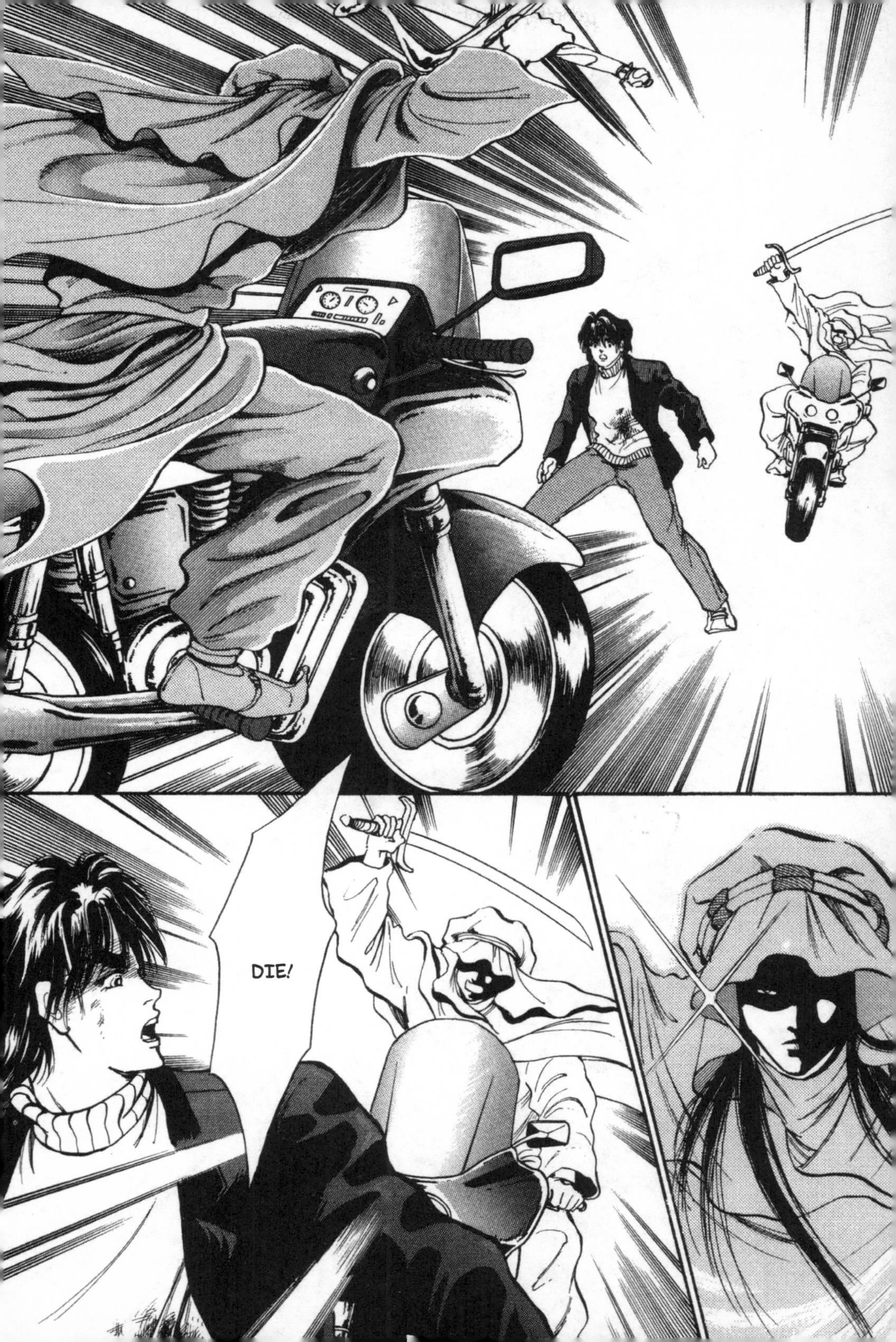
DIE!

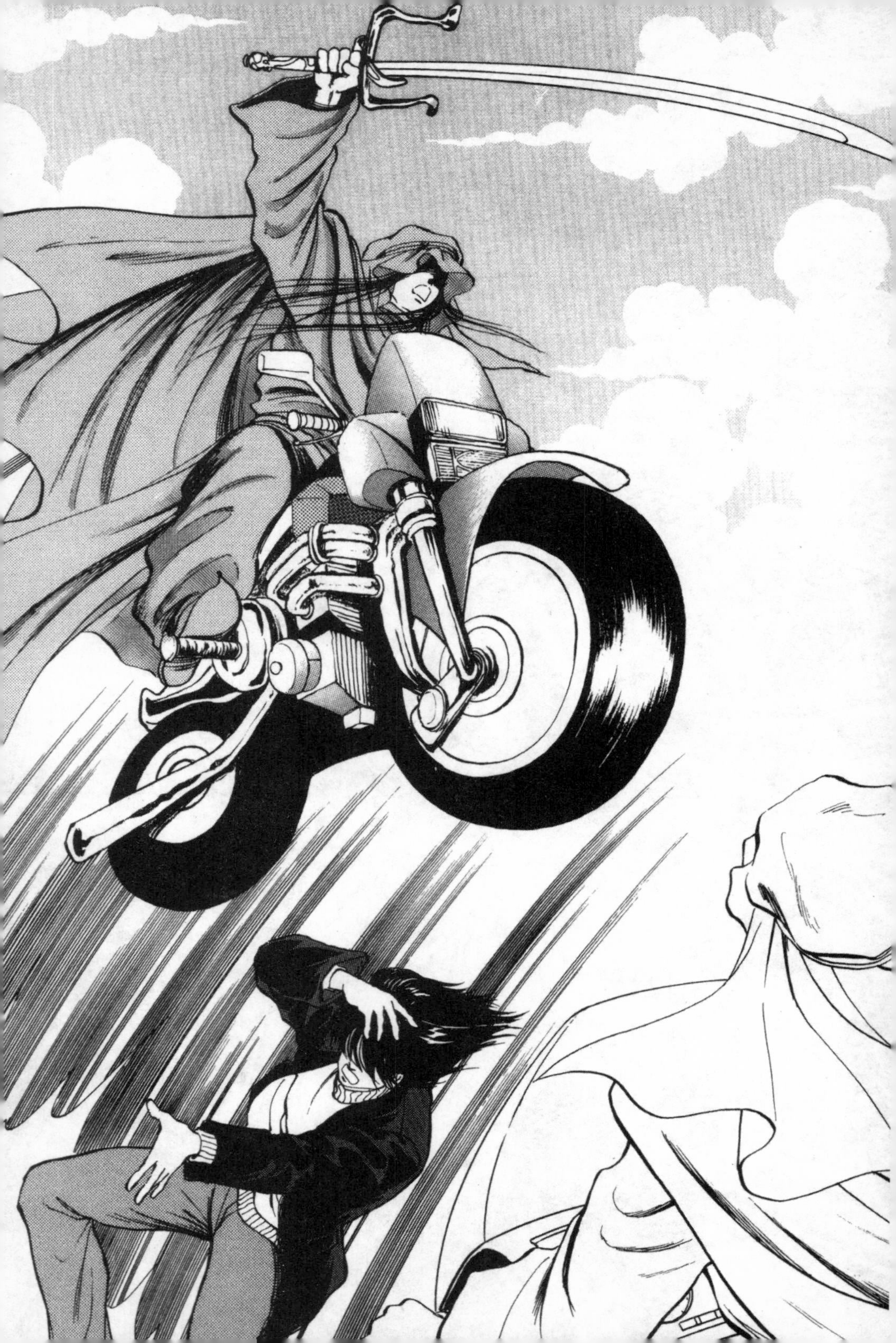

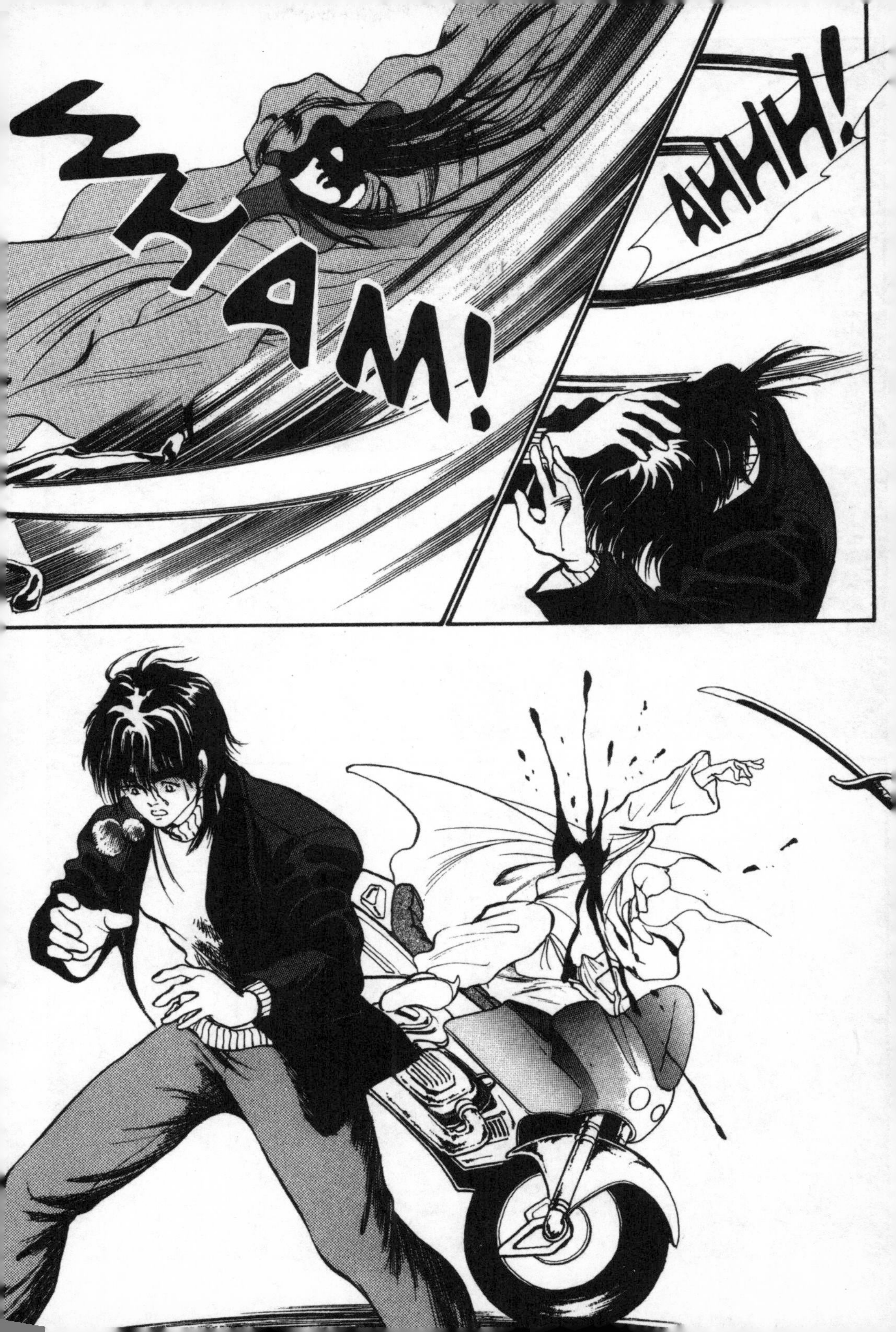

AHHH!
SHAM!

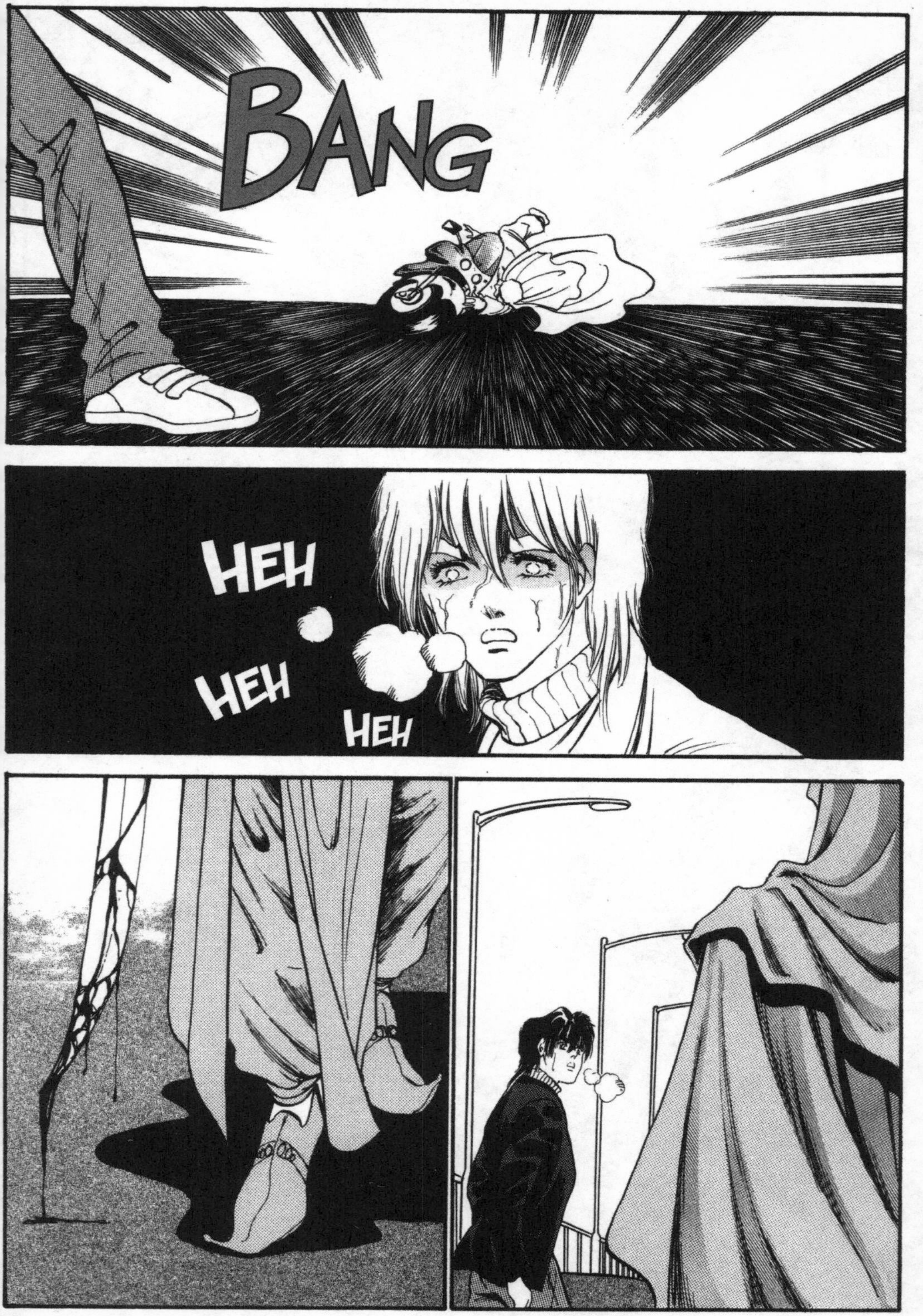
BANG
HEH
HEH
HEH

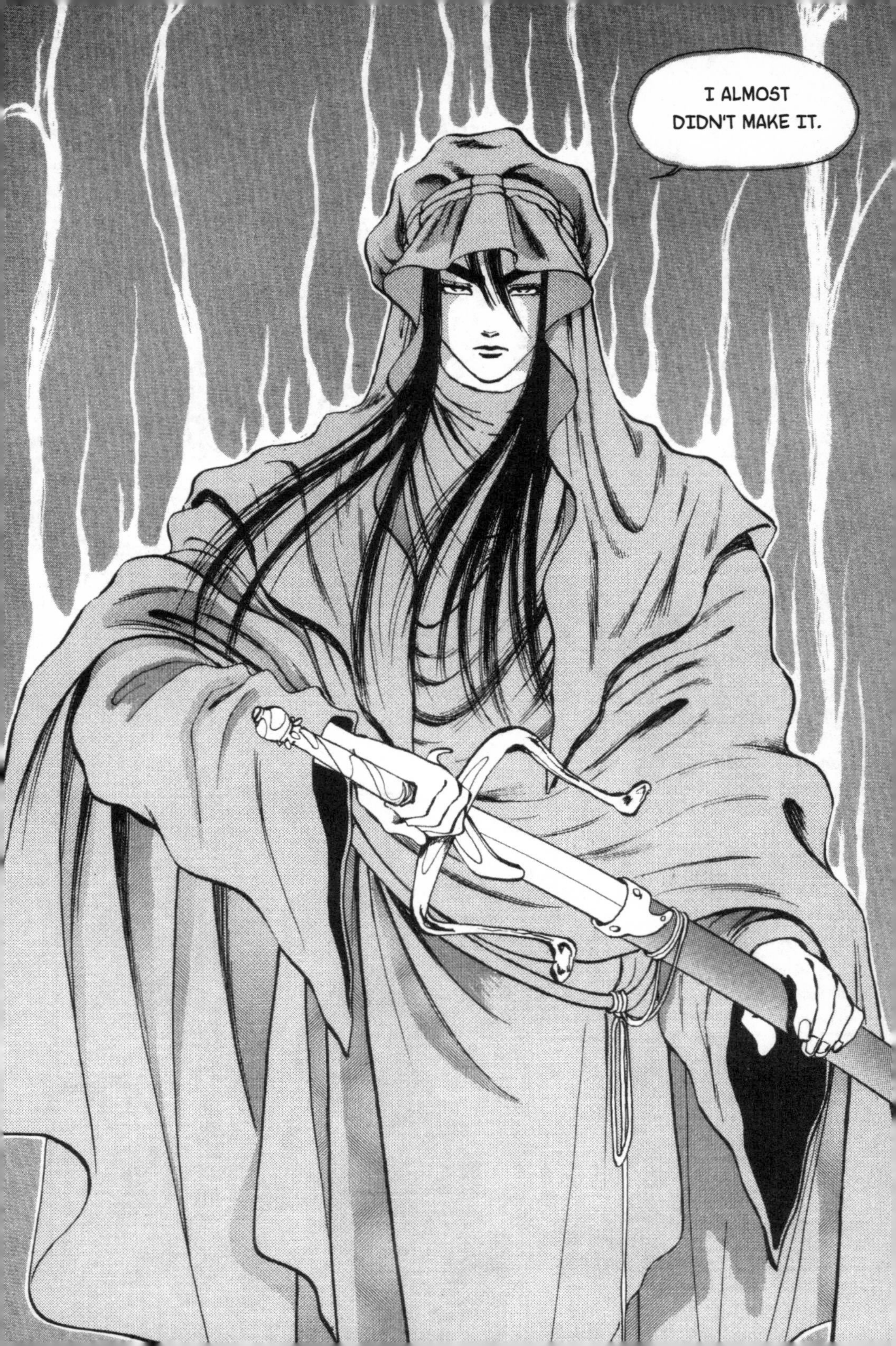
I ALMOST DIDN'T MAKE IT.

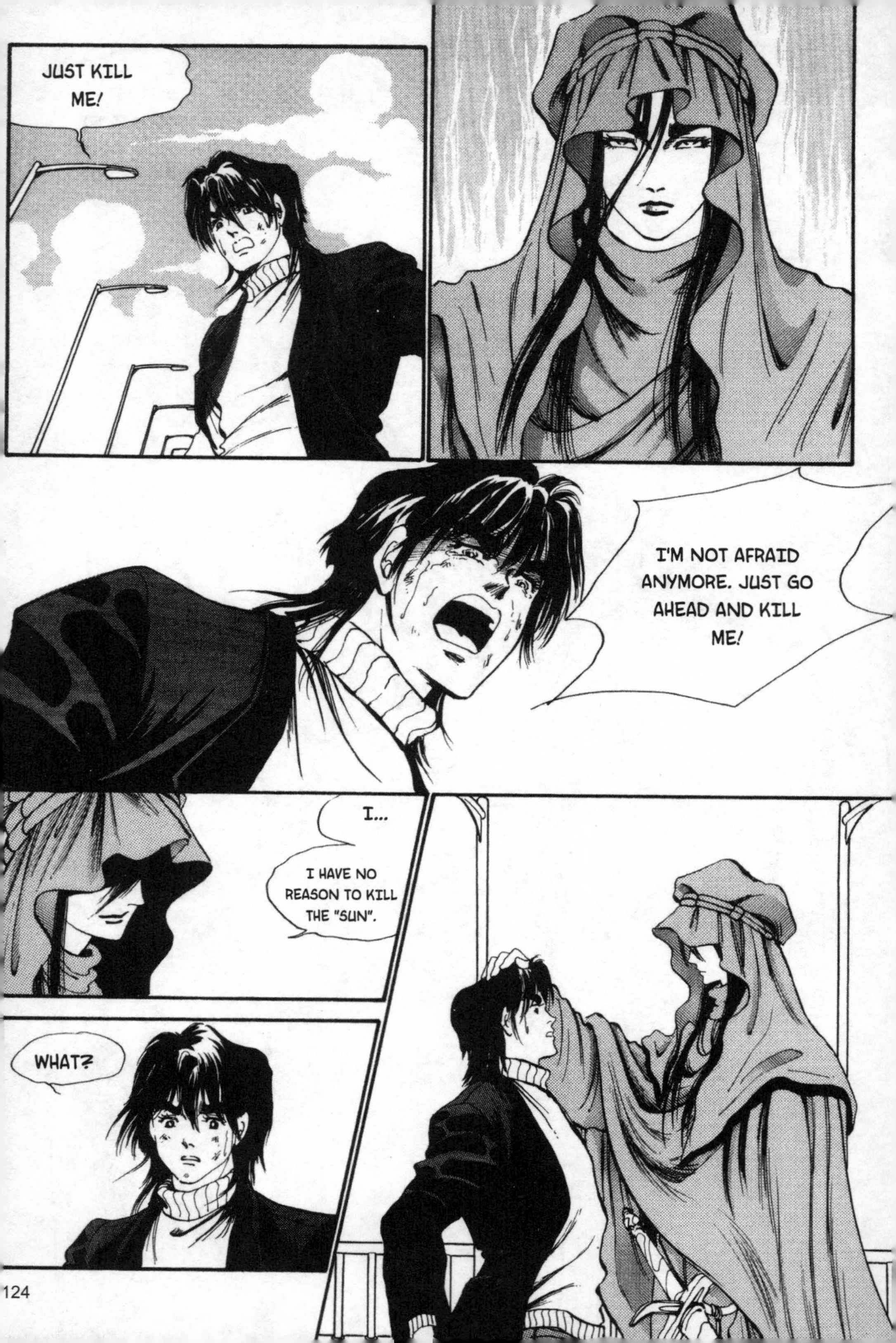
JUST KILL ME!
I'M NOT AFRAID ANYMORE. JUST GO AHEAD AND KILL ME!
I...
I HAVE NO REASON TO KILL THE "SUN".
WHAT?

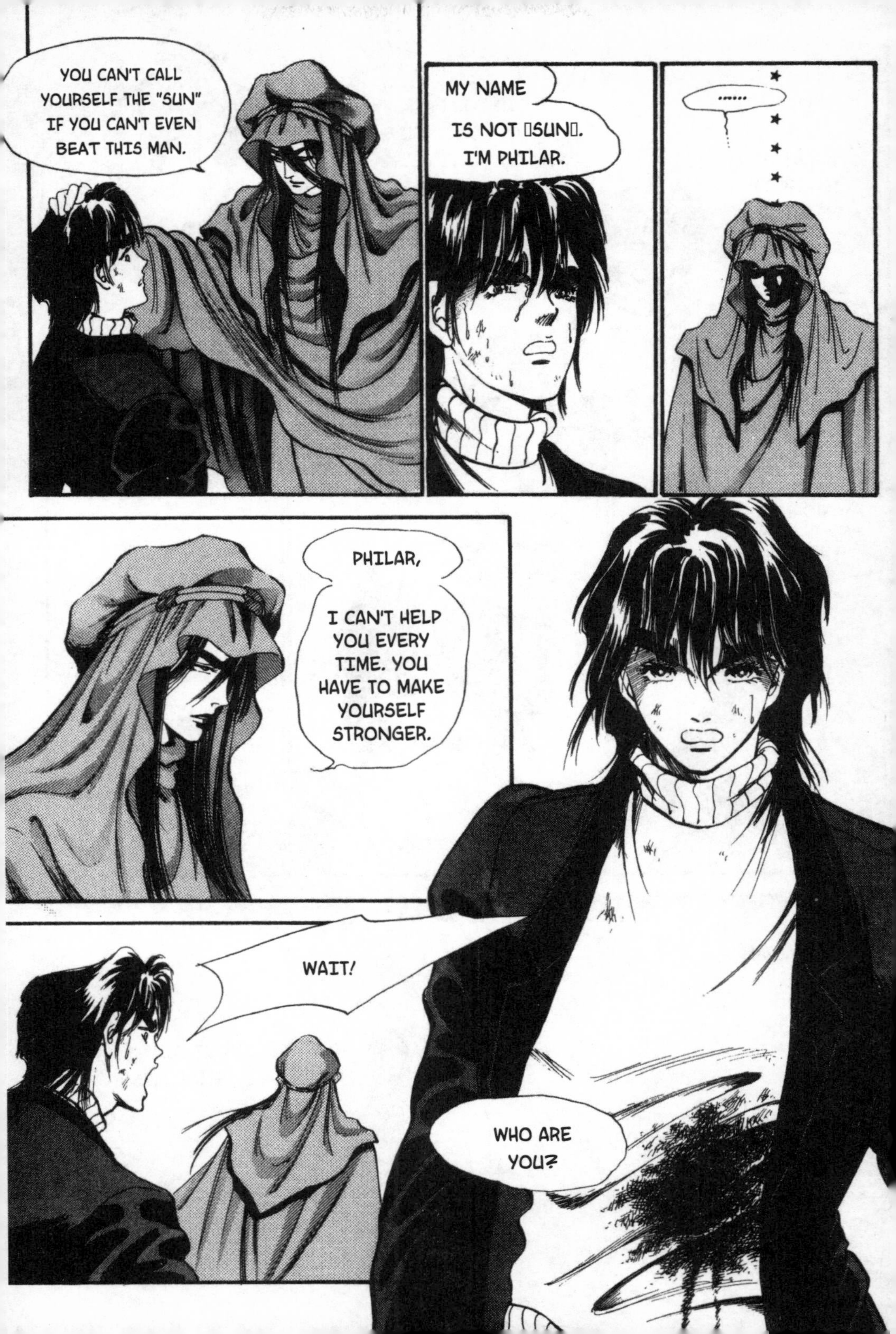

YOU CAN'T CALL YOURSELF THE "SUN" IF YOU CAN'T EVEN BEAT THIS MAN.
MY NAME
IS NOT ▯SUN▯. I'M PHILAR.
......
PHILAR,
I CAN'T HELP YOU EVERY TIME. YOU HAVE TO MAKE YOURSELF STRONGER.
WAIT!
WHO ARE YOU?

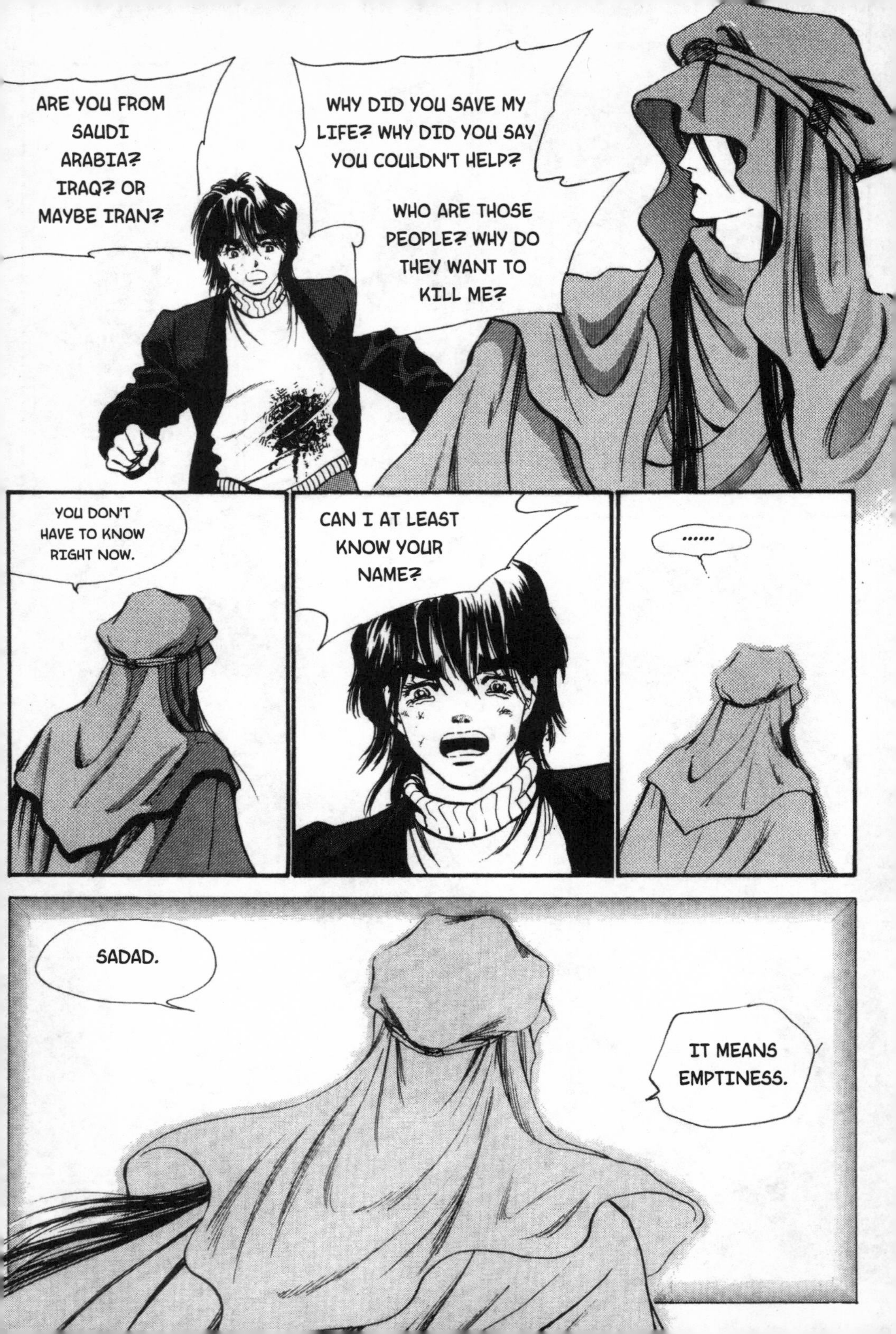
ARE YOU FROM SAUDI ARABIA? IRAQ? OR MAYBE IRAN?
WHY DID YOU SAVE MY LIFE? WHY DID YOU SAY YOU COULDN'T HELP?
WHO ARE THOSE PEOPLE? WHY DO THEY WANT TO KILL ME?
YOU DON'T HAVE TO KNOW RIGHT NOW.
CAN I AT LEAST KNOW YOUR NAME?
......
SADAD.
IT MEANS EMPTINESS.

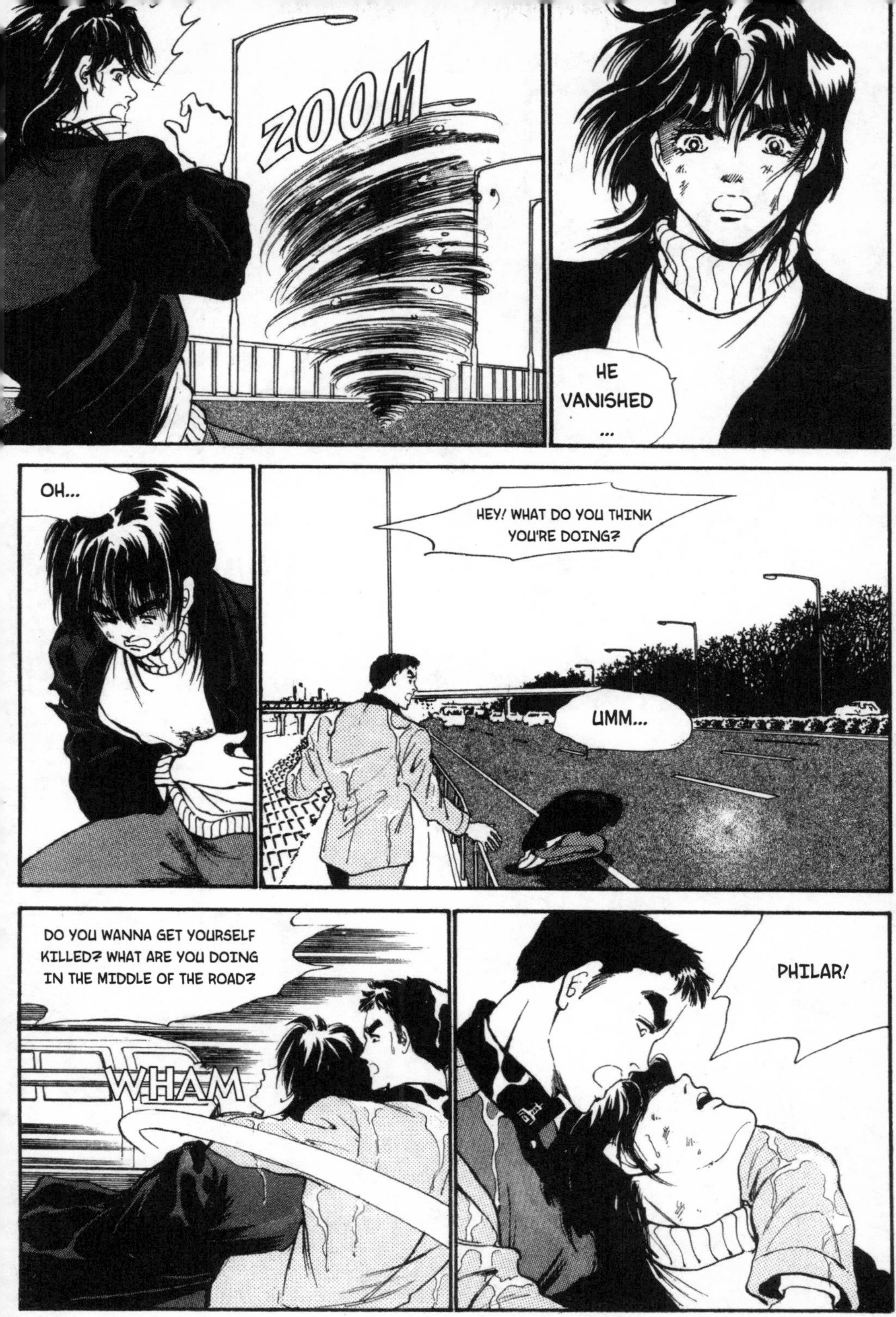
ZOOM
HE VANISHED ...
OH...
HEY! WHAT DO YOU THINK YOU'RE DOING?
UMM...
DO YOU WANNA GET YOURSELF KILLED? WHAT ARE YOU DOING IN THE MIDDLE OF THE ROAD?
WHAM
PHILAR!

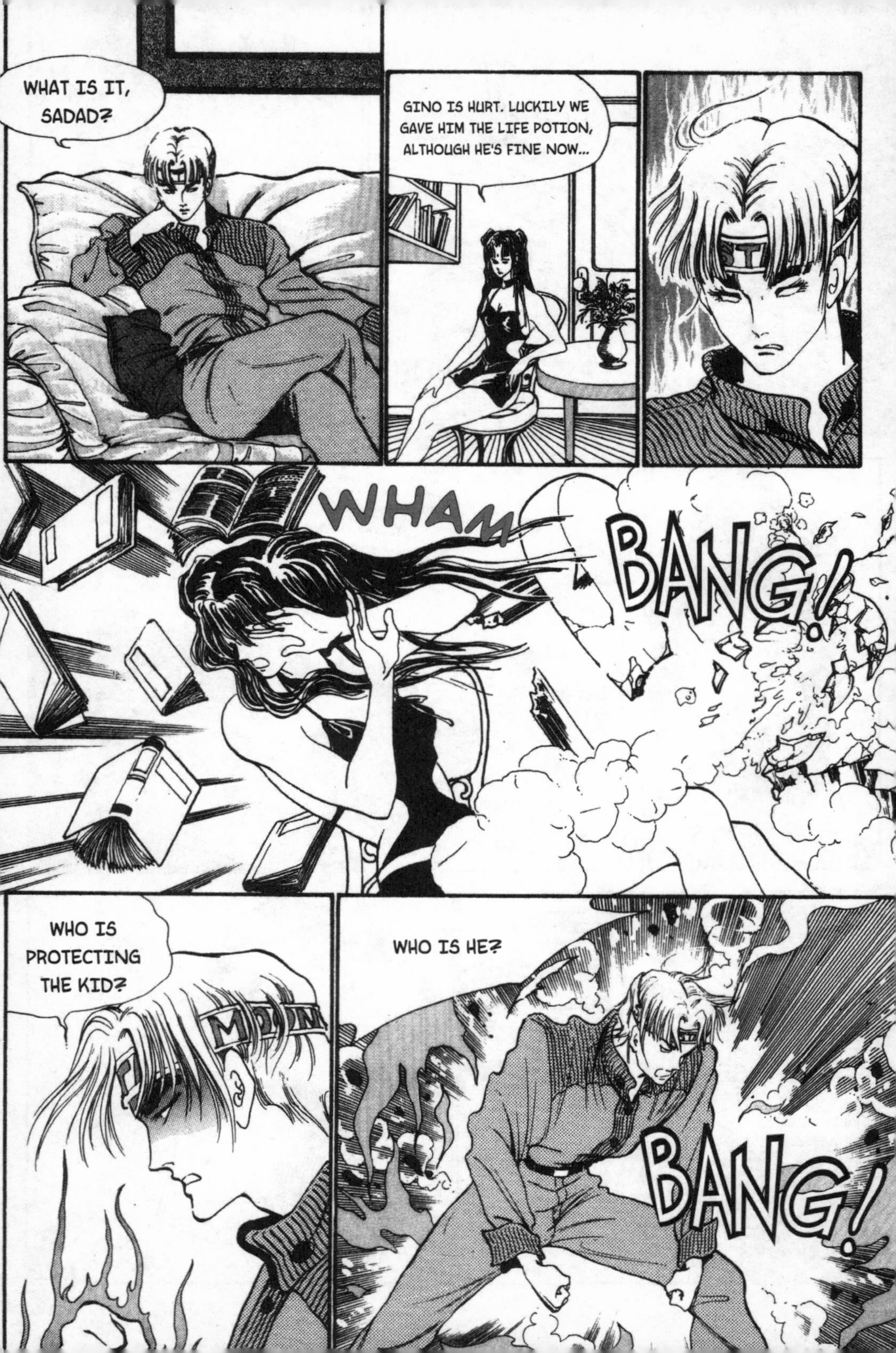

WHAT IS IT, SADAD?
GINO IS HURT. LUCKILY WE GAVE HIM THE LIFE POTION, ALTHOUGH HE'S FINE NOW...
WHAM
BANG!
WHO IS PROTECTING THE KID?
WHO IS HE?
BANG!

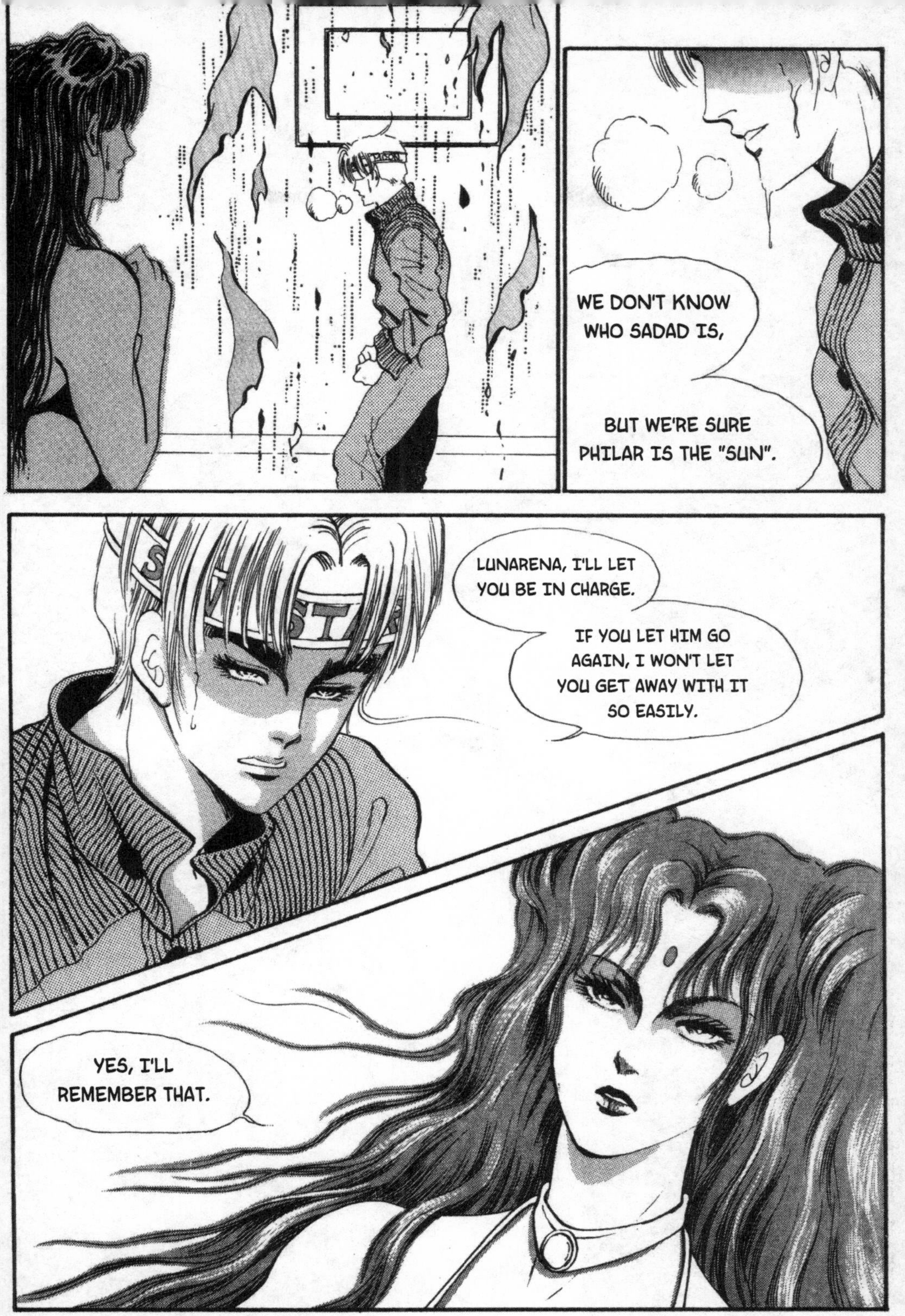
WE DON'T KNOW WHO SADAD IS,
BUT WE'RE SURE PHILAR IS THE "SUN".
LUNARENA, I'LL LET YOU BE IN CHARGE.
IF YOU LET HIM GO AGAIN, I WON'T LET YOU GET AWAY WITH IT SO EASILY.
YES, I'LL REMEMBER THAT.

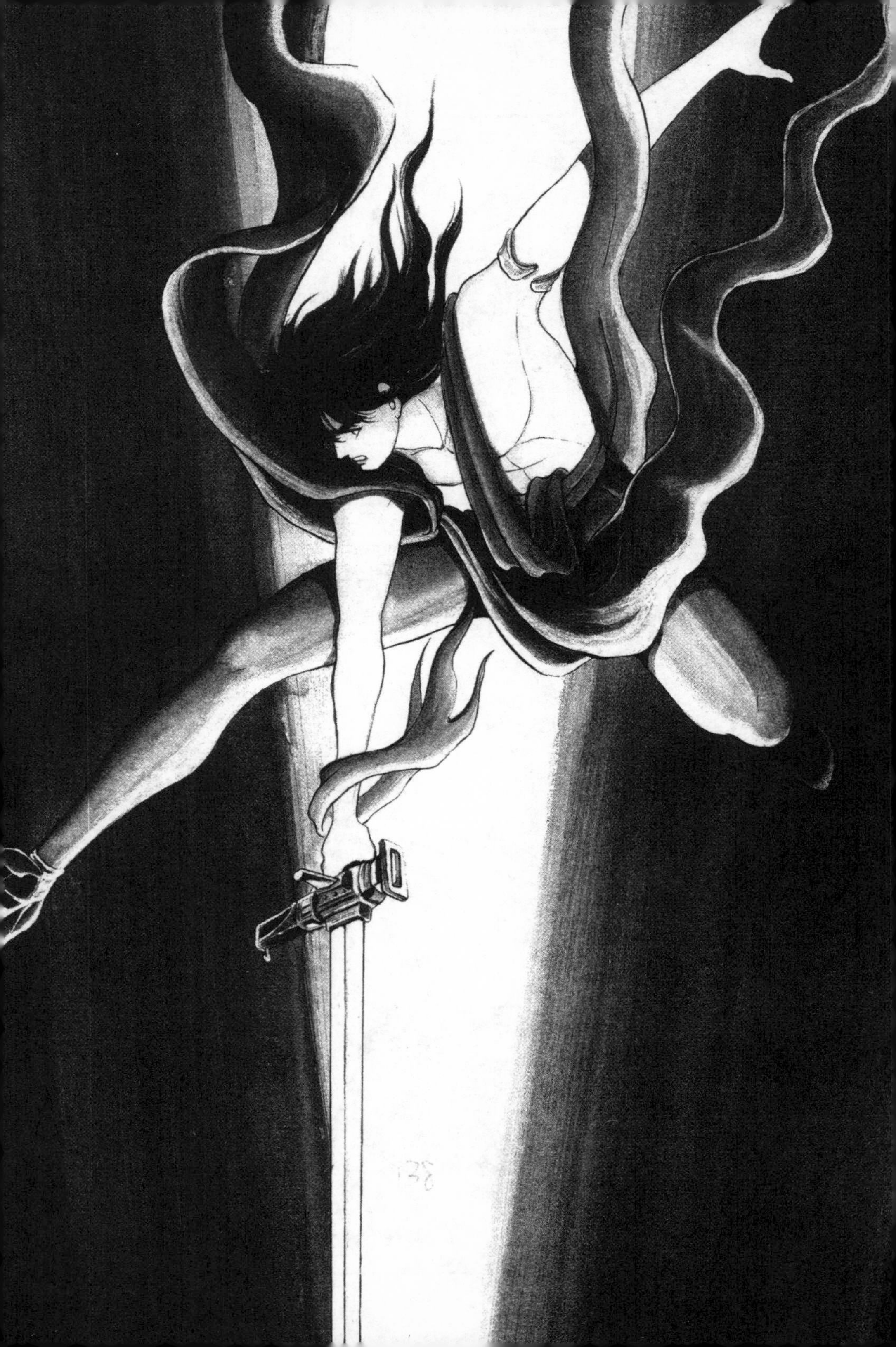

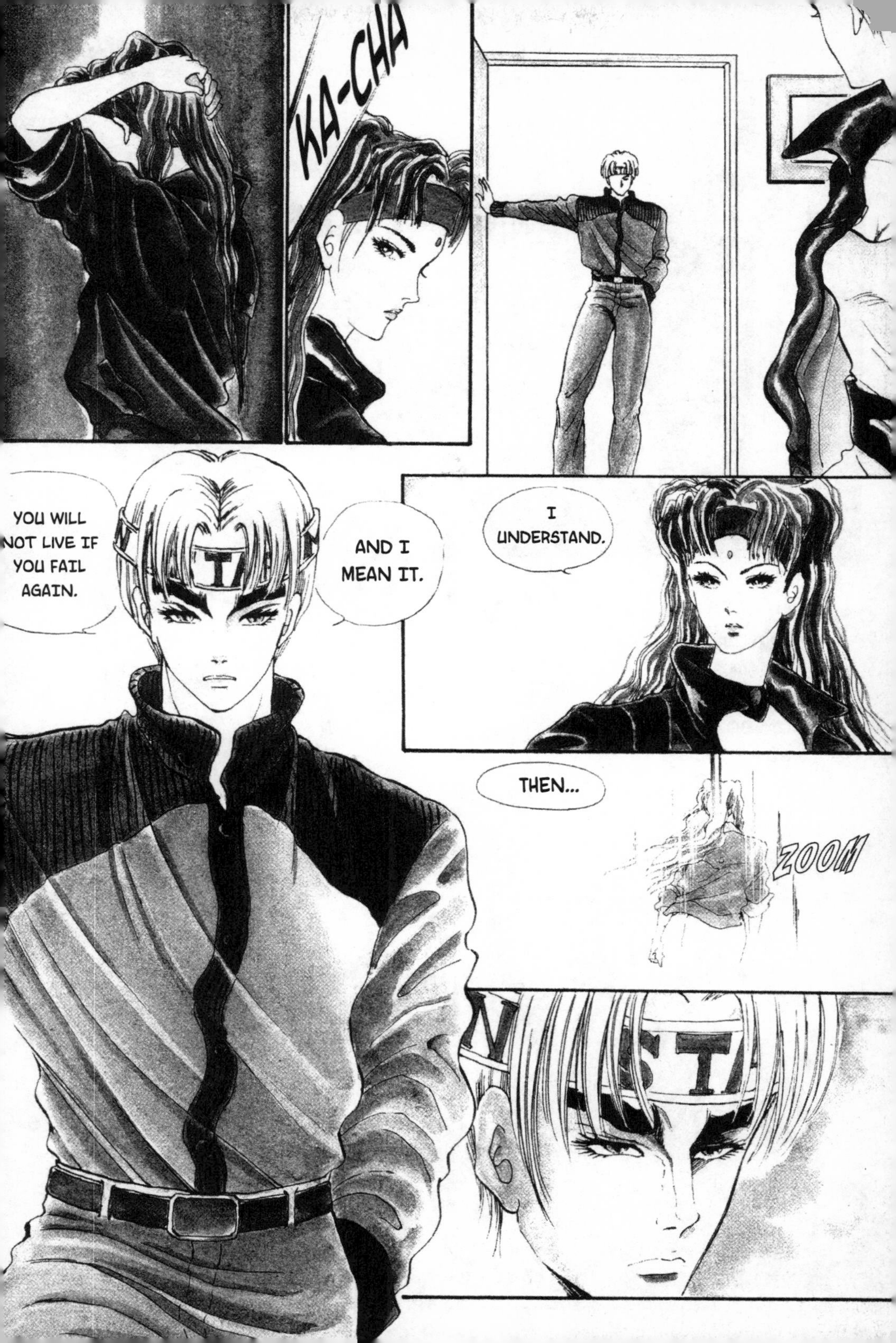
KA-CHA
YOU WILL NOT LIVE IF YOU FAIL AGAIN.
AND I MEAN IT.
I UNDERSTAND.
THEN...
ZOOM

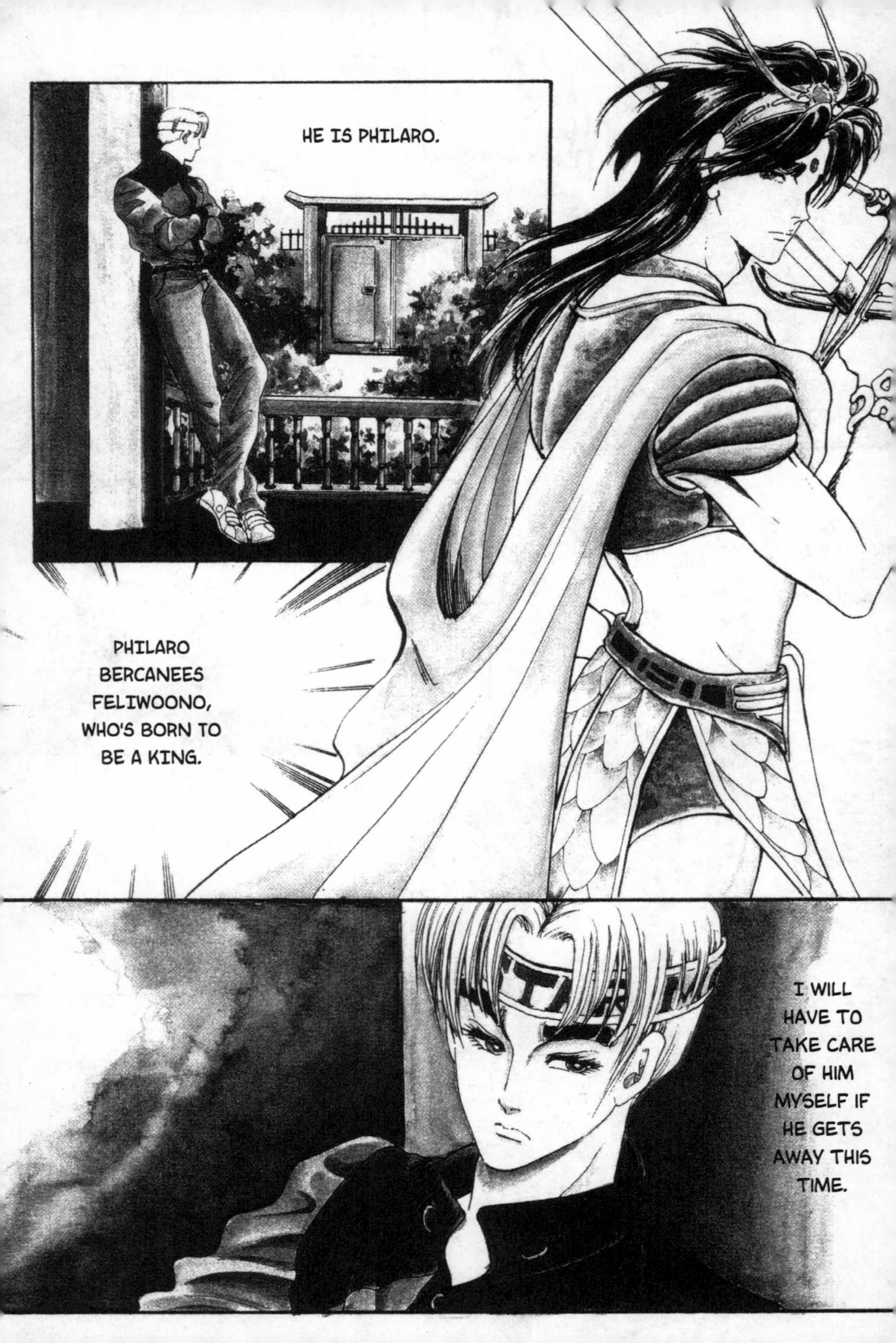
HE IS PHILARO.
PHILARO BERCANEES FELIWOONO, WHO'S BORN TO BE A KING.
I WILL HAVE TO TAKE CARE OF HIM MYSELF IF HE GETS AWAY THIS TIME.

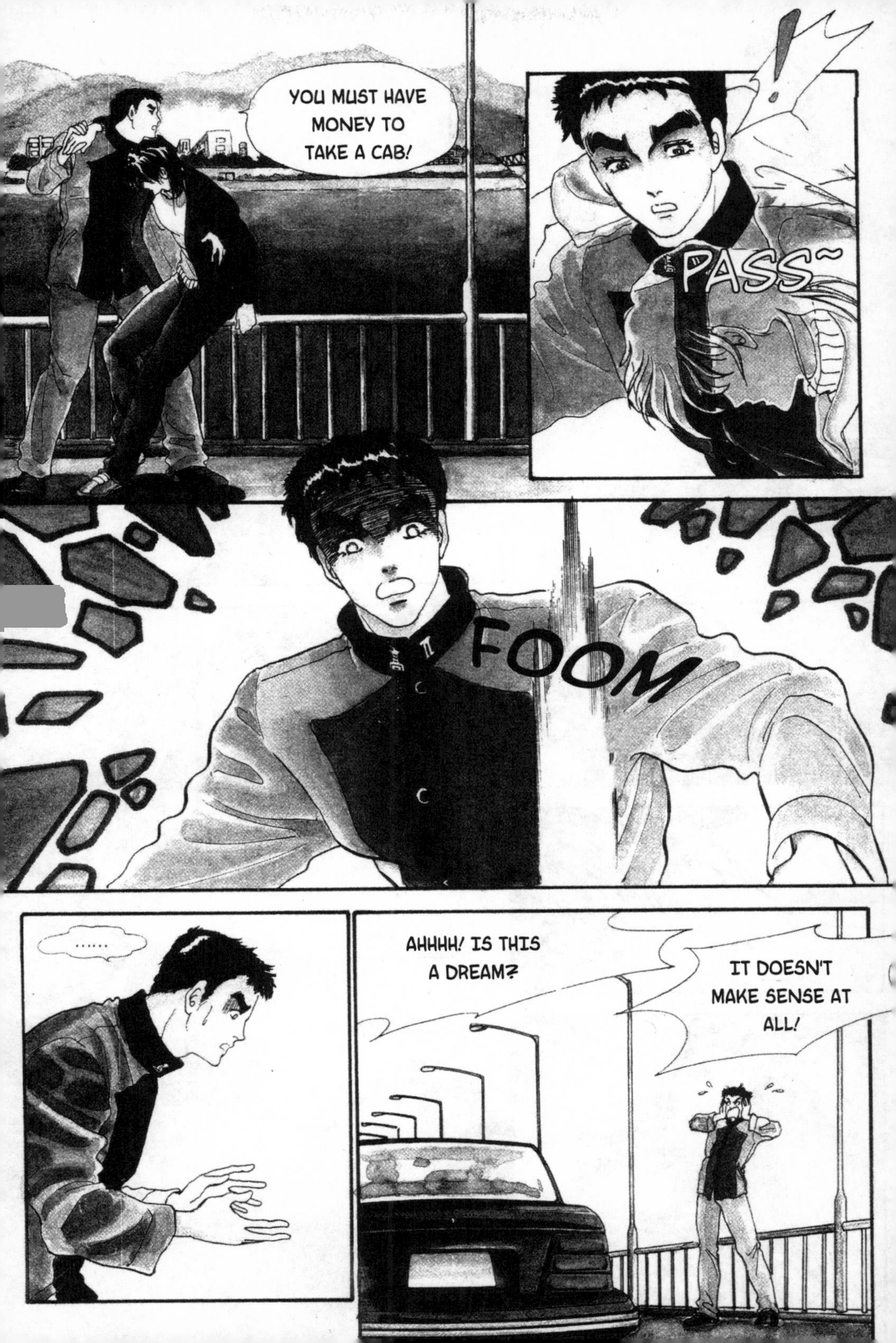
YOU MUST HAVE MONEY TO TAKE A CAB!
!
PASS~
FOOM
......
AHHHH! IS THIS A DREAM?
IT DOESN'T MAKE SENSE AT ALL!

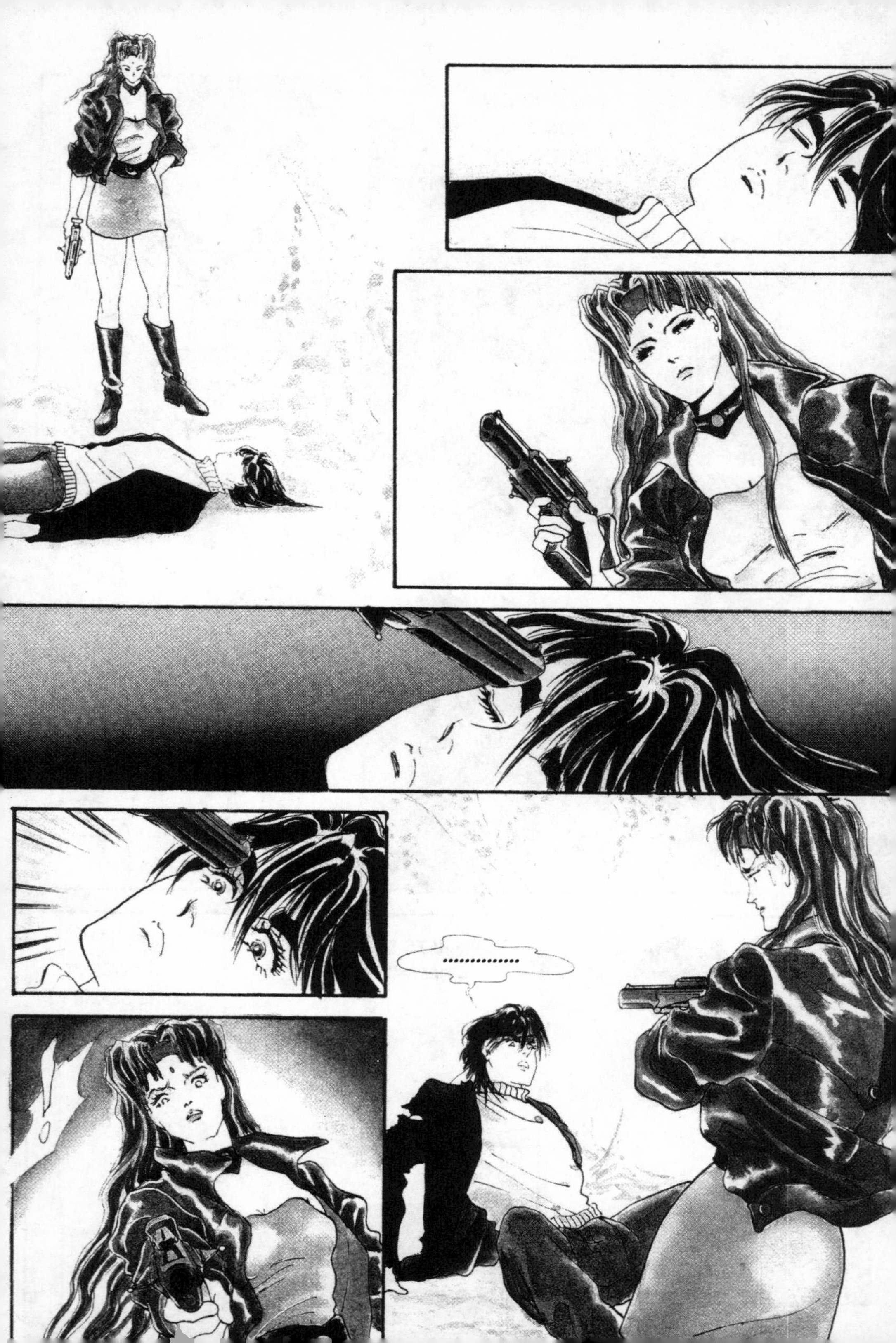
....

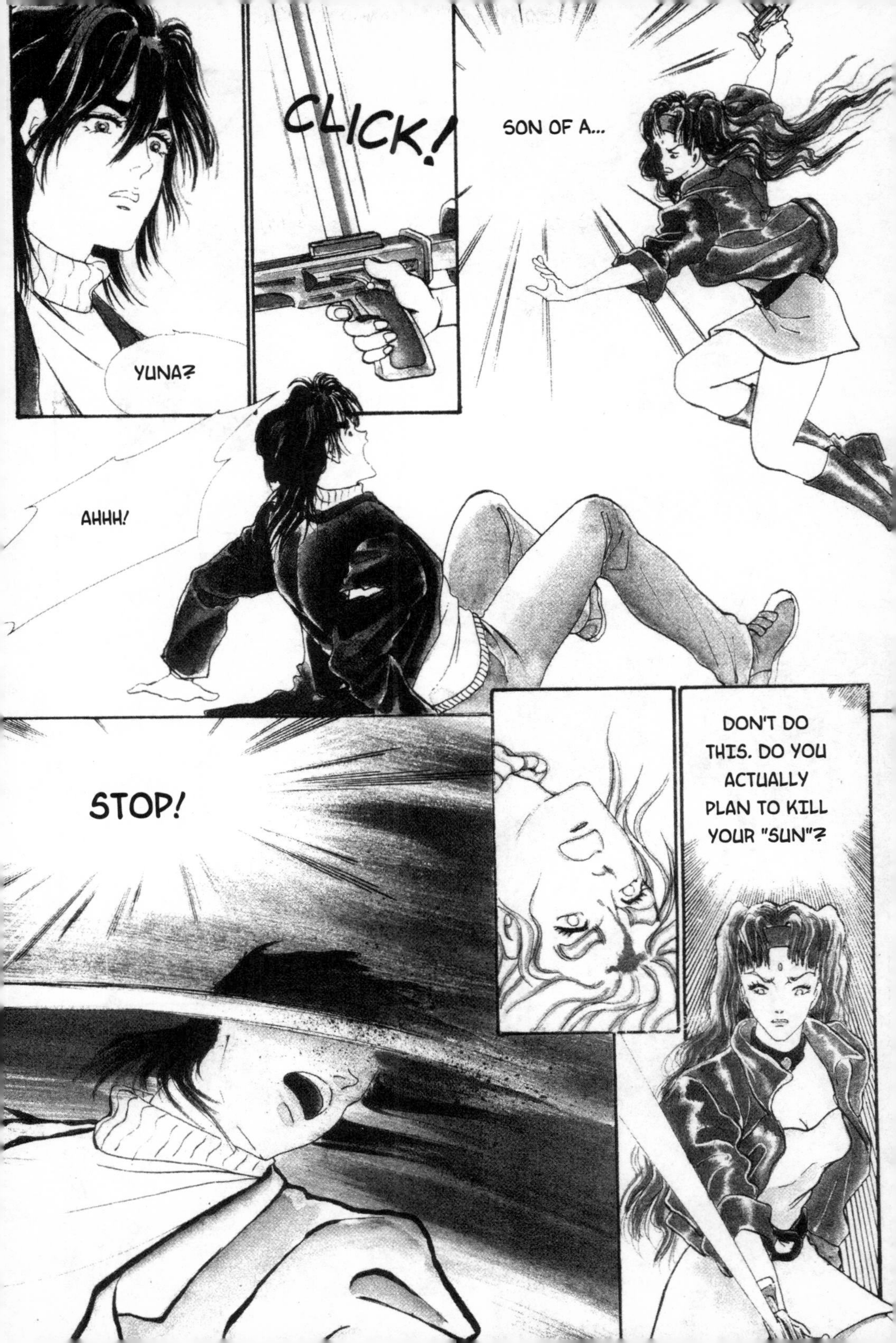
YUNA?
CLICK!
SON OF A...
AHHH!
STOP!
DON'T DO THIS. DO YOU ACTUALLY PLAN TO KILL YOUR "SUN"?

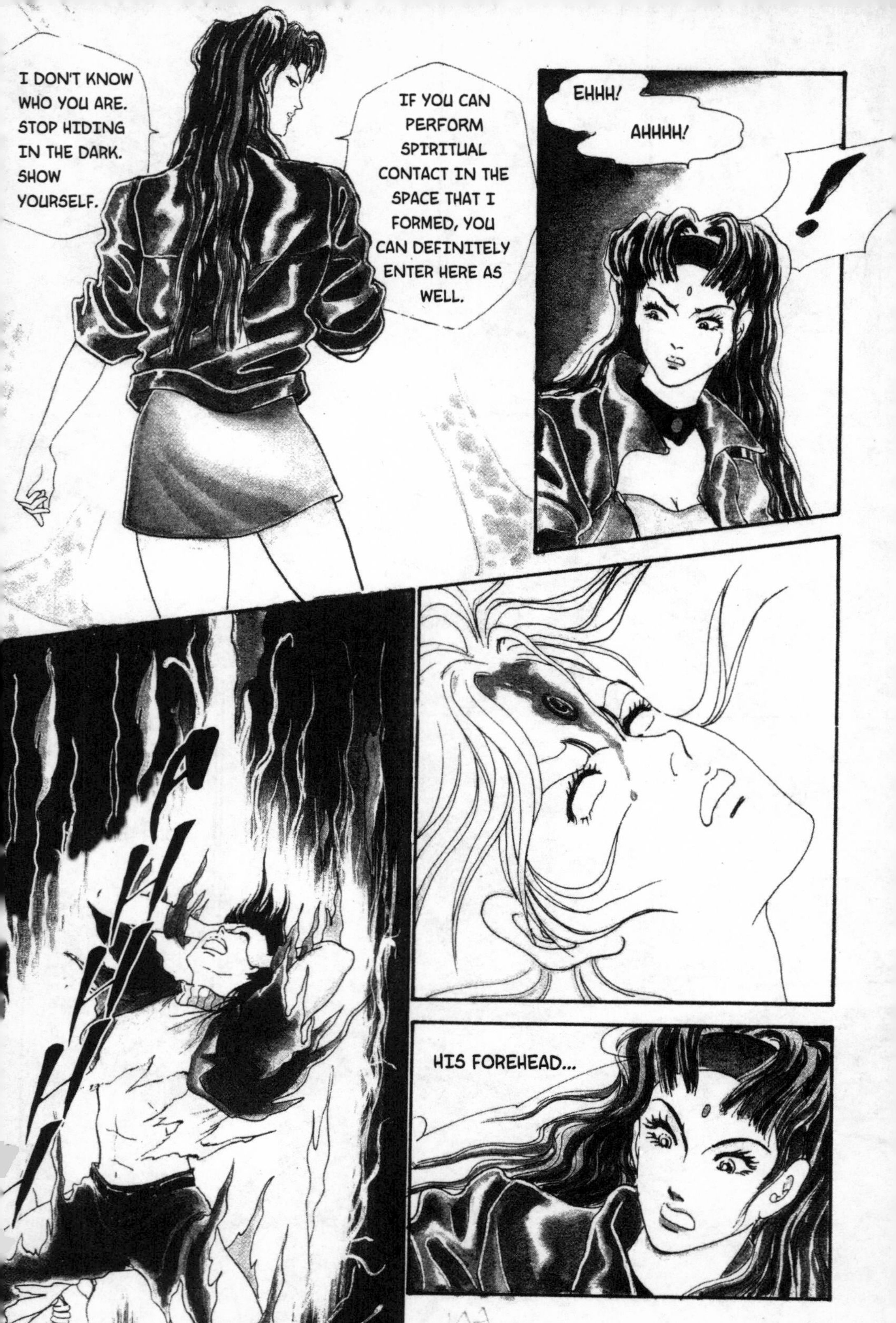

I DON'T KNOW WHO YOU ARE. STOP HIDING IN THE DARK. SHOW YOURSELF.
IF YOU CAN PERFORM SPIRITUAL CONTACT IN THE SPACE THAT I FORMED, YOU CAN DEFINITELY ENTER HERE AS WELL.
EHHH!
AHHHH!
!
HIS FOREHEAD...

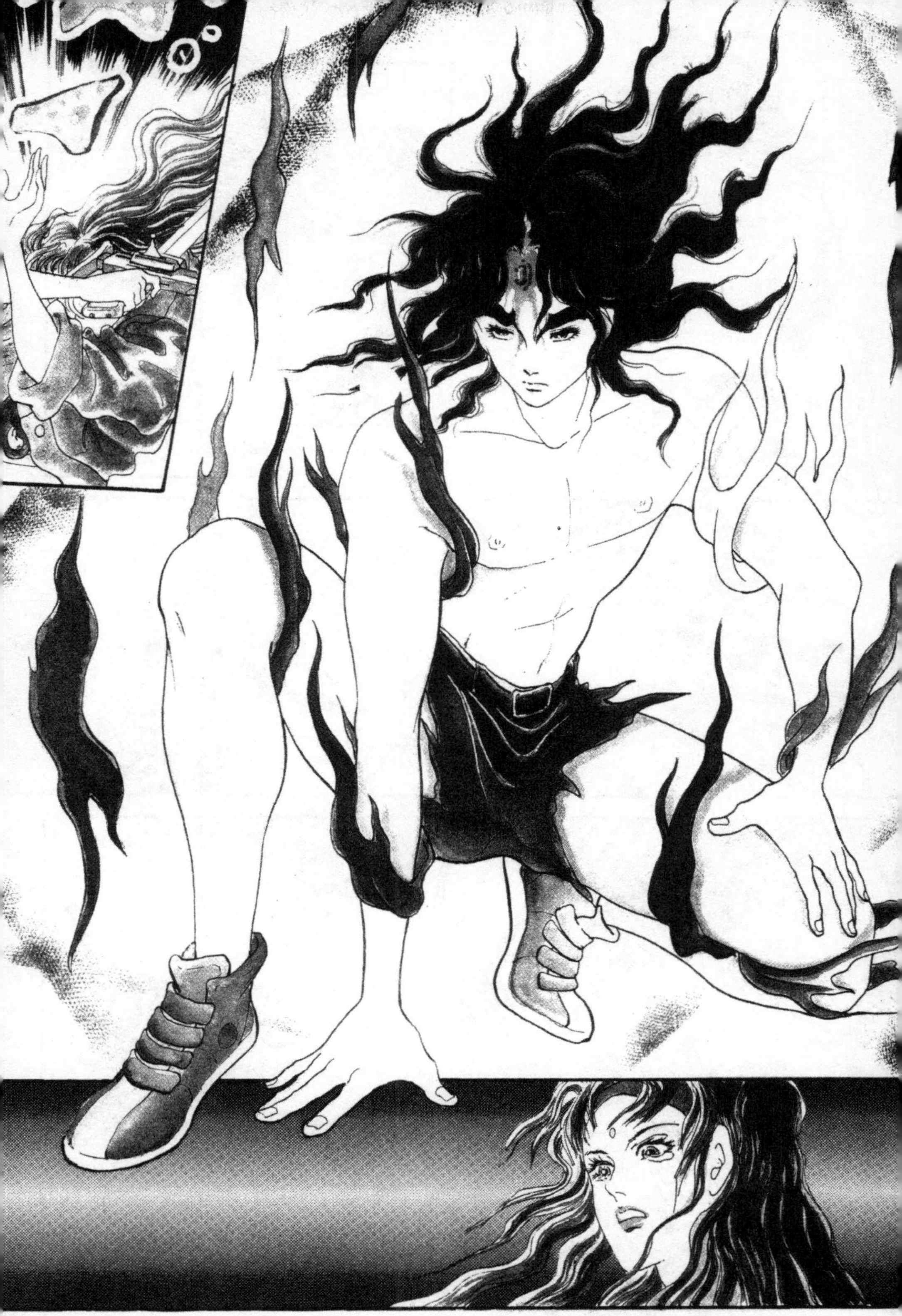

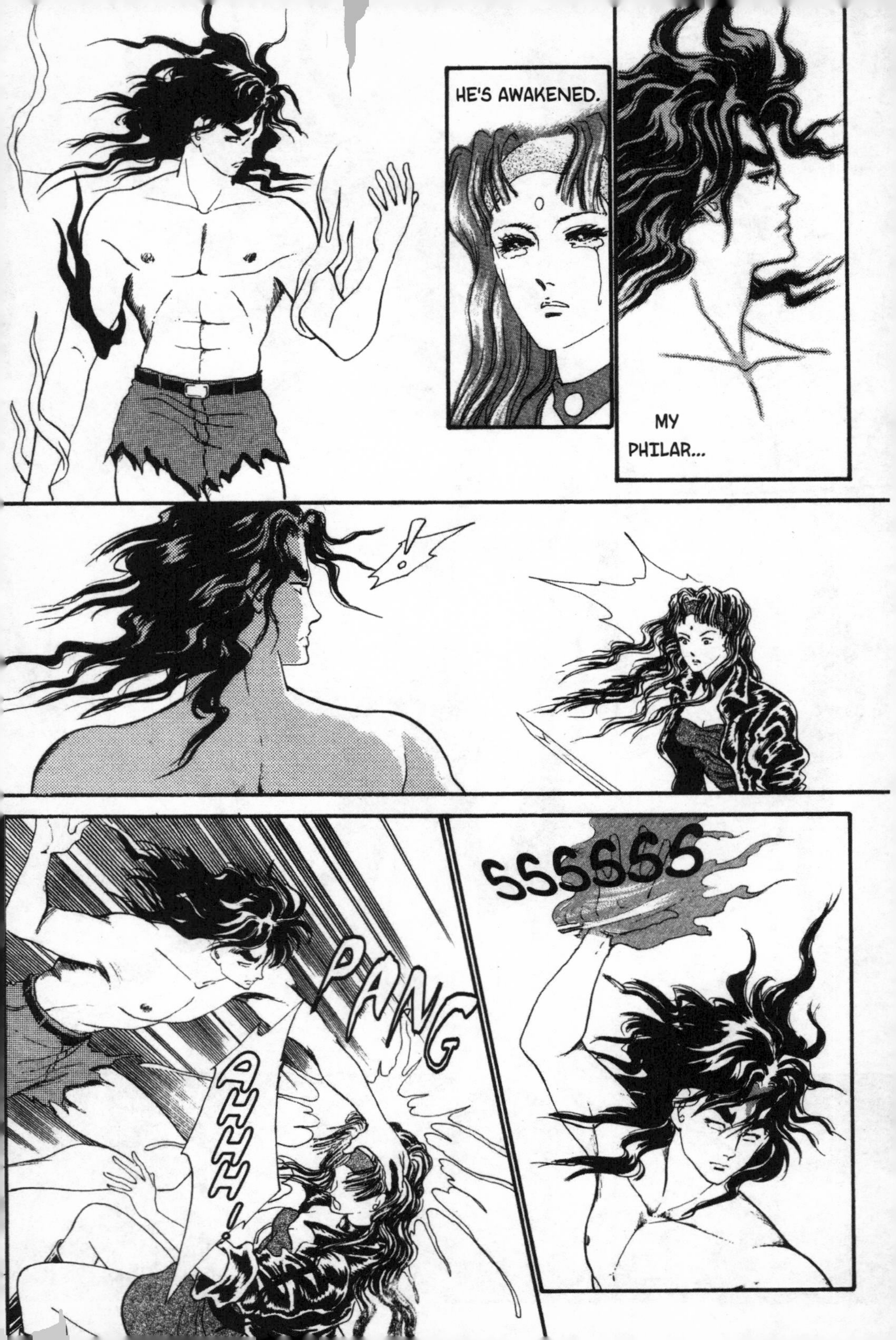
HE'S AWAKENED.
MY PHILAR...
!
PANG
AHHH!
SSSSSS

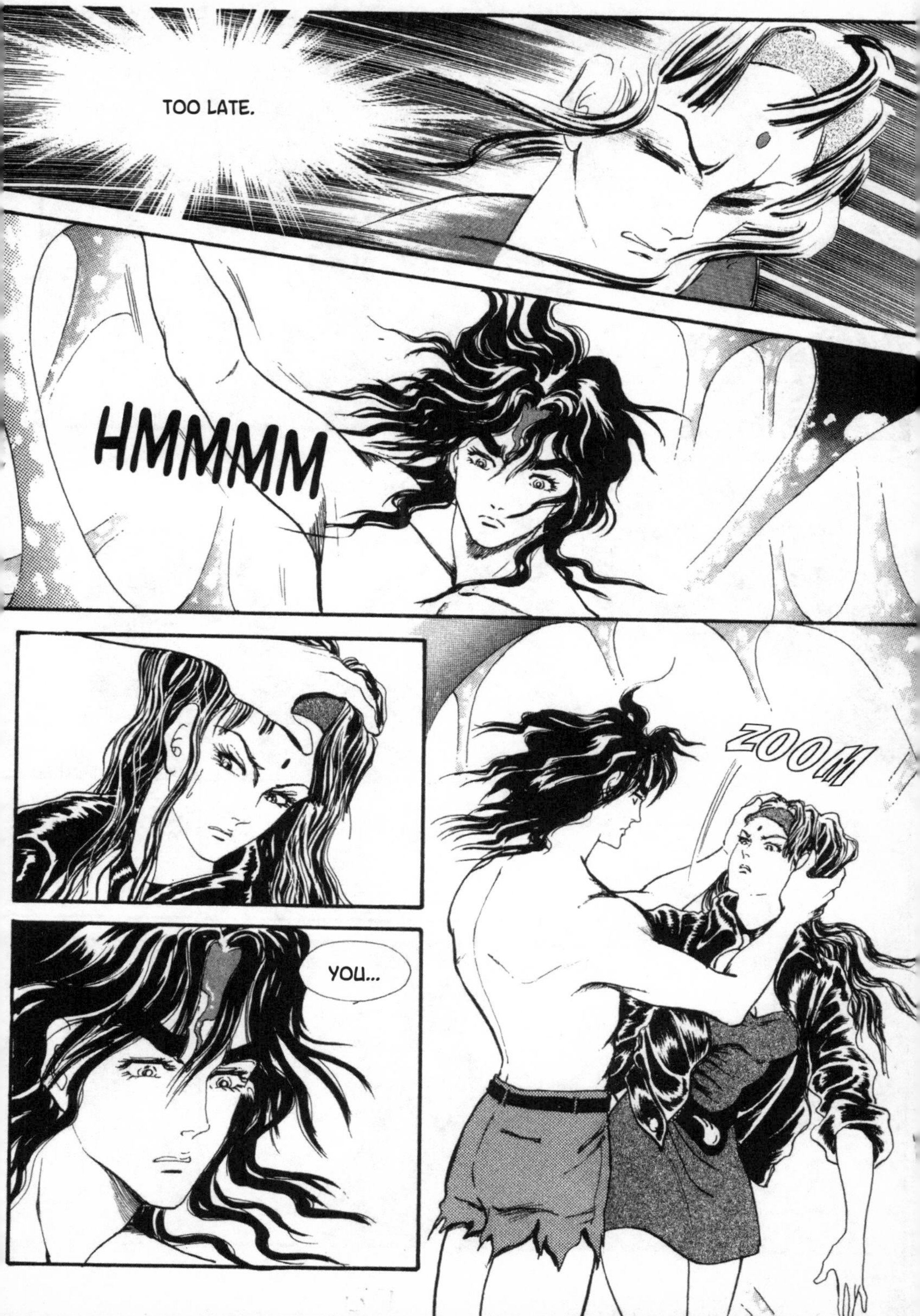
TOO LATE.
HMMMM
ZOOM
YOU...

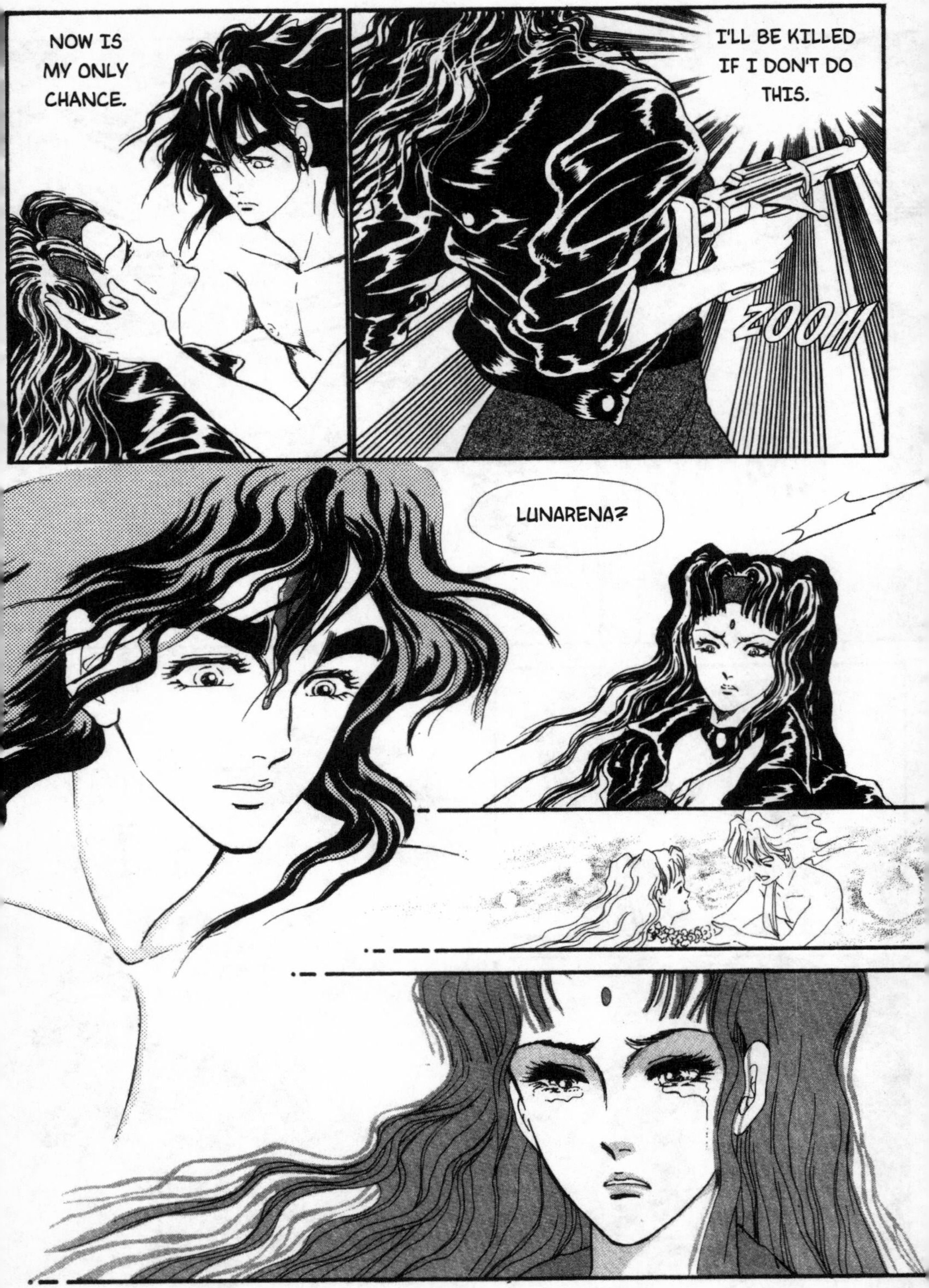
NOW IS MY ONLY CHANCE.
I'LL BE KILLED IF I DON'T DO THIS.
ZOOM
LUNARENA?

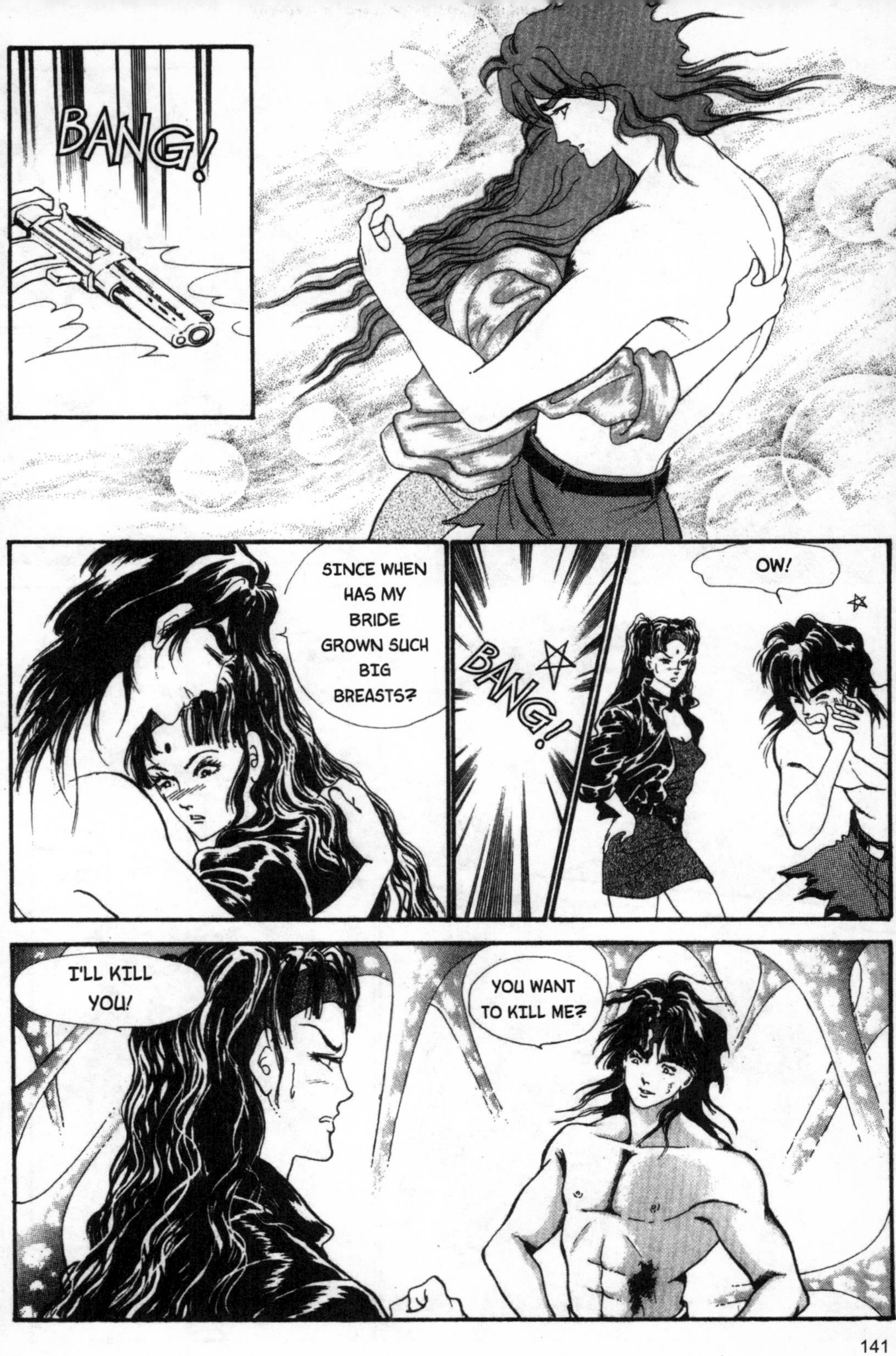
BANG!
SINCE WHEN HAS MY BRIDE GROWN SUCH BIG BREASTS?
BANG!
OW!
I'LL KILL YOU!
YOU WANT TO KILL ME?

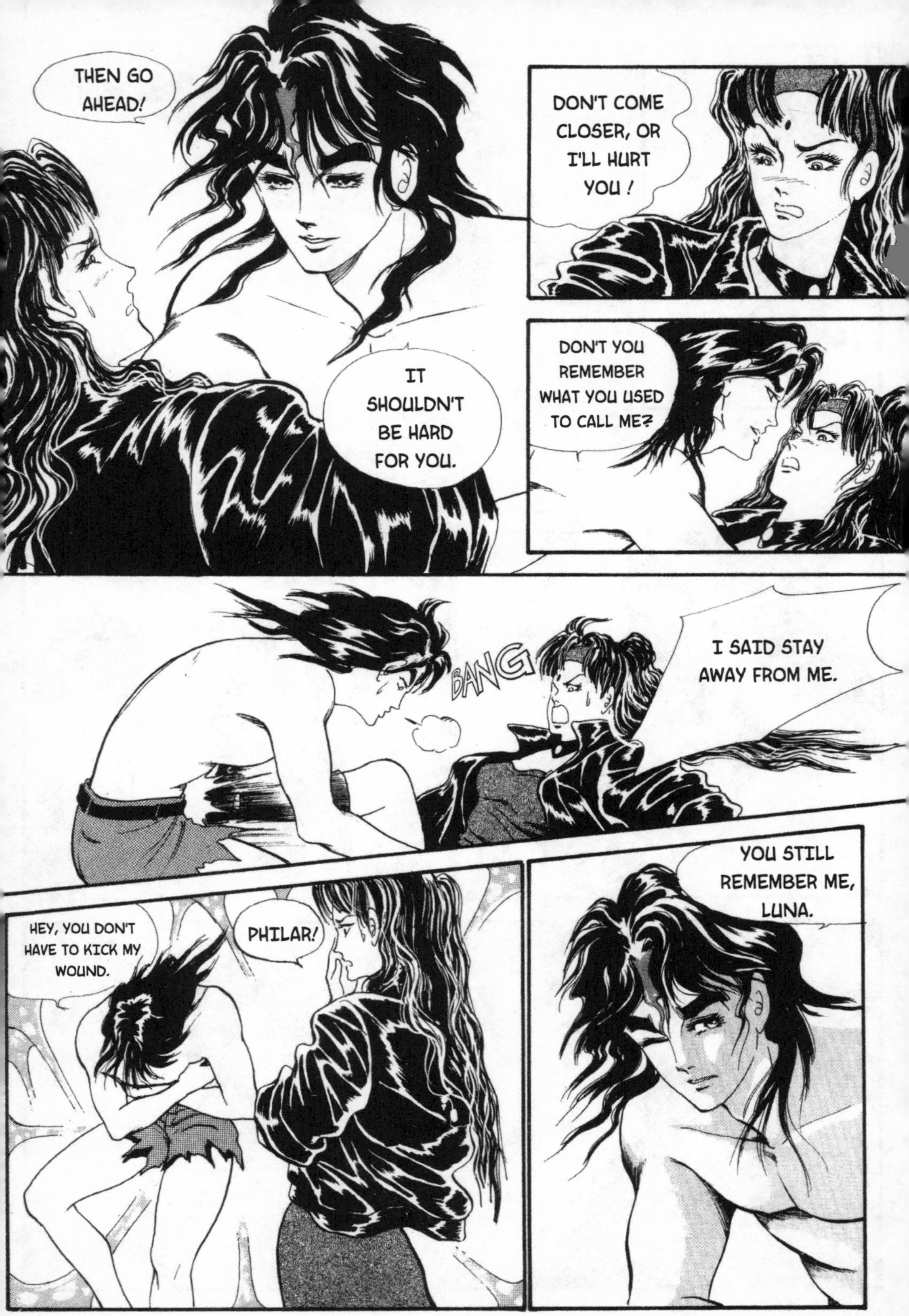
THEN GO AHEAD!
IT SHOULDN'T BE HARD FOR YOU.
DON'T COME CLOSER, OR I'LL HURT YOU !
DON'T YOU REMEMBER WHAT YOU USED TO CALL ME?
BANG
I SAID STAY AWAY FROM ME.
HEY, YOU DON'T HAVE TO KICK MY WOUND.
PHILAR!
YOU STILL REMEMBER ME, LUNA.

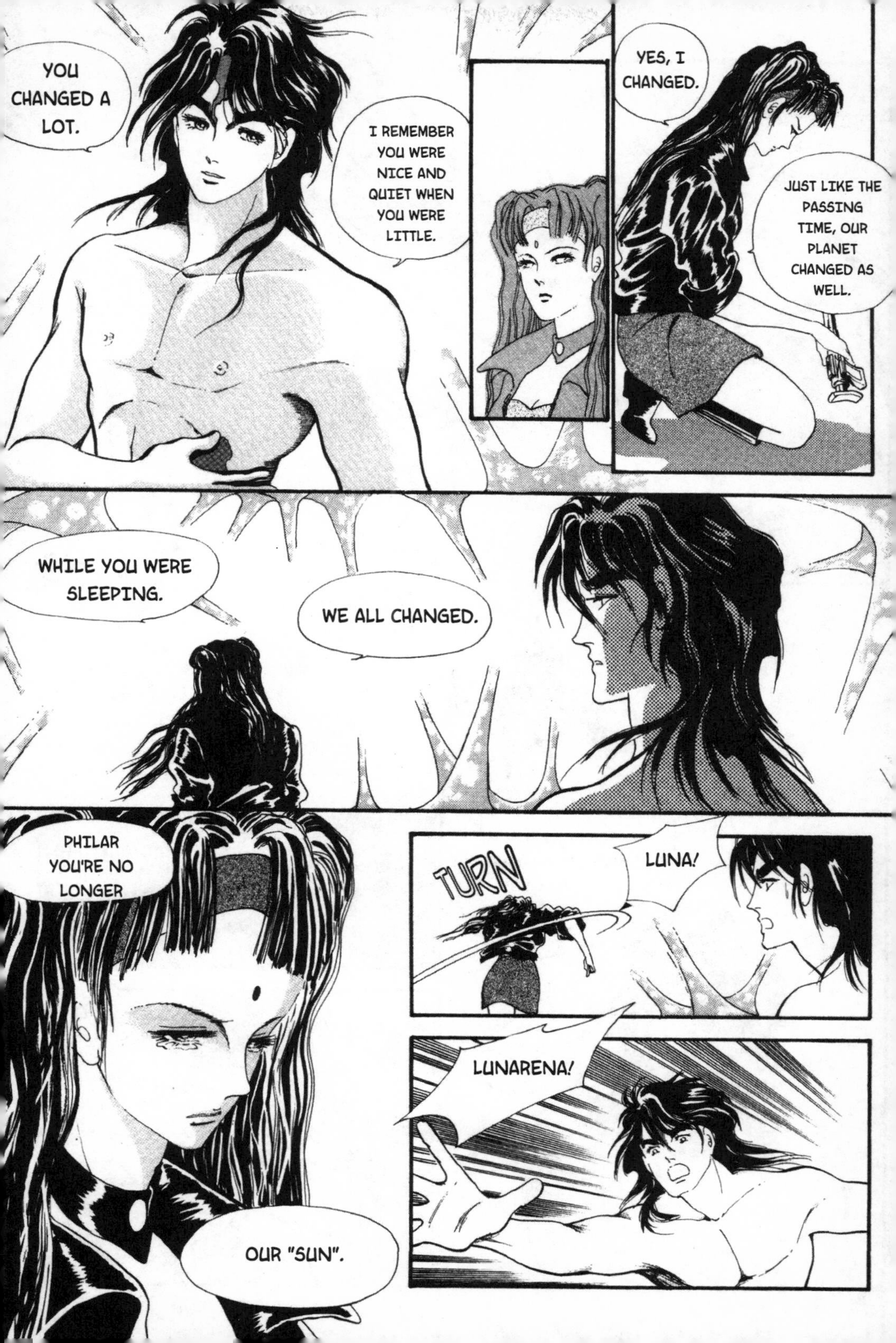
YOU CHANGED A LOT.
I REMEMBER YOU WERE NICE AND QUIET WHEN YOU WERE LITTLE.
YES, I CHANGED.
JUST LIKE THE PASSING TIME, OUR PLANET CHANGED AS WELL.
WHILE YOU WERE SLEEPING.
WE ALL CHANGED.
PHILAR YOU'RE NO LONGER
OUR "SUN".
TURN
LUNA!
LUNARENA!

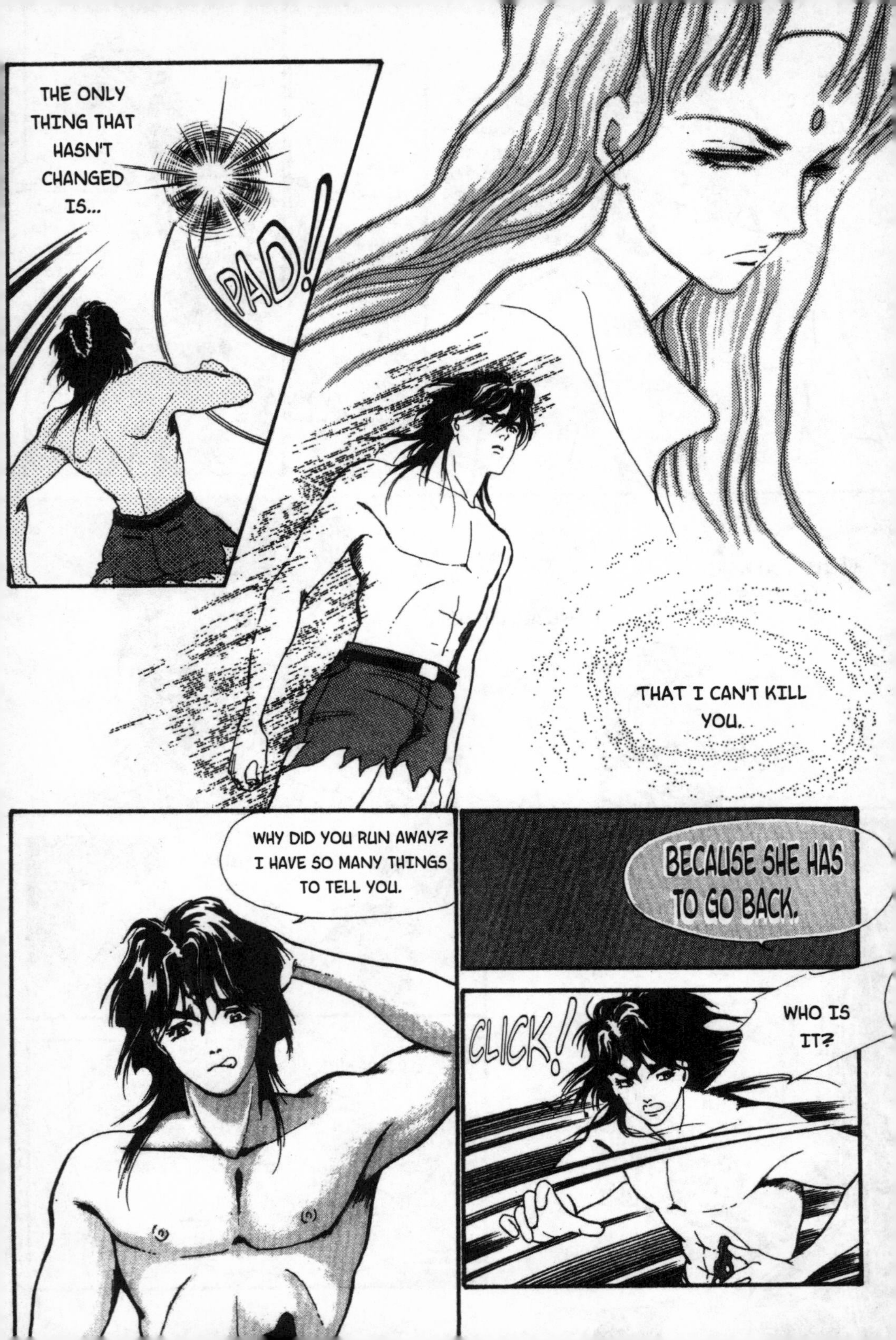
THE ONLY THING THAT HASN'T CHANGED IS...
PAD!
THAT I CAN'T KILL YOU.
WHY DID YOU RUN AWAY? I HAVE SO MANY THINGS TO TELL YOU.
BECAUSE SHE HAS TO GO BACK.
CLICK!
WHO IS IT?

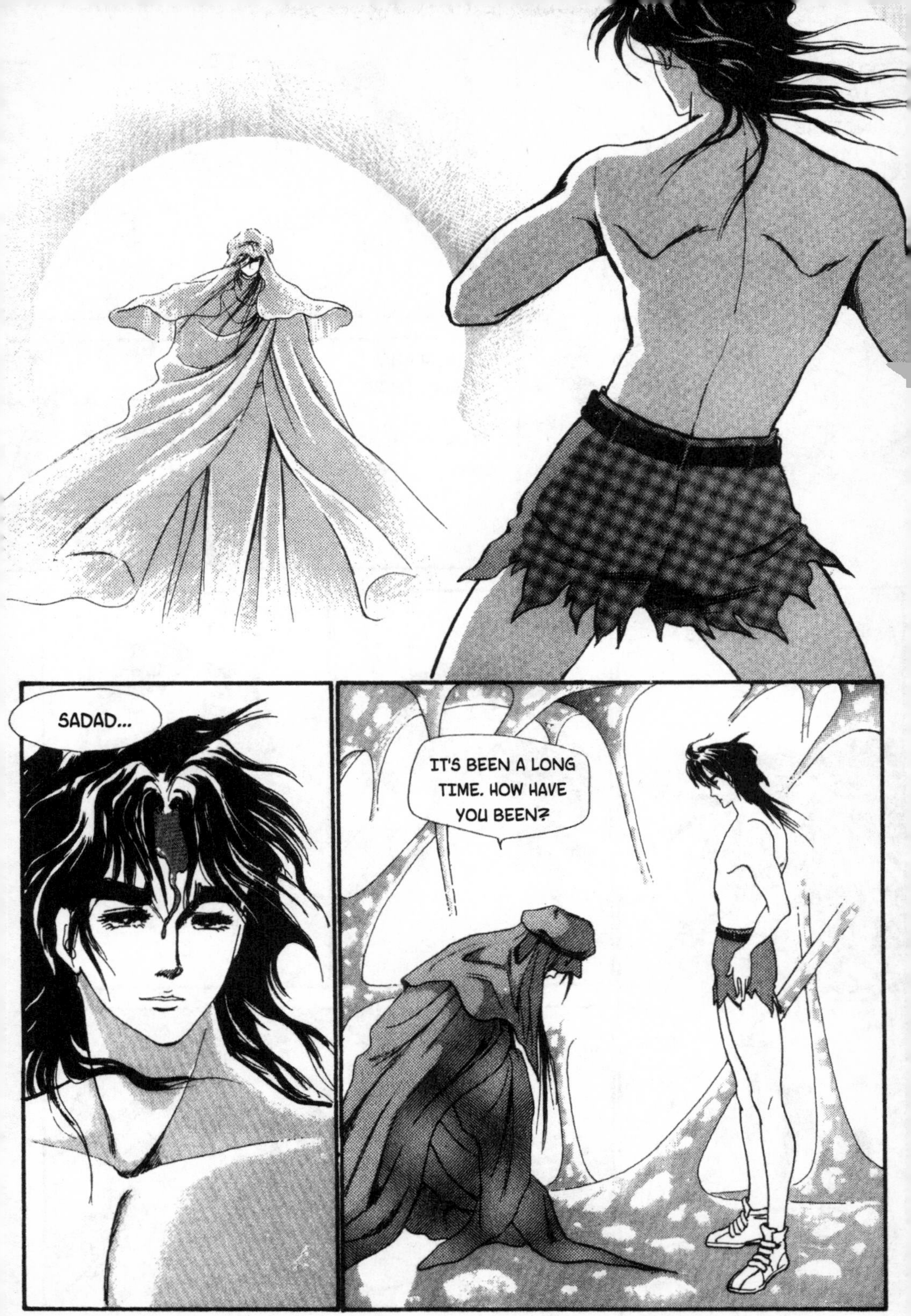

SADAD...
IT'S BEEN A LONG TIME. HOW HAVE YOU BEEN?

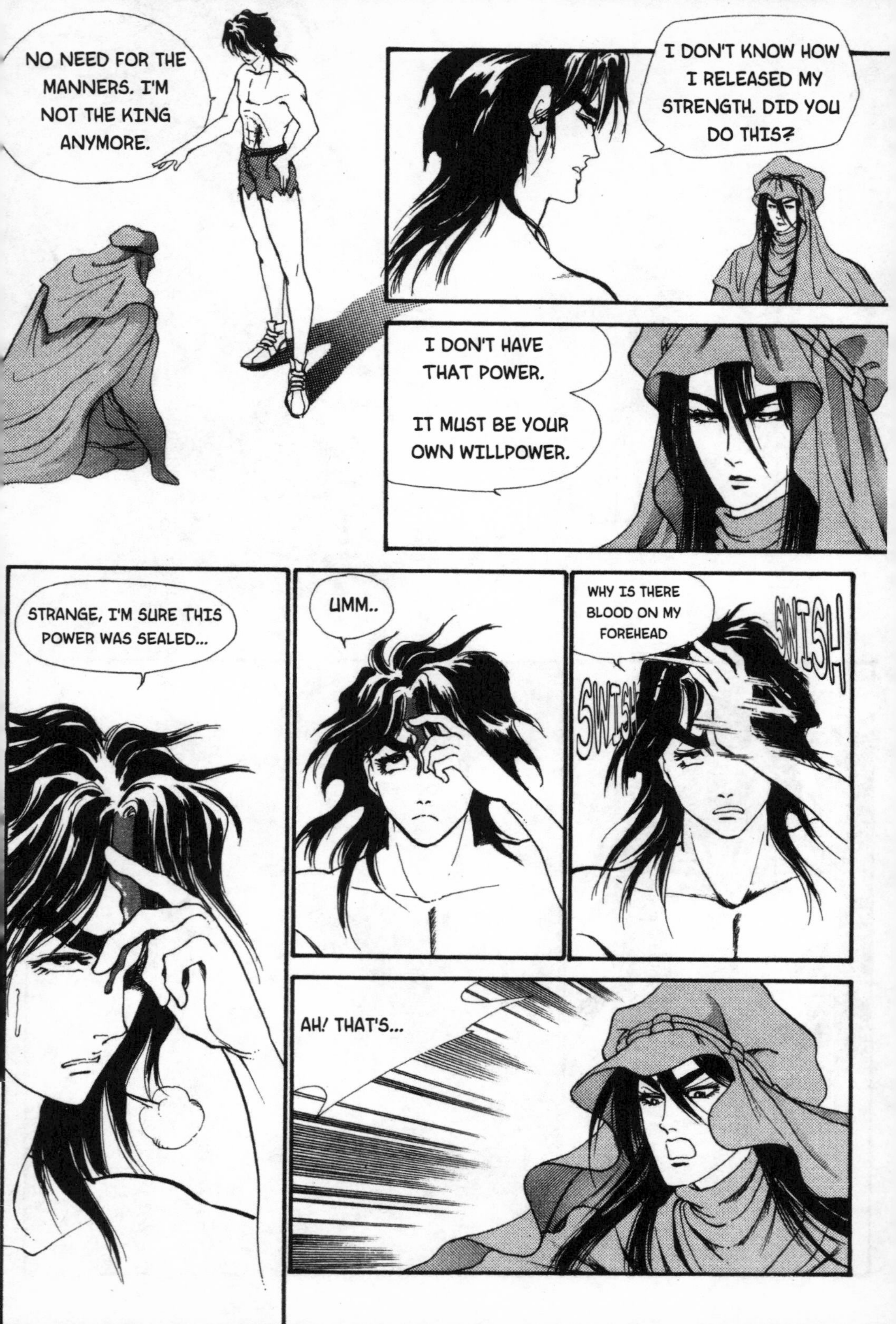
NO NEED FOR THE MANNERS. I'M NOT THE KING ANYMORE.
I DON'T KNOW HOW I RELEASED MY STRENGTH. DID YOU DO THIS?
I DON'T HAVE THAT POWER.
IT MUST BE YOUR OWN WILLPOWER.
STRANGE, I'M SURE THIS POWER WAS SEALED...
UMM..
WHY IS THERE BLOOD ON MY FOREHEAD
SWISH
SWISH
AH! THAT'S...

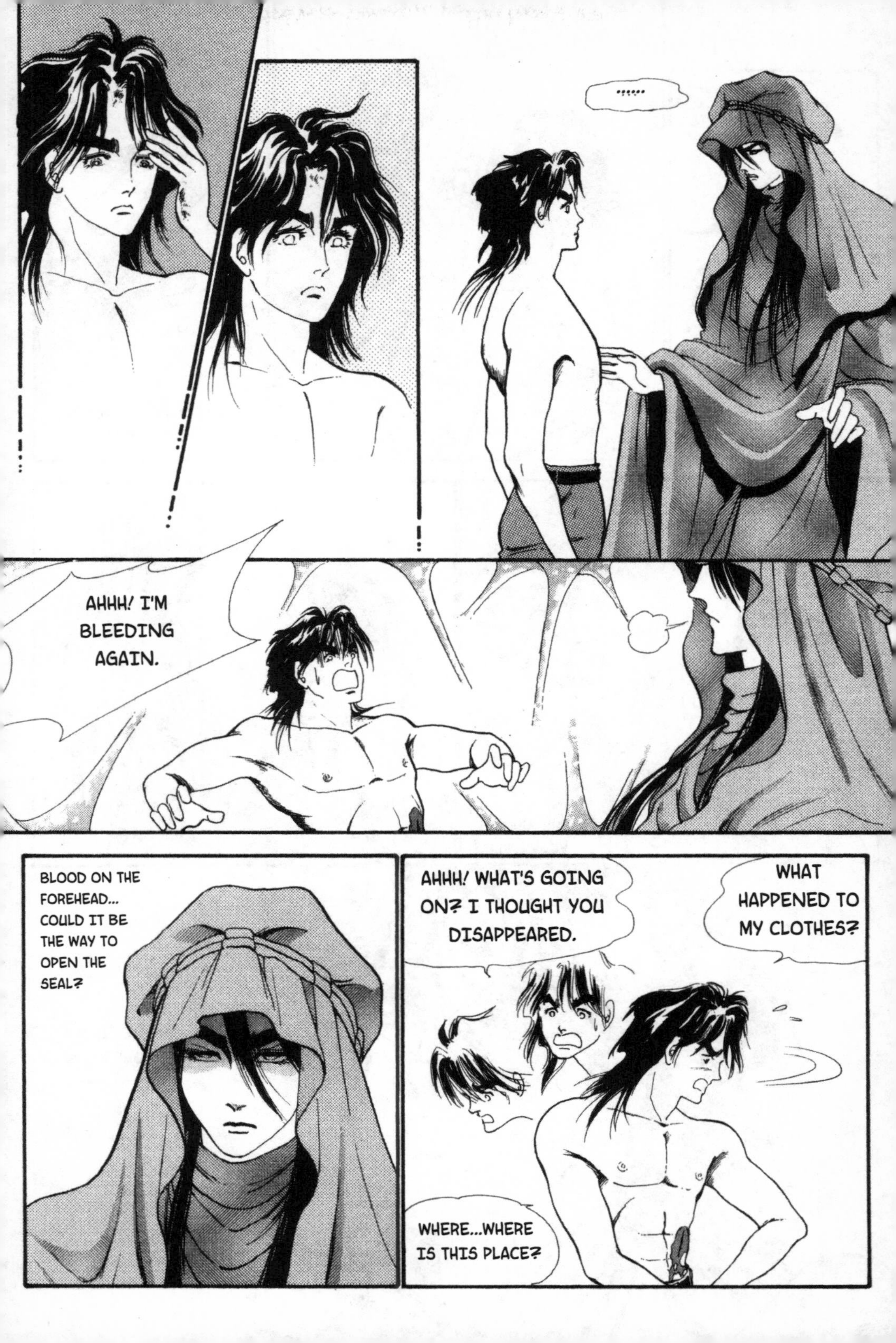
......
AHHH! I'M BLEEDING AGAIN.
BLOOD ON THE FOREHEAD... COULD IT BE THE WAY TO OPEN THE SEAL?
AHHH! WHAT'S GOING ON? I THOUGHT YOU DISAPPEARED.
WHAT HAPPENED TO MY CLOTHES?
WHERE...WHERE IS THIS PLACE?

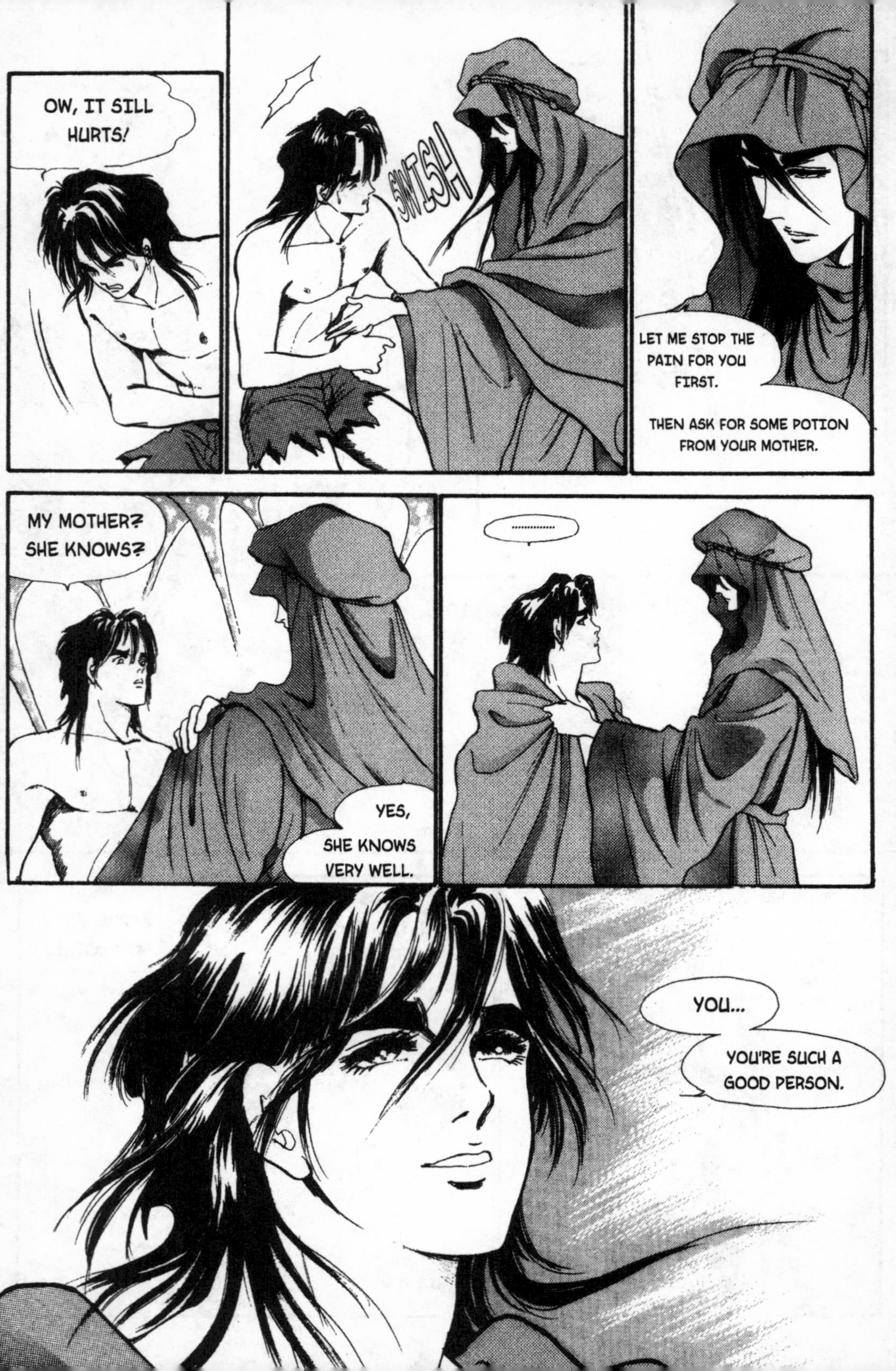
OW, IT SILL HURTS!
LET ME STOP THE PAIN FOR YOU FIRST.
THEN ASK FOR SOME POTION FROM YOUR MOTHER.
MY MOTHER? SHE KNOWS?
YES, SHE KNOWS VERY WELL.
....
YOU...
YOU'RE SUCH A GOOD PERSON.

DON'T GET SO EMOTIONAL BECAUSE OF A LITTLE FAVOR.

BUT...

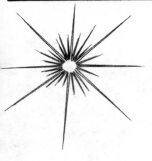

MMM... WHERE?

TIME TO OPEN THE GATE, AND YOU SHOULD GO HOME AS WELL.

YOUR HOUSE.

......

WHAT ABOUT YOU? AREN'T YOU COMING WITH ME?

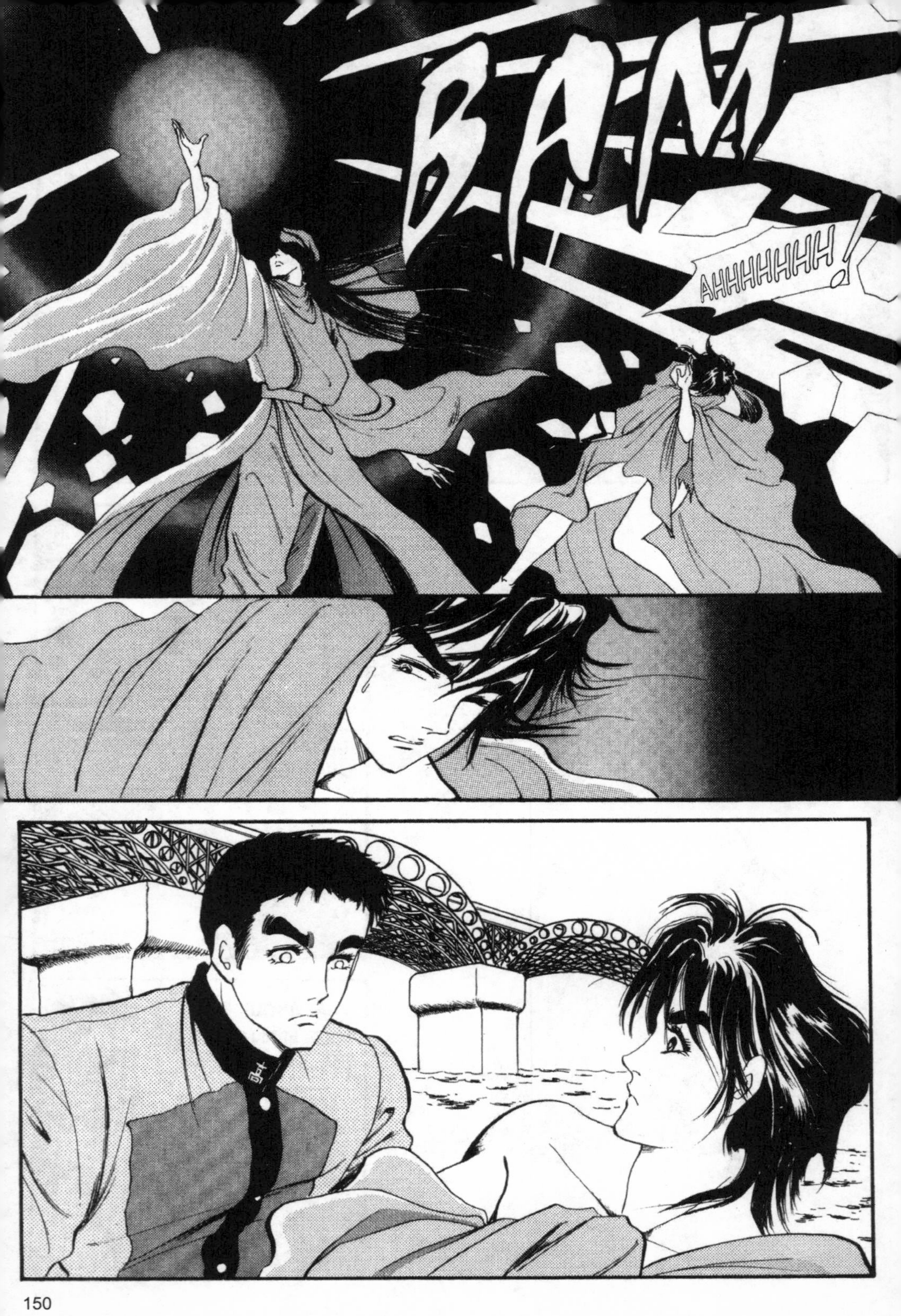
BAM
AHHHHHHH!

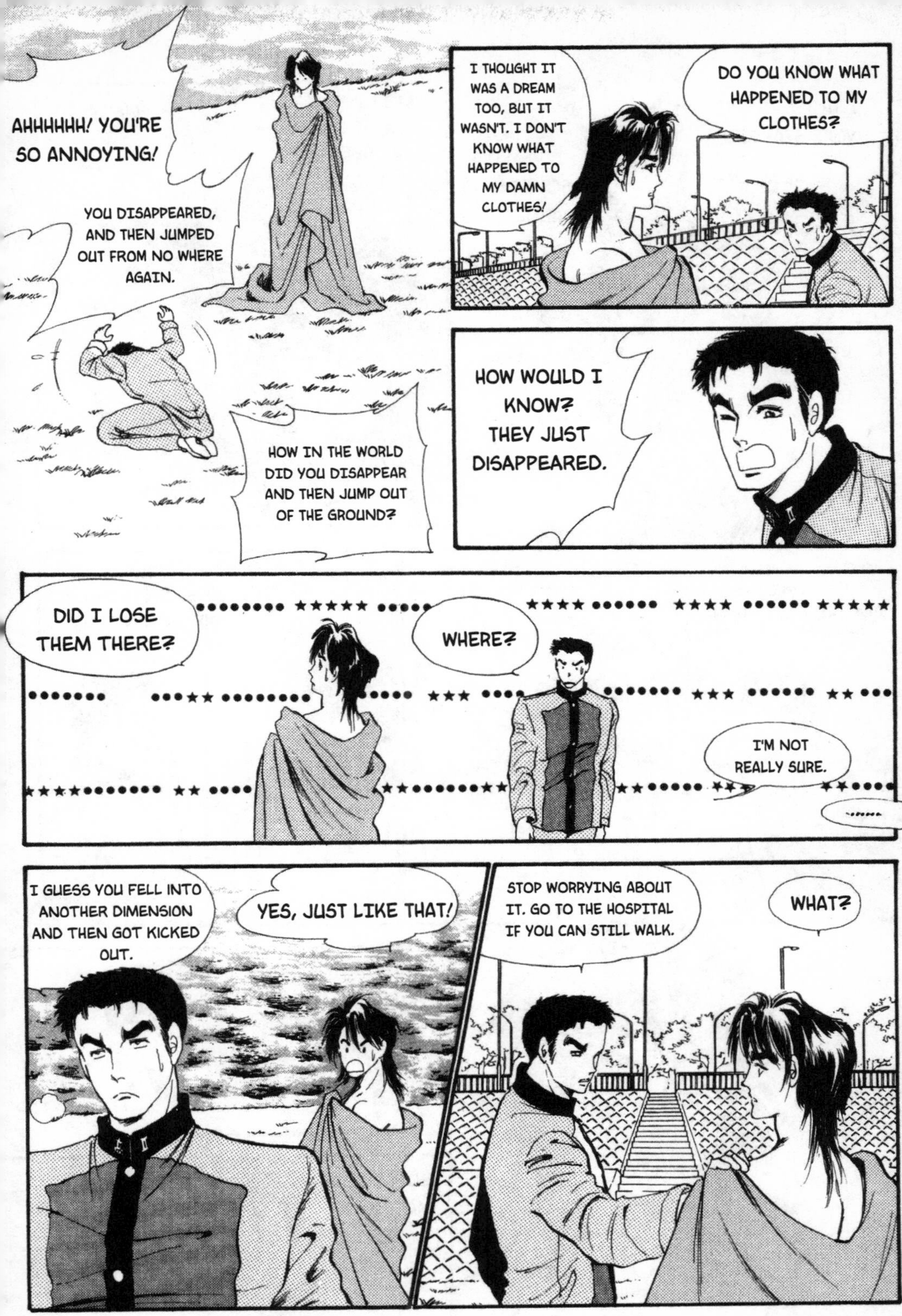
AHHHHHH! YOU'RE SO ANNOYING!
YOU DISAPPEARED, AND THEN JUMPED OUT FROM NO WHERE AGAIN.
HOW IN THE WORLD DID YOU DISAPPEAR AND THEN JUMP OUT OF THE GROUND?
I THOUGHT IT WAS A DREAM TOO, BUT IT WASN'T. I DON'T KNOW WHAT HAPPENED TO MY DAMN CLOTHES!
DO YOU KNOW WHAT HAPPENED TO MY CLOTHES?
HOW WOULD I KNOW? THEY JUST DISAPPEARED.
DID I LOSE THEM THERE?
WHERE?
I'M NOT REALLY SURE.
I GUESS YOU FELL INTO ANOTHER DIMENSION AND THEN GOT KICKED OUT.
YES, JUST LIKE THAT!
STOP WORRYING ABOUT IT. GO TO THE HOSPITAL IF YOU CAN STILL WALK.
WHAT?

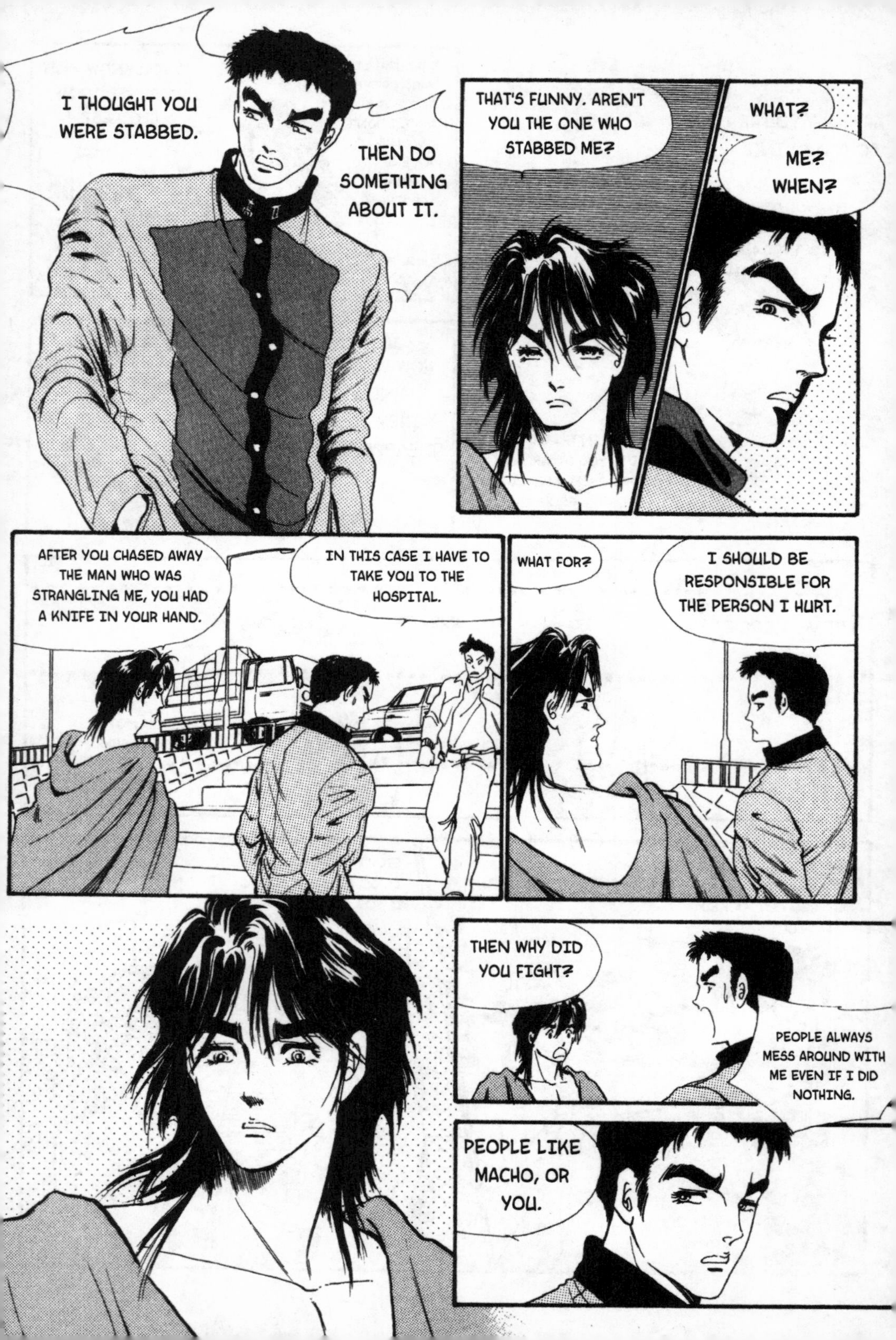
I THOUGHT YOU WERE STABBED.
THEN DO SOMETHING ABOUT IT.
THAT'S FUNNY. AREN'T YOU THE ONE WHO STABBED ME?
WHAT?
ME? WHEN?
AFTER YOU CHASED AWAY THE MAN WHO WAS STRANGLING ME, YOU HAD A KNIFE IN YOUR HAND.
IN THIS CASE I HAVE TO TAKE YOU TO THE HOSPITAL.
WHAT FOR?
I SHOULD BE RESPONSIBLE FOR THE PERSON I HURT.
THEN WHY DID YOU FIGHT?
PEOPLE ALWAYS MESS AROUND WITH ME EVEN IF I DID NOTHING.
PEOPLE LIKE MACHO, OR YOU.

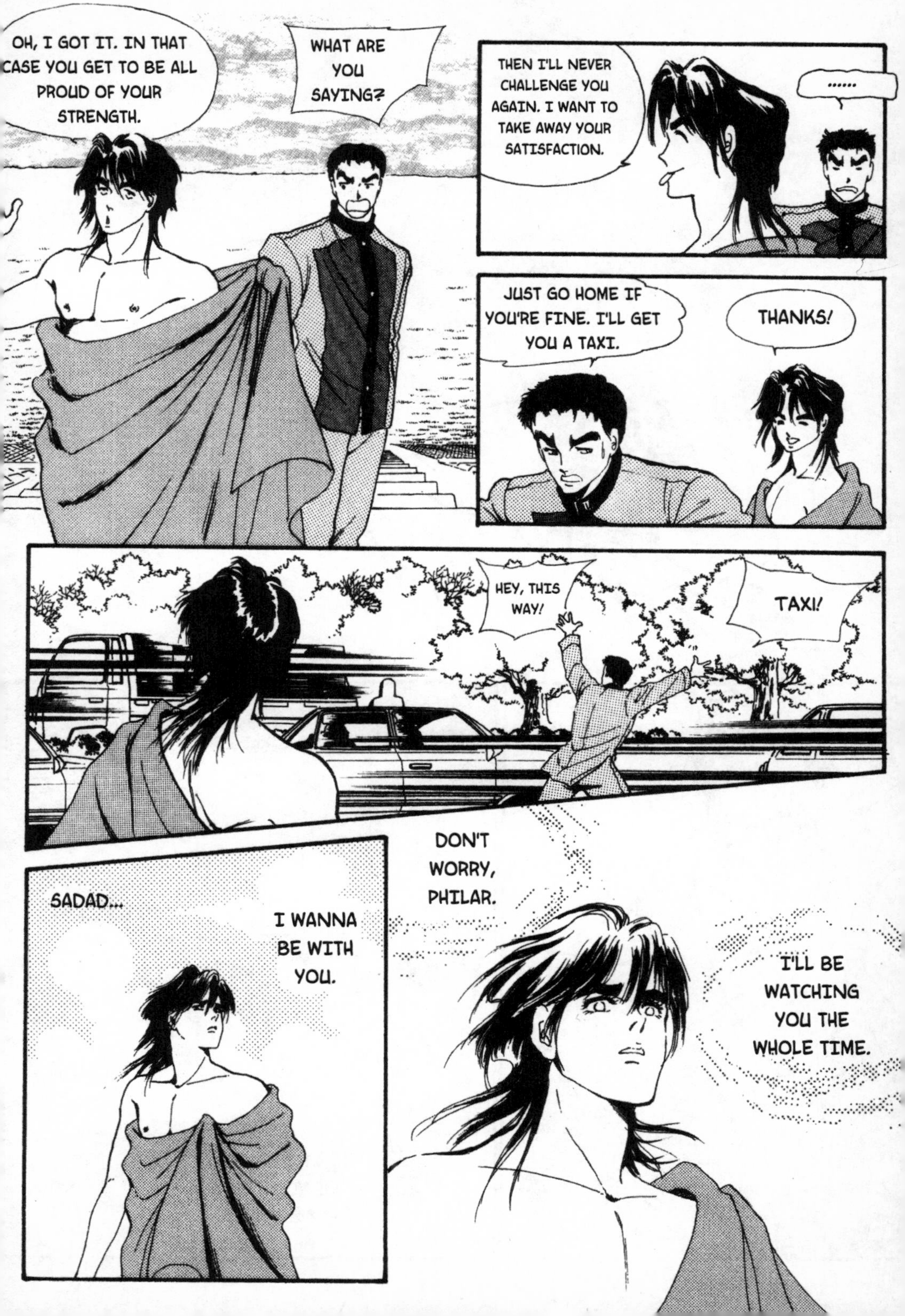
OH, I GOT IT. IN THAT CASE YOU GET TO BE ALL PROUD OF YOUR STRENGTH.
WHAT ARE YOU SAYING?
THEN I'LL NEVER CHALLENGE YOU AGAIN. I WANT TO TAKE AWAY YOUR SATISFACTION.
......
JUST GO HOME IF YOU'RE FINE. I'LL GET YOU A TAXI.
THANKS!
HEY, THIS WAY!
TAXI!
SADAD...
I WANNA BE WITH YOU.
DON'T WORRY, PHILAR.
I'LL BE WATCHING YOU THE WHOLE TIME.

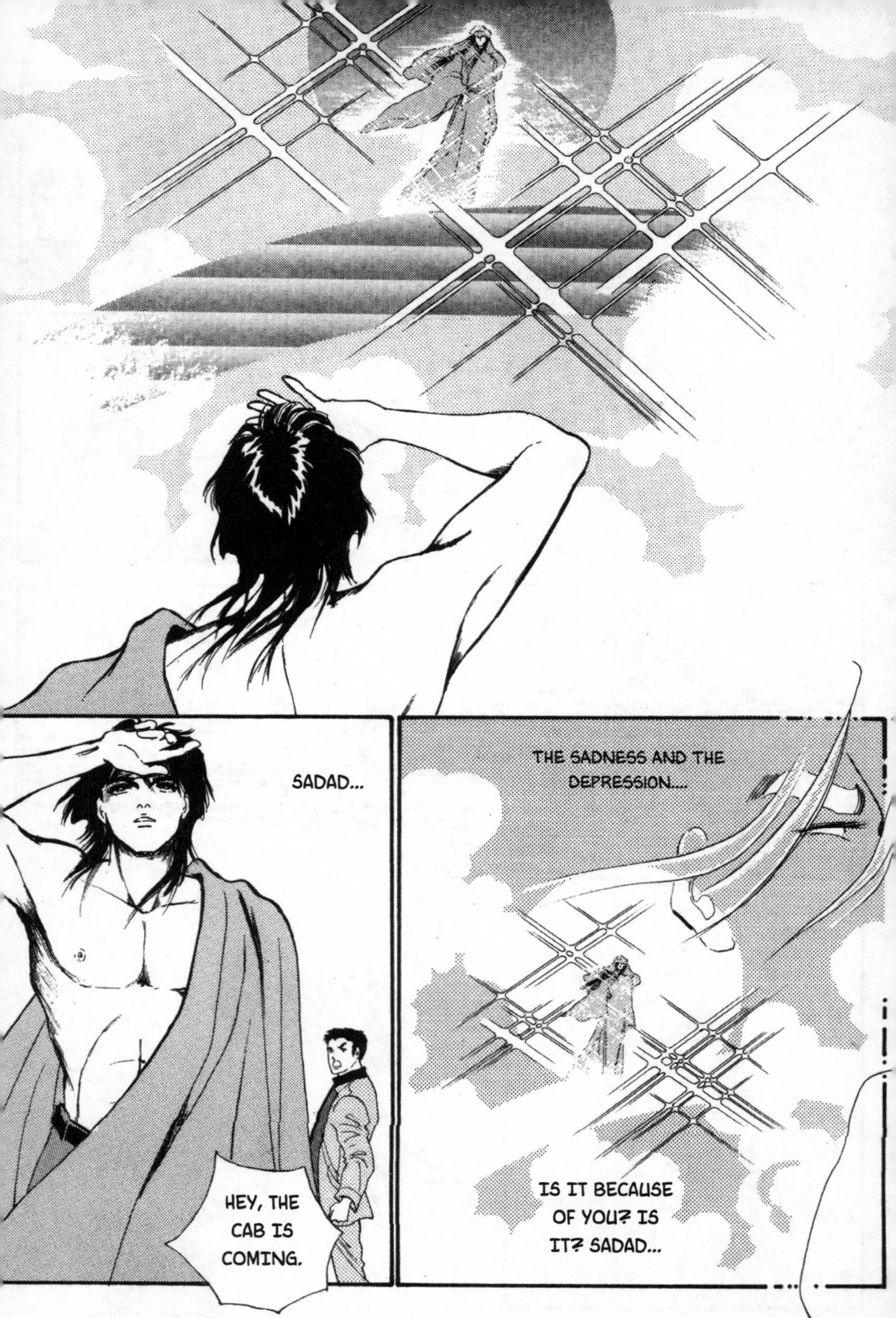
SADAD...
HEY, THE CAB IS COMING.
THE SADNESS AND THE DEPRESSION....
IS IT BECAUSE OF YOU? IS IT? SADAD...

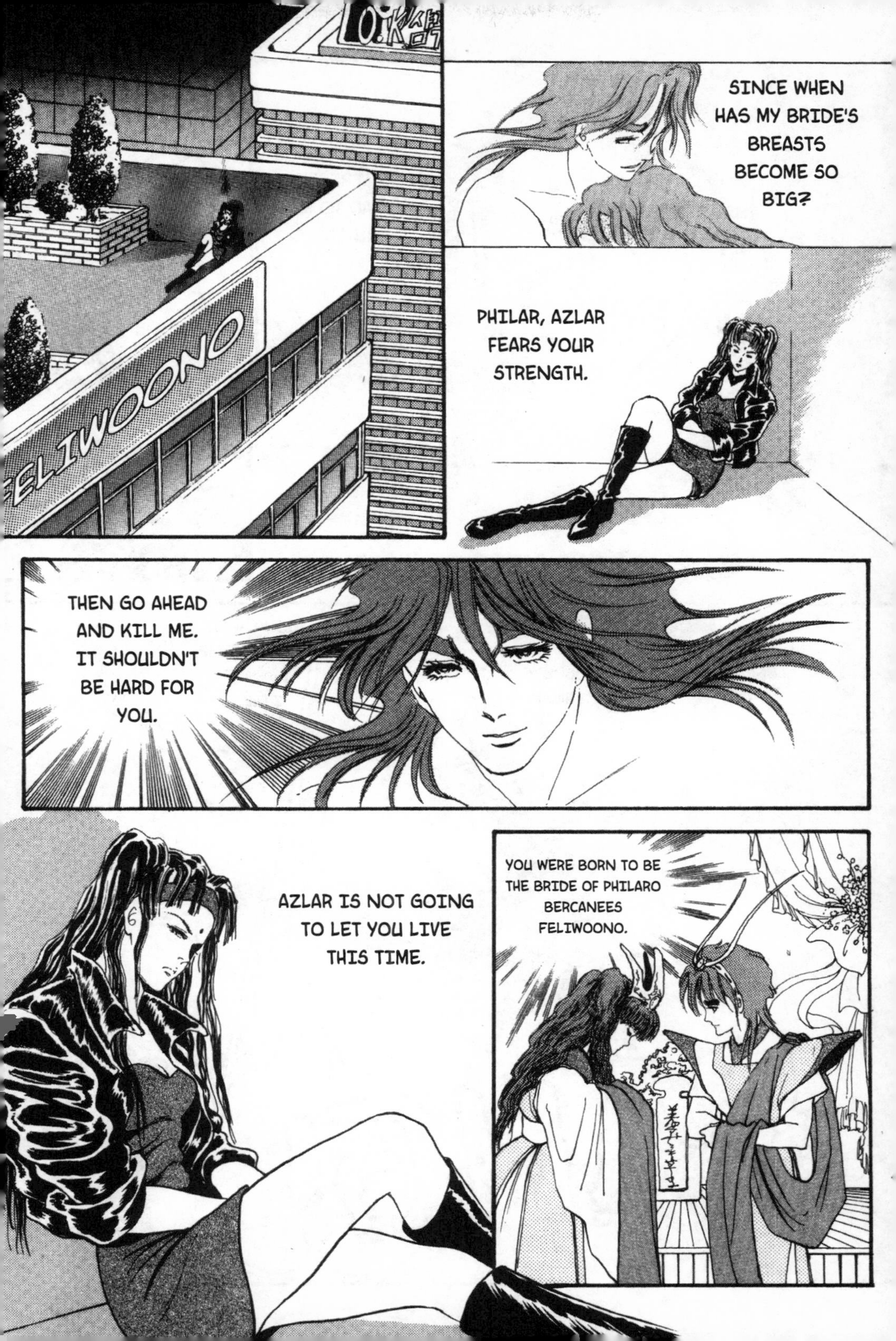
FELIWOONO
SINCE WHEN HAS MY BRIDE'S BREASTS BECOME SO BIG?
PHILAR, AZLAR FEARS YOUR STRENGTH.
THEN GO AHEAD AND KILL ME. IT SHOULDN'T BE HARD FOR YOU.
AZLAR IS NOT GOING TO LET YOU LIVE THIS TIME.
YOU WERE BORN TO BE THE BRIDE OF PHILARO BERCANEES FELIWOONO.

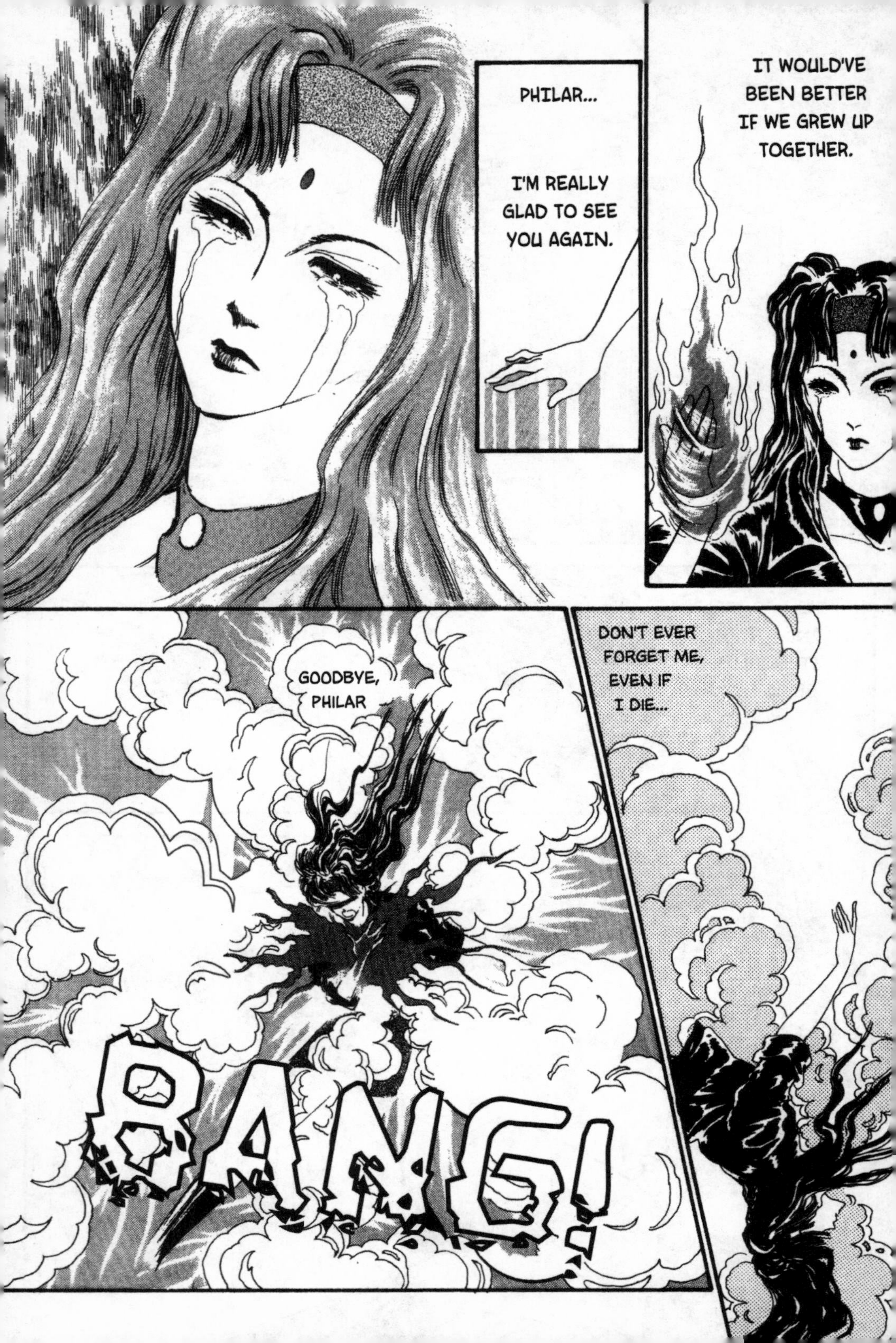
PHILAR...
I'M REALLY GLAD TO SEE YOU AGAIN.
IT WOULD'VE BEEN BETTER IF WE GREW UP TOGETHER.
GOODBYE, PHILAR
BANG!
DON'T EVER FORGET ME, EVEN IF I DIE...

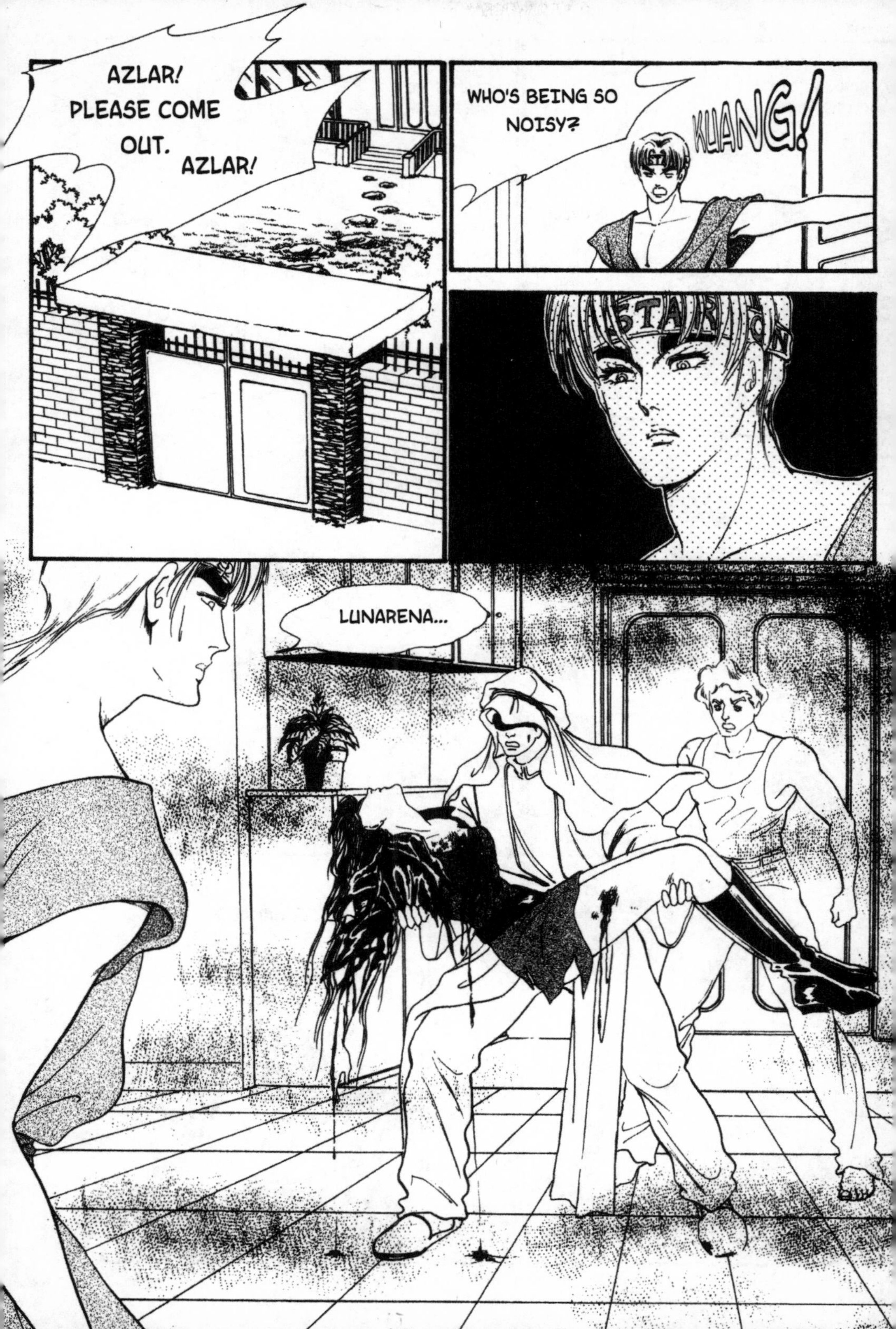
AZLAR! PLEASE COME OUT. AZLAR!
WHO'S BEING SO NOISY?
KUANG!
STAR ON
LUNARENA...

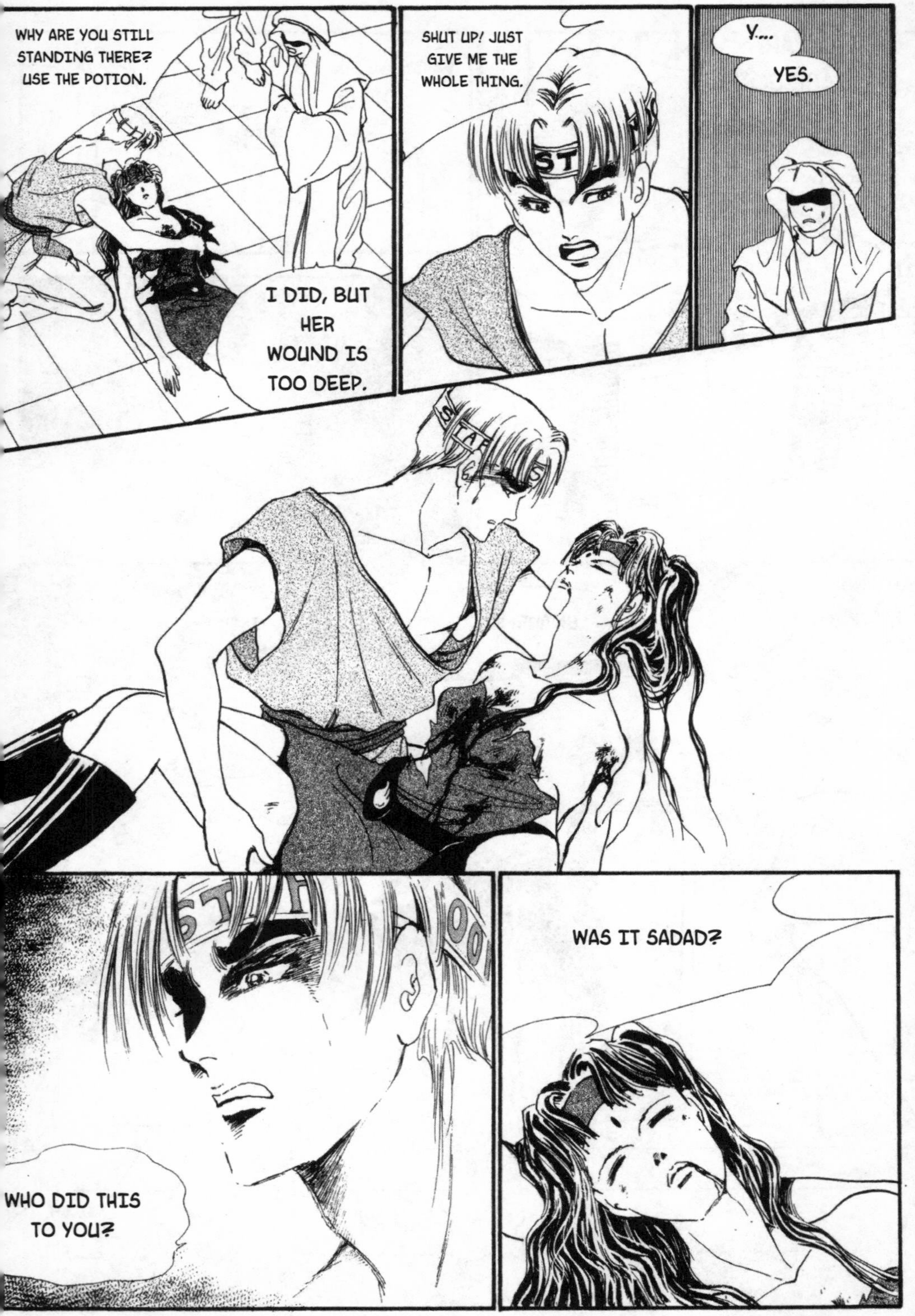
WHY ARE YOU STILL STANDING THERE? USE THE POTION.
I DID, BUT HER WOUND IS TOO DEEP.
SHUT UP! JUST GIVE ME THE WHOLE THING.
Y...
YES.
WHO DID THIS TO YOU?
WAS IT SADAD?

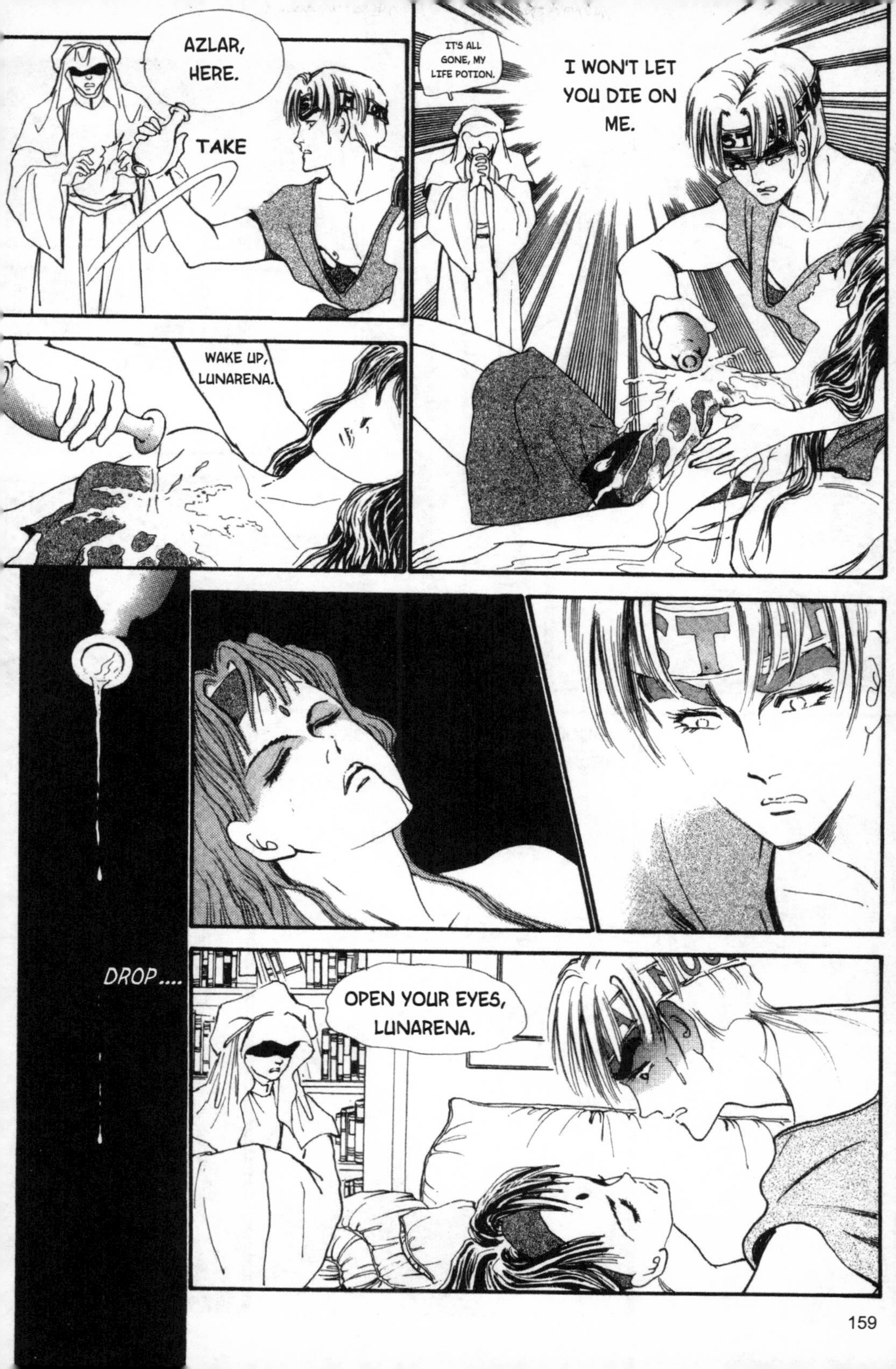
AZLAR, HERE.
TAKE
IT'S ALL GONE, MY LIFE POTION.
I WON'T LET YOU DIE ON ME.
WAKE UP, LUNARENA.
DROP....
OPEN YOUR EYES, LUNARENA.

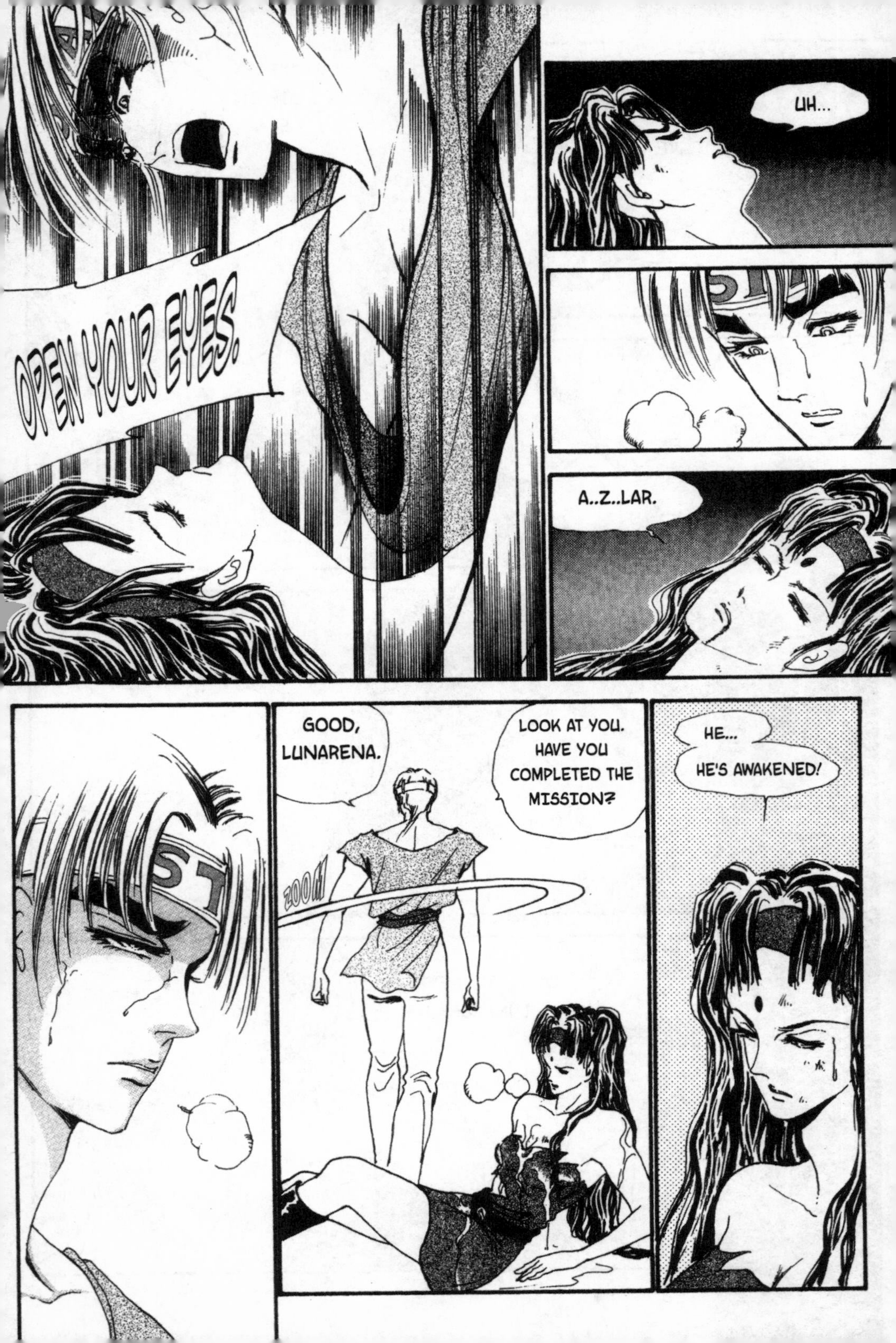
OPEN YOUR EYES.
UH...
A..Z..LAR.
GOOD, LUNARENA.
ZOOM
LOOK AT YOU. HAVE YOU COMPLETED THE MISSION?
HE...
HE'S AWAKENED!

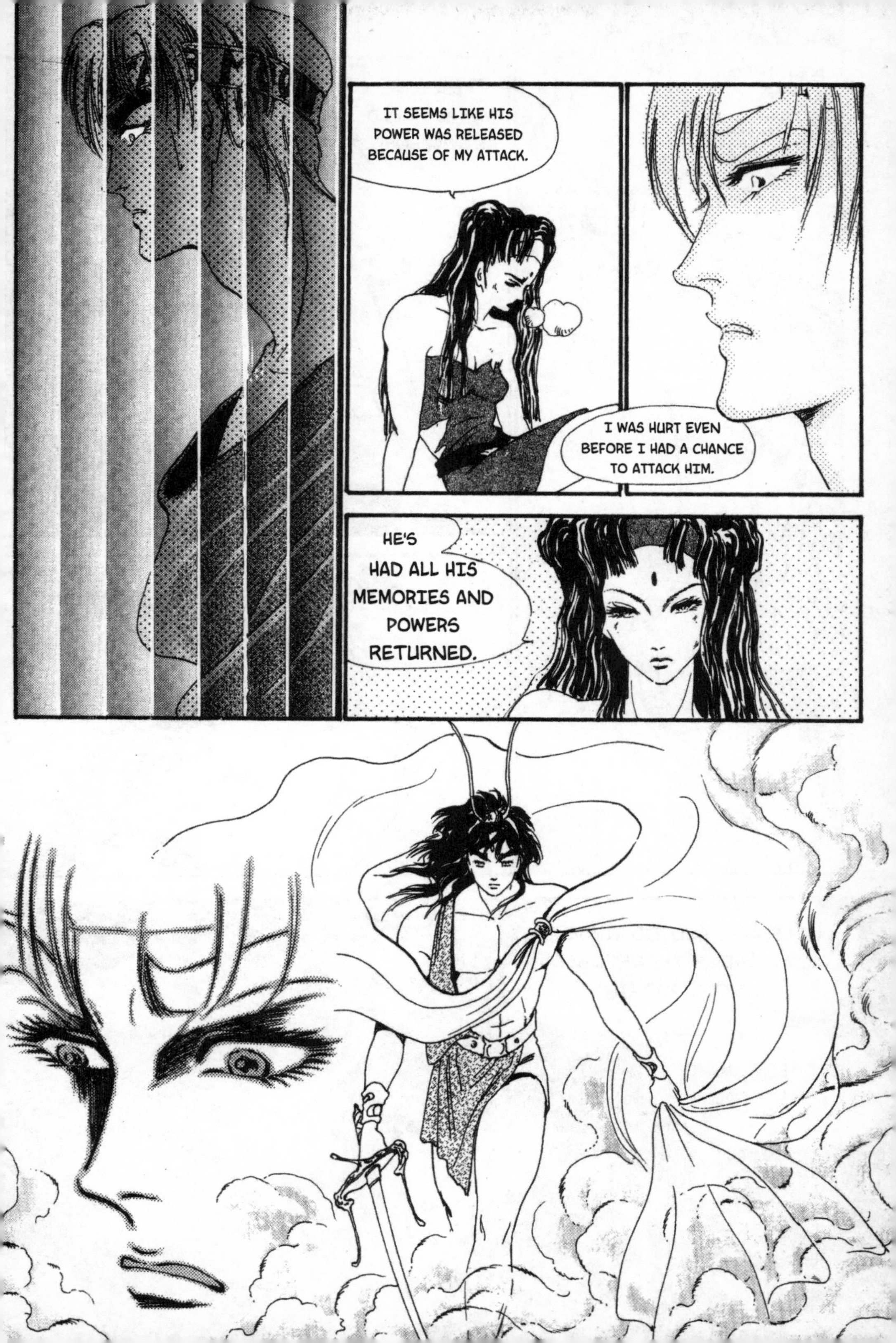
IT SEEMS LIKE HIS POWER WAS RELEASED BECAUSE OF MY ATTACK.
I WAS HURT EVEN BEFORE I HAD A CHANCE TO ATTACK HIM.
HE'S HAD ALL HIS MEMORIES AND POWERS RETURNED.

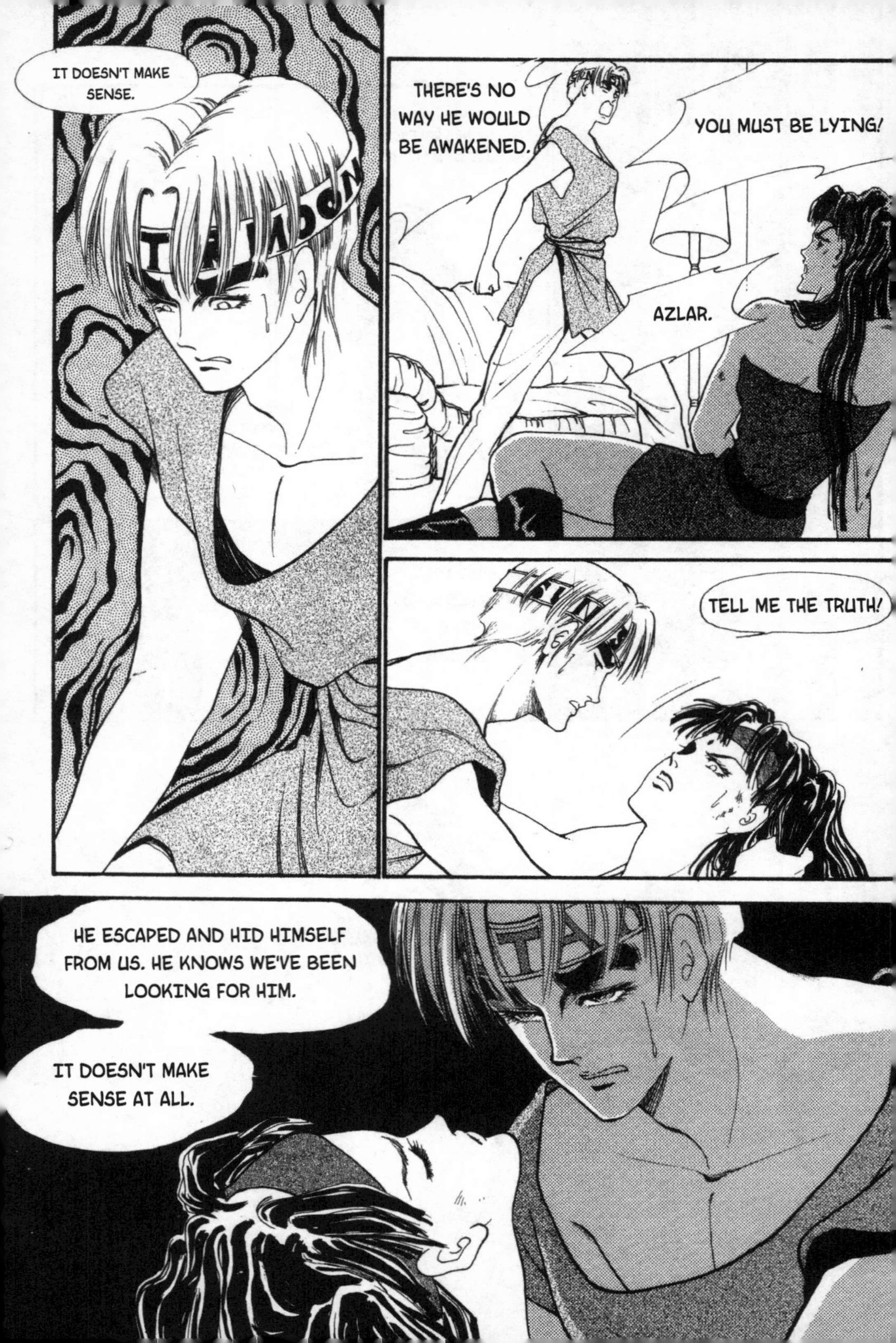
IT DOESN'T MAKE SENSE.
THERE'S NO WAY HE WOULD BE AWAKENED.
YOU MUST BE LYING!
AZLAR.
TELL ME THE TRUTH!
HE ESCAPED AND HID HIMSELF FROM US. HE KNOWS WE'VE BEEN LOOKING FOR HIM.
IT DOESN'T MAKE SENSE AT ALL.

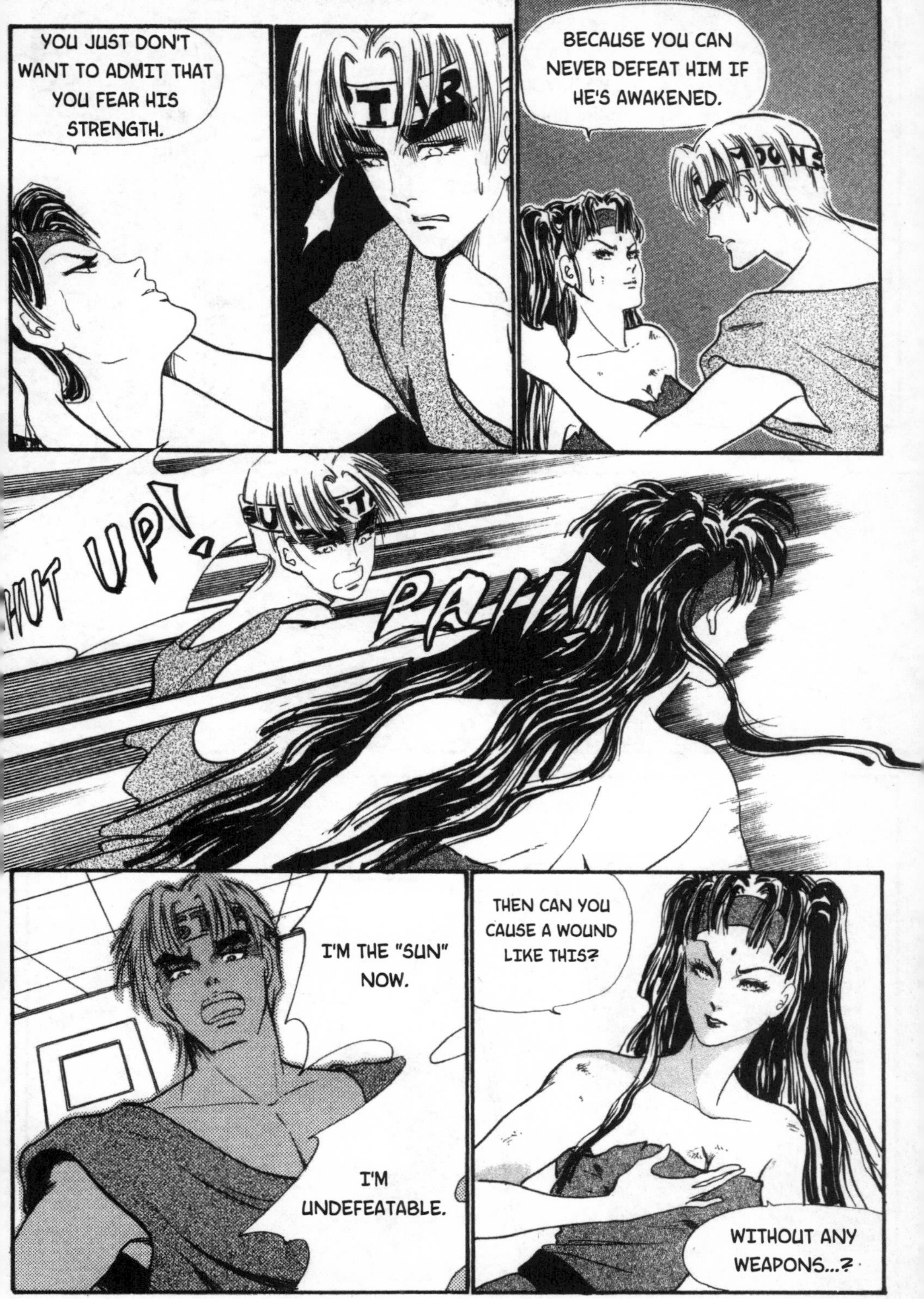

YOU JUST DON'T WANT TO ADMIT THAT YOU FEAR HIS STRENGTH.
BECAUSE YOU CAN NEVER DEFEAT HIM IF HE'S AWAKENED.
SHUT UP!
PAH!
I'M THE "SUN" NOW.
I'M UNDEFEATABLE.
THEN CAN YOU CAUSE A WOUND LIKE THIS?
WITHOUT ANY WEAPONS...?

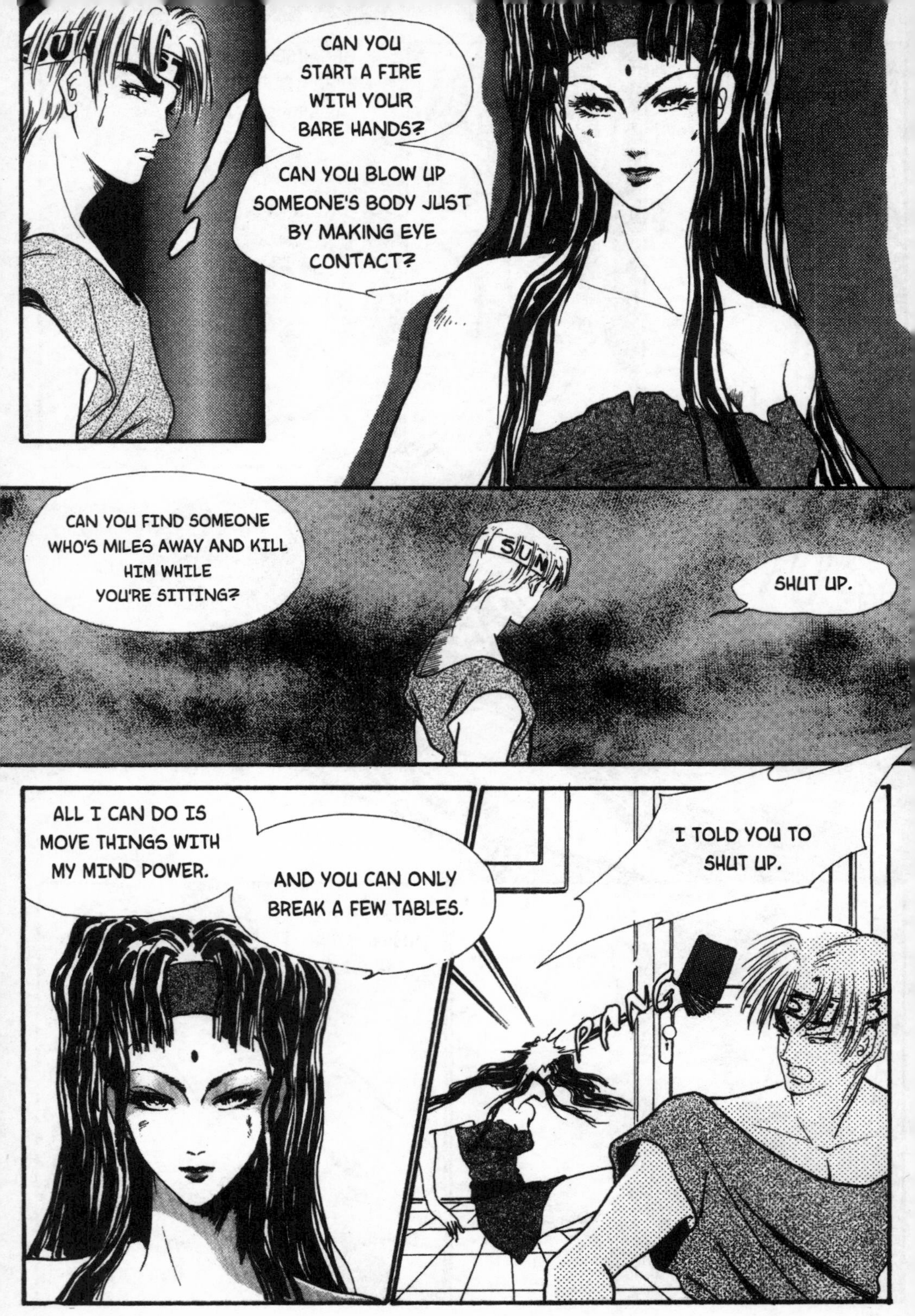
CAN YOU START A FIRE WITH YOUR BARE HANDS?
CAN YOU BLOW UP SOMEONE'S BODY JUST BY MAKING EYE CONTACT?
CAN YOU FIND SOMEONE WHO'S MILES AWAY AND KILL HIM WHILE YOU'RE SITTING?
SHUT UP.
ALL I CAN DO IS MOVE THINGS WITH MY MIND POWER.
AND YOU CAN ONLY BREAK A FEW TABLES.
I TOLD YOU TO SHUT UP.
PA-NG
SUN

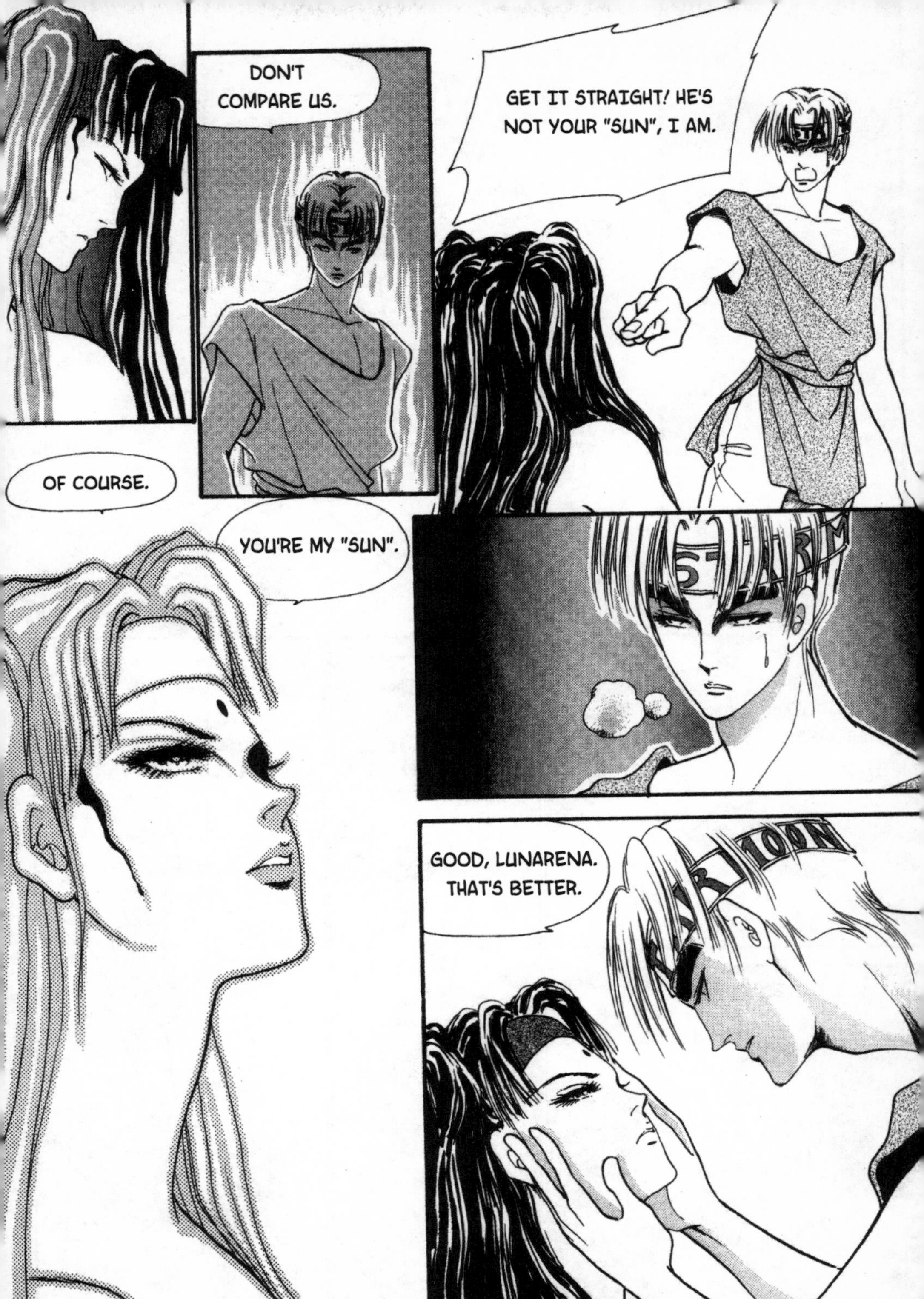

DON'T COMPARE US.
GET IT STRAIGHT! HE'S NOT YOUR "SUN", I AM.
OF COURSE.
YOU'RE MY "SUN".
GOOD, LUNARENA. THAT'S BETTER.

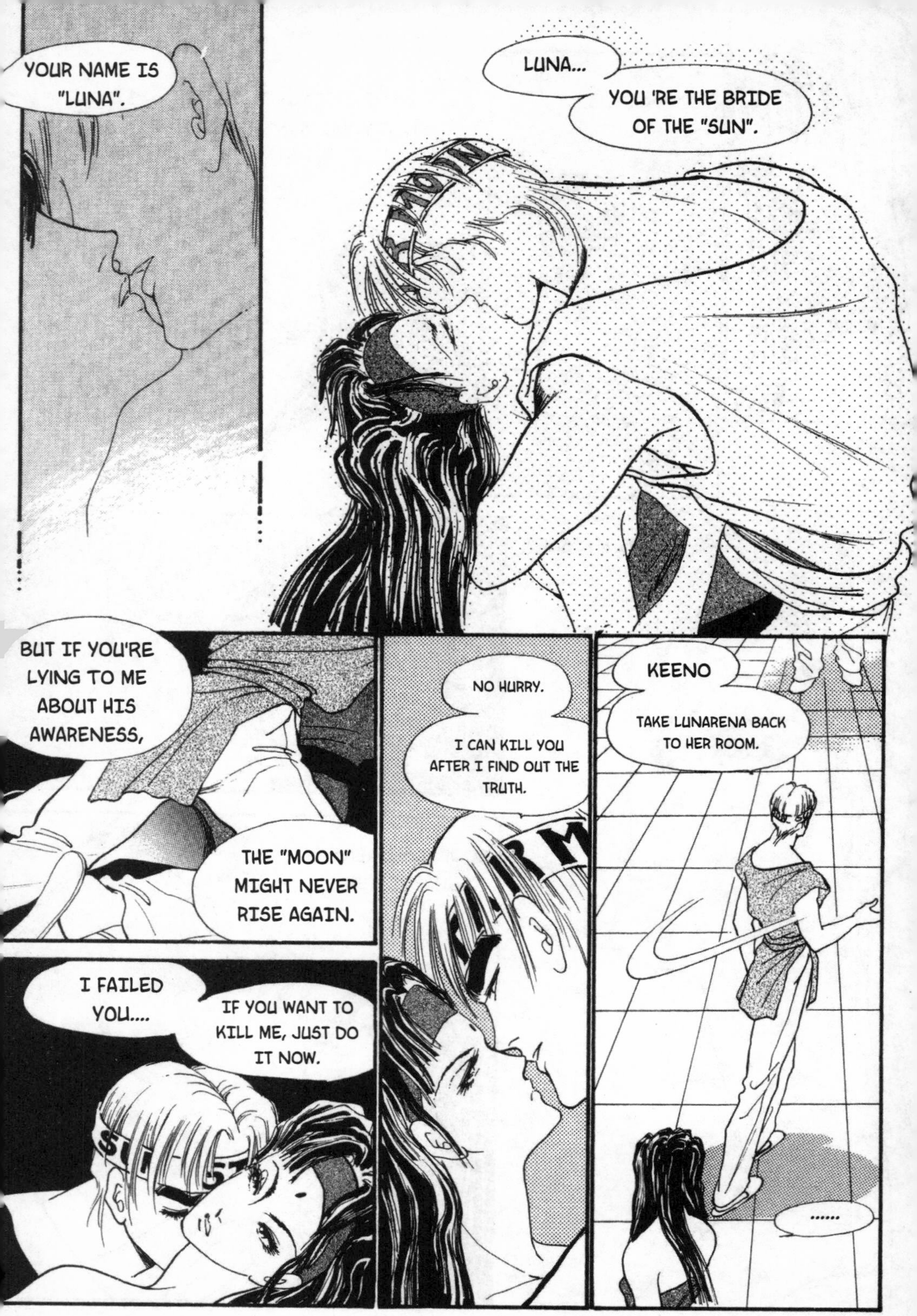
YOUR NAME IS "LUNA".
LUNA...
YOU 'RE THE BRIDE OF THE "SUN".
MOON
BUT IF YOU'RE LYING TO ME ABOUT HIS AWARENESS,
THE "MOON" MIGHT NEVER RISE AGAIN.
NO HURRY.
I CAN KILL YOU AFTER I FIND OUT THE TRUTH.
KEENO
TAKE LUNARENA BACK TO HER ROOM.
I FAILED YOU....
IF YOU WANT TO KILL ME, JUST DO IT NOW.
......

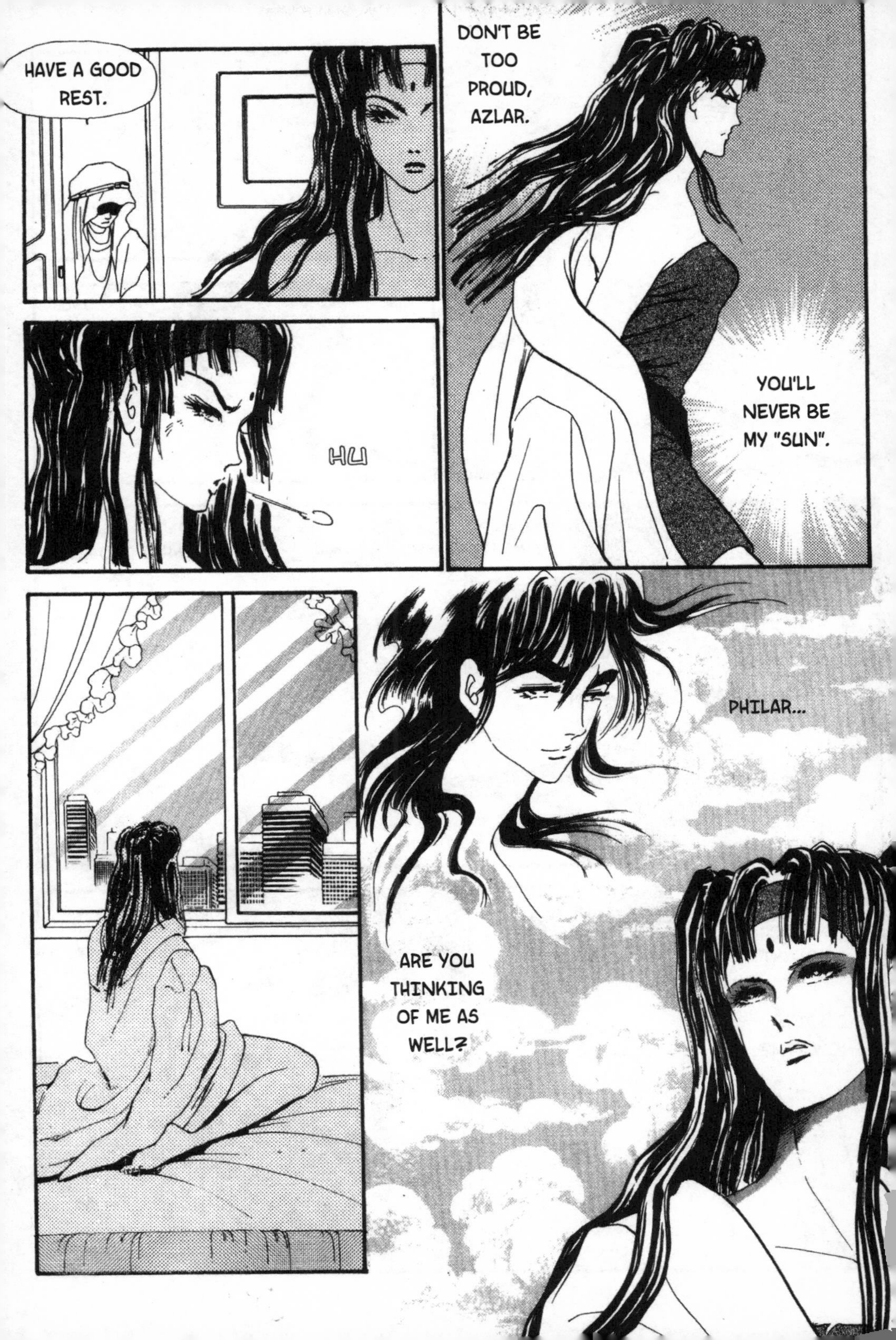
HAVE A GOOD REST.
DON'T BE TOO PROUD, AZLAR.
HU
YOU'LL NEVER BE MY "SUN".
PHILAR...
ARE YOU THINKING OF ME AS WELL?

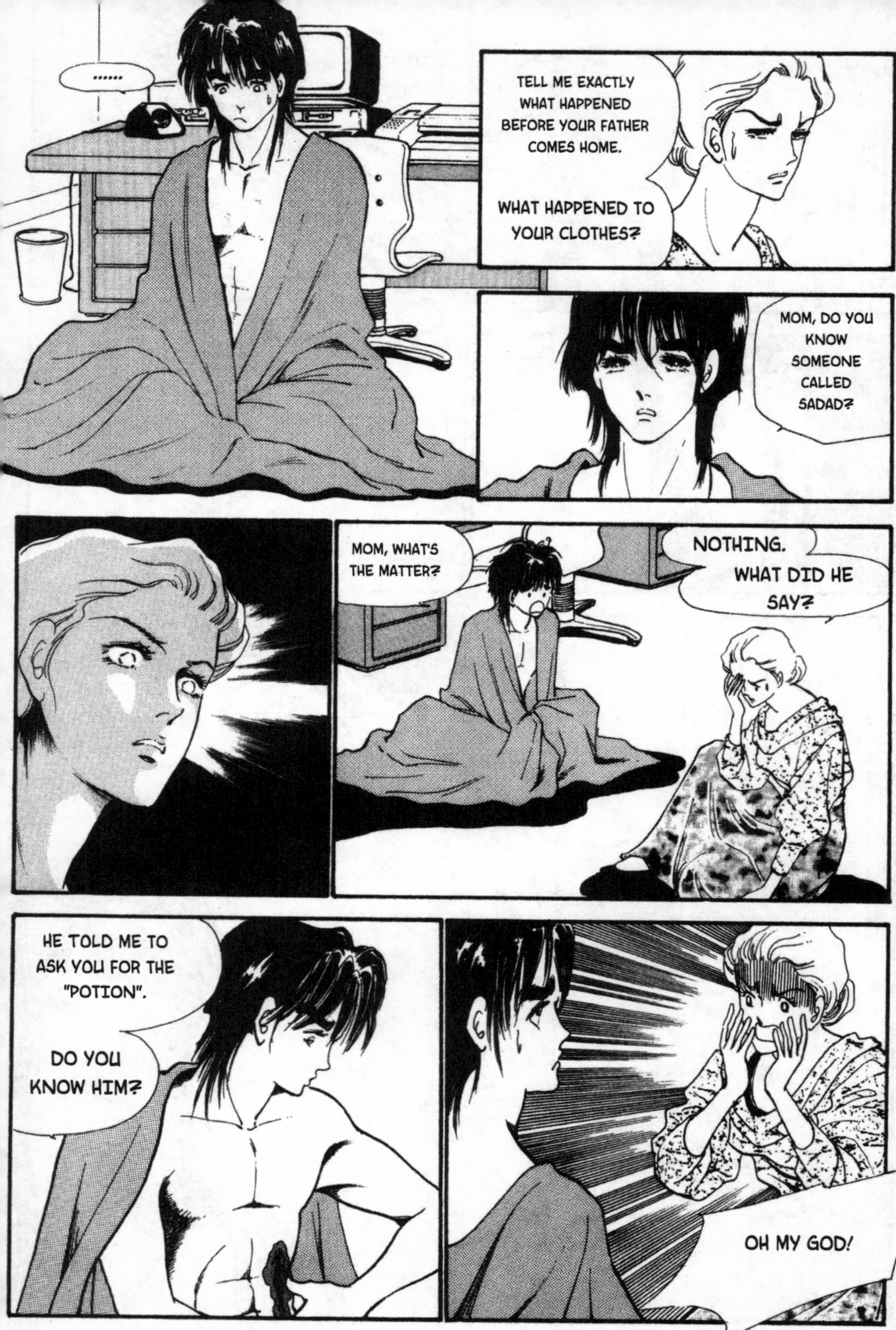
......
TELL ME EXACTLY WHAT HAPPENED BEFORE YOUR FATHER COMES HOME.
WHAT HAPPENED TO YOUR CLOTHES?
MOM, DO YOU KNOW SOMEONE CALLED SADAD?
MOM, WHAT'S THE MATTER?
NOTHING.
WHAT DID HE SAY?
HE TOLD ME TO ASK YOU FOR THE "POTION".
DO YOU KNOW HIM?
OH MY GOD!

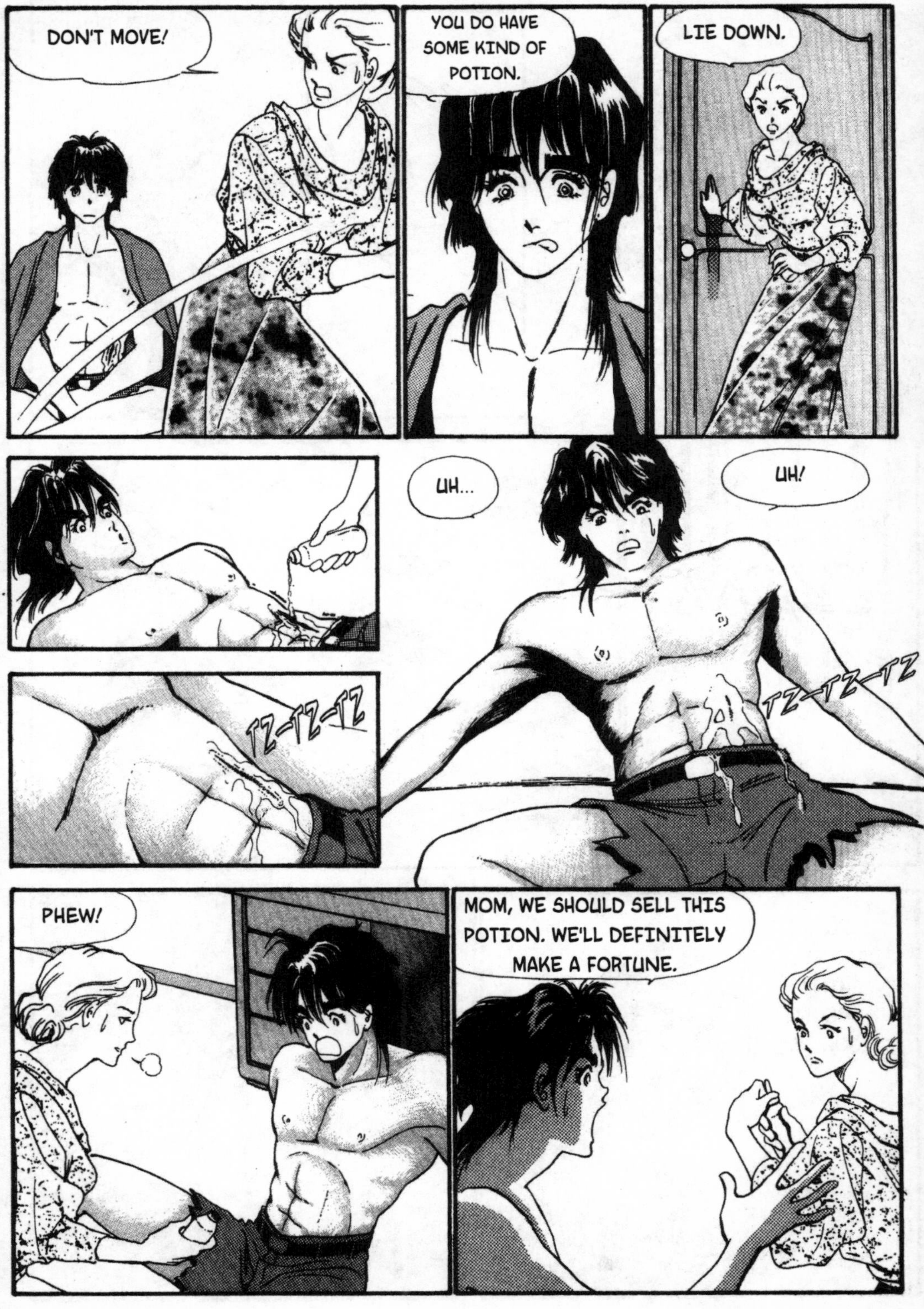
DON'T MOVE!
YOU DO HAVE SOME KIND OF POTION.
LIE DOWN.
UH...
UH!
TZ-TZ-TZ
TZ-TZ-TZ
PHEW!
MOM, WE SHOULD SELL THIS POTION. WE'LL DEFINITELY MAKE A FORTUNE.

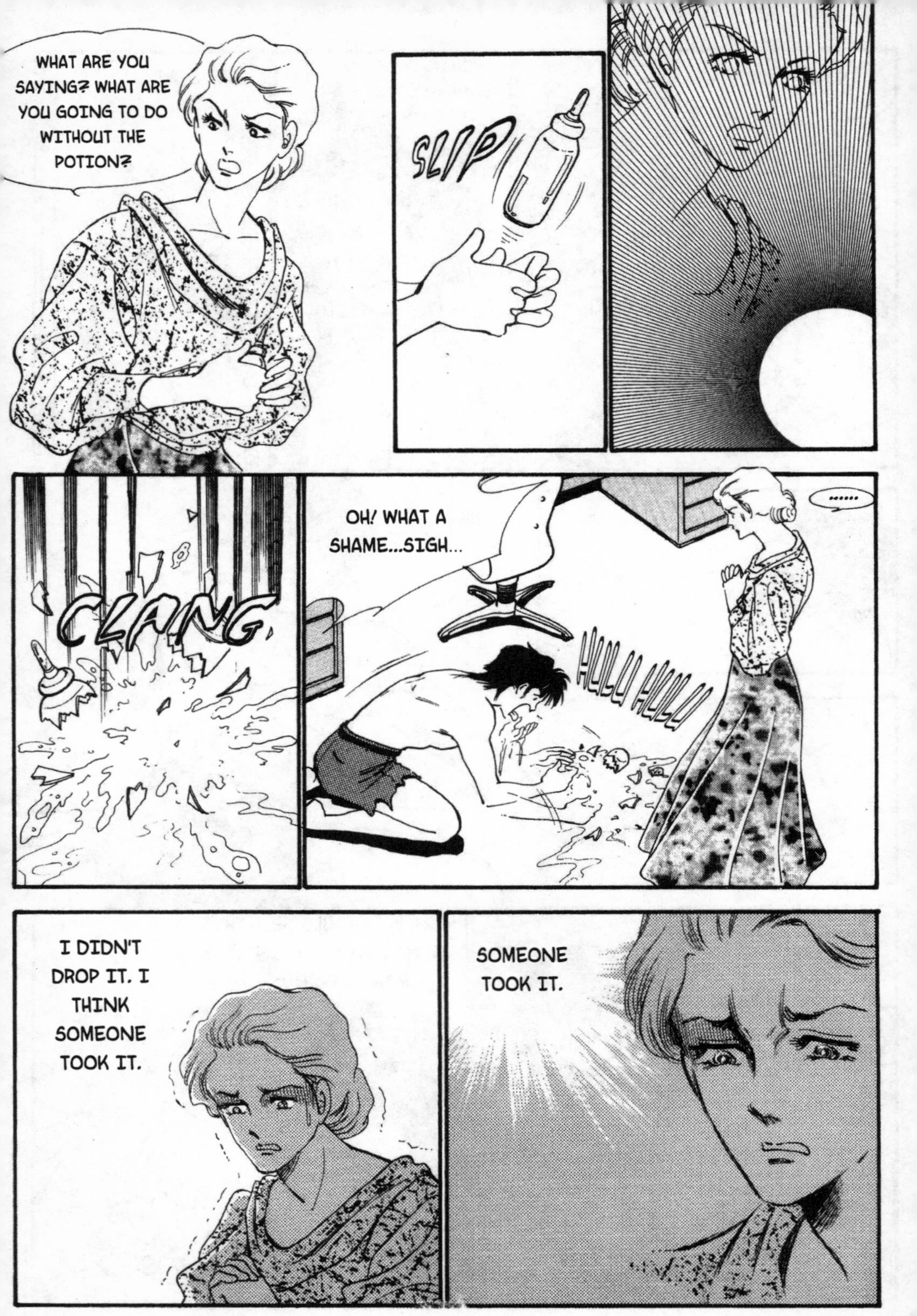
WHAT ARE YOU SAYING? WHAT ARE YOU GOING TO DO WITHOUT THE POTION?
SLIP
CLANG
OH! WHAT A SHAME...SIGH...
HULU HULU
......
I DIDN'T DROP IT. I THINK SOMEONE TOOK IT.
SOMEONE TOOK IT.

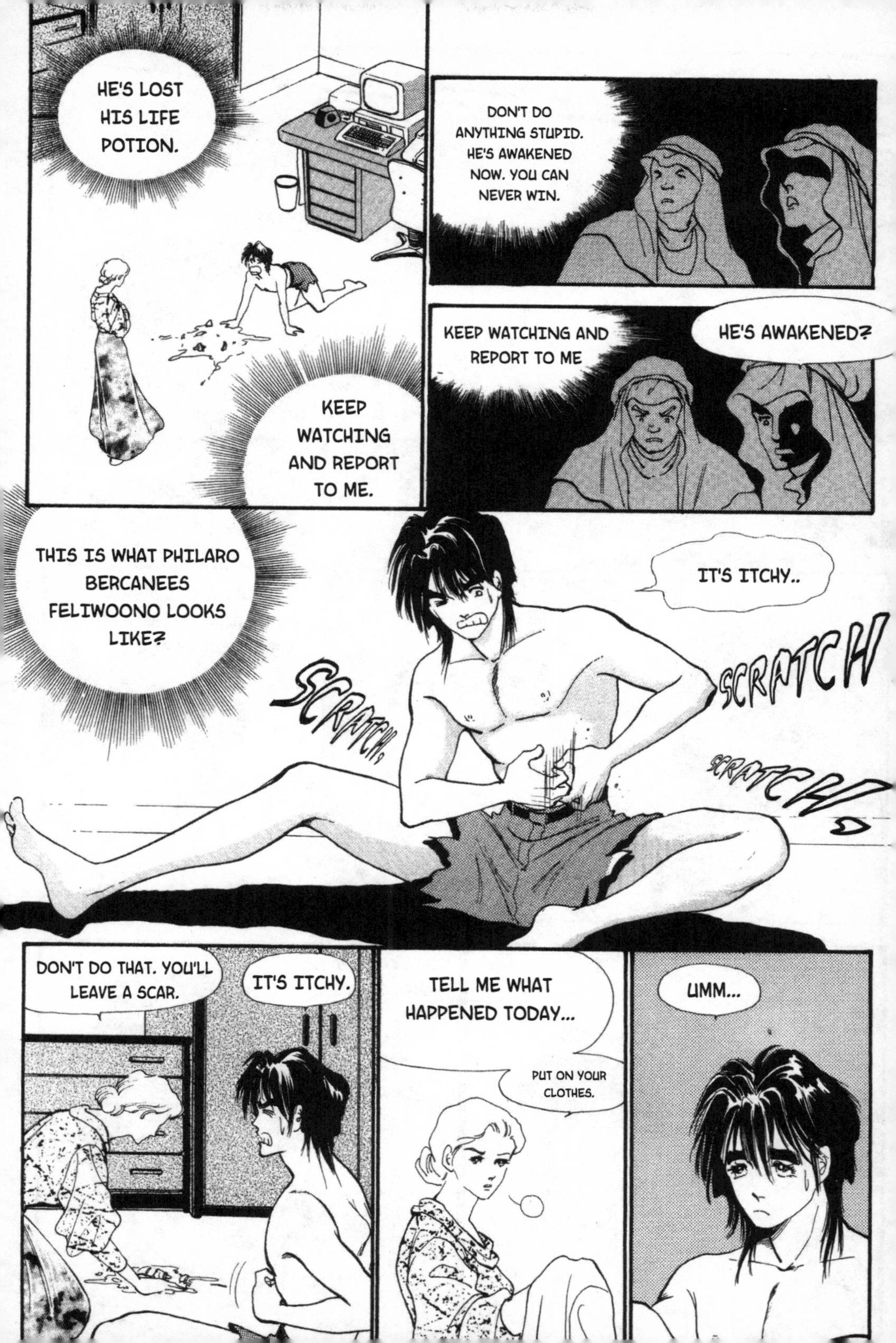
HE'S LOST HIS LIFE POTION.
KEEP WATCHING AND REPORT TO ME.
DON'T DO ANYTHING STUPID. HE'S AWAKENED NOW. YOU CAN NEVER WIN.
HE'S AWAKENED?
KEEP WATCHING AND REPORT TO ME
THIS IS WHAT PHILARO BERCANEES FELIWOONO LOOKS LIKE?
IT'S ITCHY..
SCRATCH
SCRATCH
SCRATCH
DON'T DO THAT. YOU'LL LEAVE A SCAR.
IT'S ITCHY.
TELL ME WHAT HAPPENED TODAY...
PUT ON YOUR CLOTHES.
UMM...

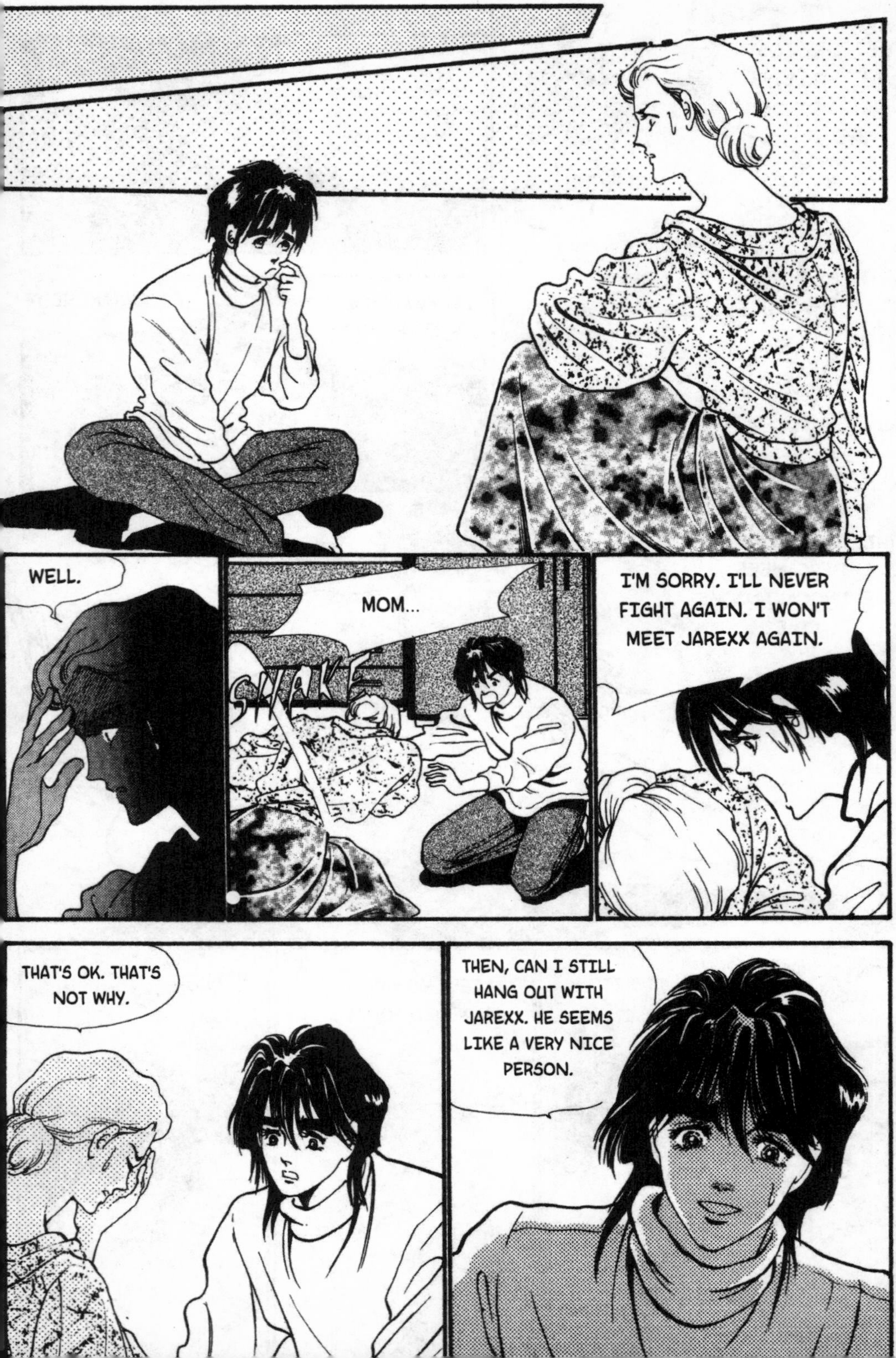
WELL.
MOM...
SHAKE
I'M SORRY. I'LL NEVER FIGHT AGAIN. I WON'T MEET JAREXX AGAIN.
THAT'S OK. THAT'S NOT WHY.
THEN, CAN I STILL HANG OUT WITH JAREXX. HE SEEMS LIKE A VERY NICE PERSON.

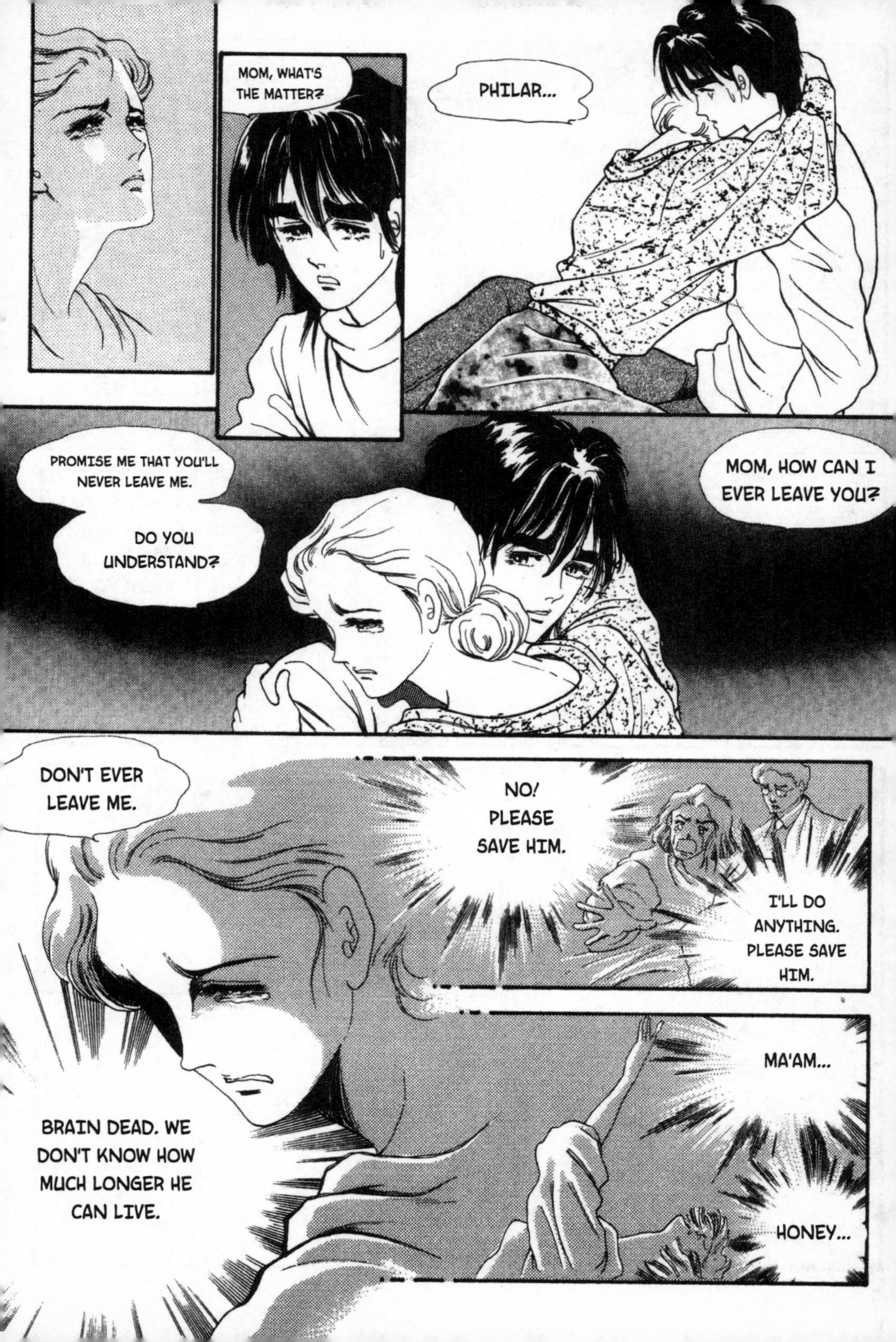
MOM, WHAT'S THE MATTER?
PHILAR...
PROMISE ME THAT YOU'LL NEVER LEAVE ME.
DO YOU UNDERSTAND?
MOM, HOW CAN I EVER LEAVE YOU?
DON'T EVER LEAVE ME.
NO! PLEASE SAVE HIM.
I'LL DO ANYTHING. PLEASE SAVE HIM.
MA'AM...
BRAIN DEAD. WE DON'T KNOW HOW MUCH LONGER HE CAN LIVE.
HONEY...

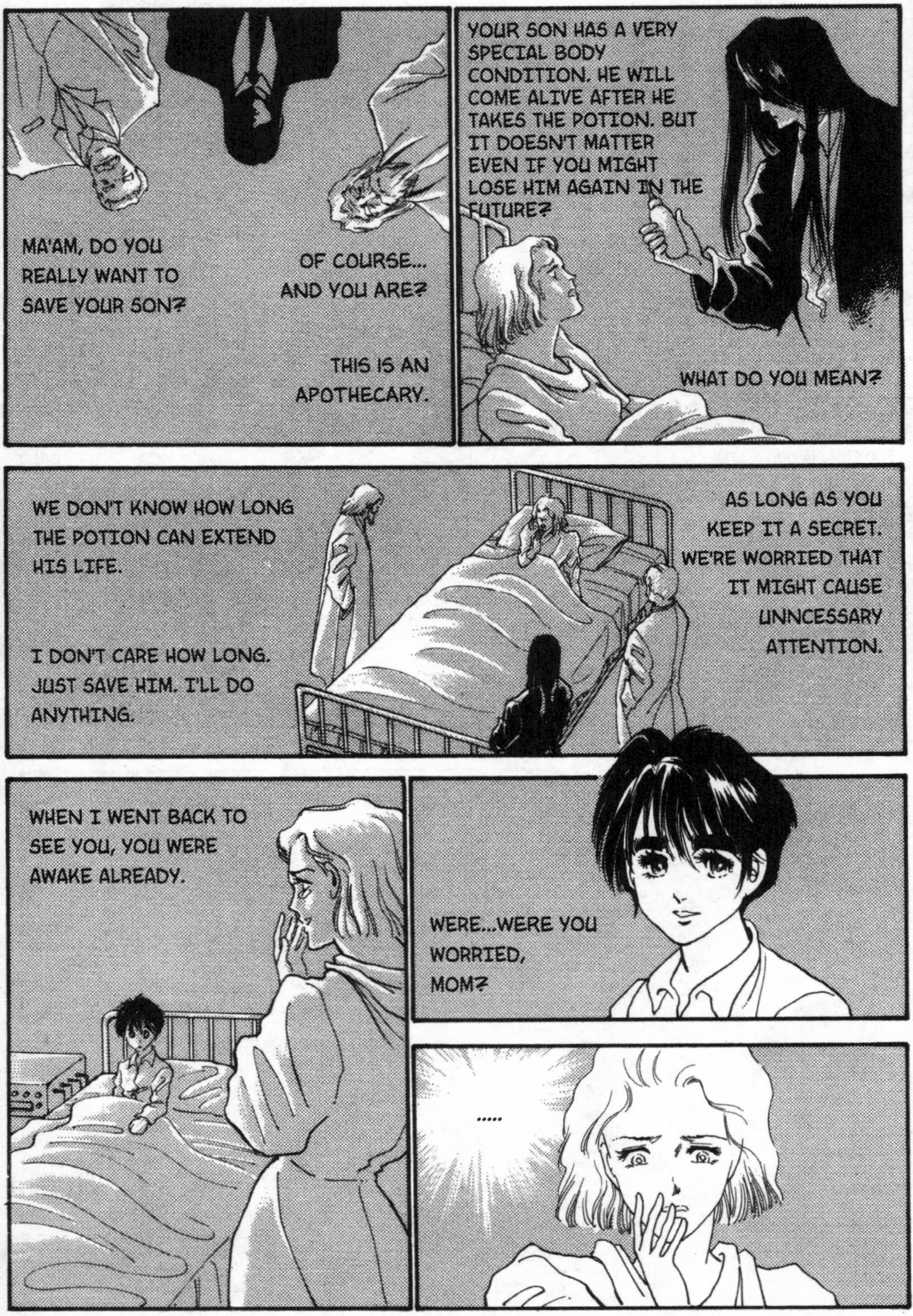
MA'AM, DO YOU REALLY WANT TO SAVE YOUR SON?
OF COURSE... AND YOU ARE?
THIS IS AN APOTHECARY.
YOUR SON HAS A VERY SPECIAL BODY CONDITION. HE WILL COME ALIVE AFTER HE TAKES THE POTION. BUT IT DOESN'T MATTER EVEN IF YOU MIGHT LOSE HIM AGAIN IN THE FUTURE?
WHAT DO YOU MEAN?
WE DON'T KNOW HOW LONG THE POTION CAN EXTEND HIS LIFE.
I DON'T CARE HOW LONG. JUST SAVE HIM. I'LL DO ANYTHING.
AS LONG AS YOU KEEP IT A SECRET. WE'RE WORRIED THAT IT MIGHT CAUSE UNNCESSARY ATTENTION.
WHEN I WENT BACK TO SEE YOU, YOU WERE AWAKE ALREADY.
WERE...WERE YOU WORRIED, MOM?
.....

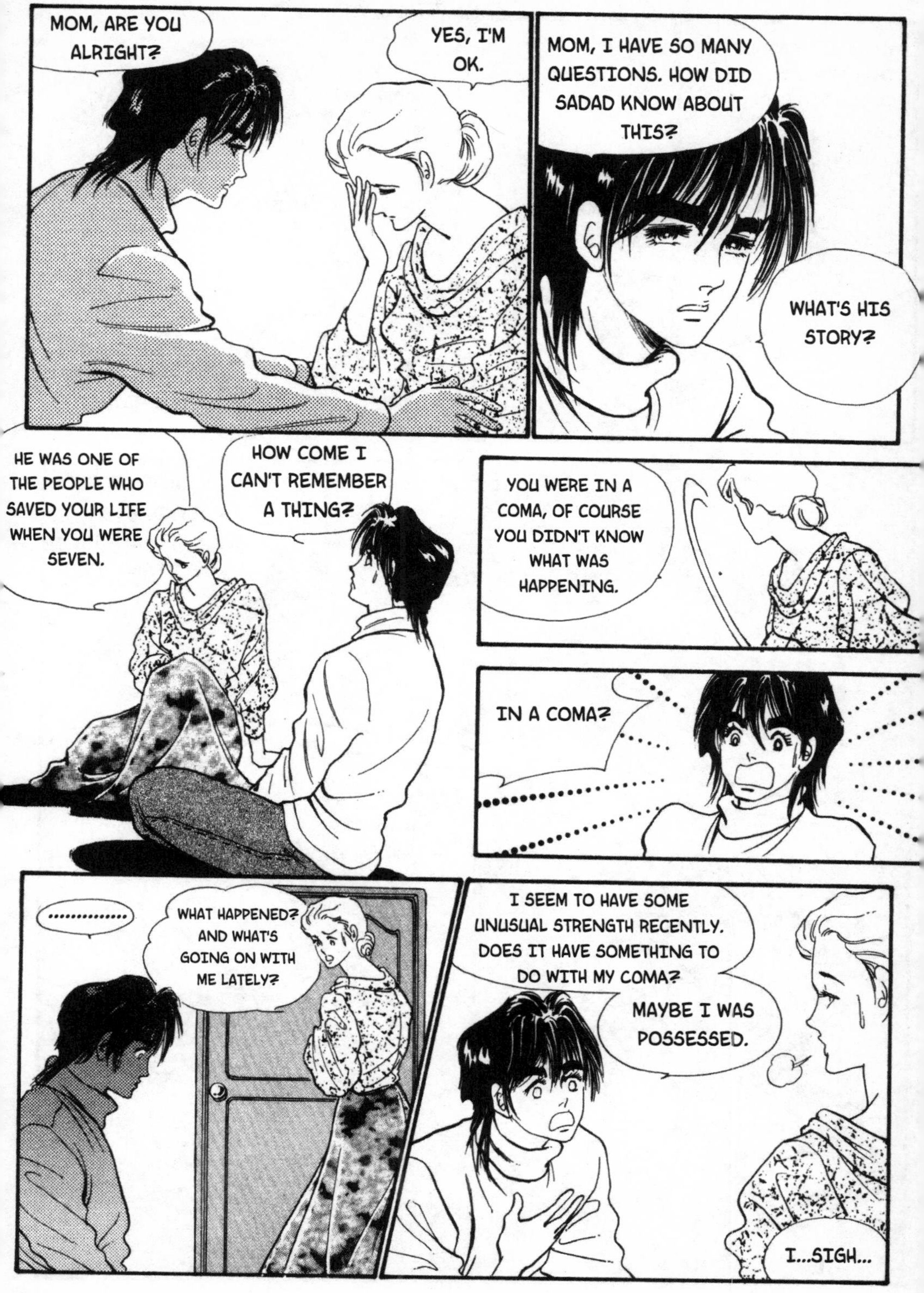
MOM, ARE YOU ALRIGHT?
YES, I'M OK.
MOM, I HAVE SO MANY QUESTIONS. HOW DID SADAD KNOW ABOUT THIS?
WHAT'S HIS STORY?
HE WAS ONE OF THE PEOPLE WHO SAVED YOUR LIFE WHEN YOU WERE SEVEN.
HOW COME I CAN'T REMEMBER A THING?
YOU WERE IN A COMA, OF COURSE YOU DIDN'T KNOW WHAT WAS HAPPENING.
IN A COMA?
....
WHAT HAPPENED? AND WHAT'S GOING ON WITH ME LATELY?
I SEEM TO HAVE SOME UNUSUAL STRENGTH RECENTLY. DOES IT HAVE SOMETHING TO DO WITH MY COMA?
MAYBE I WAS POSSESSED.
I...SIGH...

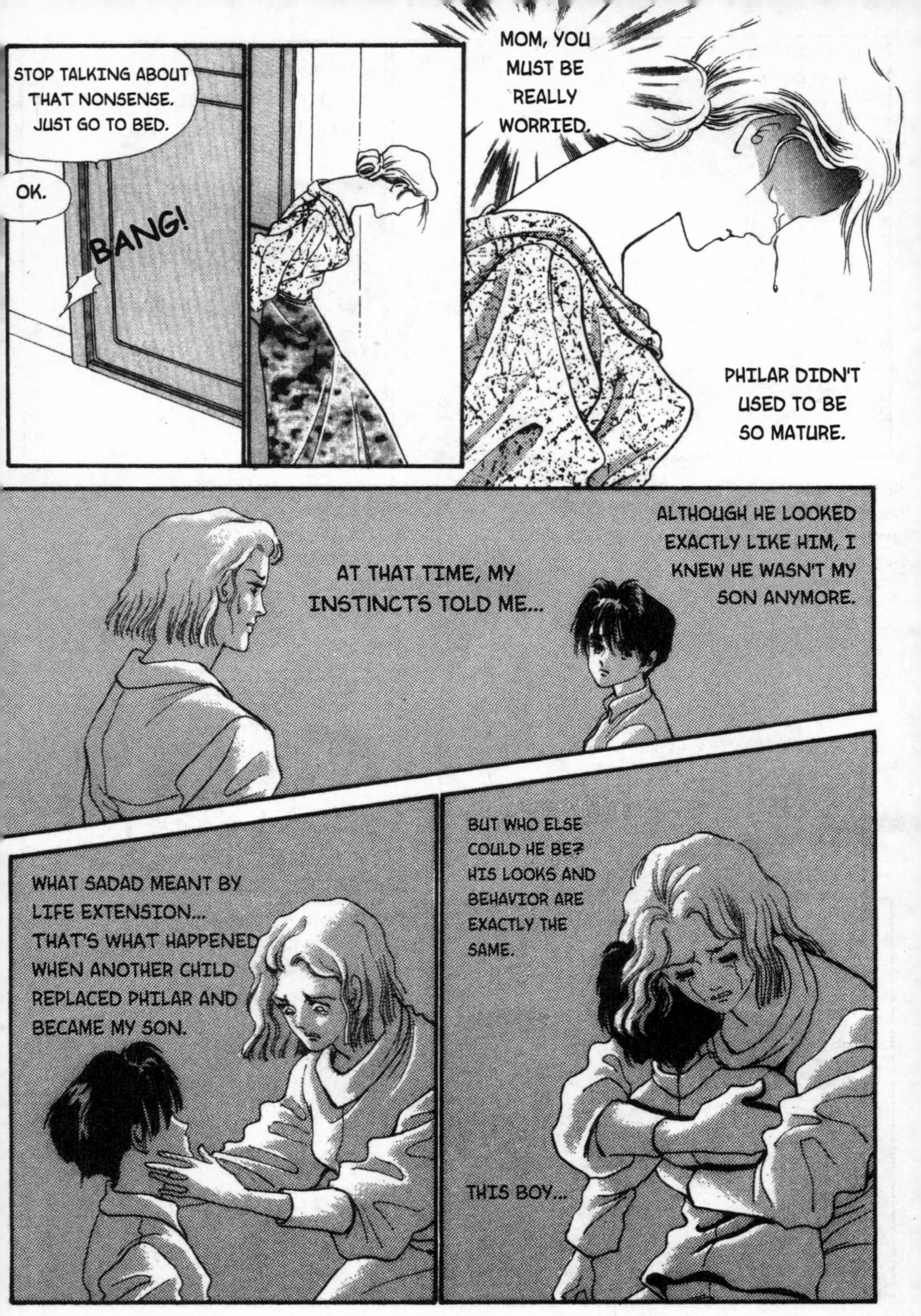
STOP TALKING ABOUT THAT NONSENSE. JUST GO TO BED.
OK.
BANG!
MOM, YOU MUST BE REALLY WORRIED.
PHILAR DIDN'T USED TO BE SO MATURE.
AT THAT TIME, MY INSTINCTS TOLD ME...
ALTHOUGH HE LOOKED EXACTLY LIKE HIM, I KNEW HE WASN'T MY SON ANYMORE.
WHAT SADAD MEANT BY LIFE EXTENSION... THAT'S WHAT HAPPENED WHEN ANOTHER CHILD REPLACED PHILAR AND BECAME MY SON.
BUT WHO ELSE COULD HE BE? HIS LOOKS AND BEHAVIOR ARE EXACTLY THE SAME.
THIS BOY...

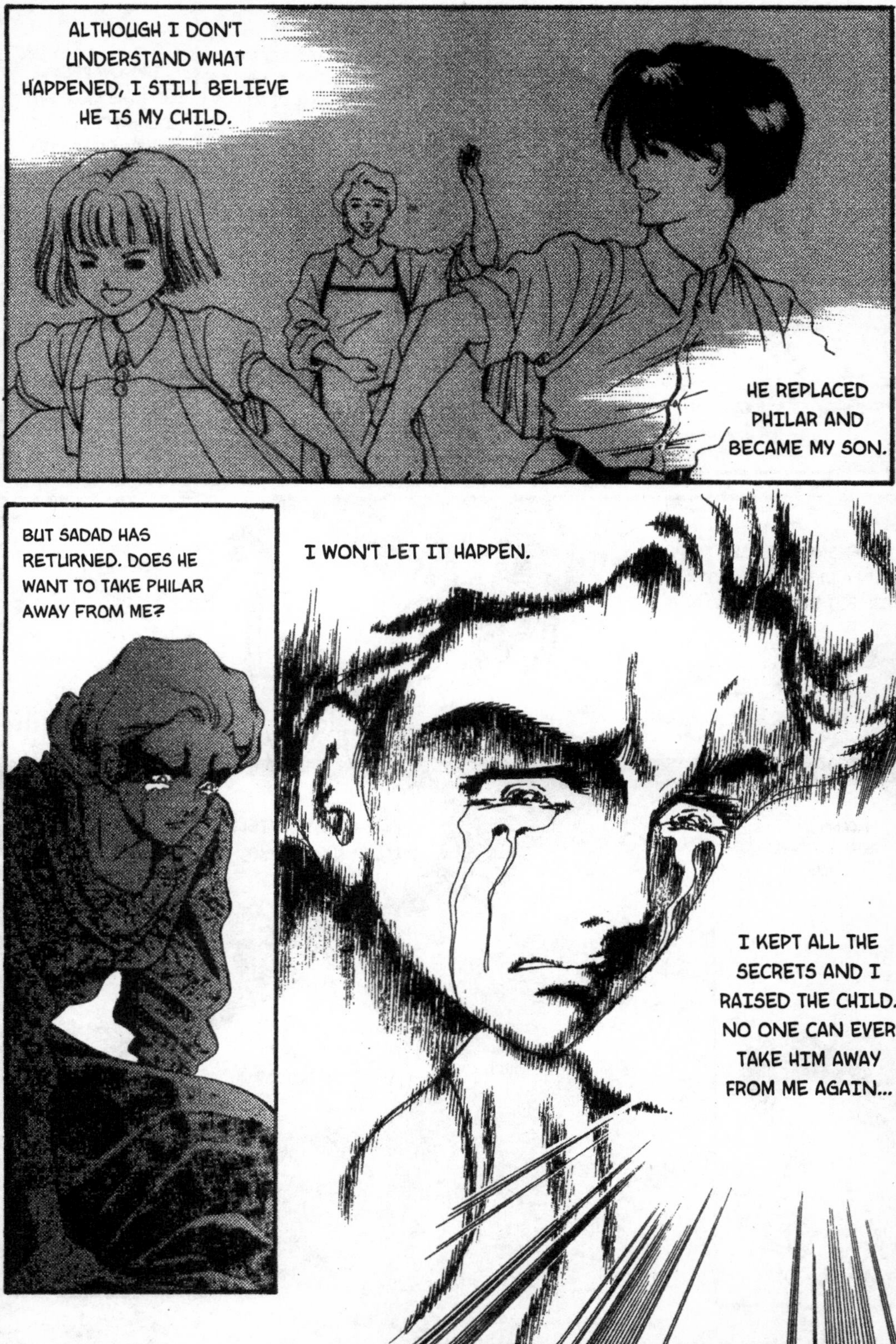
ALTHOUGH I DON'T UNDERSTAND WHAT HAPPENED, I STILL BELIEVE HE IS MY CHILD.
HE REPLACED PHILAR AND BECAME MY SON.
BUT SADAD HAS RETURNED. DOES HE WANT TO TAKE PHILAR AWAY FROM ME?
I WON'T LET IT HAPPEN.
I KEPT ALL THE SECRETS AND I RAISED THE CHILD. NO ONE CAN EVER TAKE HIM AWAY FROM ME AGAIN...

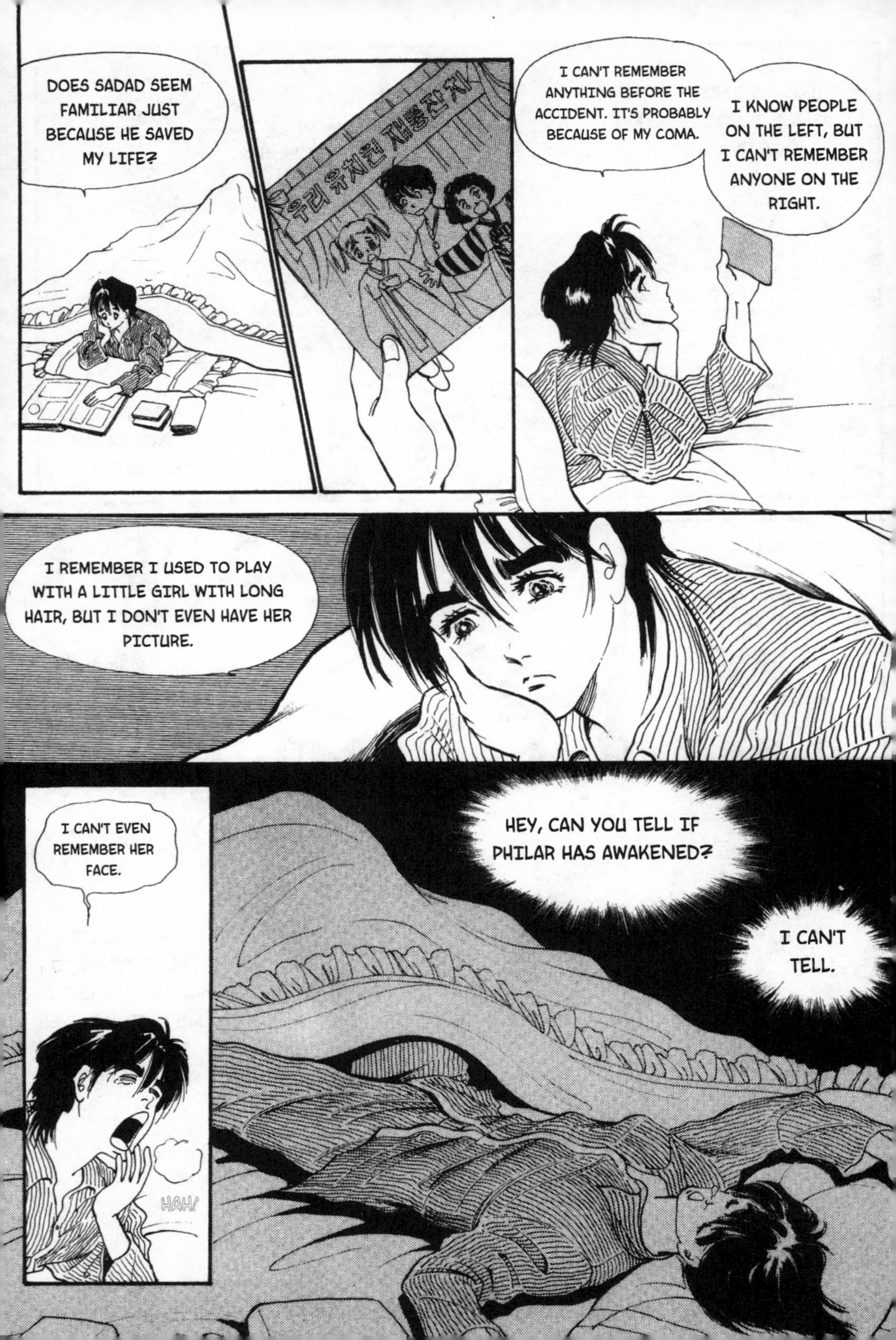
DOES SADAD SEEM FAMILIAR JUST BECAUSE HE SAVED MY LIFE?
우리 유치원 재롱잔치
I CAN'T REMEMBER ANYTHING BEFORE THE ACCIDENT. IT'S PROBABLY BECAUSE OF MY COMA.
I KNOW PEOPLE ON THE LEFT, BUT I CAN'T REMEMBER ANYONE ON THE RIGHT.
I REMEMBER I USED TO PLAY WITH A LITTLE GIRL WITH LONG HAIR, BUT I DON'T EVEN HAVE HER PICTURE.
I CAN'T EVEN REMEMBER HER FACE.
HEY, CAN YOU TELL IF PHILAR HAS AWAKENED?
I CAN'T TELL.
HAH!

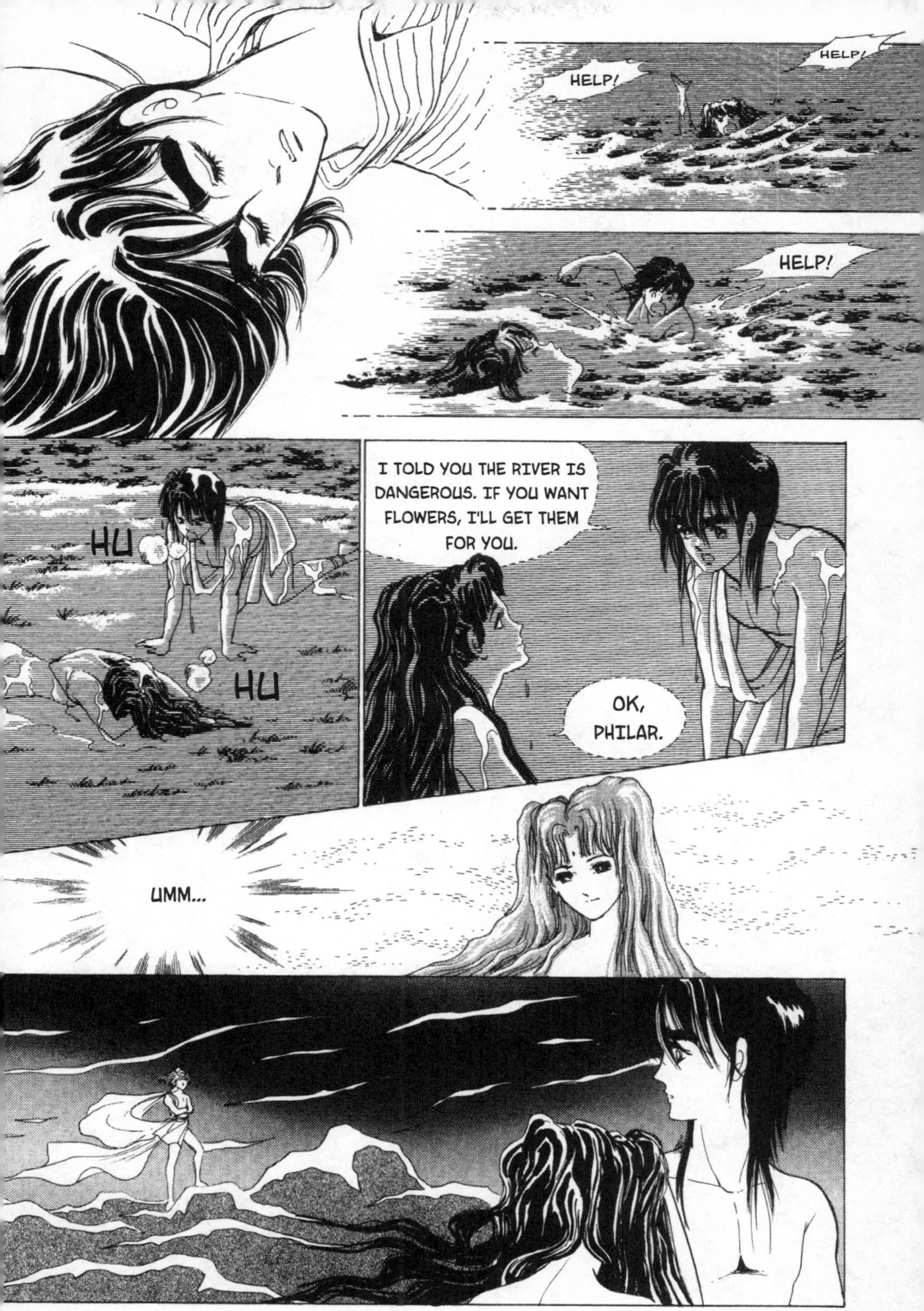
HELP!
HELP!
HELP!
HU
HU
I TOLD YOU THE RIVER IS DANGEROUS. IF YOU WANT FLOWERS, I'LL GET THEM FOR YOU.
OK, PHILAR.
UMM...

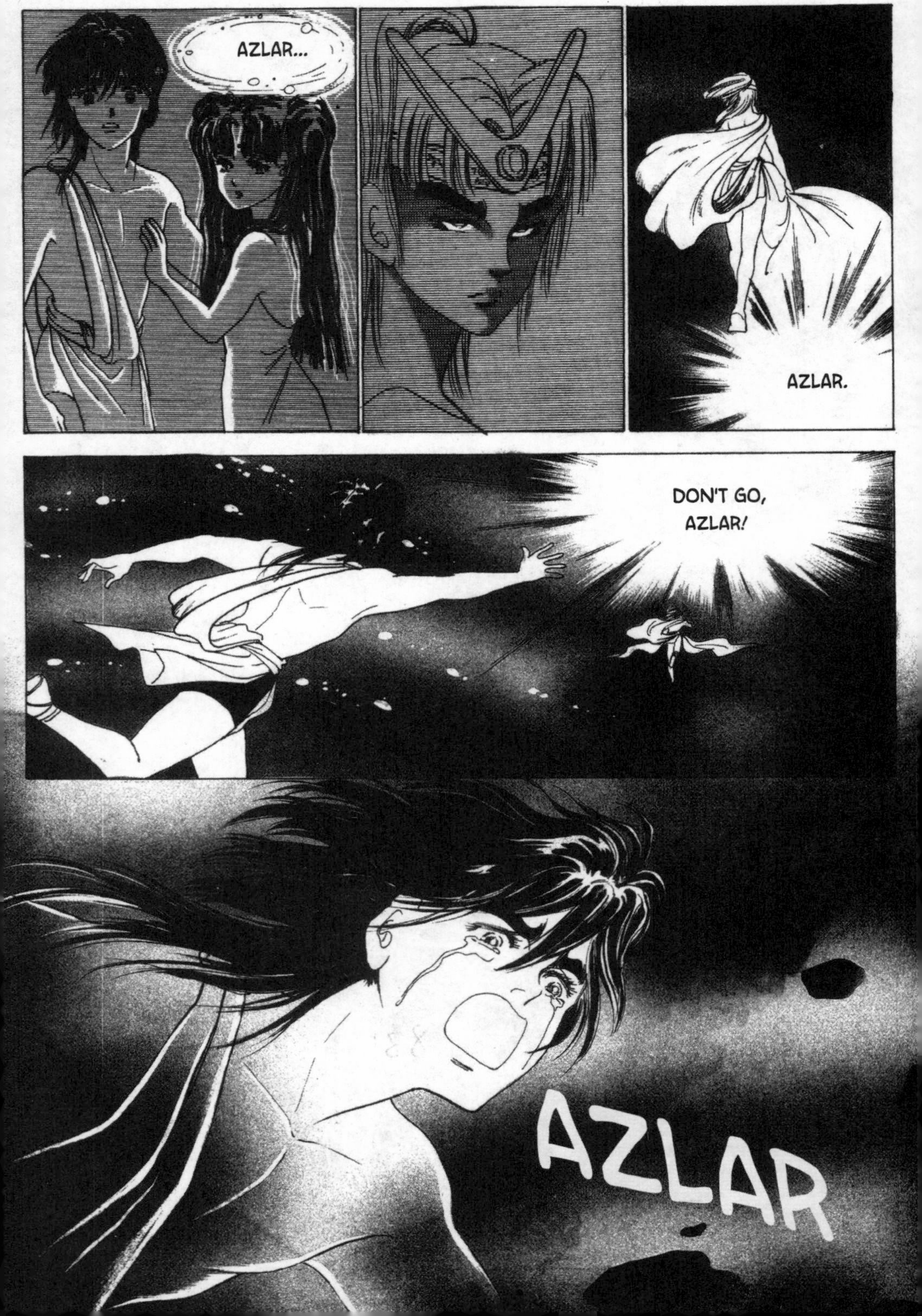
AZLAR...
AZLAR.
DON'T GO, AZLAR!
AZLAR

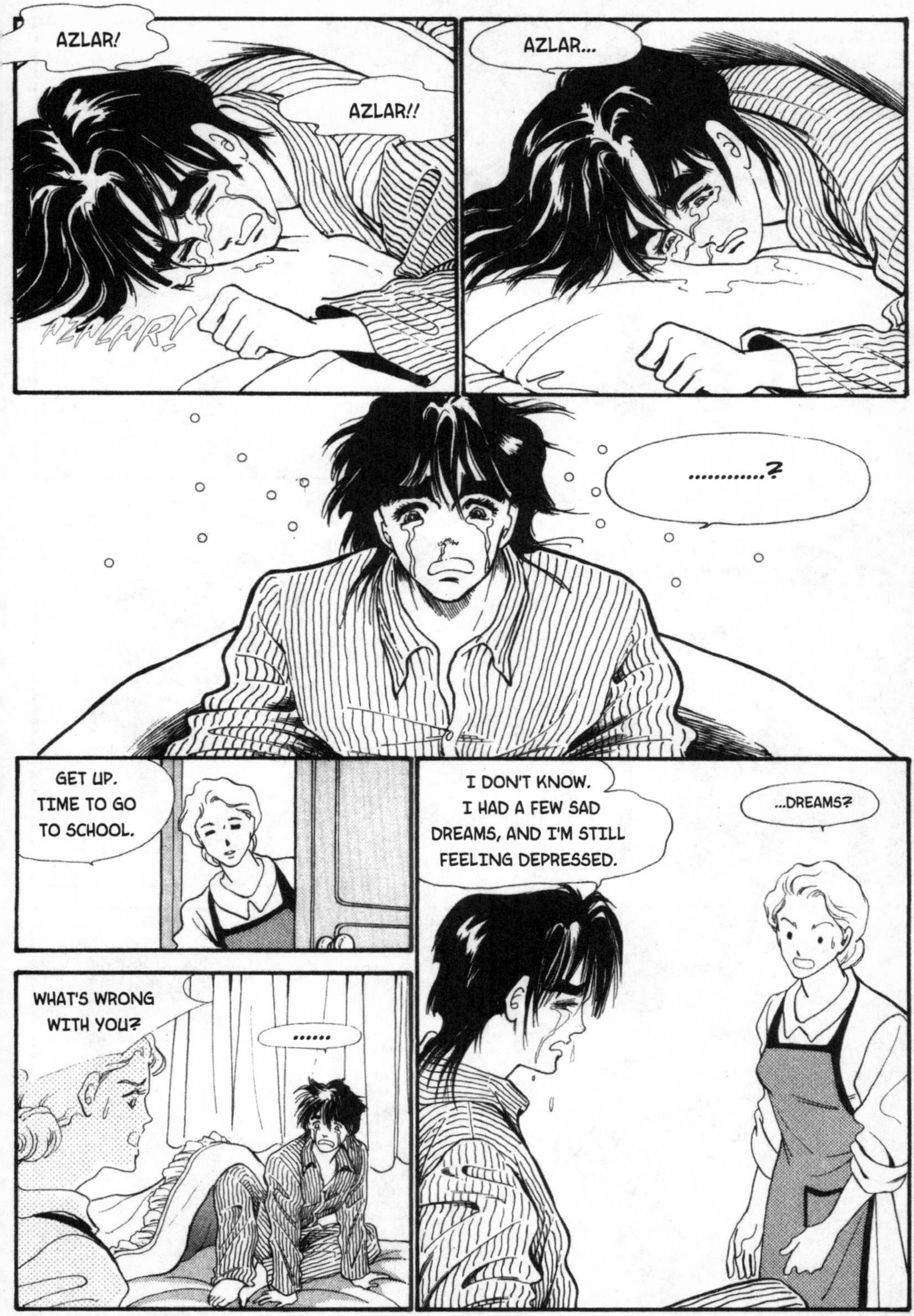
AZLAR!
AZLAR!!
AZLAR!
AZLAR...
............?
GET UP. TIME TO GO TO SCHOOL.
WHAT'S WRONG WITH YOU?
......
I DON'T KNOW. I HAD A FEW SAD DREAMS, AND I'M STILL FEELING DEPRESSED.
...DREAMS?

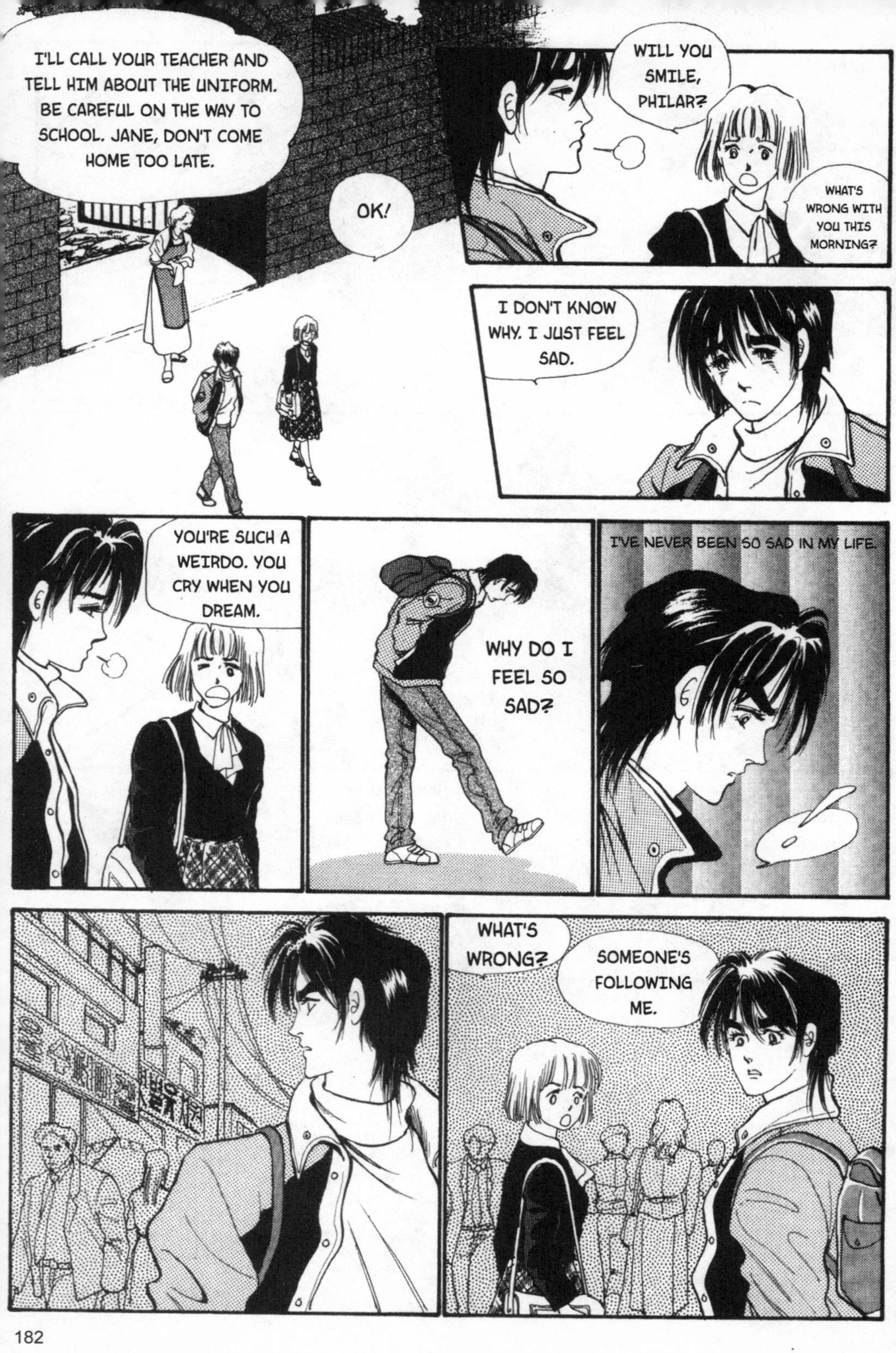
I'LL CALL YOUR TEACHER AND TELL HIM ABOUT THE UNIFORM. BE CAREFUL ON THE WAY TO SCHOOL. JANE, DON'T COME HOME TOO LATE.
OK!
WILL YOU SMILE, PHILAR?
WHAT'S WRONG WITH YOU THIS MORNING?
I DON'T KNOW WHY. I JUST FEEL SAD.
YOU'RE SUCH A WEIRDO. YOU CRY WHEN YOU DREAM.
WHY DO I FEEL SO SAD?
I'VE NEVER BEEN SO SAD IN MY LIFE.
WHAT'S WRONG?
SOMEONE'S FOLLOWING ME.

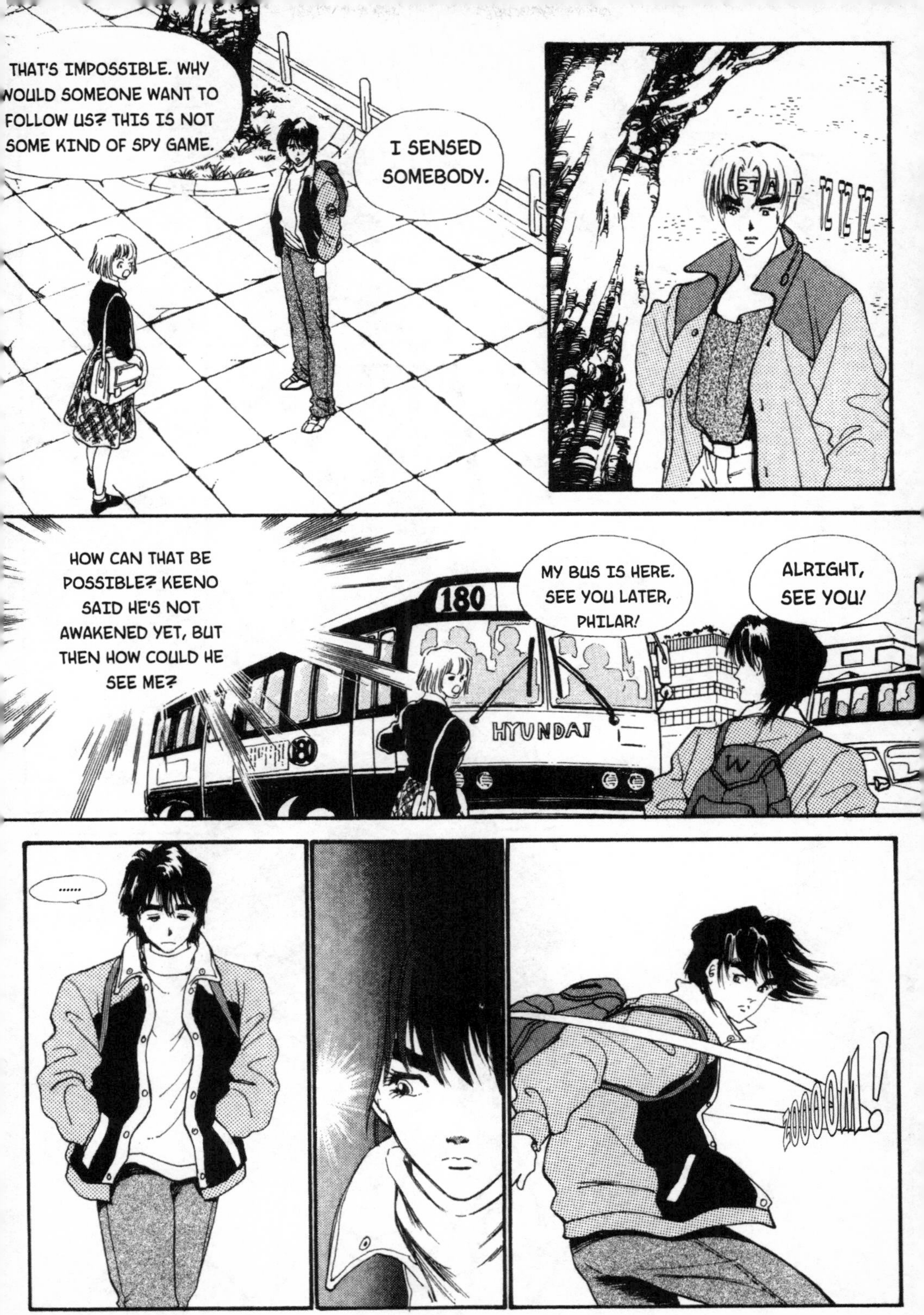
THAT'S IMPOSSIBLE. WHY WOULD SOMEONE WANT TO FOLLOW US? THIS IS NOT SOME KIND OF SPY GAME.
I SENSED SOMEBODY.
TZ TZ TZ
HOW CAN THAT BE POSSIBLE? KEENO SAID HE'S NOT AWAKENED YET, BUT THEN HOW COULD HE SEE ME?
180
MY BUS IS HERE. SEE YOU LATER, PHILAR!
ALRIGHT, SEE YOU!
HYUNDAI
......
ZOOOOM!

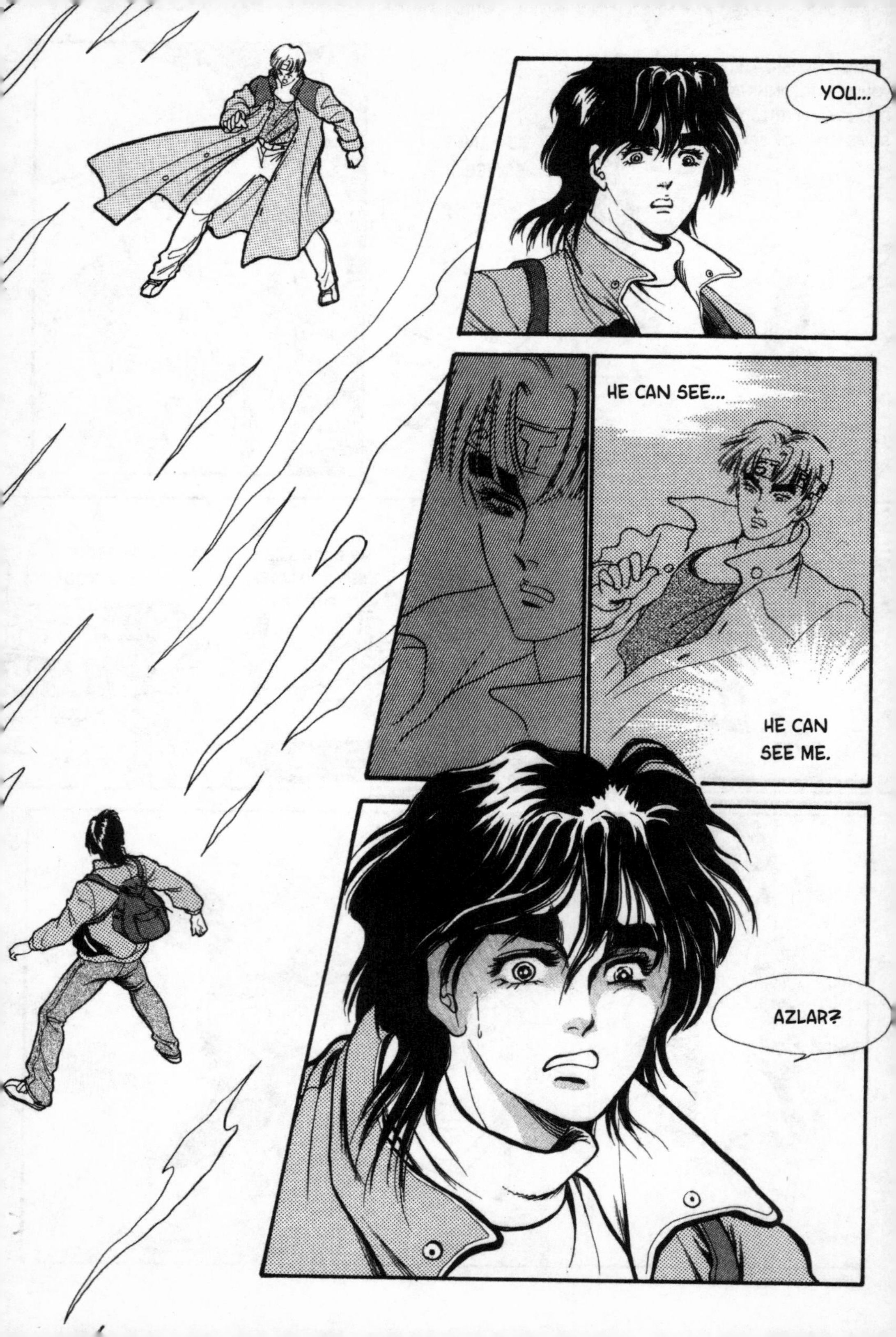
YOU...
HE CAN SEE...
HE CAN SEE ME.
AZLAR?

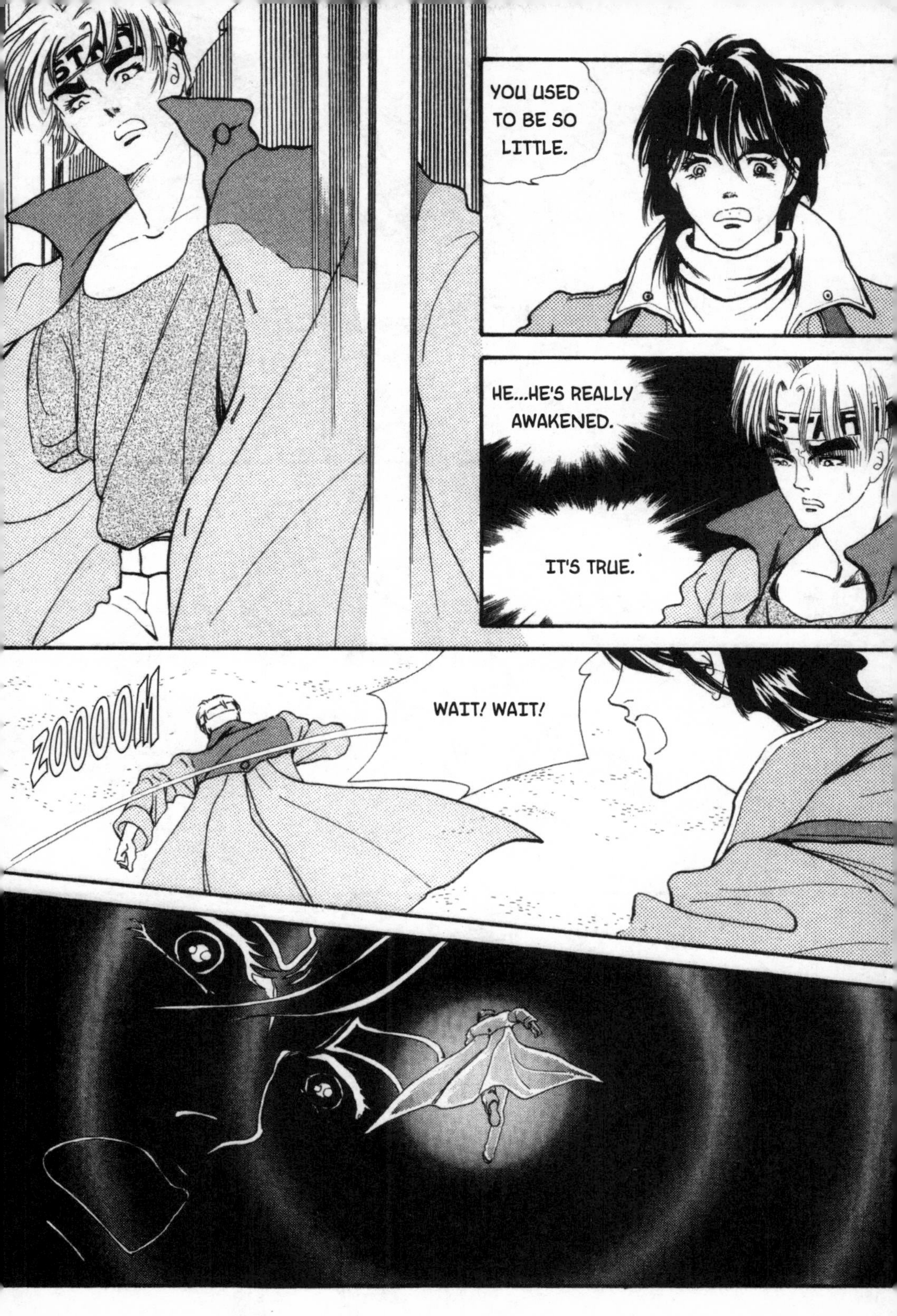
YOU USED TO BE SO LITTLE.
HE...HE'S REALLY AWAKENED.
IT'S TRUE.
ZOOOOM
WAIT! WAIT!

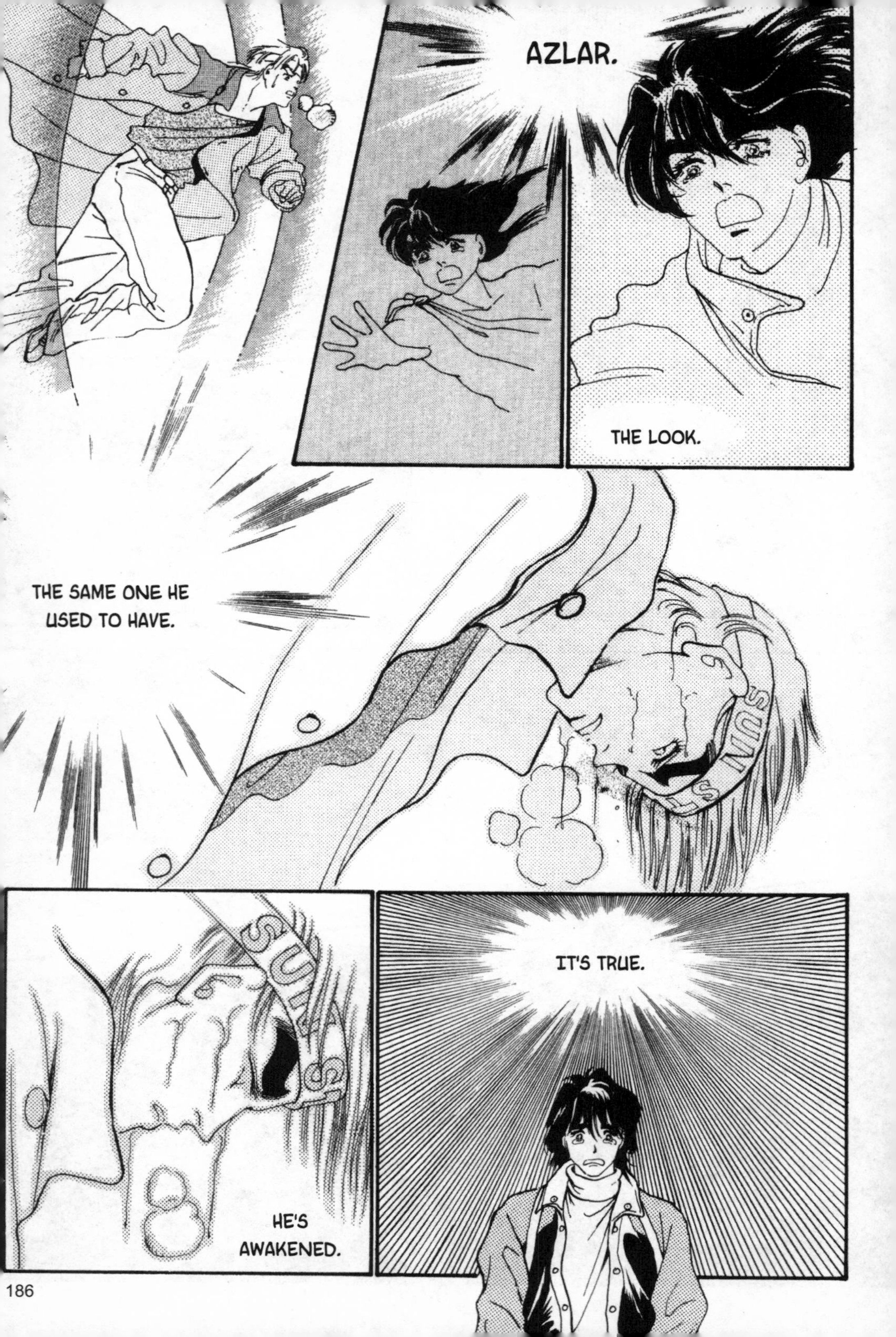
AZLAR.
THE LOOK.
THE SAME ONE HE USED TO HAVE.
IT'S TRUE.
HE'S AWAKENED.

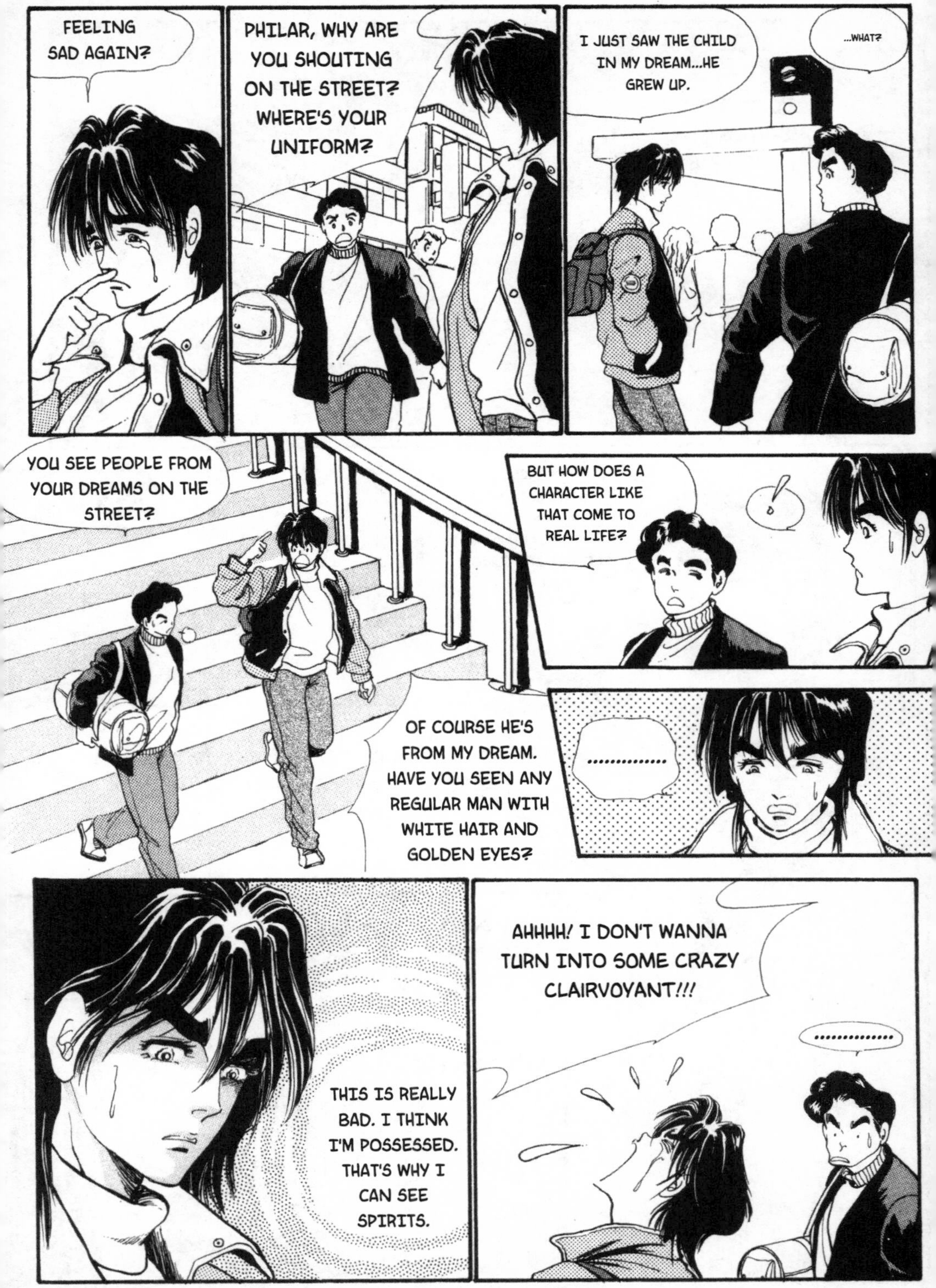
FEELING SAD AGAIN?
PHILAR, WHY ARE YOU SHOUTING ON THE STREET? WHERE'S YOUR UNIFORM?
I JUST SAW THE CHILD IN MY DREAM...HE GREW UP.
...WHAT?
YOU SEE PEOPLE FROM YOUR DREAMS ON THE STREET?
BUT HOW DOES A CHARACTER LIKE THAT COME TO REAL LIFE?
!
OF COURSE HE'S FROM MY DREAM. HAVE YOU SEEN ANY REGULAR MAN WITH WHITE HAIR AND GOLDEN EYES?
....
THIS IS REALLY BAD. I THINK I'M POSSESSED. THAT'S WHY I CAN SEE SPIRITS.
AHHHH! I DON'T WANNA TURN INTO SOME CRAZY CLAIRVOYANT!!!
....

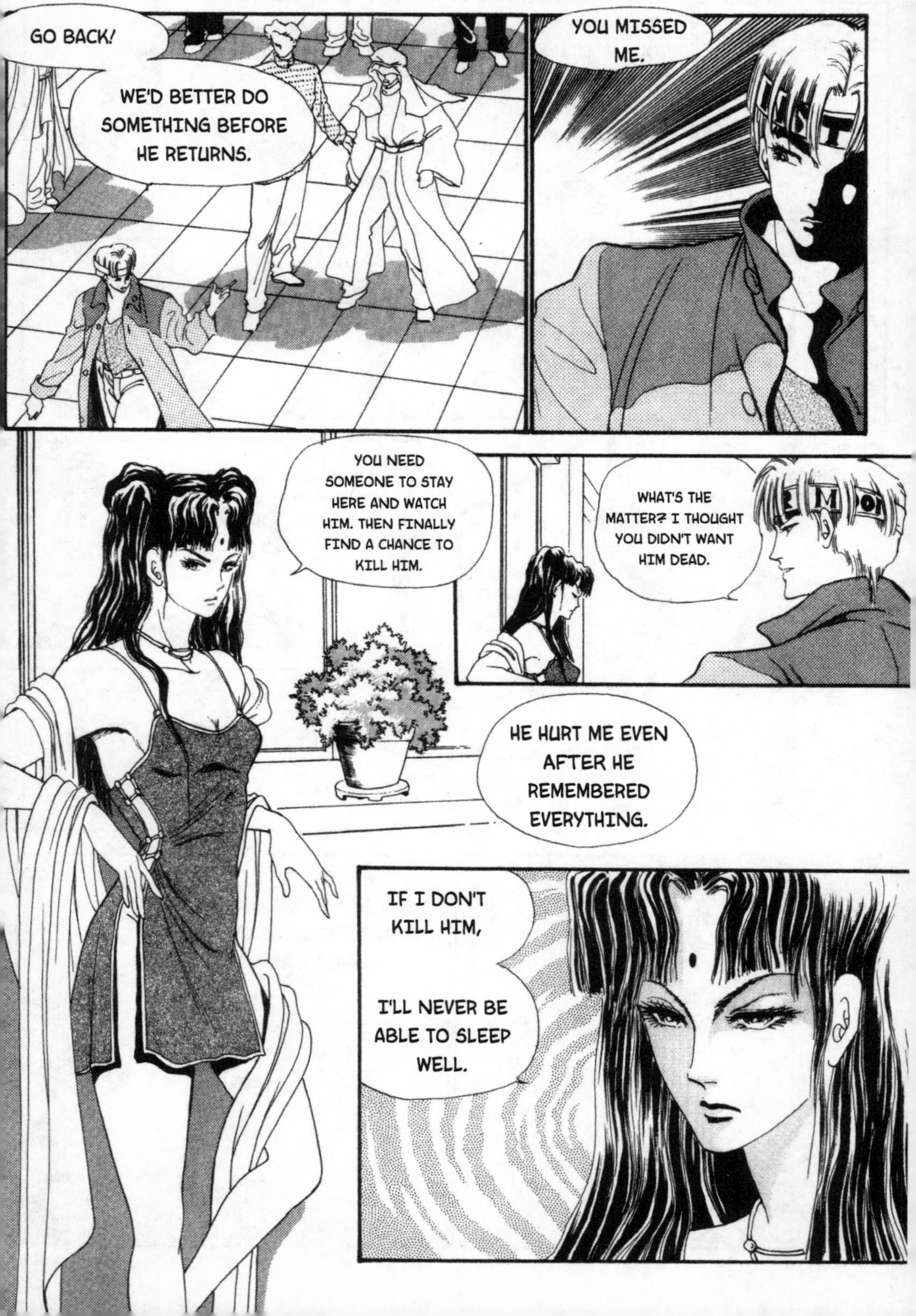
GO BACK!
WE'D BETTER DO SOMETHING BEFORE HE RETURNS.
YOU MISSED ME.
YOU NEED SOMEONE TO STAY HERE AND WATCH HIM. THEN FINALLY FIND A CHANCE TO KILL HIM.
WHAT'S THE MATTER? I THOUGHT YOU DIDN'T WANT HIM DEAD.
HE HURT ME EVEN AFTER HE REMEMBERED EVERYTHING.
IF I DON'T KILL HIM,
I'LL NEVER BE ABLE TO SLEEP WELL.

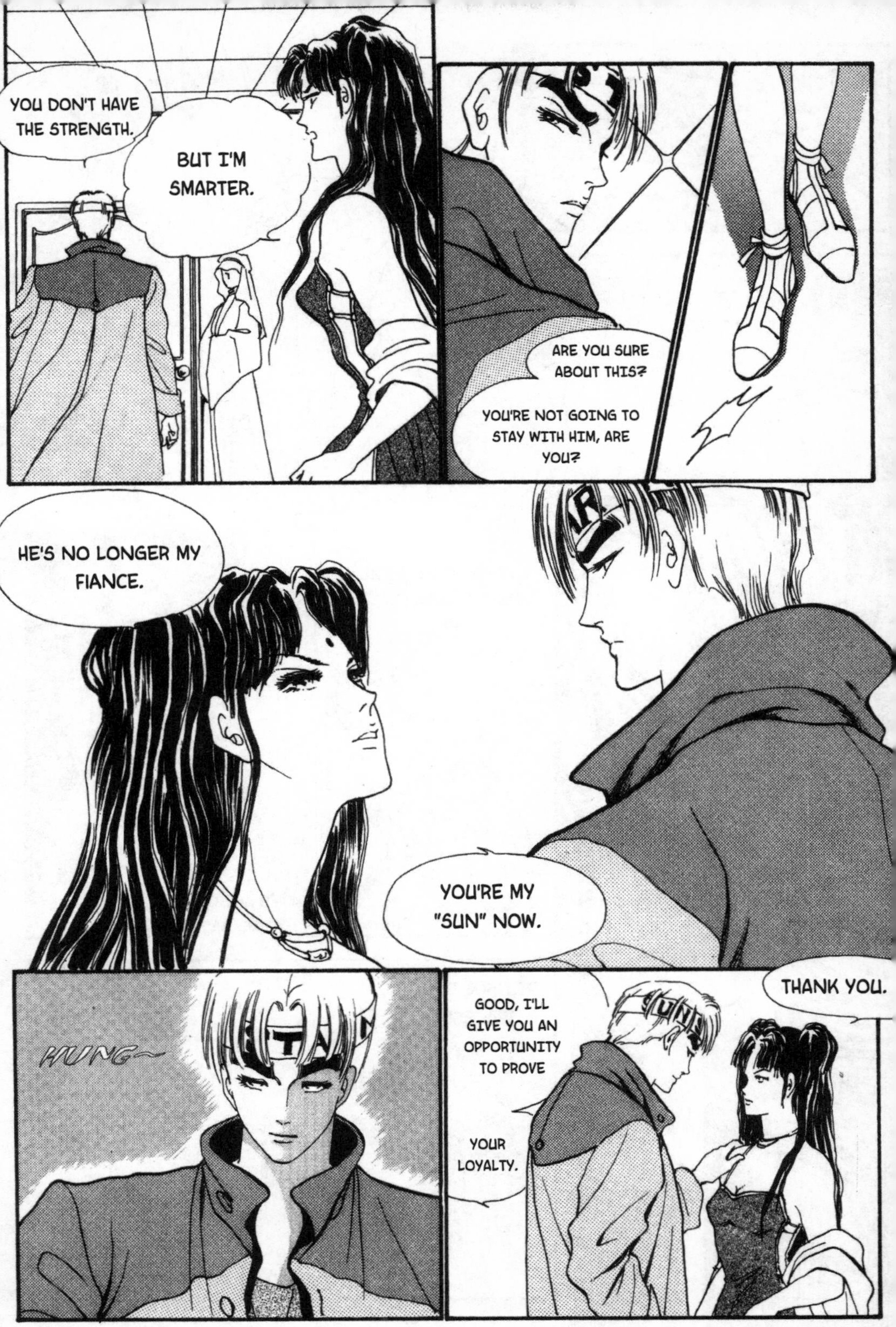
YOU DON'T HAVE THE STRENGTH.
BUT I'M SMARTER.
ARE YOU SURE ABOUT THIS?
YOU'RE NOT GOING TO STAY WITH HIM, ARE YOU?
HE'S NO LONGER MY FIANCE.
YOU'RE MY "SUN" NOW.
HUNG~
GOOD, I'LL GIVE YOU AN OPPORTUNITY TO PROVE
YOUR LOYALTY.
THANK YOU.

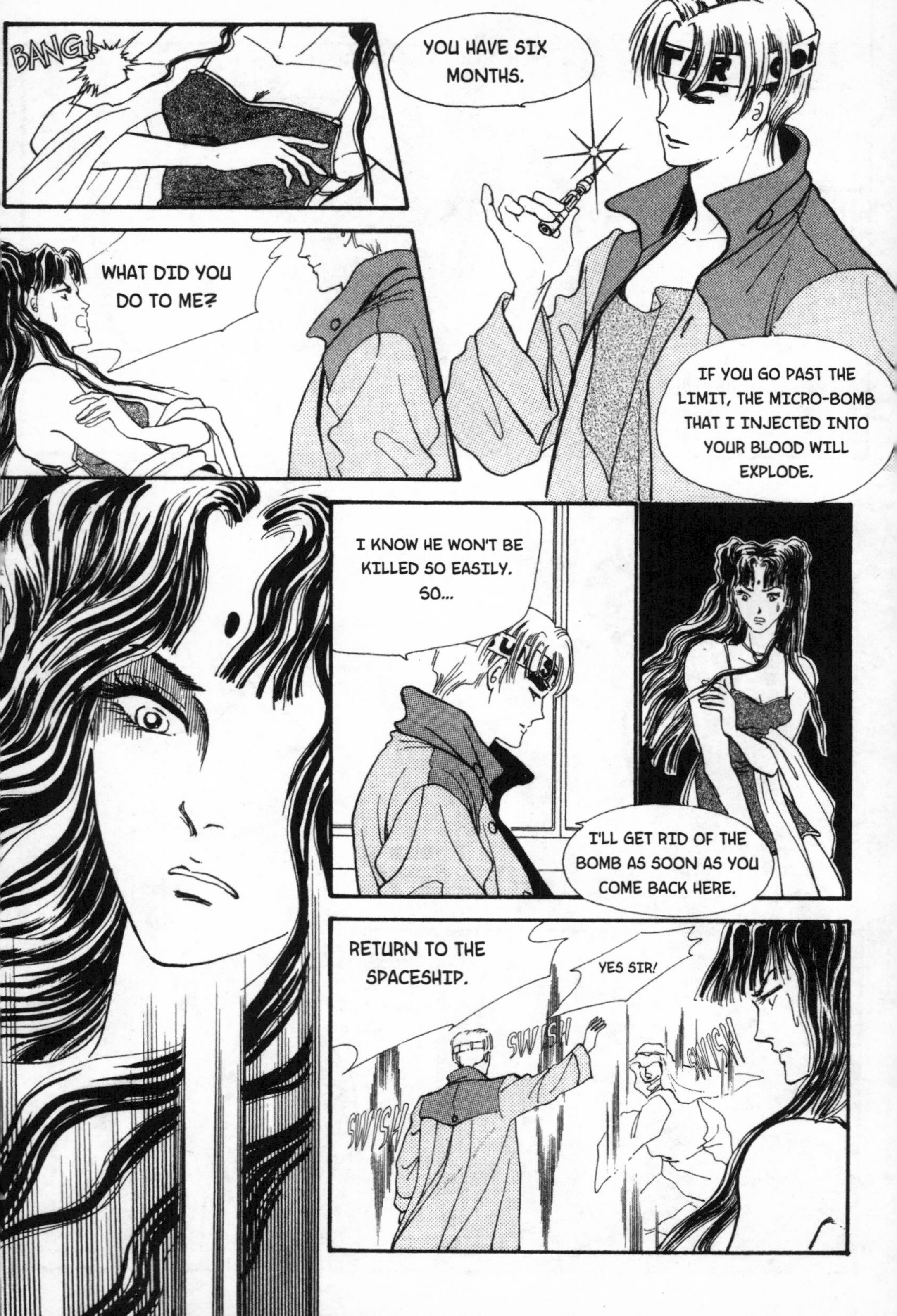
BANG!
YOU HAVE SIX MONTHS.
WHAT DID YOU DO TO ME?
IF YOU GO PAST THE LIMIT, THE MICRO-BOMB THAT I INJECTED INTO YOUR BLOOD WILL EXPLODE.
I KNOW HE WON'T BE KILLED SO EASILY. SO...
I'LL GET RID OF THE BOMB AS SOON AS YOU COME BACK HERE.
RETURN TO THE SPACESHIP.
YES SIR!
SWISH
SWISH
SWISH

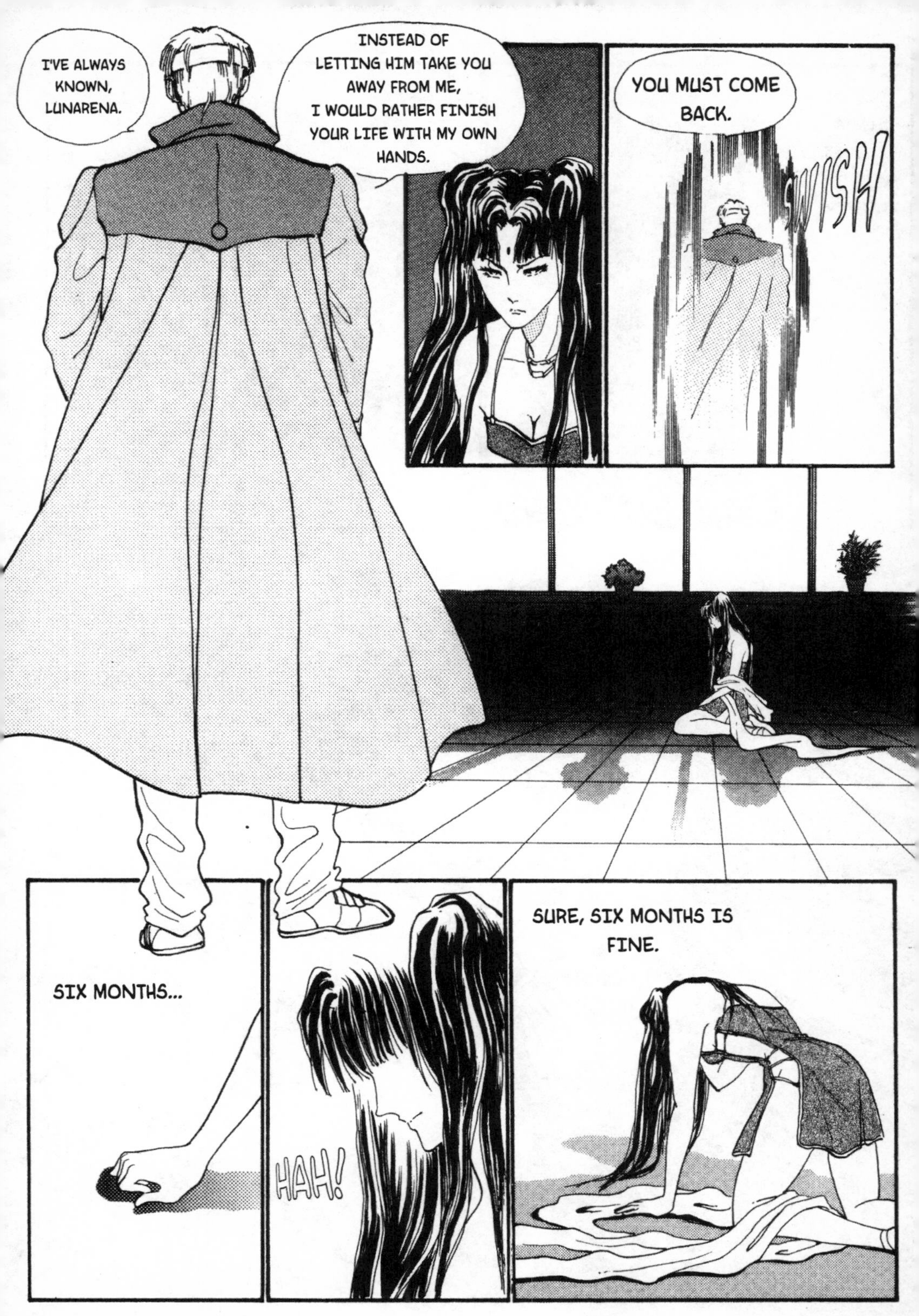
I'VE ALWAYS KNOWN, LUNARENA.
INSTEAD OF LETTING HIM TAKE YOU AWAY FROM ME, I WOULD RATHER FINISH YOUR LIFE WITH MY OWN HANDS.
YOU MUST COME BACK.
SWISH
SIX MONTHS...
HAH!
SURE, SIX MONTHS IS FINE.

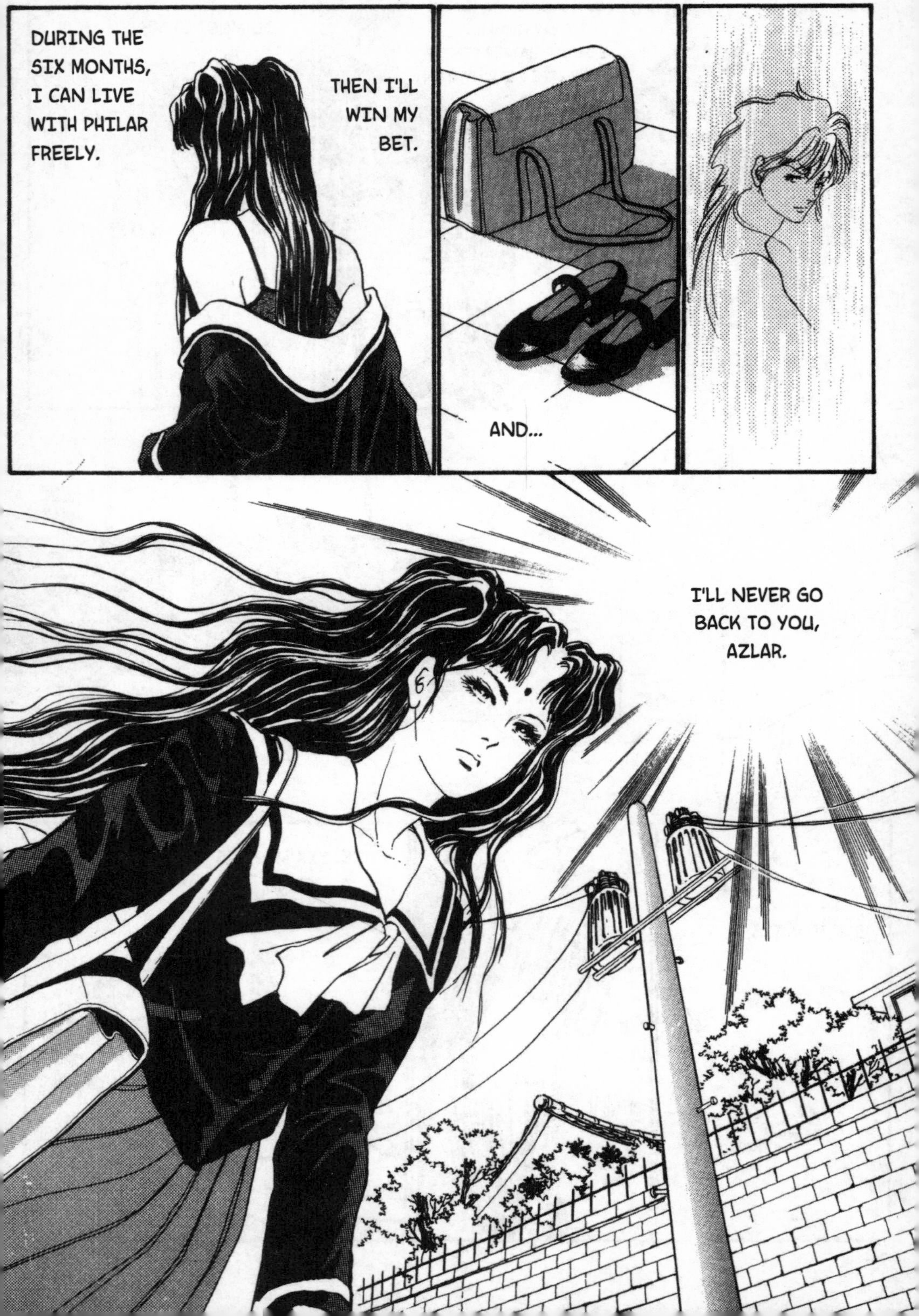
DURING THE SIX MONTHS, I CAN LIVE WITH PHILAR FREELY.
THEN I'LL WIN MY BET.
AND...
I'LL NEVER GO BACK TO YOU, AZLAR.